The Films of Walter Hill

The Films of Walter Hill

Another Time, Another Place

Brian Brems

LEXINGTON BOOKS
Lanham • Boulder • New York • London

Published by Lexington Books
An imprint of The Rowman & Littlefield Publishing Group, Inc.
4501 Forbes Boulevard, Suite 200, Lanham, Maryland 20706
www.rowman.com

86-90 Paul Street, London EC2A 4NE, United Kingdom

Copyright © 2022 by The Rowman & Littlefield Publishing Group, Inc.

All rights reserved. No part of this book may be reproduced in any form or by any electronic or mechanical means, including information storage and retrieval systems, without written permission from the publisher, except by a reviewer who may quote passages in a review.

British Library Cataloguing in Publication Information Available

Library of Congress Cataloging-in-Publication Data

Names: Brems, Brian R., author.
Title: The films of Walter Hill : another time, another place / Brian Brems.
Description: Lanham, MD : Lexington Books, [2022] | Includes bibliographical references and index. | Summary: "This book is an academic study of the work of an important American director working primarily in the action genre. The book explores the ways in which Hill's filmography reveals his point of view and intensifies classical approaches to storytelling"—Provided by publisher.
Identifiers: LCCN 2022024410 (print) | LCCN 2022024411 (ebook) |
  ISBN 9781666915280 (cloth) | ISBN 9781666915303 (paperback) |
  ISBN 9781666915297 (epub)
Subjects: LCSH: Hill, Walter, 1942—Criticism and interpretation. |
  Motion picture producers and directors—United States. |
  Motion pictures—United States—History—20th century.
Classification: LCC PN1998.3.H55 B74 2022 (print) | LCC PN1998.3.H55 (ebook) |
  DDC 791.4302/3092—dc23/eng/20220716
LC record available at https://lccn.loc.gov/2022024410
LC ebook record available at https://lccn.loc.gov/2022024411

∞™ The paper used in this publication meets the minimum requirements of American National Standard for Information Sciences—Permanence of Paper for Printed Library Materials, ANSI/NISO Z39.48-1992.

For Wild Bill

Contents

Acknowledgments	ix
Introduction: Another Time, Another Place	1
1 The Action Man	17
2 The Wild, The Hawks, and *The Warriors*	43
3 Soldiers of Misfortune	73
4 Black and White	101
5 Down These Streets of Fire	131
6 Black versus White	157
7 Last Men Standing	189
8 Partners in Crime	223
Conclusion: Terminate with Extreme Prejudice	245
Works Cited	259
Index	269
About the Author	285

Acknowledgments

Undertaking any academic study of a director's filmography is no easy task, and I was aided in this effort by a number of people, whose contributions to the work were quite valuable.

In my classes at the College of DuPage, I often teach films as a way of getting to know them better; over the past several years, my students have gotten to know the films of Walter Hill quite well, and the ideas generated in those discussions have helped shape my thinking about these works.

The editorial team at Lexington Books provided valuable guidance and support—especially acquisitions editor Jessie Tepper, who assisted with the project from its initial submission.

The book would not be the same without the insights of several actors who worked with Walter Hill on his films: Lance Henriksen, David Patrick Kelly, James Remar, William Sadler, and Sigourney Weaver. All of them were gracious enough to speak to me early in the process, which helped shape the individual chapters. I am extremely grateful for their participation, and extend my gratitude to their various management representatives, agents, and publicists, who organized the interviews.

A particular thanks goes out to Walter Hill's manager, Jeff Sanderson, who initially put me in touch with the book's subject, fielded numerous emails and calls from me, and helped organize what initially was supposed to be one conversation, and ended up being several more.

I also want to thank my wife, Genna, who heard "I've got to spend some time working on the book" more times than she can probably count and remained supportive and encouraging throughout the process of writing and revising.

Finally, I want to thank Walter Hill. He had no idea who I was when I first reached out about doing a book on him, and he was initially reluctant to talk at all, understandably believing that the work should stand on its own. After I passed my "audition" in our first conversation, he agreed to continue our discussions for as long as I needed him, and made good on that promise, even as the new film he was developing started to take more of his attention. His voice is present in his films, and I'm glad to say, throughout the book, as well.

Introduction
Another Time, Another Place

"Whenever you look at films—somebody said this a long time ago," says Walter Hill, "the director's always the hero. It's always some version in the imagination of the director of what their own virtues are. It kind of comes with the territory."[1]

In Walter Hill's films, the territory is "another time, another place," a mythic phrase that opens his 1984 film *Streets of Fire*, a hybrid of many genres. His heroes are complicated figures drawn from the seemingly opposing traditions of westerns and film noir, come to rest in the action movie that came to fruition in the New Hollywood period of the late 1960s and early 1970s, which coincided with Hill's arrival in the movie business; first, he served as an assistant director on television westerns and the cop thriller *Bullitt* (1968, Yates), before moving into screenwriting—he thinks of himself as a writer first[2]—with his big break his adaptation of Jim Thompson's novel *The Getaway*, directed by Sam Peckinpah and released in 1972. As a writer and director of his own films, Hill established a foothold in the nascent action genre, building a body of work that reflects his own interest in history, racial tensions, and the demands placed upon men by American society. Hill's respect for the history of the medium in which he works draws a line to the past, while his interest in stretching the stylistic capabilities of cinema points forward. He is a figure who links two periods of American movies by connecting the stories and methods of the past to the era in which he works.

One of the Classic Hollywood directors that Hill admires most, John Ford, repeatedly referred to a number of his films as nothing more than "a job of work."[3] The perspective Ford expressed about the practice of stepping behind the camera in that statement, oft-quoted since in the volumes of written work about Ford, surely one of the most celebrated directors in film history, demonstrates the filmmaking credo of an earlier era. The filmmakers of the Classic Hollywood era are well-known for their self-conception as craftsmen, not "artists." Hypermasculine directors like Ford sneered at such a pretentious label, as evidenced by what they purported to believe about their own creative prowess. As the old studio system began to crumble in the mid-1960s, when filmmakers like Ford were either surrendering or just barely finding ways to hang on, a new generation of directors began to infiltrate the studio backlots, given carte blanche by desperate studio chieftains who lost the pulse of the public. Spend millions on *Cleopatra* (1962), get a shrug from the audience who would rather stay home and watch television. This story has been told many times: the maverick New Hollywood generation, those wild-eyed boys who blew the bloody doors off by reaching back into movie history and blending old-style genre films with international art cinema and cooking it all in the broth of Nixon-era cynicism, delivering downer after downer, portraits of artist-surrogates-as-young-men, angry and violent and sexist and rebellious and alienated and in the end, defeated or dead. No one has done more to shape the popular perspective on the era than Peter Biskind, whose book *Easy Riders, Raging Bulls* (1998) tells a tragic story of a generation of Icaruses, brilliant artists who reinvented cinema for the hippie generation, but whose wings of wax burned away after too much of everything: sex, drugs, rock and roll, hubris, money, ego, pain, and freedom. In Biskind's telling, the era gave rise to

> a movement intended to cut film free of its evil twin, commerce, enabling it to fly high through the thin air of art. The filmmakers of the '70s hoped to overthrow the studio system, or at least render it irrelevant, by democratizing filmmaking, putting it into the hands of anyone with talent and determination.[4]

These were the "auteurs." The self-appointed ones. The film-school generation of directors who not only knew they were artists, but even knew what to call themselves, after the French had anointed Ford, Howard Hawks, Alfred Hitchcock, Orson Welles, Fritz Lang, and a number of other directors who had earned the venerable title "auteur." The film, like a novel, had to have an author, someone who was responsible for telling the story, someone whose signature was visible in every image the way Ernest Hemingway's terse language expressed its author's tough personality in every syllable.

Biskind's story is a compelling one. But it is also only part of the story. The characters he leans on—Dennis Hopper, Martin Scorsese, Bob Rafelson, Jack Nicholson, Francis Ford Coppola, Hal Ashby—reflect the story of the era. White, male, straight. Recent works of scholarship, like Maya Montanez Smukler's *Liberating Hollywood*, which examines the contributions of female filmmakers to the 1970s American cinema scene, have attempted to correct the historical record by examining the contributions of lesser known, but essential figures of the New Hollywood period. In Smukler's convincing study, she argues that this retrospective view has "fostered a popular and romantic historicization of 1970s Hollywood as an era of extraordinary potential for young filmmakers," but the result was "the open door for 'almost anyone' to enter the ranks and direct feature films was entered primarily by white men."[5] Smukler brilliantly states her book's intention: "neither to rewrite the history of American cinema during the 1970s nor to construct a separate history of women directors in the period," calling her work "an *expansionist* and *integrationist* film history."[6] Smukler's keen observation is that the full story of the New Hollywood period has not yet been told, despite the number of studies that have been devoted to the period.

Walter Hill registers two brief mentions in Biskind's book. In one, he is a friend of De Palma's dropping by the beachfront hangout house where the Movie Brats got high and talked about their favorite directors,[7] and in the other, he is an also-ran noted for the violence in his films alongside Schrader, Scorsese, and De Palma.[8] Biskind has nothing to say about Hill's work. His book is hardly the only one to virtually ignore Hill, however. Ryan Gilbey's *It Don't Worry Me: The Revolutionary American Films of the Seventies* doesn't mention Hill once.[9] The same is true of Peter Lev's *American Films of the 70s: Conflicting Visions*, where Hill is absent entirely.[10] In Lev's contribution to *American Cinema of the 1970s: Themes and Variations*, Hill is only a "writer/producer" of *Alien* (1979, dir. Ridley Scott), and he is mentioned nowhere else in the book.[11] Editor Stephen Prince's follow-up, *American Cinema of the 1980s: Themes and Variations*, fares no better; Hill is mentioned only once in the book, in Prince's introduction, as the director of *The Long Riders* (1980), one of "a few good westerns" made in the decade.[12] Jonathan Kirshner's *Hollywood's Last Golden Age* references Hill once for his screenplay for the detective comedy *Hickey & Boggs* (1972), which he dismisses as "not much concerned with explaining every little thing (or, for that matter, some bigger things)."[13] Drew Casper's study of the New Hollywood period ends with 1976, but does manage to mention Hill's screenwriting contributions to Sam Peckinpah's 1972 film *The Getaway*[14] and even notes the director's development of a consistent theme in what Casper calls "the adult male's rite of passage that raised issues of masculinity,"[15] an unelaborated encapsulation of Hill's *Hard Times* (1975), the bare-knuckle boxing film that would be his directorial debut. Perhaps most surprising is Hill's omission from Derek Nystrom's *Hard Hats, Rednecks, and Macho Men*, a study of masculine types in American films of the 1970s and 1980s focusing on class.[16] A number of Hill's characters from *Hard Times*, *The Driver* (1978), *The Warriors* (1979), *The Long Riders*, and especially *Southern Comfort* (1981), would have fit the bill.

Many of Hill's contemporaries bear the influence of filmmakers from the Classic Hollywood generation, most especially Howard Hawks. Another Hawks admirer, John Carpenter, has benefited from the association, according to Ian Conrich and David Woods.[17] Those who have studied Carpenter, like Robert C. Cumbow, "make no apology" for his auteur status.[18] The number of published works on Carpenter's cinema speak to his acceptance as an important American filmmaker, despite his consistent work in so-called low genres like science, fiction, and horror. Unlike Carpenter, Hill has been ignored up to now, likely owing to his long residency in the action genre, which has not yet developed a substantial body of critical study or legitimacy. In fact, it is not too heavy a lift to substitute Hill's name for Carpenter's in Conrich and Woods's following sentence about Carpenter: "A B-movie aesthetic of sensationalistic, uninhibited and confident genre filmmaking has continually been a mark of Carpenter's productions, but this may explain why his movies have been both applauded and dismissed, and why he has received little academic attention."[19] Genre was one path for Carpenter's admission into the auteur club; Barry Keith Grant sees Carpenter's contribution alongside Hill's: "In the 1980s, along with Walter Hill, [Carpenter] was instrumental in the development of the new action film, as distinct from the traditional adventure or disaster film."[20]

Carpenter's work stands on its own, of course, but the director's admiration of Hawks likely helped serious academics to consider his films beyond the level of their genre in the first place. Hill's work also reveals devotion to Hawks, one of the original auteurs in the eyes of the *Cahiers du Cinema* crowd. One of its members, critic and director Jacques Rivette, was impressed by Hawks's ability to blend comedy and drama "so that each, rather than damaging each other, seems to underscore their reciprocal relation: the one sharpens the other."[21] For Rivette and a number of subsequent critics studying Hawks's films, their focus on men of action made the strongest impression. When Rivette watched Hawks's *Red River* (1948), he saw the "*actions* that he films, meditating on the power of appearances alone."[22] Hawks, according to Rivette, turned his commitment to narrative economy and stylistic rigidity into organic fluidity: "The smooth, orderly succession of shots has a rhythm like the pulsing of blood, and the whole film is like a beautiful body, kept alive by deep, resilient breathing."[23] Andre Bazin, dean of the *Cahiers du Cinema* magazine, argued that "the formal intelligence of Hawks's direction masks intelligence, full stop."[24] The French critics knew that Hawks's surface simplicity would deter others from taking his work seriously, especially in contrast to the visual and aural ostentatiousness of Hitchcock or the grandiosity and mythmaking of Ford. Bazin's assertion that Hawks's films are deceptively deep justifies the value of seeing Hawks separately from the genres in which he works; whereas Hitchcock and Ford can be seen obviously elevating the thriller and the western to new artistic heights, Hawks's work might be easily mistaken for slumming if not given proper consideration.

The case for Hawks as auteur rested on a number of ideas, including Peter Wollen's observation that "in film after film, Hawks repeated himself, albeit giving each repetition a new twist, a new flavor."[25] His signature became visible through his repeated reliance on actors, narrative situations, themes, staging, visual style, and gestures, all of which built on his previous work without undercutting the individual film in which they appeared. Like the filmmakers who would follow him, Hawks "stole not only from himself, but from other directors too."[26] Critics studying Hawks's work have found a consistent voice across these numerous genres; Manny Farber calls him "the key figure in the male action film because he shows a maximum speed, inner life, and view, with the least amount of flat foot."[27] Because of his profound influence on Hill, Hawks remains an essential ancestor of the action film. His direct, deliberate style became a lodestar for budding directors in the 1970s and 1980s, the foundational decades for the development of modern action cinema. Farber's discussion of Hawks echoes praise for the finest action films, as his work offers "striking photography, a good ear for natural dialogue, an eye for realistic detail, a skilled inside-action approach to composition, and the most politic hand in the movie field."[28]

In a 2013 interview with *The AV Club*, Walter Hill expressed his fondness for Hawks: "I think one of the great masters was [Howard] Hawks. And I think Hawks rather impatiently answered, when being asked certain questions—'Will he live or will he die?'—'That's drama.' Once you're in that situation, that's the fundamental business of an action film. I like being an action director. It's kind of what I've always wanted, really."[29] Hill follows Hawks in using genre as a viable space for his own personal self-expression. In Hill's estimation, the masters transcended the genre space in which they worked:

> John Ford and Howard Hawks are beyond genres. Even so, I always felt that genre film-making was going to be my home, but I also understood that you couldn't go on making them the way they used to do—there's no challenge. If you were just gonna go at it the way the old guys did, then you were going to run up against the fact that they did it better than you ever could—not surprising, since they had invented the genres themselves. My generation found you had to use the old genres in new ways, pull them inside out.[30]

Hill's self-awareness also shows up in the films themselves, each of which, as John Patterson says, "pull a whole lot of conventions inside out, and offer a concentrated, high-octane dose of bracingly violent action-poetry, one after another."[31] Hill follows deliberately in the footsteps of giants, but still finds ways to make his work personal by specifying their universal themes. His references to Hawks and others are more than mere glosses on film history; they place his work in conversation with the work of others who came before him. Rivette's encapsulation of Hawks's cinema, in which "Human actions are weighed and measured by a master director preoccupied with man's responsibilities,"[32] is also true of Hill's films.

Though Hawks made a number of films in various genres, his work in westerns and war films, which chronicle groups of men and their hierarchical relationships, made the most lasting impact on Hill. The importance of professionalism defines many of Hawks's key works; characters in his landmark film *Rio Bravo* are obsessively preoccupied with male efficacy. John Wayne's John T. Chance, a town sheriff keeping a murderer locked in his jail while fending off a gang's attempts to spring him, is the ultimate professional man, judged by his actions. Dean Martin's Dude spends the film negotiating his past reputation as "the best" with his current one as the town drunk. The film hinges on key questions: will Dude be good enough? Will Chance approve of him? Will the two rediscover their mutual admiration for the other's abilities? Hill reappropriates these themes throughout his work. In *Southern Comfort*, two members of a group of National Guardsmen develop a grudging respect for each other amidst a survival crisis.

Hill was also influenced by Sam Peckinpah, who, through his innovative, confrontational work, became a kind of upperclassman guiding freshmen across Hollywood's moviemaking campus. Like Ford before him, Peckinpah worked frequently in westerns, but his major contribution to cinema was to completely rewrite the rules for on-screen violence, experimenting first in *Major Dundee* (1965) and then reaching full-scale onslaught in the extraordinarily bloody elegy for the dying west, *The Wild Bunch* (1968). Peckinpah's editing disrupted normal patterns of continuity. His free implementation of Soviet-style montage and chaotic, disorienting approach to shooting wild melees of action revolutionized the way subsequent filmmakers portrayed violence on screen. He used slow-motion at will, resulting in what Stephen Prince called "aestheticized violence" that manifested Peckinpah's "intensely felt personal relationship to the problem of violence, in both his personal life and in his perception of the tragedy of American history."[33] Hill's apprenticeship while collaborating with Peckinpah on *The Getaway* left a lasting impression, obvious in his stylistic employment of slow motion and deliberate restaging of some of Peckinpah's most famous cinematic moments.

From Peckinpah, Hill adopts the sense of a world slipping away along with the expressionistic approach to shooting film violence. In Peckinpah's second feature *Ride the High Country* (1962), he demonstrated his awareness of the genre's past, casting Randolph Scott and Joel McCrea, yesterday's western heroes, in lion-in-winter roles that lamented the passing of an era. Hill worked closely with Peckinpah on *The Getaway* and draws a contrast in their disparate uses of slow motion. According to Hill, Peckinpah "used the slow motion to extend reality, and to make things more real, and I was trying to use slow motion as kind of a nightmare."[34] Peckinpah's films, but especially *The Wild Bunch*, made a lasting impact on Hill's work, most obviously in his 1987 film *Extreme Prejudice*, cowritten by Hill's friend John Milius. Set on the border between Texas and Mexico, the oppositional relationship between childhood friends turned Texas Ranger and drug kingpin, recalls the duality of outlaw and mercenary posse leader in *The Wild Bunch*. Two friends, driven apart by circumstance, are pulled back together by their competing responsibilities. The climax of *Extreme Prejudice* takes place at the kingpin's Mexico hideout, exploding into a melee of machine gun violence clearly indebted to Peckinpah's chaotic climax in *The Wild Bunch*, which ends with a courtyard full of bullet-riddled bodies. Both thematically and stylistically, Hill moves in Peckinpah's wake, just as he does with Hawks. Actor James Remar considers Hill "a great student of film" who "knows movies from the bottom up," owing to his beginnings as a screenwriter and an assistant director.[35]

Hill's films arrive between the elimination of the Production Code rules but before the advent of digital effects that strained the suspension of disbelief almost to its breaking point. Following Hawks's example, a number of his films that focus on groups of men rely on wide and medium shots, emphasizing the collective reactions of men as they jockey for position against each other in the masculine hierarchy. To William Sadler, Hill "embodies an old-fashioned style of moviemaking that you don't see anymore."[36] In *The Warriors* and *Southern Comfort*, this stylistic choice reflects Hill's finely tuned sense of how groups of men interact, where roles are constantly in flux. This deceptively simple approach contrasts mightily with Hill's similar adoption of Peckinpah's aestheticized violence captured in slow motion and with fragmented editing. A particularly brutal execution in *The Long Riders*, when the James Gang draws down on a pair of Pinkerton agents responsible for killing their younger brother, bears the mark of Peckinpah; the cacophony of rifle fire sends the agents flying backward through a plate glass window at half speed, the glass shattering around them. It is a moment of undeniable beauty, but contrasted sharply with the savagery of the violence. It is moments like these that lead actor David Patrick Kelly to suggest that Hill's movies bridge the gap between "art movies and action movies—that there could be real substance to action movies, more than just entertaining and lowbrow culture. There's big ideas in there about society at large."[37]

This Hawks-Peckinpah axis of style defines much of Hill's early work, but his 1984 film *Streets of Fire*, which bills itself as a "rock and roll fable," upends the apple cart. Though Hill's subsequent films still make use of the straightforwardness favored by Hawks and the aesthetics of Peckinpah to establish their basic cinematic grammar, his post–*Streets of Fire* films also show increased willingness to experiment with other stylistic devices. After 1984, Hill is more likely to shoot scenes with Dutch angles unmotivated by staging. In these later films, Hill also increasingly deploys wide-angle lenses in close-ups, which distort his characters' faces by warping the frame at the edges. His adventurousness only grows as he enters the 1990s. His 1992 thriller *Trespass*, in which a pair of white Arkansas firemen hunt for buried gold in an abandoned East St. Louis warehouse only to run afoul of a group of Black drug dealers, mixes diegetic image sources; one of the gangsters captures the events through the lens of his handheld camcorder, through which Hill shows them plotting to flush out the barricaded firefighters. The film's release was delayed by the 1992 uprising in Los Angeles in the aftermath of the "not guilty" verdict in the trial of the police officers caught on video beating up Rodney King.[38] Hill continued such stylistic experimentation in *Wild Bill*, in which he uses narrative flashbacks and surrealistic dream sequences shot on video and converted to black-and-white film to express his anti-hero's ambivalence to the trail of bodies left in his wake which simultaneously built his legend and haunt his nights.[39] Hill's sensibility has leaned even further into his long-stated admiration for comic books and graphic novels in recent years, as his director's cut of *The Warriors* adds comic panel flourishes to its opening scene and important transitions,[40] but also in *Bullet To The Head*, an adaptation of a graphic novel, and *The Assignment*, which was released in tandem with a graphic novel version penned by Hill himself. *Streets of Fire*, as a hybrid work drawing from westerns, noir, and musicals, was the film that liberated Hill to explore new narrative and stylistic territory. Actor Lance Henriksen values his collaborations with Hill, which produced "the joy of working with a guy who thinks in epic terms."[41]

Though Hill's directorial debut *Hard Times* does not appear until 1975, his contributions as screenwriter to *Hickey & Boggs*, *The Getaway*, and *The Thief Who Came to Dinner* (1973, Yorkin) demonstrate his early participation in the New Hollywood story. During the latter half of the 1970s, when the studio system is beginning to reassert its dominance on the strength of blockbusters, Hill begins to direct in earnest, with 1978's *The Driver* and 1979's *The Warriors*, followed by *The Long Riders* in 1980 and *Southern Comfort* in 1981. Though Hill's chosen genre, the action film, would be more likely to find a home alongside the blockbusters than the "personal art films" associated with Scorsese, De Palma, and others, Hill uses the genre to explore crucial themes of interest to him while balancing the commercial needs of adhering to, and ultimately delivering on, its essential conventions. His films are not the uncompromising, often self-indulgent art films of his contemporaries; they balance the needs of profit and personality in ways that sometimes foreclose their possibilities.

Studies of action cinema of the 1980s have tended to focus on the decade's bigger, more obvious objects—the films of muscle-bound stars like Arnold Schwarzenegger and Sylvester Stallone, signifying for Susan Jeffords "a resurgence of both national and masculine power."[42] Schwarzenegger wore a loincloth and brandished a sword for *Conan the Barbarian* (1982, Milius) *Conan the Destroyer* (1984, Fleischer) before moving on to *The Terminator* (1984, Cameron), in which Schwarzenegger's villainous cyborg is an unstoppable force powered by the actor's chiseled physique. The Austrian-born actor carried this invulnerable reputation into *Commando* (1985, Lester), a self-conscious kidnap-and-rescue mission undertaken with a heavy ironic wink, and in the science fiction-action hybrid *Predator* (1987, McTiernan). Stallone, meanwhile, spent the decade playing John Rambo in the relatively grounded *First Blood* (1982, Kotcheff), the Vietnam-minded, "Do we get to win this time?" sequel, *Rambo: First Blood Part II* (1984, Cosmatos), and joining the mujahedeen to fend off the Soviets in Afghanistan in *Rambo III* (1988, MacDonald). Together, Schwarzenegger and Stallone redefined the action hero in their bodybuilder images, emphasizing his physical strength and resistance to pain. Hill's action cinema makes little use of these muscular heroes; his 1988 collaboration with Schwarzenegger, *Red Heat*, would largely downplay his actor's physique by covering him in a Russian police officer's uniform. By the time Hill would work with Stallone in 2012's *Bullet To The Head*, the actor was no longer in peak physical condition, a fact emphasized by his on-screen fight with future Aquaman Jason Momoa.

As an action director of the late New Hollywood period and early blockbuster era, Hill performs an important transitional function between two historical movements in cinema, while also entrenching the action film as a viable genre. Just as Ford's contributions to the western demonstrated that it could be a serious mode of storytelling with 1939's *Stagecoach*, which Barry Keith Grant called "the first 'adult western,'"[43] Hill's mature work in what has been perceived as an immature genre elevates the action film to a space for artistic expression. Hill takes the influence of the action film's progenitors and instantiates their stylistic and thematic approaches as genre conventions. Modern action film tropes, including slow motion, extremity of violence, contests of masculinity between mismatched partners, gun-to-the-head hostage standoffs, and others, all become conventions through Hill's repeated deployment of them. His presence during the historical moment when action films proliferated is no accident; those who come after following his example whether they know it or not.

Though the Classic Hollywood period, action lived inside other film genres—war films, westerns, and certain kinds of noir—rather than existing on its own.[44] Hill's action films bear the mark of westerns or noir, and often implement varying degrees of both simultaneously. In his 1996 film *Last*

Man Standing, a gunslinger rides into a dusty Prohibition-era town, fusing the Classic Hollywood western with the story of Akira Kurosawa's *Yojimbo* (1961). The setting of *Last Man Standing* is definably western, but the voice-over and tough guy attitude lends it a touch of noir. Hill preceded it with *Geronimo: An American Legend* (1993), a film clearly indebted to John Ford's cavalry trilogy, made up of *Fort Apache* (1948), *She Wore a Yellow Ribbon* (1949), and *Rio Grande* (1950), both in its subject matter and in Hill's largely classical approach to the material. His next feature, 1995's *Wild Bill*, starring Jeff Bridges as infamous gunslinger "Wild Bill" Hickok, explores the myth of the western anti-hero. This work in the 1990s, not to mention *The Long Riders*, has led critics like John Patterson to mark Hill "the unofficial conservator of the never quite moribund western genre [. . .] perhaps because he considers all his movies to be westerns at heart."[45] His move into westerns in the 1990s, long his favorite genre, at a time when audiences were decidedly moving away from them, shows either an increasing commitment to his own artistic expression or a dulling of his commercial instincts—perhaps it is some combination of both.

Noir has been just as influential over Hill's work, as he has regularly adopted the urban settings and chiaroscuro lighting of Classic Hollywood thrillers. He says, "I was a great fan of film noir when I was a kid. And I've strived for a touch of that darkness."[46] Hill's interest in noir should come as no surprise, given the New Hollywood filmmakers' preoccupation with revisiting old genres and films with fresh, newly cynical perspective. Hill's career begins in the 1970s and peaks in the 1980s, a time which saw neo-noir films update the genre's thematic and stylistic conventions for their own era. They employed self-conscious callbacks to the noir films that made up a loose, disconnected movement defined most effectively through its shared mood of anxiety and dread, feelings which resonated deeply in the 1970s and 1980s. Hill shows the influence of noir throughout his work, but most especially in 1989's *Johnny Handsome*, a crime thriller about a grotesque thief who undergoes reconstructive plastic surgery in an effort to get revenge against the hoods who crossed him and killed his partner in a job gone bad. Hill returns to the same narrative device in his most recent film, 2016's *The Assignment*, for which he courted controversy over the central plot conceit: a male assassin is unwillingly given reconstructive surgery that turns him into a woman. The assassin uses his body and new identity to get revenge against the doctor who performed the surgery, a narrative structure that drew accusations of transphobia. *Johnny Handsome* and *The Assignment*, like many noir films, are about the loss of self.

Despite narrative and stylistic evolution, Hill's work has remained consistent in its interest in male relationships in groups or in partnerships. Many of his early films, including *The Warriors*, *The Long Riders*, and

Southern Comfort, examine the complex battles over leadership and the performance of masculinity that sustain groups of men. By placing his male groups in crisis, Hill watches how they succumb to outside pressure, often through dissolution. While Hawks's groups of men often came together to fend off threats or reconcile their differences, Hill often breaks apart, reflecting a New Hollywood-inspired revisionist approach to earlier cinema. Though the Warriors make it back to Coney Island alive, they lose key members of the gang along the way; the National Guardsmen in *Southern Comfort* are not so lucky, as all but two are killed by the Cajun trappers hunting them, and the survivors are bloodied physically and emotionally by the trauma they have experienced. Hill's decision to cast real-life sets of brothers to play the brother-outlaw teams in *The Long Riders* goes beyond gimmickry; when one of the men makes a foolhardy mistake or fails the group, his brother's decision to stand by him or abandon him carries additional emotional weight, transmitting his divided loyalty to the audience through self-conscious play upon star image. Hill's subsequent turn to two-man partnerships narrows his focus, but not his resolve to explore the complicated dynamics of power, respect, and failure that govern homosocial interactions.

Often in Hill's films, these group and partnership dynamics achieve an additional layer of political relevance through their multiracial focus. Across Hill's work, he demonstrates consistent interest in issues of racial discontinuity that hearken back to the history of American race relations, including the bloody history of slavery and the injustice of Jim Crow segregation, along with the still persistent wealth gap between white and Black Americans. Hill is the white filmmaker of the New Hollywood era who is not only most interested in issues of race, but also the one who most consistently walks the walk by actually populating his films with a number of actors of color. According to Sigourney Weaver, "Walter is so comfortable with what America really looks like."[47] His action-comedy *48 Hrs.*, which cast Eddie Murphy in his first film role, foregrounds racial difference between Murphy's charming convict Reggie Hammond and top-billed Nick Nolte's gruff police detective Jack Cates. The friction between the two men not only stems from their respective positions on opposite sides of the law, but also their overt racial roles, which becomes fodder for dialogue. Hill does not simply let the casting do the work; his characters directly participate in the often ugly racial discussion, all the more remarkably so in a film that became one of Hill's most commercially successful, but also spawned less adventurous pairings in imitators. Many of Hill's successive films, including his comedy *Brewster's Millions* (1985) and his blues drama *Crossroads* (1986), continue the director's interest in racial difference before he returns to the Hammond-Cates pairing in *Another 48 Hrs.* (1990), this time with the newly empowered Murphy producing and earning top-billing over Nolte. The aforementioned *Trespass* features a predominantly Black cast, as does Hill's return to the boxing genre with *Undisputed* (2002), a film that equates sport with the imprisonment and commodification of Black men's bodies. Among his contemporaries, Hill has been the white director most willing to venture into racially troubled waters.

Hill has made a number of important individual films across his long career; sometimes, those films have met their moment, and sometimes, they haven't. He has only intermittently achieved critical and commercial success simultaneously; often, both have been fleeting, with his biggest artistic risks (such as *Streets of Fire* and *Wild Bill*) opening to failure. Hill's vision of cinema sometimes seems ill-suited to the moment in which he is working; it is as if he would have been more comfortable working as a studio director under contract at Warner Brothers, alongside the filmmakers of the Classic Hollywood system that he admires. Commercial success, however, is just one measure of a film director; it can and should be divorced from artistic success.

This book is supported by extensive interviews conducted with Walter Hill throughout the first half of 2021, totaling nearly fifteen hours of conversation. In other interviews and in the conversations for this book, Hill demonstrates his tendency to see his work through the prism of an accumulated history of other sources of inspiration. He is quick to quote maxims and words of wisdom from his forebears, and his films are shaped by literature, philosophy,

Figure I.1 Actual history and cinema history suffuse the films of Walter Hill. They are kept alive through references to and engagement with other times and other places; in Wild Bill (1995), gunfighter *Wild Bill* Hickok (Jeff Bridges) leans back in a chair, as Wyatt Earp (Henry Fonda) had done in *My Darling Clementine* (1948, Ford). *Source: Screenshot captured by author.*

history, comic books, and above all, other films. He would likely bristle at being called an intellectual, and his films hit at the gut-level, but the fusion of Hill's wide-ranging interest in culture, history, and art with a definably commercial medium of expression leads to some tensions and, yes, compromises, in his work.

This text assumes that there is validity to the auteur idea, but acknowledges, as Hill himself certainly would, that the director does not act alone, but is supported by a number of essential collaborators who participate in a film's authorship. Auteurism in Hollywood is also complicated by the demands of the system, which mostly places profit above personality; because Hill reached his greatest success in the late 1970s and 1980s, alongside the rise of the blockbuster, his films are inevitably shaped and no doubt compromised by the needs of capital. With any film artist, authorship is potentially speculative territory. Hill's collaborators, however, paint a consistent picture: he is a writer and director who communicates his ideas directly and with specificity, but such efficiency complements a deeper interest in human failings. This book also features interviews with actors Lance Henriksen, David Patrick Kelly, James Remar, William Sadler, and Sigourney Weaver, who praise his inventive dialogue and sure hand as a director who knows what he wants and yet creates a space for collaboration.

The book takes as its vantage point what we might call "qualified auteurism"; it represents an attempt to reveal the artist at work without assigning him the full responsibility for a totalizing vision. Chapter 1 begins not with Hill's debut feature *Hard Times*, but with his sophomore effort *The Driver*, and contextualizes his career in the action cinema to which he belongs. Chapter 2 examines how his third film *The Warriors* reveals the twin influences of Hawks and Peckinpah. Next, I place Hill in the New Hollywood moment in a study of two of that period's defining ideas—genre revisionism and the Vietnam War—in *The Long Riders* and *Southern Comfort* in chapter 3. An exploration of the racial tensions in *48 Hrs.* and its sequel *Another 48 Hrs.* follows in chapter 4, supported by an analysis of a history of Black performers on screen. The book's pivot point comes with chapter 5 on *Streets of Fire*, which also sends Hill's career into a series of different artistic directions. Though the book's first several chapters generally run chronologically with Hill's career, its second half deviates from that trajectory and collects several films by their thematic, stylistic, or generic identity, beginning with a study of the filmmaker's approach to issues of race and wealth in chapter 6, which covers *Hard Times, Undisputed, Brewster's Millions, Crossroads*, and *Trespass*. Hill's numerous westerns form the basis of chapter 7, as each of his efforts—*Geronimo, Wild Bill, Broken Trail*, and *Last Man Standing*—ties to the history of one of Hollywood's most important genres. Chapter 8 follows a similar path, examining the role of place as a signature theme of film noir in Hill's *Red Heat, Bullet to The Head, Johnny Handsome*, and *The Assignment*. The conclusion offers a close reading of *Extreme Prejudice* in isolation as a representation of Hill's themes, style, and an example of an action film that hybridizes westerns and film noir. Throughout, the reader will find Hill's work placed into conversation with the films of Hollywood genres past in an effort to draw lines of continuity between the filmmaking traditions of the studio era and New Hollywood and the consistent themes and conventions of genre cinema.

Hill's films, like those of his New Hollywood contemporaries, acknowledge the history of the medium, but they are also overshadowed by it. For a writer and director whose films are so clearly assembled products, drawn from earlier eras of cinema and heavily inspired by the works of other filmmakers, there is a risk. His adoption of themes and style that defined the cinema of an earlier era might imperil his own artistic vision. Are Hill's films his own, or are they simply retreads of those that came before? Are they hollow exercises in imitation and repetition, or do they reflect his perspective? Can any director be original in the wake of the incredible influence and cultural power of Classic Hollywood? These might be the wrong questions. Hill's self-conscious conversation with film history may undermine his originality, but maybe originality is overrated—an unattainable goal more theoretical than practical. His work acknowledges the importance of history, but the films do not stop there. They transplant contemporary concerns to different historical periods or alternative worlds, aspiring to the mythic rather than the real. From the 1930s of *Hard Times* to the nightmare New York of *The Warriors*; from the bayou-as-Vietnam of *Southern Comfort* to the western deserts of *Geronimo*; from the midnight rides of *The Driver* to the rock and roll jams of *Streets of Fire*; Hill's work is firmly rooted in another time, another place.

NOTES

1. Walter Hill, interview with the author, 26 January 2021.
2. Ibid.
3. Joseph McBride, *Searching for John Ford* (New York: Faber & Faber, 2003), 101.
4. Peter Biskind, *Easy Riders, Raging Bulls* (New York: Touchstone Books, 1998), 17.
5. Maya Montanez Smukler, *Liberating Hollywood: Women Directors and The Feminist Reform of 1970s American Cinema* (New Brunswick, NJ: Rutgers University Press, 2019), 7.
6. Ibid, 15.
7. Biskind, 232.

8. Biskind, 383.

9. Ryan Gilbey, *It Don't Worry Me: The Revolutionary American Films of the Seventies* (New York: Faber & Faber, 2003).

10. Peter Lev, *American Films of the 70s: Conflicting Visions* (Austin, TX: University of Texas Press, 2000).

11. Peter Lev, "Movies and the End of an Era," in *American Cinema of the 1970s: Themes and Variations*, ed. Lester D. Friedman (New Brunswick, NJ: Rutgers University Press, 2007), 246.

12. Stephen Prince, "Introduction: Movies and the 1980s," *American Cinema of the 1980s: Themes and Variations*, ed. Stephen Prince (New Brunswick, NJ: Rutgers University Press, 2007), 17.

13. Jonathan Kirshner, *Hollywood's Last Golden Age: Politics, Society, and The Seventies Film in America* (Ithaca, NY: Cornell University Press, 2012), 169.

14. Drew Casper, *Hollywood Film 1963-1976* (Malden, MA: Wiley-Blackwell, 2011), 304.

15. Ibid, 233.

16. Derek Nystrom, *Hard Hats, Rednecks, and Macho Men: Class in 1970s American Cinema* (New York: Oxford University Press, 2009).

17. Ian Conrich and David Woods, "Introduction," in *The Cinema of John Carpenter: The Technique of Terror*, ed. Ian Conrich and David Woods (London: Wallflower Press, 2004), 2.

18. Robert C. Cumbow, *Order in the Universe: The Films of John Carpenter*, Second Edition (Lanham, MD: Scarecrow Press, 2000), 1.

19. Conrich and Woods, 3.

20. Barry Keith Grant, "Disorder in the Universe: John Carpenter and the Question of Genre," in *The Cinema of John Carpenter: The Technique of Terror*, ed. Ian Conrich and David Woods (London: Wallflower Press, 2004), 11.

21. Jacques Rivette, "The Genuis of Howard Hawks," in *Howard Hawks: American Artist*, ed. Jim Hillier and Peter Wollen (London: British Film Institute, 1996), 26.

22. Ibid, 28, emphasis in original.

23. Ibid, 28.

24. Andre Bazin, "How Could You Possibly be a Hitchcocko-Hawksian?" in *Howard Hawks: American Artist*, ed. Jim Hillier and Peter Wollen (London: British Film Institute, 1996), 33.

25. Peter Wollen, "Introduction," in *Howard Hawks: American Artist*, ed. Jim Hillier and Peter Wollen (London: British Film Institute, 1996), 2.

26. Ibid, 3.

27. Manny Farber, "Underground Films," in *Howard Hawks: American Artist*, ed. Jim Hillier and Peter Wollen (London: British Film Institute, 1996), 35.

28. Ibid, 36.

29. Walter Hill, "Walter Hill on the Anti-Buddy Movie and the Evolution of the Action Film," interview by Scott Tobias, *The AV Club*, February 1, 2013, https://film.avclub.com/walter-hill-on-the-anti-buddy-movie-and-the-evolution-o-1798236038.

30. Walter Hill, "Walter Hill: A Life in the Fast Lane," interview by John Patterson, *The Guardian*, July 17, 2014, https://www.theguardian.com/film/2014/jul/17/walter-hill-action-movie-interview.

31. John Patterson, "Walter Hill: A Life in the Fast Lane," interview by John Patterson, *The Guardian*, July 17, 2014, https://www.theguardian.com/film/2014/jul/17/walter-hill-action-movie-interview.

32. Rivette, 29.

33. Stephen Prince, *Savage Cinema: Sam Peckinpah and the Rise of Ultraviolent Movies* (Austin, TX: University of Texas Press, 1998), 48.

34. Walter Hill, "Slow Motion: Walter Hill on Sam Peckinpah," on *The Long Riders*, DVD, Kino Lorber, 2017.

35. Interview with the author, 26 January 2021.

36. Interview with the author, 22 February 2021.

37. Interview with the author, 25 January 2021.

38. Jane Galbraith, "Coincidences Cause Director to Tread Lightly With 'Trespass,'" *Los Angeles Times*, December 28, 1992, https://www.latimes.com/archives/la-xpm-1992-12-28-ca-2070-story.html.

39. Michael Sragow, "Realized Ambitions," *The Atlantic*, December 1995, https://www.theatlantic.com/magazine/archive/1995/12/realized-ambitions/376504/.

40. Imagine filmmaker Richard Linklater's process of animating over previously shot footage for *Waking Life* (1995) and *A Scanner Darkly* (2003), except applied to select sequences rather than the entire film, and done retrospectively.

41. Interview with the author, 6 February 2021.

42. Susan Jeffords, *Hard Bodies: Hollywood Masculinity in the Reagan Era* (New Brunswick, NJ: Rutgers University Press, 1994), 21.

43. Barry Keith Grant, "Introduction: Spokes in the Wheels," in *John Ford's Stagecoach*, ed. Barry Keith Grant (New York, Cambridge University Press, 2003), 2.

44. Noir's own "genre" status has long been contested, of course. By the time Hill goes to work in the 1970s, noir has become a kind of genre at least enough to engender imitation.

45. Patterson, https://www.theguardian.com/film/2014/jul/17/walter-hill-action-movie-interview.

46. Walter Hill, "Walter Hill's Dark Visions," interview by John Stanley, SF Gate, May 27, 2007, https://www.sfgate.com/entertainment/article/Walter-Hill-s-Dark-visions-2558469.php.

47. Interview with the author, 13 April 2021.

Chapter 1

The Action Man

"I'm an action director," says Walter Hill.[1] He embraces the designation, the label carrying more than a little of an echo of John Ford's famous self-declaration upon meeting new people: "I'm John Ford, and I am a director of westerns," the printed legends report him saying.[2] Like many directors of the New Hollywood generation, Hill admires Ford greatly, holding him alongside a number of other filmmakers who continue to shape the historical boundaries of the Classic Hollywood studio era, including Howard Hawks, Fritz Lang, Raoul Walsh, and others. Though he might bristle at the application of the term, Hill's work is undoubtedly informed by these filmmakers' embodiment of the "classical" style of moviemaking that held the studio system together.[3] Though Hill's films are likewise informed by the postmodern mood coursing through the veins of his fellow New Hollywood directors and are sometimes afflicted by the anxiety of belatedness that preoccupies many contemporary film artists, he reaches for the classical most often.

There is more than a little irony in the juxtaposition of Hill's self-definition as an "action director" and his fondness for the old masters. For one thing, though the films of Ford, Hawks, Lang, Walsh, and others contain a number of scenes of action—the thrilling chase through the desert in *Stagecoach* (1939, Ford) comes to mind, but so too do the safari scenes in *Hatari* (1962, Hawks) as the characters gather up a number of dangerous animals—the action genre as we know it today did not really exist for much of the studio era. Action was not a genre, but a storytelling device that livened a movie up through an escalation of the dramatic stakes. Action could be found in westerns, or combat films, or swashbucklers, or adventure films, and on and on. Noir films sometimes relied on action, as well, but have a similarly tenuous generic identity, notoriously hard to pin down and characterize without a litany of on-the-one-hands and on-the-other-hands. Action was a tool—it couldn't sustain the entirety of a film narrative, let alone codify into a successful formula that could be endlessly repeated into a cycle, and then a genre. Action's mutability has no doubt shaped the genre, which for Yvonne Tasker are "more or less hybrids, drawing on and combining generic plots, settings and character types from sources including science-fiction, the western, horror, the epic, war films, crime cinema and thrillers, disaster movies, swordplay and martial arts, even comedy."[4]

Beginning in the mid-1960s, the tectonic plates that sat beneath the film industry started to shift, creating a seismic disruption that ushered out the old studio system and heralded the arrival of a new, younger group of filmmakers who were not bound by the classical system, but had instead approached cinema as an art form worth studying, rather than a craft learned through apprenticeship or, in another of Ford's immortal phrases, "a job of work."[5] These new filmmakers were aided in their efforts by the abolition of the Hollywood Motion Picture Production Code, a system of self-censorship regulations that had stood with only minor changes since it began to be enforced by the Production Code Administration in 1934. After the Code lost its legitimacy in the mid-1960s, its edifice assaulted by a series of broadsides from piquant directors who chafed under its restrictions, it was eventually replaced by the ratings system, more or less as we know it today. This new system of regulation retired the old "dos," "don'ts," and "be carefuls" in favor of an after-the-fact label that placed the responsibility on the film audience, as opposed to in the paternalistic hands of the Production Code Administration, staffed stem-to-stern with Catholic moralizers. Suddenly, language that had heretofore been prohibited from issuing forth from the mouths of characters could suddenly be heard, in four-lettered glory. Gone too were the fine restrictions on screen morality, which tightly regulated a system of rewards and punishments to be doled out to characters who behaved well or badly, respectively. Films could now depict sexual themes and offer images of movie stars in the nude, a piercing of the veil that the PCA had thrown down around all but the most oblique reference to the sex act. Gone were the romantic swells of music and the whisper of suggestion, replaced by the genuine article—two movie stars, their naked bodies once only imaginable, now stretched hundreds of feet wide on the silver screen. It wasn't the same as it used to be, but it would do.

The doors were also thrown open to new depictions of screen violence, which obliterated the Code's hand-wringing concerns about excessive depictions of "brutality."[6] The subject of action films is violence—as long as the Code remained in place, with even nominal prohibitions against the portrayal of violence, action would be limited. In light of these changes, says J. David Slocum, "The 1960s and early 1970s was the golden age of American film violence, a fact understood by filmmakers and critics at the time and celebrated since."[7] During the 1970s, the action film as we know it today is born, cohering into a genre with specific conventions, tropes, character types, visual style, and notable artists. Genre theorist Steve Neale offers an accounting of those generic properties: "a propensity for spectacular physical action, a narrative structure involving fights, chases and explosions, and in addition to the deployment of state-of-the-art special effects, an emphasis in performance on athletic feats and stunts."[8] Author Eric Lichtenfeld ties the emergence of the genre as crucial to the changes taking place in Hollywood during the 1970s, especially in its representation of evolution of other genres that relied on action as a narrative device: "it liberated the warrior heroes of American cinema from the foreign battlefields of combat films and the long-gone frontier of the western."[9] Yvonne Tasker makes the same contention, but specifically emphasizes the action cinema's financial prowess: "Action has emerged as a pre-eminent commercial genre of the New Hollywood cinema."[10] The proliferation of action-oriented blockbuster filmmaking, represented especially in the 2010s by the ubiquity of the superhero film makes Tasker's point for her.

Walter Hill has seen it all. His career as a film artist began in the late 1960s as an assistant director on *Bullitt* at the dawn of the action genre, and he has been both a bystander to and participant in these dramatic changes up through the release of *The Assignment* (2016). As a self-defined action director, Hill's works have consistently been at the forefront of the action genre. While a screenwriter working for Sam Peckinpah on *The Getaway* in 1972, Hill established an identity as a man who could confidently handle an action story, giving propulsive drive to the narrative that was then expounded upon by the film's director, with his own poetic and nightmarish approach to screen violence. Shortly thereafter, he made his own directorial debut with *Hard Times* in 1975, a bare-knuckle boxing film set during the Great Depression in New Orleans, with action star Charles Bronson, fresh off his vigilante turn in *Death Wish* (1974, Winner), in the leading role. But it was with the release of *The Driver* in 1978 that Hill really established his action bonafides. Despite the film's financial failure, its impact on action cinema was profound as the first of a cycle of overtly stylized 1980s crime thrillers, relying heavily on noir conventions, shot through with a neon-drenched visual aesthetic. Hill's early contributions to the action genre in his various capacities as assistant director, screenwriter, and then director, reveal how his career will embody one of what Lisa Purse argues are the action film's central concerns, "its persistent and detailed attention to the exerting body, a focus which shapes its audio-visual aesthetics as much as its characterization and narrative design."[11] The breakneck car chase of *Bullitt*, the thrilling shootouts of *The Getaway*, the bare-knuckle boxing matches of *Hard Times*, and the multiple car chases and gun battles of *The Driver* testify to Hill's presence in the heady early days of the action genre, when its scenes and character types were still being worked out. He defined their conventions for a number of future filmmakers, who would imitate the work he did. Car chases would become essential action film set pieces, with notable presence in films of the moment like *Gone in 60 Seconds* (1974, Halicki), as well as more recent films like *The Bourne Supremacy* (2004, Greengrass). Though *The Getaway* was certainly not the first heist picture, its influence led to a remake from Hill's screenplay in 1994, directed by Roger Donaldson, and the similarly themed *The Town* (2010, Affleck), among many others. The working class milieu of Depression-era New Orleans in *Hard Times* no doubt shapes the Appalachian-set *Out of the Furnace* (2013, Cooper), which centers around an underground bare-knuckle boxing ring. In 2011, Nicolas Winding Refn would lift the character and the basic story of Hill's *The Driver* for his own self-consciously designed 1980s crime thriller *Drive*, the titular connection more than a little obvious. So too would Edgar Wright in *Baby Driver* (2017), heavily indebted to Hill's film.

However, there is a long distance between the emergence of the action genre in the 1970s and the infusion of its generic identity into the dominant force in Hollywood in the early 2020s. The 1980s are really the action genre's classical period, when the genre has been codified into a very specific set of films and is driven by a number of highly bankable stars, including Arnold Schwarzenegger and Sylvester Stallone, who appear in several films that show off what Susan Jeffords calls their "hard bodies" in her book of that title, which finds an inextricable link between the image of masculinity portrayed by these film stars and the muscular approach taken to political action by then-president Ronald Reagan.[12] Characters like Schwarzenegger's Terminator and Stallone's Rambo, in Jeffords's estimation, showed how Reagan and the film industry moved as one: "both Reagan and Hollywood participated in the radical shift away from the attitudes, public policies, and national concerns that characterized the late 1970s and the Carter administration."[13] The release of John McTiernan's *Die Hard* in 1988 announced a different kind of masculinity that, for Martin Flanagan, "represented a movement away from the model of the cruel, intractable hero, aligning the character with the wisecracking star persona of Bruce Willis and shifting the emphasis slightly from body to voice."[14] The shift is embodied by Willis's everyman police officer John McClane, who must do battle with a group of terrorists who are holding his wife hostage in a Los Angeles skyscraper, with little more than his wits and his bare feet to keep him alive. *Die Hard*'s influence was so profound that a number of imitators quickly sprang forth, refashioning the everyman-hero-against-the-villains-in-a-public-space narrative into a repeatable formula; the legacy of *Die Hard* is visible in *Under Siege* (1992, Davis), *Passenger 57*

(1992, Hooks), *Speed* (1994, De Bont), *Sudden Death* (1995, Hyams), and *Air Force One* (1997, Petersen), not to mention the film's own four sequels.

Hill's action work throughout the 1980s remains stubbornly outside both traditions. While Purse reminds us that contemporary action films have "always incorporated and repurposed tropes from other popular genres, most obviously the western, but also melodrama, romance, science fiction and horror to name the most common,"[15] they most often tend to subsume those influences beneath the more overt trappings of the action genre. The film *Commando* (1985, Lester), for instance, is a vigilante rescue movie which borrows its premise from *The Searchers* (1956, Ford), sending its hero John Matrix (Arnold Schwarzenegger) to South America to retrieve his kidnapped daughter from the villains who have abducted her. The film is replete with gunfights, chases, and especially its fervent display of Schwarzenegger's body. It also exemplifies the action genre's refusal to take itself seriously, most often manifest in the pithy one-liners given to its heroes after dispatching the antagonists in particularly gruesome ways, a trope borrowed from James Bond movies. In *Commando*, Schwarzenegger's Matrix tells one criminal, "I like you, Sully. That's why I'm going to kill you last"; after breaking the neck of another thug in the plane seat next to him, Matrix tells a flight attendant, "He's dead tired"; after dropping a crook off a cliff, he reports to his partner, "I let him go"; the coup-de-grace of the film comes when he impales the primary villain with a pipe, and tells him, "Let off some steam." Such a comedic approach to death and dismemberment comes to dominate impressions of the action cinema, evidence that the genre trivializes violence by rendering it farcical. By contrast, Hill's lone collaboration with Schwarzenegger, the cop thriller *Red Heat*, self-consciously avoids the goofier aspects of the muscle-bound star's screen persona, situating the action and his character's reactions to it in the real world.

Neither did Hill make a version of *Die Hard*, with his films throughout the 1980s generally avoiding the singular protagonist in favor of the internal dynamic of a group, as in *The Warriors*, *The Long Riders*, and *Southern Comfort*. His other action films of the period focus on the relationship between two partners, as in *48 Hrs.*, its sequel *Another 48 Hrs.*, and *Red Heat*. Despite the absence of an action hero, as embodied most frequently in the genre by Schwarzenegger and Stallone, and later Willis, the central narrative concerns of all three of these films root them firmly in action cinema, which feature similar circumstances articulated by Purse: "in an environment fraught with risk and danger, it is the body poised between mastery and loss of control that holds our attention."[16] While the "hard bodies" of Schwarzenegger and Stallone protected them from true narrative danger—they may suffer violent attacks, injuries, and torture, but their ultimate fate is never really in question—Hill's groups are not so lucky. Because he largely avoids the casting of these "hard body" types, or deliberately downplays those elements of their personae, Hill's action films both exist inside the genre's classical period and outside of it. He likewise plays self-consciously on Willis's screen persona in their film together, *Last Man Standing*, in which the *Die Hard* star plays a taciturn, even sullen anti-hero; as Willis's John Smith decimates the henchmen of two rival gangs fighting for control of a dead western town, he largely keeps his mouth shut and lets his guns do the talking.

Die Hard and its numerous imitators mostly design action around gun fights, which offer audiences a spectacle of violence that makes the human body vulnerable to bullets. Though many filmmakers are associated with such gun violence, Hong Kong director John Woo, who came to Hollywood in the 1990s, brought a new approach to shooting gun violence that leaned into the aestheticized approach of Sam Peckinpah, foregrounding his action heroes' acrobatics using extreme slow-motion. In his Hong Kong films *A Better Tomorrow* (1986), *A Better Tomorrow II* (1987), *The Killer* (1989), and *Hard Boiled* (1992), Woo offers what David Bordwell calls "expressive amplification of action," which "seeks to characterize each chase or fight quite emotionally."[17] The stylistic excess of Woo's cinema, which he pioneered in Hong Kong and then replicated in his American action films *Hard Target* (1993), *Broken Arrow* (1995), and especially *Face/Off* (1997), situates action alongside melodrama, a similarly borderless technique that shapes much of Hollywood cinema while also moonlighting as a genre of its own. According to Barry Langford, "a renovated melodramatic mode combining aspects of both blood-and-thunder and modified melodrama characterizes the most important contemporary Hollywood genre, the action blockbuster."[18] For Richard Pope, the somewhat precarious properties that the action film shares with melodrama make it "indeterminate and always already subject to reiteration and reorientation."[19] Perhaps it is action cinema's alignment with the melodrama that has led many to dismiss it as little more than empty spectacle rooted in chaotic, mindless violence. And yet, there is no denying the genre's success with audiences, giving it what Scott Higgins calls "the double distinction of being both one of the most popular and most popularly derided of contemporary genres."[20] Of the fifteen highest grossing movies of the 1990s, more than half rely significantly on action sequences, and several combine their action with highly melodramatic storytelling devices.[21]

Hill's films rarely revel in the balletics of a gunfight, as do John Woo's, but instead portray violence as sudden, shocking, and often shattering to his characters. His characters' final confrontations with the antagonists, as in the standoff between Jack Cates (Nick Nolte) and Albert Ganz (James Remar) in *48 Hrs.*, are over quickly—Cates shoots once, which surprises Ganz, and then fires again, bringing him down. Hill does not include images that Woo is notorious for: a cool cop or criminal, an automatic pistol in each hand, sailing through the air in slow motion while firing. Many subsequent directors have followed in Woo's footsteps, aestheticizing the moment of violence, but Hill's interest is not in the act of gunplay itself; his films instead examine the limits of violence. As an art form, cinema has long been consumed by its ability to display the violent act, a trend which Stephen Prince argues "is tied to the medium's inherently visceral properties."[22] Action films can tend to let the viewer off the hook, a concern expressed by Devin McKinney, who laments that, more often than not, screen violence "seems to come equipped with its own escape hatch, its own assurance that involvement can be avoided."[23] This trend has only accelerated in the era of CGI, which strains the bounds of physical credulity, sending its action heroes—even the ones who don't wear capes—diving off buildings, leaping over impossibly wide chasms, and surviving untrammeled peril.

Hill's films are more earthbound, rooted in the physical impact of violence on the human body that accentuates pain and horror. Though he avails himself of the Peckinpah-esque slow motion shot, he adapts it to suit his own purposes: in *The Long Riders*, he strains slow motion far beyond Peckinpah's use of the technique, dwelling intently on the physical pain of the gunshots that perforate his James Gang; in *Southern Comfort*, a fatally maimed National Guardsman screams in agony as he is impaled by a booby trap set by the bayou's Cajuns, seeking vengeance against the interlopers; in *Red Heat*, a veteran cop is gunned down during a shootout, the force of the bullet's impact slamming his body to the floor of a train station hallway; in *Bullet to The Head*, a pair of hitmen assassinate their bare-chested target, the bullets registering on his flesh in a visual display that refuses to sanitize the violence. Even Hill's most stylized approach to violent action, *Last Man Standing*, acts as a kind of parody of the action pioneered by John Woo, as Willis's Smith blows a gangster away in the film's first gunfight, sending him flying some thirty feet back on impact. Hill himself describes this approach to violent action as rooted in the story he is telling, with each sequence he designs "particular to the narrative and character" of each individual film, acting as "an extension of the characters," which determines their construction.[24] In his approach, directing an action sequence requires strict adherence to "the same principles that apply to any dramatic scene."[25] Hill's action movies attempt to resolve a longstanding tension in the action genre, one reminiscent of that facing the musical, which is the competing devotion to spectacle and narrative. They contrast mightily with the prevailing trend in action cinema that dominated the 1980s, most readily exemplified by the filmmaking team of producers Jerry Bruckheimer and Don Simpson, and director Tony Scott, whose films have, according to Lorrie Palmer, "come to symbolize an abandonment of plot and character in favor of excess and spectacle, the centrality of surface over substance."[26]

Hill's action films reconcile these tensions—when they do provide action scenes that feel like spectacle, as in other action films, those sequences are constrained by the terrestrial, an impulse rooted in Hill's admiration for classical directors. The relative absence of pure spectacle in Hill's action cinema has led to its omission from most critical studies of the genre, even in those of its classical period. His films, though certainly action movies, do not earn serious attention from Susan Jeffords or Yvonne Tasker in their studies of the body in the action genre. Neither Hill nor any of his films rate an indexical mention in either *Hard Bodies* (Jeffords's book) or *Spectacular Bodies* (Tasker's), likely because of their refusal to engage in the same kind of display of the male body that each argues is essential to the action genre; this is not to criticize Jeffords or Tasker, but to point out that Hill's films, because they are less easy to categorize, have escaped the attention of even the most serious scholars who have studied the action cinema.[27] In their refusal to make the action hero an object of spectacle, Hill's action films offer an alternative vision of what the action cinema can accomplish. In Scott Higgins's estimation, considering "narrative and spectacle as oppositional, and the emphasis on the genre's apparent subversion of classical qualities, have clouded our historical understanding of the action film."[28] This is the gap into which Hill's work has fallen.

Hill's action movies are (mostly) about men, though. According to Lisa Purse, "Action cinema is traditionally masculinist, heavily invested in reinforcing dominant constructions of masculinity as active, physically strong, rational and powerful, values which, as we have seen, are predominantly embodied in the figure of the white heterosexual male."[29] Richard Dyer agrees, but extends the masculine world of the action cinema to the spectator as well, focusing on its ability to create "extreme sensation" for men.[30] Hill's films repeatedly place men in peril, stranding them in desperate survival situations in which a dramatic struggle is exacted upon them. The gang in *The Warriors* must fight its way back home to Coney Island through hostile territory, fighting off challenges from rival groups; the Guardsmen in *Southern Comfort* are picked off one by one as they wander around the Louisiana swamp where they have lost their way; a small-town sheriff crosses the border into Mexico, finding himself in the sun-drenched lair of a drug kingpin in *Extreme Prejudice*; firemen hunting for gold in an abandoned warehouse find themselves trapped by an East St. Louis drug dealer and his crew in *Trespass*. Most action films vest ultimate authority in the action hero, whose triumph over the terrorists, thieves, gangsters, and drug dealers who are the genre's most frequent villains, restores a kind of conservative order.

Hill's films don't do this. Rather than seeking to uphold this status quo through adherence to the genre's potential for conservatism, his movies deconstruct male behavior in their depiction of failure and desperation. Hill says that action is valuable because its films

> define the ultimate dilemma. As Hawks put it: "Will he live or will he die? That's drama." Within that context, you can develop ideas through characters that ask themselves questions and try to work out answers that have some real weight. I think as long as they're at a fairly rudimentary level, action films do that very well.[31]

Throughout his work, the survival narrative places his male characters in a heightened situation, in which their codes of honor and habituated approach to masculinity break down under stress. The braggadocio and hyper-exaggerated virility of *The Warriors*' Ajax (James Remar) gets him caught by the police; the greed and racism of Don (William Sadler) in *Trespass* gets him killed; wallowing in self-pity, drug dealer Cash Bailey (Powers Boothe) in *Extreme Prejudice* is unable to imagine a path back to respectability, and forces his childhood best friend Jack Benteen (Nick Nolte) to gun him down. Delivered within the action genre, they exemplify Hill's assessment of his own cinema: "One of my most consistent themes is that macho ethics don't work."[32]

While Hill rarely features a singular hero, his partnerships often bring racial division into sharp relief, as in the action-comedies *48 Hrs.* and its sequel, *Another 48 Hrs.*, which pair the white cop Jack Cates with the Black convict Reggie Hammond (Eddie Murphy). Often credited—or blamed—for inaugurating the mixed-race buddy cop film that others would imitate, Hill's films foreground racial difference in a more confrontational way than many of its descendants, which often simply rely on it for humor or, at their most cautious, ignore it altogether. Both of the *48 Hrs.* films undermine the image of the white male cop, Cates, by offering Reggie as a foil, who spends much of the narrative of both films poking holes in the white man's definition of self. The mixed-race partnership appears again in *Bullet to the Head*, as hitman Jimmy Bobo (Sylvester Stallone) must team up with the Korean-American cop Taylor Kwan (Sung Kang) to find the men responsible for the murders of their respective partners; their racial difference creates additional layers of tension that reproduce the cop-criminal divide of *48 Hrs.*, but also a generation gap made manifest through each man's comfort level with technology—Stallone was sixty-six, and Kang was forty. His boxing film *Undisputed* (2002) features two Black protagonists, professional fighter George "Iceman" Chambers (Ving Rhames) and Monroe Hutchen (Wesley Snipes), who battle for supremacy in a jailhouse boxing match. Though action films frequently feature diverse casts, Hill's films directly engage racial issues, demonstrating their refusal to position the white male action hero as the ultimate authority. Films like *Die Hard* validate McClane's go-it-alone approach by contrasting his instincts with the foolish police bureaucrats who underestimate the terrorists who are holding his wife hostage, picking up on the half-cop, half-vigilante character established by *Dirty Harry* (1971, Siegel).

What Lichtenfeld calls "the *Die Hard* model"[33] would eventually be displaced around the turn of the millennium by an increased emphasis in action cinema on highly digitized spectacle, given the dramatic advancements in computer generated imagery (CGI) that had been coming in fits and starts since the early 1990s. While individual successes like *Terminator 2: Judgement Day* (1991, Cameron) and *Jurassic Park* (1993, Spielberg) undoubtedly impressed audiences, their heavy reliance on CGI was a marker of their innovation. According to Jose Arroyo, this shift towards CGI spectacle had a substantial impact on the action cinema's generic stability: "contemporary Hollywood cinema, as represented by action/spectacle, is substantially different from Hollywood cinema of the '70s in terms of its industrial infrastructure, economics and aesthetics. Individually, each of these might constitute only a difference in degree, but cumulatively they suggest a difference in kind."[34] In some sense, the action cinema that grew in the 1970s and cohered into a classical period in the 1980s has slipped back into an earlier period, when action was less a full-fledged genre than a tool used by filmmakers to accelerate story.

Hill responded to this shift towards spectacle by stepping further away from it, finding refuge in the genre most associated with the past—the western. Hill's frequent collaborator, screenwriter Larry Gross, captures some of the ambivalence that many action filmmakers felt upon seeing such spectacles take center stage in the 1990s:

> Whatever you call this genre—the movie-as-Theme-Park, the movie-as-Giant-Comic-Book, the movie-as-Ride—I call it simply the Big and Loud Action Movie. For better or worse, it has been a central economic fact, structuring all life, thought, and practice in Hollywood at least since the late 70s.[35]

In a prophetic aside, written in 1995, Gross hastens to add, "This will not change soon."[36] Many of Hill's action films rely on western conventions: *The Long Riders*, obviously, is a James Gang western; the final shootouts in *48 Hrs.*, its sequel, and *Red Heat* all draw on the genre's typical climactic standoffs; *Extreme Prejudice* reworks a common trope, which takes the violent action south to Mexico. Beginning in 1990s, Hill situates his action in the western genre itself, rather than allowing the western's conventions to shape his action films. The Apache western *Geronimo: An American Legend* (1993) shares a war film sensibility with *The Warriors* and *Southern Comfort*, the violent action rooted in the struggle between Geronimo (Wes Studi) and the U.S. Cavalry. Though based on a play, his western *Wild Bill*

(1995), which follows the legend of Wild Bill Hickok (Jeff Bridges), includes a number of additions made by Hill, chief among them a climactic gunfight in which Wild Bill faces down a gang of mercenaries who have, until the film's final moments, held him and his friends hostage in a saloon. In each case, the western genre lends the violent action a kind of authenticity tied inextricably to the past, eschewing the prevailing trend in Hollywood toward bigger and brighter spectacle, aided by advancements in technology. *Last Man Standing*'s fusion of noir and western conventions similarly shows a sensibility rooted in another time, another place; as action films were getting bigger and louder, it seems as though Hill's were getting more esoteric and personal.

After the year 2000, CGI began to take a much more prominent place in action cinema, especially given the narrative demands of the ascendant comic book and superhero film adaptation. What started as a cycle of films with *X-Men* (2000, Singer) was soon followed by *Spider-Man* (2002, Raimi) and *Batman Begins* (2005, Nolan), before becoming a full-fledged genre with the first film in the Marvel Cinematic Universe, *Iron Man* (2008, Favreau). Lichtenfeld argues that these superhero films are inseparable from the technological advancements that made them possible, a historical development that coincided with a change in the action film genre, as it sought new ways to tell stories about heroes and villains. In his interpretation of the history, he argues that

> in the 1990s, however, the comic book film would be increasingly co-opted by the fantastical form of the action genre for at least two reasons: the genre would exhaust the models that differentiated it from superhero adventures (the *Die Hard* model, the buddy film, etc.); and the genre's aesthetics would increasingly emulate those of the comics, just as it would emulate those of the video game.[37]

This is more or less where the state of the action cinema stands in the early years of the 2020s, with the stylistic aesthetics and narrative construction of the superhero film forming an empire upon which the sun never sets. Studios other than Disney, which purchased the Marvel Cinematic Universe in 2010, have sought to replicate its success, with an industry-wide shift towards franchise filmmaking, although they have experienced varying degrees of success and failure—mostly the latter.

Hill's work in the action genre has come further and farther between in the twenty-first century, with another western made as a miniseries for the AMC television network, *Broken Trail* (2006), a three-hour epic that concludes with a gunfight between the film's rugged cowboys and a group of road agents and bandits. The 2012 Hill-Stallone film *Bullet to The Head* completed a kind of de facto trilogy with *Red Heat* and *Last Man Standing*, each a self-conscious take on the action hero persona of Schwarzenegger and Willis, respectively, the trio of stars most associated with the genre in its classical era. In addition to its reliance on noir conventions that Hill has explored before, it represents a response to a new era in one respect, with a few moments of CGI-aided action—in one effects gag, a crook is run over by a car; in another, Jimmy's house blows up; digital effects also permeate the gun battles, taking the place of traditional squibs on actors' bodies and embedded in the set. Though far from the CGI-driven spectacles of modern action cinema, the presence of digital effects shows that even Hill's traditional roots are not immune to their intrusion. Hill's controversial 2016 revenge thriller *The Assignment* stars Michelle Rodriguez as assassin Frank Kitchen, a man who is given sex reassignment surgery by a deranged doctor (Sigourney Weaver); the low-budget film was largely dismissed upon its release, falling into a crevasse where many similarly austere action efforts now end up, finding a spare audience through on demand or streaming services. Rodriguez's appearances in *Furious 7* (2015, Wan), budget $190 million, and *The Fate of the Furious* (2017, Gray), budget $250 million, on either side of *The Assignment*, budget $5 million,[38] exemplify the trends in action film, as the middle where Hill made a comfortable living for many years is hollowed out, leaving polarized extremes. In the early 2020s, the action genre—to say nothing of the industry as a whole—stands at something of a crossroads. Interest in the Marvel Cinematic Universe might be showing signs of waning, a decline that could potentially be accelerated by the loss of salience of its images of city-wide destruction as cultural memory shifts from the aftermath of 9/11 to the aftermath of the COVID-19 pandemic. Whether the Hollywood blockbuster, which according to Barry Langford, "seems largely uninterested in any plot element except as a narrative ruse through which to deliver explosions, chases and gunfights, the bigger the better,"[39] can continue to rely on these conventions, remains to be seen.

Hill is given to saying that most of his films are westerns in one sense or another. He has made a number of direct westerns, of course, but his self-definition as an action director shows the importance of noir to his work. When Hill begins working in cinema, the genre conventions of the action film are still in the process of being codified. Lichtenfeld argues that action films bring together "conventions of the western with conventions of *film noir*,"[40] and that "the developing action film reconciled two genres that might otherwise seem starkly opposed."[41] Imagine a western sheriff dropped into the urban space of film noir. That character might not be fated to die, as so many noir protagonists are, but instead may be able to intervene, as a western lawman might, restoring some sense of order, however temporarily, to the fallen urban environment, with justice delivered at the business end of a gun. Action film heroes are cops, detectives, or FBI agents, in many cases, but above all, they are professionals who can bend the environment they inhabit to their will through sheer force of their ability to accomplish something. Action films are about bodies in motion, and in them, action men move.

In *The Driver*, Hill, working from his own script, situates many of these hybridized conventions and themes, common to both westerns and noir, in the titular character, who is given no other name than Driver, played by Ryan O'Neal. Though Hill would spend a considerable portion of his subsequent action films concerned with the group dynamics of a cohort of male action heroes or the complicated relationship between two male partners, *The Driver* is mostly localized to the single, central character. As embodied by O'Neal, Driver is detached, cold, and, in keeping with the conventions of the action film as they have subsequently taken shape, highly professional. Though *The Driver* is not Hill's first film, it establishes many of the themes and stylistic approaches that he will take throughout his career. *Hard Times* is a confident debut, but *The Driver* is more recognizably an action film in the sense that the genre would be defined in its classical era, the 1980s. In its overt use of archetypal characters, location shooting, and especially in its centralizing of the action in one of its most important pieces of iconography, the car, *The Driver* in many ways sets the prototype that many other action filmmakers working in the 1980s will follow.

CAR CHASES

Perhaps more than any other single type of action sequence, action films are prominently associated with the car chase, which functions in some respects in the same way as a show-stopping number in MGM musicals. This strong association has roots in the 1970s, where car chases became regular features of the action cinema, both beginning to grow together. There is a long history of chase sequences going back to the silent cinema, of course, but according to Tico Romao, "it is only in the 1970s that the car chase became Hollywood's action sequence *par excellence*."[42] This is no historical accident—the car chase begins to appear more commonly in the 1970s alongside the action genre itself, with these types of sequences helping to codify the conventions of the genre.

The narrative and stylistic conventions of car chases primarily begin to appear on screen in the 1970s thanks to some specific formal decisions made by teams of filmmakers working in the newly developing action genre. One of the most notable is William Friedkin's *The French Connection* (1971), which stages a breakneck chase through the streets of New York City, with the film's pseudo-vigilante police detective "Popeye" Doyle (Gene Hackman) behind the wheel of a commandeered car, in hot pursuit of an assassin who has taken a shot at him and then boarded an elevated train. Hackman did some of his own driving through the city streets, which the production did not close down to clear traffic, lending the scene an intense degree of authenticity, as well as danger.[43] Romao argues that "the tendency to film actors in actual moving vehicles instead of resorting to staging such scenes in a studio using rear screen projection"[44] is one of the defining features of the new interest in car chases in the 1970s, infusing them with neorealist immediacy. Other formal innovations, like Friedkin and cinematographer Owen Roizman's decision to place the camera on the bumper of the car to simulate the speed of the vehicle racing through crowded streets, help give the scene its energy and likewise set a kind of template that later filmmakers would eagerly follow. The car chase in *The French Connection* would prove extraordinarily influential on American cinema, but would also find purchase in the Italian police thrillers of the 1970s, known as the *polizieschi*. Many steal Friedkin's centerpiece action sequence, including the overtly titled *The Italian Connection* (1972, Di Leo), *The Violent Professionals* (1973, Martino), and *Street Law* (1974, Castellari), just to name a few.

The French Connection does not feature the first dramatic car chase of the period, however—that distinction is generally awarded to Peter Yates's *Bullitt*, on which Walter Hill served as an assistant director. This police thriller, in which Detective Frank Bullitt (Steve McQueen) must protect a witness against the mob, pivots around a crucial car chase through the streets of San Francisco, its dramatic hills and sun-drenched vistas lending the intense sequence a contrapuntal aesthetic beauty. In an interview with director and admirer Edgar Wright, Hill says he "was there for every shot" of the car chase, with his primary responsibility being crowd control, protecting innocent bystanders from wandering into danger. In his recollection, the chase took "a little over two weeks" to shoot, with the most impressive dimension to Hill being the effort that Yates made to "shooting from inside the cars," which, in his estimation, lent the scene its propulsive power.[45] Coming midway through the film, the car chase is undoubtedly *Bullitt*'s most memorable sequence, especially because of its novelty. Yates's reliance on long lenses helps to establish a relationship between the cars in motion and their environment, a manifestation of Romao's contention that authentic space is one determining factor in the rise of car chases as a dramatic device. Before the chase begins, Bullitt gets into his own parked car and notices another, with a pair of shady-looking characters, waiting across the street, watching him. After a close-up of McQueen, Yates cuts to a wide shot of his car pulling out, heading beneath a highway overpass; without cutting, Yates's camera zooms out slowly, and the car following Bullitt pulls into the frame, heading beneath the same overpass. Yates pans, dutifully following the trajectory of the car as it trails Bullitt out of frame.

This kind of stylistic film grammar might seem basic, and in some sense, it is. However, Yates's specific handling of the cars in their environment, through a mixture of cutting and moving camera shots (either physical movements like panning and tracking or lens adjustments made with a zoom), sets the logic that many filmmakers will subsequently follow when bringing car chases to the screen. Hill is absolutely right in his observation that a number of the shots appear inside the cars themselves—the vast majority of them do, in fact. Many of the shots show each of the characters—Bullitt, the driver of the follow car, or its passenger—but many more reflect those characters' points of view as they move through the city. Romao sees these interior shots as crucial to defining the emotional stakes of the scene, arguing that "these interior views are not restricted to a limited number of camera positions, but are taken from a range of different camera setups, once again reinforcing the placement of characters in the midst of the action."[46] In Romao's view, these shots obviate the need for process work like rear projection, emphasizing the location shooting and thereby underlining the authenticity of the sequence, a sense doubly increased by the presence of the skilled driver McQueen in the car. According to Romao, "The fact that Steve McQueen did his own stunt driving in several scenes is highlighted in a number of interior shots in which his face is rendered partially visible through the angling of the vehicle's rearview mirror."[47]

The scene's tempo accelerates alongside its dramatic tension when Bullitt evades his pursuers and suddenly appears behind them, his Mustang materializing in their rearview mirror. As it moves more quickly, Yates drops out the musical score and replaces it with the symphony of squealing tires that would come to be such a defining feature of later car chases. He also adheres to a general tradition of cutting that many later filmmakers will use in order to establish a clear sense of geographical relationship: a shot of the pursued car racing past a corner, then a cut inside the pursuer's car, and then back to the same corner with the pursuer speeding around it. This type of editing pattern helpfully establishes a visual sense of space, which is crucial to an audience's understanding of the narrative stakes. A failure to maintain spatial orientation is where some filmmakers, when shooting and editing chase scenes, slip into narrative incoherence. Such stylistic features are crucial for maintaining the audience's emotional involvement in the story and the experience of the characters, essential for preserving the car chase's grounding in narrative, rather than allowing it to drift into the realm of the purely spectacular. Romao suggests,

> The emotional effectiveness of the car chase depends upon its anchorage in a wider, compelling narrative. Yet it is not only in this manner that one can demonstrate the narrative significance of pursuit sequences; the chase can be

taken one step further by speaking of the inherent narrative dimension of the pursuit structure itself and its ability to generate the emotional experience of suspense.[48]

When Bullitt finally runs the other car off the road and it explodes in a fireball after the case has left the city for the highways outside it, the narrative stakes mean something—it is not just action for action's sake, but a tremendous release of pent-up tension that has been built in the audience over the preceding seven minutes.

Drive, He Said

Action films are about the line between chaos and control. After his front-row seat to the execution of a car chase, perhaps the first of its kind, in *Bullitt*, Walter Hill took what he learned and applied it to *The Driver*. He remembered the number of interior shots taken by Yates, which formed the backbone of the sequence and used the same approach in his two primary car chases. "What made the *Bullitt* chase remarkable was not just stunts. It was the technique of shooting from inside. You really felt it was a rollercoaster ride as well as something you were observing. I made damn sure that when I was doing *The Driver* I filmed an enormous amount of inside shots," he told Edgar Wright.[49]

The Driver features two chase sequences—one opens the film and one concludes it. Hill was motivated to do the film by his frequent collaborator, producer Lawrence Gordon, who suggested that instead of doing a film about a robbery, they do one focused on "the getaway driver," to which Hill immediately responded, "Say no more."[50] He describes the resulting screenplay for *The Driver* as "stylized."[51] Between the two car chases, which each showcase Driver's professionalism, his maneuvers behind the wheel carried out with cool efficiency, he is drawn into a criminal scheme orchestrated by the film's primary antagonist, the Detective (Bruce Dern), who wants to bring him down by any means necessary.

Hill's film, like the crime thrillers which would follow in its wake, tends to be associated with its heavy use of style. And yet, what stands out about *The Driver* is its stylistic austerity, deliberately imposed through the withholding of traditional narrative information, including character names, but also a general instinct to deny spoken dialogue. As Driver, O'Neal speaks very few lines, restricted mostly to his function as a quiet, professional getaway driver who lets his skill behind the wheel do the talking for him. The film's wordless opening minutes show Driver boosting a car from a garage, with the title of the movie fading over the image of him peeling out in subdued white text. He collects his clients, a pair of thieves who have just robbed an underground casino, but is spotted by a woman credited as The Player (Isabelle Adjani) while he waits in the alley with the engine running. He takes off with his clients in the backseat, and the getaway begins.

Throughout the chase sequence, Hill's screenplay remains committed to verbal austerity, with Driver barely uttering a word as the police begin to pursue them. O'Neal, who gave diametrically opposed performances in a pair of screwball comedies for Peter Bogdanovich, *What's Up Doc?* (1972) and *Paper Moon* (1973), each with manic chase scenes of their own, here does almost nothing, situating his character in quiet reserve, with his face tightly controlled and his voice on an even keel. This performative austerity makes Driver into a kind of western archetype, a reversal of that genre's tendency towards verbose, charismatic outlaws whose verbal dexterity echoes the danger they represent. In John Ford's *The Man Who Shot Liberty Valance* (1962), for example, Lee Marvin generates much of Liberty's menace through the delivery of his lines of dialogue, with John Wayne's Tom Doniphon, not a lawman, but certainly a representative of a kind of western order, much closer to the strong, silent type. In *The Driver*, the verbose, charismatic villain is actually The Detective, the representative of law and order, while the outlaw, O'Neal's getaway driver, has more of the traditional qualities of the western hero. This reversal of the conventions of the western is just one example of Hill's career-long investigation of the genre, even in films that do not seem, at least on their surface, to have much in common with westerns.

Figure 1.1 The archetypal driver (Ryan O'Neal) in Walter Hill's sophomore feature. *The Driver* (1978) speaks few lines and is given little backstory; what we learn about him is conveyed through his professionalism behind the wheel. *Source: Screenshot captured by author.*

From a stylistic standpoint, it is clear that Hill learned much from watching Yates work on *Bullitt*. Working in the post–*French Connection* period, he also borrows from Friedkin, placing the camera on the front of a car as it weaves through traffic, the lens close to the pavement below as it races by just beneath the frame. Hill likewise follows the cutting patterns established by Yates, offering shots of Driver's blue Ford Galaxie intercut with shots of the police cruisers chasing after him. He includes a specific shot that echoes *Bullitt*, with the camera placed at the bottom of a dramatic hill (the film was shot in Los Angeles, not San Francisco), waiting patiently for Driver and his two pursuers to reach the bottom. This comparatively lengthy shot (12 seconds) shows that Hill does not only rely on frenzied cutting to generate intensity but is willing to vary the duration of shots in order to build and release tension. Instead of a cut, he brings another car into an intersection halfway up the hill, which Driver and the police must both avoid, horns blasting.

Above all, car chases are about the accelerating intensity of movement, which Hill explores through a slight stylistic evolution from Yates's approach in *Bullitt*. While Yates relied on a number of interior shots to make the chase thrilling, he tends to cut outside the car for hairpin turns, which show off the cars in motion. Though Hill follows the same strategy throughout much of this opening chase in *The Driver*, he also keeps the camera inside the Galaxie for some of those turns, which make the view of the city outside the windshield spin wildly out of control, its red stoplights and dots of white in the windows of skyscrapers swirl into a manic blur. This is an especially effective approach in one section of the chase where the Driver maneuvers into a parking garage, and the concrete walls seem to rush towards the front windshield, the camera sitting in the backseat. Later, Driver's Galaxie is pinned between two police cruisers on a straightaway. As they try to box him in, Driver shows the first sign of physical strain, wincing slightly on contact with the passenger side police car; Hill cuts outside the cars to a wide shot as Driver rams the officer, his car flipping up onto its side and scraping along the loading dock of a vacant warehouse before coming to a screeching halt, its siren knocked off.

It isn't all speed, however. Hill controls the scene's tension by backing off, allowing Driver to momentarily escape from his police pursuers after causing a wreck and racing into an industrial park to hide in the dark. He flicks the lights off and waits in silence with the engine running, anticipating the appearance of the police cars at the intersection ahead. Contemporary directors, who have escalated car chase sequences to the point of near absurdity, often decline to include moments like this where the audience can experience a different emotion from total exhilaration. The approaching sirens on the soundtrack eventually reignite the suspense—Driver will be discovered—and once the police cruisers turn the corner, Hill cuts to a dramatic close-up of the gear shift, which Driver yanks into place, followed by a shot outside the car of the lights flicking back on, and then the squeal of the tires as Driver floors the gas. It is at this point that Driver's clients, largely quiet until this moment, begin to yell as police bullets make impact with the windshield. Driver, in keeping with the western archetype from which Hill draws, doesn't say a word.

The stylization of *The Driver* is aided by the absence of characters in the story that are not part, at least in some way, of the criminal underworld in which it is set. In this, there are echoes of Robin Wood's observation about Howard Hawks's *Rio Bravo* (1959) that the film's town is entirely focused on the narrative demands without much attention paid to making it feel populated with real people: "inhabitants appear only when the narrative demands their presence."[52] *The Driver* takes place in a similarly hermetically sealed Los Angeles that feels more like a mythical representation of The City, where the characters are isolated within their own archetypal narrative. This certainly seems the case in one of the film's most important scenes, when the double-dealing thieves Teeth (Rudy Ramos) and Glasses (Joseph Walsh) put Driver's skills to the test in an underground parking garage, and he repays their skepticism with a smash-and-crash bumper-car ride that seems to break apart the vehicle piece by piece with pinpoint precision, all with them screaming inside. A similar scene occurs in John Boorman's revenge thriller *Point Blank* (1967), in which Walker (Lee Marvin) seeks information about his former partner, who double-crossed him and left him for dead, by taking a potential informant on a nightmarish joyride around the streets of San Francisco, barely dodging oncoming cars and ramming the car's front and back ends into pillars underneath a highway overpass. The entire film is predicated on Walker's suicidal death wish—he is so bent on revenge that he seems not to care whether he lives or dies—that the scene is given a kind of manic energy by sheer force of Marvin's reckless abandon. In a similar scene with Stacy Keach behind the wheel in *Street People* (1976, Lucidi), he taunts his terrified passenger with each successive impact of the car.

In Hill's hands, the scene is propelled by contrast between the quiet, professional control of Driver and the terrified screams of the passengers, Teeth, Glasses, and another driver, Fingers (Will Walker) as he careens the vehicle around the garage at top speed, slamming it into walls and concrete pylons. In keeping with Wood's observation about Hawks's desolate Rio Bravo, the garage in *The Driver* is incomprehensibly vacant, without another car or person in sight. Teeth asks Driver a quintessentially Hawksian question: "How do we know you're that good?" Driver simply responds, "Get in," which Hill follows with a smash cut to a highly disorienting shot taken from inside the car, the neon green glow of the parking garage swirling through the windshield, tires squealing on the soundtrack. As in many Hawks films, whether a man is "good" can only be proven through action, which Driver ably demonstrates with his precise control of the car, which he first navigates expertly through the garage's many concrete pillars and obstacles, missing each one. It is only when he decides to smash the car deliberately that he begins making contact with the walls and pylons, but first dragging each side's mirrors against a series of water pipes, bursting them at their spigots. Driver chooses each impact carefully, but without a single line of dialogue, over the protestations of Glasses, who shouts that he has had "enough of this shit!" from the backseat. It is too late, of course. Once asked to prove that he is "good" enough, in typical Hawksian fashion, Driver must take it all the way. Noel Carroll sees this reliance on a Hawksian framework as essential to understanding the film's central character and typical of New Hollywood directors' tendency to quote and reference their way through narrative. For him, Hill's films are limited because they "only appear to make sense in the light of the Hawksian cult of the professional."[53]

In his choice of setting, Hill improves upon the chaos of similar, earlier scenes because the garage's ceiling bears down on the car; shots taken from inside the car looking out through the windshield seem oppressively claustrophobic, and each bounce of the car threatens to send launch the image straight into the concrete above. This creativity extends to the final chase sequence, with Driver and The Player in a red pickup truck, trying to evade the vengeful Teeth and his new driver, The Kid (Frank Bruno). From beginning to end,

Figure 1.2 In a setup borrowed from Howard Hawks. Driver proves his skills to a skeptical group of prospective clients. Stylistically, Hill generates excitement by keeping the camera inside the car as Driver strategically smashes his way through an abandoned parking garage. *Source: Screenshot captured by author.*

the chase sequence lasts more than twelve minutes, but features the same acceleration and deceleration of pace that Hill demonstrates in the opening scene. Teeth and The Kid pursue Driver and The Player across town in a car chase that is shot and edited similarly to the one that began the film, but eventually, they find their way to an empty warehouse—more of that Hawksian desolation—where the chase slows to a crawl. Once inside, it is unclear who is chasing whom, with Driver suddenly shifting into an aggressive position while The Kid hides his car among the stacks of unpacked crates and shipping containers stored inside the building. Again, dialogue is almost totally absent, even when the chase abandons the exciting noise of squealing tires and roaring engines. Hill is supremely confident in his ability to control the narrative through images, relying on attention to visual detail and management of the physical space.

To conclude the chase sequence, Hill relies on narrative doubling, restaging the game of chicken that more or less decided the police pursuit that opened the film. He adds an element of danger because the standoff takes place in an interior space, with the warehouse's main floor the runway, lined by an access trench on one side. When Driver and The Kid each floor it, hurtling towards each other at top speeds, Hill uses all the grammar of cinematic car chases at his disposal, with shots from inside each car looking out the front windshield at the other vehicle fast approaching, wide shots of them racing ahead, and reaction shots of the drivers and passengers, before cutting to a wide shot to show the incredibly well-executed stunt of The Kid's car bailing out of the chicken game, hitting a piece of machinery, and flipping over as it crashes upside down into the access trench. Still reluctant to use violence, but aiming a gun at his vanquished foe, Driver gives Teeth a chance to quit: "Give up," he says, before firing once Teeth raises his gun. This exchange is yet another invocation of the western, a restaging of its climactic gunfights, but in a contemporary, noir-infused setting. The presence of The Kid also recalls westerns, as Driver lets him go after recognizing his archetypal self in him. Their final exchange echoes the final scene of George Stevens's *Shane* (1953), when the wounded gunfighter hero (Alan Ladd) imparts some farewell advice to young Joey (Brandon De Wilde): "Joey, there's no living with . . . with a killing. There's no going back from one. Right or wrong, it's a brand. A brand sticks. There's no going back. Now you run on home to your mother, and tell her . . . tell her everything's all right. And there aren't any more guns in the valley." When Joey notices Shane is injured and bleeding, Shane persists: "I'm all right, Joey. You go home to your mother and father and grow up to be strong and straight. And, Joey . . . take care of them, both of them." Characteristically terse, Driver looks at the Kid and says, "Go home," which is a much more efficient—Hill might say "stylized" again—way to express the same sentiment.

Influence

Though *The Driver* did not succeed in its initial run with critics or audiences, it undoubtedly found an audience among fellow filmmakers. Making his feature debut in 1981 with *Thief*, Michael Mann draws upon the same narrative and stylistic tools. Mann's safecracker Frank (James Caan) is likewise a professional, though one who has much more trouble containing his combustible emotions. The film's many nighttime Chicago exteriors capture the moment of the late 1970s and early 1980s when streetlights read on celluloid as a kind of neon blue-green, giving the crime thrillers made in this particular period the look of a near alien world. Mann's ostentatious use of color would likewise drive his work in *Manhunter* (1986), adapted from the Thomas Harris novel *Red Dragon*, featuring a similarly professional character, the FBI profiler Will Graham (William Petersen), who is in just as emotionally precarious a place as Frank. The year before, Petersen was behind the wheel in another of cinema's most dramatic car chases, the centerpiece of William Friedkin's thriller *To Live and Die in LA* (1985), a daytime race through the concrete basin of the Los Angeles river that culminates in a breathless sequence of wrong-way highway driving, as Petersen's reckless Secret Service agent tries desperately to avoid being caught by the police after botching a plan to rob a drug courier. Each of these films follows in *The Driver*'s footsteps, with the visual and aural aesthetic of the 1980s established by Hill in 1978.

Those are films of stylistic excess, however, which sets them apart from Hill's quiet, efficient approach. Mann's and Friedkin's protagonists are men on the edge, whose emotional volatility makes them dangerous, even when they wear a badge. Driver is firmly in control throughout the film, underlined by his understated humiliation of The Detective in the film's final scene. Though Mann and Friedkin picked up on Hill's visual style, their interest in heavily interventionist filmmaking associates their films with the 1980s—their electronic scores are a big reason why—while Hill's film seems more dislocated in time. The 1980s aesthetic of Mann and Friedkin is ostensibly what director Nicolas Winding Refn was chasing with *Drive* (though the film is officially based on a novel by James Sallis), which borrows Hill's central protagonist, known only as Driver—as played by Ryan Gosling, the character is similarly taciturn, with Gosling imitating O'Neal's austerity. Refn imbues his Driver with a few more mannered characteristics, however, Gosling drives with an unlit match in his mouth and wears a signature bomber jacket emblazoned with an embroidered scorpion on the back, a far cry from O'Neal's non-descript black suit and light blue button-down shirt. Refn's references to *The Driver* are most overt in the film's opening sequence, a restaging of the getaway that opens Hill's film. He is nothing if not attentive to detail, with Gosling's Driver in the front seat and his two passengers in the backseat, just as Hill placed them. Refn likewise picks up on Hill's acceleration and deceleration of tension and speed, as his Driver pulls over and flicks his lights off to hide in a parking spot as a patrol car creeps through the intersection ahead. Once Driver's car is spotted by a helicopter, the chase kicks into high gear, and Refn deploys the fundamental cinematic grammar of the car chase, with clear influence specifically from *The Driver*—he repeats Hill's tendency to place the camera inside the car on screeching turns, cutting between Driver, the passengers in the back, and shots of the car racing through Los Angeles, even traveling some of the same roads that appear in Hill's film.

Refn's Driver is also highly professional, with a police scanner that telegraphs their every move to him, which allows him to evade the helicopter's spotlight; he also oscillates between the scanner and the radio broadcast of a Los Angeles Clippers basketball game, monitoring it closely. Refn comes close to restaging Hill's game of chicken between Driver and the police cruisers when his Driver is stopped at a red light, a patrol car waiting in the other left turn lane across the intersection. The moment builds tension before Driver hits the gas after the light turns green, peeling out and igniting the cop's sirens. As in *The Driver*, this moment precedes the conclusion of the chase, as Refn's Driver pulls into the parking garage at the Staples Center just as the Clippers game ends, knowing that fans will soon be streaming out of the stadium and he can easily disappear into the crowd. *Drive* demonstrates the lasting influence of Hill's film—even in a pastiche like Refn's, Hill's efficiency of style incites what will give way to visual and auditory excess, especially its brutal violence.

Whatever the reception of *The Driver*, financially or critically, Walter Hill had arrived as an action director. As the action genre began to cohere, Hill was there to help usher in its classical period, though he would do so by making markedly different films from those "hard-bodied" efforts launched by major stars of the era. Action films have historically been dismissed by the critical community, and continue in large part to be so today, for a variety of reasons. Yvonne Tasker argues that because they are "deemed noisy and brash, judged empty at best and politically reactionary at worst, action films have consistently failed to meet the markers of aesthetic and cultural value typically applied within contemporary film culture."[54] The action genre used to share this space, a critically outcast forbidden zone, with the horror film, which has long been considered a low genre, but has gained traction in the academic and critical community for its unique ability to explore "the return of the repressed."[55] The horror film has also been rescued from the critical doghouse by the authorial presence of the genre's undeniably great artists, including John Carpenter, Wes Craven, David Cronenberg, and George A.

Romero. The application of the somewhat contentious term "elevated horror" has also invited contemporary filmmakers like Jordan Peele, Ari Aster, Jennifer Kent, and Robert Eggers into the conversation as serious artists who use the genre to tackle substantial political or emotional issues.

The action film's critical reevaluation is yet to come. Hill's adherence to the stylistic approaches of classical filmmakers blends with his adoption of new techniques, creating an action cinema that is coherent, which also demonstrates a balance between the chaos of violence and the quiet of its aftermath. Above all, Hill's films must be understood as the work of a self-proclaimed "action director," but one who stands astride the Hollywood of the past and the Hollywood of the present.

NOTES

1. Walter Hill, interview with the author, 26 January 2021.
2. Joseph McBride, *Searching for John Ford*, 482.
3. David Bordwell, Janet Staiger, and Kristin Thompson, *The Classical Hollywood Cinema*, New York: Columbia University Press, 1985.
4. Yvonne Tasker, "Introduction," in *Action and Adventure Cinema*, ed. Yvonne Tasker, Wiley Blackwell, 2015, 4.
5. McBride, 5.
6. "Appendix I: The Hollywood Motion Picture Production Code of 1930," in *Pre-Code Hollywood: Sex, Immorality, and Insurrection in American Cinema 1930-1934*, ed. Thomas Doherty, 355.
7. J. David Slocum, "Introduction," in *Violence and American Cinema*, ed. J. David Slocum, Routledge, 2001, 6.
8. Steve Neale, "Action-Adventure as Hollywood Genre," in *Action and Adventure Cinema*, ed. Yvonne Tasker, Routledge, 2004, 72.
9. Eric Lichtenfeld. *Action Speaks Louder: Violence, Spectacle, and The American Action Movie*, Revised and Expanded Edition. Middletown, CT: Wesleyan University Press, 2007, 2.
10. Tasker, 1.
11. Lisa Purse, *Contemporary Action Cinema*, Edinburgh University Press, 2011, 2.
12. Jeffords, Susan. *Hard Bodies: Hollywood Masculinity in the Reagan Era*, 19.
13. Ibid, 15.
14. Martin Flanagan, "Get Ready For Rush Hour: The Chronotope in Action," in *Action and Adventure Cinema*, 112.
15. Purse, 2.
16. Ibid, 3.
17. David Bordwell, "Aesthetics in Action: Kungfu, Gunplay, and Cinematic Expressivity," in *At Full Speed: Hong Kong Cinema in A Borderless World*, ed. Esther C.M. Yau, University of Minnesota Press, 2001, 86.

18. Barry Langford, *Film Genre: Hollywood and Beyond*, Edinburgh University Press, 2005, 49.

19. Richard Pope, "Doing Justice: A Ritual-Psychoanalytic Approach to Postmodern Melodrama and a Certain Tendency of the Action Film," *Cinema Journal* 51, no. 2 (2012), 114.

20. Scott Higgins, "Suspenseful Situations: Melodramatic Narrative and the Contemporary Action Film," *Cinema Journal* 47, no. 2 (2008), 74.

21. Brooke Bajgrowicz, "The 15 Highest-Grossing '90s Movies Of All Time (According To Box Office Mojo)," Screenrant, 5 June 2020, https://screenrant.com/grossing-90s-movies-box-office-mojo/.

22. Stephen Prince, "Graphic Violence in the Cinema: Origins, Aesthetic Design, and Social Effects," in *Screening Violence*, ed. Stephen Prince, Rutgers University Press, 2000, 2.

23. Devin McKinney, "Violence: The Strong and the Weak," in *Screening Violence*, 108.

24. Walter Hill, interview with the author, 12 March 2021.

25. Ibid.

26. Lorrie Palmer, "'Cranked' Masculinity: Hypermediation in Digital Action Cinema," *Cinema Journal* 51, no. 4 (2012), 4.

27. Though Tasker devotes considerable attention to Schwarzenegger's late 1980s output, she does not mention *Red Heat* at all: 80–83. Jeffords extensively examines the actor's other 1988 film, *Twins* (Reitman), 92–95.

28. Higgins, 75.

29. Purse, 133.

30. Richard Dyer, "Action!," in *Action/Spectacle Cinema*, ed. Jose Arroyo, BFI Publishing, 2000, 18.

31. Walter Hill, "Last Neotraditionalist Standing," interview by Giulia D'Agnolo Vallan, *Film Comment* 49, no. 1 (January 2013), 56.

32. Ibid, 60.

33. Lichtenfeld, 286.

34. Jose Arroyo, "Introduction," in *Action/Spectacle Cinema*, xvi.

35. Larry Gross, "Big and Loud," in *Action/Spectacle Cinema*, 3.

36. Ibid.

37. Lichtenfeld, 286–287.

38. Budget figures taken from IMDBPro, and are thus subject to what is reported by the studios.

39. Langford, 234.

40. Lichtenfeld, 2.

41. Ibid.

42. Tico Romao. "Guns and Gas." In *The Hollywood Action and Adventure Film*. Malden, MA: Wiley Blackwell, 2015, 131.

43. William Friedkin, *The Friedkin Connection: A Memoir*, Harper Perennial, 2013, 170–182.

44. Ibid, 132.

45. Walter Hill, "Edgar Wright and Walter Hill Discuss *The Driver*," Interview by Edgar Wright, *Empire*, 13 March 2017. https://www.empireonline.com/movies/features/edgar-wright-walter-hill-discuss-driver/.

46. Romao, 132.

47. Ibid, 133.

48. Ibid, 143.

49. Hill interviewed by Wright.

50. Hill, interview with the author, 5 February 2021.

51. Ibid.

52. Robin Wood, "*Rio Bravo*," in *Howard Hawks: American Artist*, ed. Jim Hillier and Peter Wollen, BFI, 1996, 91.

53. Noel Carroll, "The Future of Allusion: Hollywood in the Seventies (And Beyond)," *October* 20 (1982), 68.

54. Tasker, "Introduction," 2.

55. Though not original to Robin Wood, his reliance on this phrase to describe horror cinema is highly influential over academics attempting to read the genre more critically.

Chapter 2

The Wild, The Hawks, and *The Warriors*

In the final scene of Walter Hill's dystopian gangland adventure film *The Warriors*, the surviving members of the eponymous gang, having fought their way through the New York City night back home to Coney Island after being wrongfully accused of murdering a would-be gangland messiah, stand on the beach, their names cleared and the real murderer exposed. The leader of the victim's gang, The Riffs, stares out from behind his aviator sunglasses and says, in admiration of their ability to survive the night, "You Warriors are good. Real good." The leader, Swan (Michael Beck), corrects him: "The best."

The exchange demonstrates how deeply Walter Hill internalizes the language and sensibility of his cinematic forebears. The Riffs' leader's compliment is, in the cinema of Howard Hawks, the highest honor that can be paid. In Hawks's adventure film *Only Angels Have Wings* (1939), a pilot dies because he "just wasn't good enough." In *Rio Bravo* (1959), the despairing alcoholic Dude (Dean Martin), carrying the pain of lost love, worries that he isn't "good enough anymore" and won't be of any use to Sheriff John T. Chance (John Wayne) in protecting the jail from outlaws who want to lay siege to it. These two examples, from a pair of Hawks's most famous and acclaimed films, stand in for a larger filmography consumed by the search for the "good," with its achievement the highest ideal imaginable in Hawks's self-contained worlds. The director himself speaks relentlessly in the same terms as his characters; in conversation with Joseph McBride, Hawks says, "I'm interested first in the action and next in the words they speak. If I can't make the action good, I don't use the words."[1] Hawks was consistent, though—he used the same standard for the work of other directors. To McBride, he recalls a conversation he had with young admirer William Friedkin after seeing *The Birthday Party* (1969), which Hawks did not like. He gave Friedkin some advice, and then, pleased with the results, relayed the highest honor a Hawks character can bestow: "And I said, 'Do something that's entertaining. People seem to like chase scenes. Make a good chase. Make one better than anyone's done.' And he did it in *The French Connection*. Did a good job of it."[2]

Those who study Hawks know that he expected this aspirational "goodness" of his collaborators, as well, including longtime screenwriting partner Leigh Brackett, who worked on *The Big Sleep* (1946), *Rio Bravo*, *Hatari!* (1962), *El Dorado* (1967), and *Rio Lobo* (1970) for Hawks. According to Peter Wollen, "when he hired Leigh Brackett, sight unseen, Hawks expected her to be a man. She turned out to be a woman, but she was 'good', she was professional."[3] Brackett would supply the characters with Hawks's outlook, carrying on the tradition of "good" men that populate so many of his films. Many of Hawks's critical admirers apply his standard to his films. Andrew Sarris, for instance, argues that Hawks's style "is good, clean, direct, functional cinema, perhaps the most distinctively American cinema of all."[4] Though the action genre would not cohere into its contemporary form until after Hawks had stopped making films, he is undoubtedly one of its ancestors. As French New Wave director and *Cahiers du Cinema* critic Jacques Rivette described Hawks's cinema,

> It is actions that he films, meditating on the power of appearances alone. We are not concerned with John Wayne's thoughts as he walks towards Montgomery Clift at the end of *Red River*, or of Bogart's thoughts as he beats somebody up: our attention is directed solely to the precision of each step—the exact rhythm of the walk—of each blow—and to the gradual collapse of the battered body.[5]

Rivette sees the relentless focus on action in Hawks's cinema in every individual choice:

> There seems to be a law behind Hawks's action and editing, but it is a biological law like that governing any living being: each shot has a functional beauty, like a neck or an ankle. The smooth, orderly succession of shots has a rhythm like the pulsing of blood, and the whole film is like a beautiful body, kept alive by deep, resilient breathing.[6]

Walter Hill strongly believes that "film needs to move along—that's part of the storytelling process."[7] This is certainly a Hawksian tendency, and one that the director himself expresses to Joseph McBride, describing his working methods in brutally efficient terms: "I try to tell my story as simply as possible, with the camera at eye level. I just imagine the way the story should be told, and I do it."[8] This is something that Hill believes Hawks shares with another of the studio era's great masters, Raoul Walsh, who made films driven by the same sense of methodical purpose, which relied heavily on action as a narrative device. In Hill's estimation, Walsh was "a perfect exemplar" of "one of the great traditions of American filmmaking," in which "every shot advances the story—there is no wasted motion."[9] In his own work, Hill says, "I wish I could live up to it. I try."[10] Hill's awareness of Walsh and Hawks, never far from his mind, demonstrates a kind of continuity with the past that makes up the classical impulse that stretches across much of his filmography. In this way, Hill shares a reverence for studio era Hollywood with his contemporary Peter Bogdanovich, who is associated with classicism more than any other New Hollywood director thanks to his self-conscious adoption of the narrative and stylistic approach of directors like Ford, Hawks, Sturges, and Capra, whose ghosts hang over every film he makes. According to Rivette, "Hawks gives the modern sensibility a classical conscience."[11] The same might be said of Hill's works, which are infused with the efficiency and professionalism that defines the Classic Hollywood cinema but feel contemporary in their use of stylistic flourishes more associated with modernist filmmakers.

Though the simplicity and directness of Hawks is never far from Hill's mind, he is also a student of the man with whom he worked on his first major screenwriting effort, *The Getaway*—Sam Peckinpah. Stephen Prince sees Peckinpah as

> the crucial link between classical and postmodern Hollywood, the figure whose work transformed modern cinema in terms of the stylistics for rendering screen violence and in terms of the moral and psychological consequences that ensue, for filmmaker and viewer, from placing brutality at the center of a screen world.[12]

Hill is not alone in his admiration for Peckinpah, especially in his depictions of violence through jagged montage editing that simultaneously crafts a narrative and formal assault on the audience in many of his most important works, chief among them *The Wild Bunch* (1969). Prince speaks to the dramatic power of the director's contributions to cinema, especially as they would be employed in action films:

> Though he did not innovate them, the slow motion violence and exploding squibs that are closely identified with his work have now become the normative techniques for rendering screen violence. More than any other American director, Peckinpah made slow motion the requisite format for capturing and extending the action of violent gun battles, and he coupled this with an extremely kinetic mode of montage editing.[13]

Peckinpah's use of slow motion inserts throughout the opening and closing battle sequences of *The Wild Bunch* would be heavily influential on the action cinema; most action films made in the 1980s and beyond contain slow motion images, most often during gunplay. In *Above the Law* (1988, Davis), a Chicago cop (Steven Seagal) sees his partner (Pam Grier) gunned down by gangsters—she flies backward down a set of stairs in slow motion, the moment stretched out for high drama. Many of the other Seagal movies of the 1980s and early 1990s rely on similar slow motion techniques, despite the presence of different directors, demonstrating the marriage of slow motion to the genre—Peckinpah's influence permeates the action film, detached from the toolbox of any given filmmaker and available to all.

Unlike Hawks, who had a very lengthy and stable career, Peckinpah made only fourteen features, many of which were mutilated in editing during conflicts with the studios who financed them, including *Major Dundee* (1965), *Pat Garrett and Billy the Kid* (1973), and even *The Wild Bunch*, not universally regarded as a masterpiece or even available in Peckinpah's preferred cut until it was remastered and re-released in 1995, long after the director's death. Far from Hawks's efficiency, Peckinpah was self-destructive and impulsive, which affected his work on many films as he descended into alcoholism. His film *Bring Me the Head of Alfredo Garcia* (1974) offers something of a nightmare autobiography, with one of his frequent collaborators Warren Oates cast as a hole-in-the-wall piano player wasting away in a Mexican cantina who bears more than a passing resemblance to the film's director.[14] And yet, there is the dramatic power of his skill, cohering most fully in *The Wild Bunch*, which tells the story of a group of outlaws being left behind by the changing of the West, modernizing too quickly for them to keep up. According to Prince, the film "is an epic work, and it has had an epic impact on American cinema."[15] As a whole, Peckinpah's work ought to be seen as a response to the classical tradition practiced by Ford and Hawks, imbued with a cynicism that was at least in part a product of the 1960s and '70s when Peckinpah did most of his notable work. In Wheeler Winston Dixon's estimation,

> In contrast to [John] Wayne's heroism and victories in the westerns of Ford and Hawks, there are no easy victories in the world of the Peckinpah western; in fact, there are no victories at all. There is only the struggle, and the search, for some solidity within the confines of a rapidly changing and often overtly hostile landscape, and the certainty that time, and the human span of years, are quickly becoming exhausted.[16]

Look no further in Peckinpah's work for this despairing worldview than in the final apocalyptic battle of *The Wild Bunch*, in which the gang of outlaws led by Pike (William Holden) commit a kind of suicide-by-Mexican-army, staging a violent melee that culminates in the free use of a machine gun, a symbol of modernity, that leaves every member of the group dead, their bodies torn apart by bullets. They take most of the army with them, the courtyard where the battle takes place a killing field awash in blood. Formally, the scene is a furious explosion of cinematic style, with Peckinpah's reliance on montage editing and slow motion infusing the violence with a kind of moral outrage—intended by the director as a wake-up call to an audience that he thought had fallen into complacency despite the ongoing catastrophe of the Vietnam War—that was sometimes lost in the cacophony of gunfire. The violence in *The Wild Bunch*'s final scene—a strategy also used in the film's opening, during which the Bunch are ambushed during a robbery—was also meant to respond to the tradition of screen violence that Peckinpah felt sanitized the real experience of pain and suffering that bullets could bring to the human body. Prince calls this kind of violence, which was the normative mode throughout the studio era, "*clutch-and-fall*. [. . .] The defining feature of this mode lies in the victim's response. The victim takes the bullet with little to no physical reaction, even if the shot is fired at close range."[17] Take the conclusion of Hawks's *Red River* (1948) for an example of this tendency. The dictatorial cattle baron Tom Dunson (John Wayne), relieved of his herd by his adopted son Matt Garth (Montgomery Clift), stalks into town, aiming to settle up with Matt, by violence if necessary. Matt's friend Cherry (John Ireland), a gunfighter who joined the cattle drive and sided with Matt during the mutiny, intercepts Dunson and pulls his gun. Hawks has been dollying the camera back with Dunson as he strides into the image's foreground, with Cherry in the background, still visible in deep focus. When Cherry calls out Dunson, he whirls around and the two men fire simultaneously, each taking a shot. Cherry is so far in the shot's background that when Ireland clutches and falls, no physical impact of the bullet is visible on his body; Dunson, meanwhile, is staged with his back to the camera, and Wayne similarly clutches, his character hit in the side. While another man rushes into the shot to tend to the fallen Cherry, Dunson turns back to face the camera and strides towards it, Wayne holding his left side to obscure the bloodless bullet wound.

Peckinpah's approach to screen violence represented a dramatic shift away from its more austere depictions during the studio era by directors like Hawks, who found Peckinpah's work objectionable: "I'm getting goddamn sick of these pictures, you know, nothing but violence. Peckinpah and I believe in exactly the opposite thing."[18] Hawks saw himself as an entertainer, someone responsible for, in the end, telling a good story. Peckinpah's films are shockingly brutal and confrontational to the point of inducing profound discomfort, especially in their portrayals of violence. In contrast to Hawks, Prince argues, "Most films do not hold viewers accountable for, or implicate them in, the violent spectacles they witness. Peckinpah's films do, and this is one reason for their controversial nature."[19] For a filmmaker like Hawks, who plied his trade in the period of the Production Code, the austere approach to violence is natural; by the time Peckinpah comes along, he has grown frustrated with the unwillingness of the cinema to confront violence as a social problem.

Walter Hill's films synthesize the artistic inclinations of these two diametrically opposed directors in an attempt to reconcile the distance between the classicism of Hawks and the modernism of Peckinpah. David Desser suggests that "Hill is very much the patrilineal descendent of Hawks and Peckinpah. He works exclusively in those masculinist genres that have come to be associated with Hawks and, especially, Peckinpah."[20] Sometimes dismissed as a pale imitator of Peckinpah thanks to his films' staging of violence and occasional reliance on slow motion, Hill's work is equally driven by the kind of Hawksian commitment to efficiency and narrative economy. Hill's attempts to reconcile these two traditions create a dialectical cinema that becomes about, in addition to the films' individual narratives, the uneasy tensions between classicism and modernism. After all, Peckinpah's stylistic experiments in screen violence, as Prince observes, have now become the norm, with screen action almost always represented through some deployment of jagged montage, slow motion, and exploding squibs (practical or CGI). The mainstream cinema's accommodation of techniques like Peckinpah's, which were considered radical disruptions in form when *The Wild Bunch* was released, demonstrates the power of classical storytelling—like the blob, it can absorb all it touches, growing stronger all the time. Over time and through repetition, even the most adventurous stylistic innovation can be added to the classical storyteller's toolkit. In bringing together the diverging traditions of Hawks and Peckinpah, Hill makes Peckinpah's techniques into a stylistic norm acceptable to the mainstream cinema.

In *The Warriors*, Hill juxtaposes the classicism of Hawks to the modernism of Peckinpah for the first time, moving beyond the self-imposed stylized austerity of *The Driver*, which drew comparisons to the French gangster film *Le Samourai* (1967, Melville) for its similarly stoic protagonist and reserved approach to narrative. With *The Warriors*, Hill begins a cycle of three films, with *The Long Riders* and *Southern Comfort* to follow, that are heavily focused on the internal dynamics of a group, a typical Hawksian theme. In Hawks's group films, the members of the group negotiate the specific roles that determine the power dynamics and hierarchies which they must obey. According to Manny Farber, Hawks is

> powerfully interested in the fraternal groups that he sets up, sticking to them with an undemonstrative camera that is always eye level and acute on intimate business, and using stories that have a straight-ahead motion and develop within a short time span.[21]

In Hawks's groups, the pecking order is usually decided by who is "good enough" and who isn't, a theme that becomes central to *The Warriors*. Groups were important to Peckinpah, as well, whose explorations of leadership and the uneasy camaraderie within groups of men in *Major Dundee*, *The Wild Bunch*, and *The Killer Elite* (1975) might be considered almost Hawksian. Desser argues that "Hawks's homosocial legacy was carried forward in American cinema by Sam Peckinpah."[22] However, while *The Warriors* borrows the Hawksian group to propel the narrative, Hill is more interested in Peckinpah's use of form, including the reliance on montage editing and slow-motion to depict instances of violence, territory into which he would eventually tread more overtly in the two group films to follow, *The Long Riders* and *Southern Comfort*.

THE WARRIORS AND HOWARD HAWKS

Based on the social realist novel of the same title by Sol Yurick, Walter Hill's third feature is a dystopian nightmare that imagines a New York City fallen deeply under the control of warring gangs, who fight for ownership of the city's neighborhoods block by block. Hill's relentless action thriller draws heavily upon the mythical story of *Anabasis* (as does the source novel), written by Xenophon, the Ancient Greek soldier who found himself cut off from his homeland with his army, and had to fight his way back through enemy lines. To Desser, *The Warriors*' reliance on these mythic influences take the film beyond the social realism of Yurick's novel, creating "a mythic realm of transcendent action and redemptive romance."[23] Desser argues that "if the mythical rather than the historical is the dominant mode of the film, so too the mythical replaces the contemporary."[24] At the risk of trivializing its subject matter, Hill strips societal conscience away from the film, eliminating any overt reference to poverty, prejudice, or the absence of a secure governmental safety net or other societal infrastructure that might have kept The Warriors or the film's other gangs from falling into delinquency. There are no moralizing adults, no concerned teachers, no good-hearted and noble police desperate to intervene. Instead, he leaned into artificiality: "I was very conscious of—I now want to move to a comic book approach" and drew inspiration from Fantomas, the masked French criminal popular in serials first appearing in 1911, as well as the like-themed film *Judex* (1963, Franju). Hill made a conscious effort to abandon the social realist tone of Yurick's novel, because he "didn't think it would hold," and decided to make the entire film "comic book-like." However, he was inspired by a scene from Yurick's novel in which one of the characters is reading a comic book based on the story of Xenophon; lightning struck, and he decided that this approach would be the best way to productively heighten the themes he wanted to explore, placing the action in a dystopian, near-future New York City that, given the state of the city's finances and general environment throughout the 1970s, didn't seem like too distant a possibility.[25] In the original cut of *The Warriors*, the comic book aesthetic permeates the film, creating a context that shapes the actors' exaggerated performances, the visual style, and especially the colorful depictions of the various gangs who interrupt The Warriors' journey back to Coney Island. Hill returned to the film in 2005 for a Special Edition DVD release in which he makes the comic book style more overt, adding an opening narration (which he himself performs) that explicitly invokes the story of Xenophon and including a series of comic book panel animations that bridge scenes together through dissolves, with the panels overlaid on the images of a subway train pulling into a platform or one of his actors in close-up.

As ever, Hill's work is dependent upon genre. Eric Lichtenfeld sees *The Warriors* as a pastiche, cobbled together "from the western, noir, martial arts movies, jungle adventures, and the combat film."[26] With the exception of the martial arts film, which came into being alongside other action films in the 1970s, Howard Hawks worked in each of the genres Lichtenfeld lists. Unlike John Ford, who became strongly identified with the western (though he did work in other genres), Hawks developed a reputation as something of a genre tourist, moving freely from gangster films to comedies to war films to adventure movies to westerns to musicals, building a varied body of work that shows consistency of theme and style across several genres, not confined to one or two. One of those themes is action, which makes his work deceptively simplistic, masking a deeper interest in his many subjects: says Farber, "no artist is less suited to a discussion of profound themes than Hawks, whose attraction to strutting braggarts, boyishly cynical dialogue, and melodramatic fiction always rests on his poetic sense of action."[27] Following in Hawks's footsteps, Hill's cinema is driven by action, but the epochal shift from action-as-storytelling-mode to action-as-genre means that Hill works in a different context. He consistently borrows Hawksian themes, language, and narrative situations, as well as visual style, especially in the group films, where he generally favors wider compositions that privilege the whole ensemble of characters, rather than close-ups that emphasize one hero.

In an essay expressing discomfort at the New Hollywood filmmakers' reliance on allusion to the classical era, Noel Carroll argues that "the exact increments of Hill's allusion to Hawks are more difficult to pinpoint than are allusions made to a scene or a camera movement or even to a story; there is no structural element, no object or image that we can hone in on that is being imitated."[28] However, closer examination of them reveals exactly these kinds of allusions (style, narrative, themes, structure, and more). Recall Hill's creation of a sealed narrative environment in *The Driver*, a space within which the story takes place, but only participants in the narrative itself are allowed to enter. Hill eschewed the tendency to make the world of his film feel lived in with the addition of extras or other environmental details that lend a movie verisimilitude, which heightens its artifice. Lichtenfeld sees a similar dynamic at work in *The Warriors*, in which New York City

> seems to exist solely as a stage for gang action, and as a space that exists only to be traversed. This effect is completed by the film's almost total lack of extras. There are no "civilians" on these streets, only combatants. Thus the city is a ritualized space; it exists as a dream state. And as a dream state, spatial orientation begins to fold in on itself, despite the linearity of the Warriors' journey.[29]

In *The Driver*, the closed narrative world resonates with Driver's own self-imposed isolation—in one scene, he lies on his bed in silence, seemingly waiting for the next narrative development that demands his participation to begin—but the film is little interested in plumbing the depths of its central character's psychology. Instead, Hill creates a mythic figure not unlike the western gunfighters of the past. The similar rejection of verisimilitude in *The Warriors*, despite the film's New York City locations, creates another mythic space that embodies the story of Xenophon invoked by the narrative and the comic book aesthetic that Hill self-consciously adopts.

Figure 2.1 In *The Warriors* (1979), the titular gang retreats to the safe haven of Coney Island, fighting their way through a New York City bereft of all civilians; only dangerous rival gangs populate the streets. *Source: Screenshot captured by author.*

Comic books are structured in panels; like the film frame, they offer a specific vision of a character in the midst of performing an action. Also like a film frame, they exclude what falls beyond the lines formed by the borders of the image. A comic book represents a series of overt decisions on the part of the artists: what to show and what not to show. The film director's job is much the same, with the borders of the frame conveying narrative information about the characters and the world who appear within it, to the exclusion of what falls without. In this sense, comic books have much in common with the Hawksian tradition of American cinema to which Hill aspires, in that each panel, which must be carefully placed and drawn, must be used to advance the story. In their ruthless narrative efficiency, comic books offer a stylistic equivalent to Hawks's contention that the visual dimension of cinema should take primacy over dialogue: "when you leave the dialogue out and make visual stuff, the visual stuff has so much more impact because you hadn't used it before."[30] Hawks describes the same demands placed on comic book artists, thinking first in images and panels, and executing moments of action within those panels for maximum dramatic effect. Henri Langlois sees Hawks's cinema in terms of its director's tendency towards a streamlined cinematic experience: "His works, then, are stripped bare almost to the point of abstraction—but it as if they are made of concrete."[31] Each film frame in Hawks offers only what is "essential. The truth of the dialogue, the truth of the situations, the truth of the subjects, of the milieux, of the characters: a dramaturgy derived from an agglomeration of facts, words, noises, movements, situations, as a motor is assembled. There is nothing superfluous: no stopping, no meandering, no fleshing out."[32]

The main narrative action of *The Warriors* concerns the gang's efforts to fight their way back to Coney Island; along the way, they get into a series of scrapes with other gangs who want to apprehend them to collect on the bounty placed on them by the Riffs after the death of would-be leader Cyrus (Roger Hill). The film raises the narrative stakes, however, by eliminating the gang's leader, Cleon (Dorsey Wright), in the aftermath of Luther's (David Patrick Kelly) assassination of Cyrus and his subsequent blaming of The Warriors. In the film's opening sequence, before The Warriors board the subway train bound for Cyrus's meeting in the Bronx, Hill establishes Cleon as a strong leader who gives his gang clarity of purpose. When Swan (Michael Beck) expresses concerns ("We ain't even been to the Bronx before," he says), Cleon reassures him: "No sweat." Cleon tells his gang that he gave his word that "the Warriors would uphold the truce," agreeing not to bring any guns or other weapons to the meeting, emphasizing his honor—a man's word, in the world of these gangs, has to mean something. He also makes sure, before they depart, that one of his members brings the spraypaint, so they can tag a wall with graffiti: "I want everyone to know The Warriors were there," he says, showing concern for the reputation of his outfit. Cleon seems universally respected by the other Warriors, with the exception of the group's malcontent, Ajax (James Remar), who represents a challenge to Cleon's leadership, which will intensify after Cleon is killed and Swan takes charge. When Ajax excitedly suggests that they might get to "waste a few heads along the way," Cleon won't have it: "You just soldier and keep your mouth shut." Cleon's death after the assassination upends the Warriors' internal group dynamics, and they are intermittently separated on their way back to Coney Island, with some members of the group chased down by rival gangs and others drawn into temptation by women, in an echo of the sirens from Homer's *Odyssey*. In Cleon's absence, Swan struggles to hold the group together, but eventually succeeds, but at a cost—Fox (Thomas G. Waites), who isn't good enough, is killed in a fight with a police officer, and Ajax, who is too chaotic for the gang to control, is arrested while propositioning a woman in Central Park, who turns out to be an undercover cop. Ajax isn't good enough either, his sexual appetites and impulses getting the better of him.

The removal of Cleon from the narrative not only casts the gang's internal dynamics into disorder, but also demonstrates Hill's adaptation of a Hawksian principle, which he articulated to Joseph McBride: "That's a trick I use all the time. To make a business dangerous, you hurt somebody in the beginning."[33] In *Only Angels Have Wings*, this narrative function is served by the death of Joe (Noah Beery Jr.), who crashes his plane in the South American mountains when he can't find the runway through the dense fog just twenty minutes in, which establishes the danger that dominates the rest of the film; any time one of the pilots goes up, he might die. Hawks foregrounds the danger into outright immediacy in *Hatari!*, his African safari film, in which one of the team, which gathers animals from the savannah and sells them to zoos, is gored by a black rhino in the film's opening scene, even before its credits sequence. The racing film *Red Line 7000* likewise opens with a dramatic, fiery crash. These scenes of danger, where even the crew's ostensible leader can be killed, imperil the entire cast of characters, lending a sense of urgency to each of Hawks's scenes. For a director who prized forward motion above all, this tendency became a crucial Hawksian device for establishing and then escalating tension.

Hill follows a similar approach in many of his own films, both behind the camera and where he serves as a screenwriter. Before *The Warriors* went into production, Hill provided extensive but ultimately uncredited rewrites (working in the final stages with regular collaborator David Giler) on *Alien* (1979, Scott). The film's point of view shifts dramatically throughout the narrative; it opens in the spaceship, Nostromo, and introduces the first crewman to rise from cryosleep, Kane (John Hurt), subtly establishing him as the film's protagonist. However, Kane is the first crew member to be incapacitated when the alien in its larval form attaches itself to his face; he is killed during one of the most memorable dinner scenes in film history when his chest explodes, the alien in its new form bursting its way through his rib cage. Kane's sudden removal from the narrative prompts another point of view switch to Captain Dallas (Tom Skerritt), who is then himself killed by the alien. The film shifts point of view yet again to Ripley (Sigourney Weaver), who is the last survivor. The deaths of similar characters in *Aliens* (1986, Cameron) and *Alien 3* (1992, Fincher), on which Hill served as producer and writer, show the influence of this Hawksian tendency—anyone can die at any moment.

Behind the camera, Hill repeats this strategy in *Southern Comfort*, when the first of the National Guardsmen to be killed is Lieutenant Poole (Peter Coyote), the unit's commanding officer and the only one of the men with real combat experience. In *The Warriors*, the gang reckons with the death of Cleon first by lapsing into uncertainty; disoriented after their narrow escape from the melee at the rally, they regroup in a cemetery, unsure of what to do next. Swan, undifferentiated early in the film from any other member of the gang, takes charge. This is a crucial narrative move on Hill's part, which parallels the script for *Alien*, which does the same thing with Ripley; he does not telegraph that Swan is the real protagonist of the film by filtering the opening sequences before Cleon is killed through his point of view. Swan emerges as the gang's leader only in the aftermath of Cleon's death; as a result, his leadership is not foreordained by the film's style and feels much more tenuous. Hill establishes real tension by inviting the audience to consider the effectiveness of Swan's leadership, and whether he is good enough for the job, enacting a key Hawksian theme.

Throughout his early work, Hill evinces a preference for a judicious use of close-ups, preferring instead to rely on wider compositions that accommodate multiple members of the cast rather than placing them in isolation. Though Hawks by no means had a monopoly on this visual style, which was common to many studio era directors, he definitely favored it. Of close-ups, Hawks said, "I use them wherever I think you need them for emphasis. But I get awful sick of the trend in television where it's all made in close shots. And some of the best scenes that you make are in long shot."[34] Note Hawks's application of his all-important standard of quality—the long shots are often "the best." Hill relies on this type of two- and three-shot framing throughout *The Warriors* (and will reprise it in both *The Long Riders* and *Southern Comfort*) but the presence of stylistic continuity between the two directors is best demonstrated through a pair of analogous scenes—one from Hawks's *Air Force* and one from *The Warriors*.

Both *Air Force* and *The Warriors* are about all-male groups of fighters doing battle after the loss of their leader. Andrew Sarris suggests that *Air*

Force represents a crucial shift for Hawks: "Hawks's technique, confronted with epic material for the first time, reveals a new incisiveness in exploiting the calculated symbolism of a plane around which events swirl during its odyssey."[35] Three-quarters of the way through *Air Force*, the Mary Ann's Pilot (John Ridgely) is killed when the plane is ambushed by a group of Japanese fighters; the plane is also badly damaged during the rough landing at the army airfield where the crew finds brief respite after the attack. After the scene in which they say goodbye to the Pilot, who dies in the hospital, the military commander of the airfield is notified that someone has been stealing airplane parts from the wreckage of other downed bombers. He charges out to have a look, and finds the crew of the Mary Ann hard at work attempting to repair their hopelessly damaged plane. Lasting roughly two minutes, this scene comes immediately after the death of the Pilot, and in typical Hawksian fashion, the crew has responded to his death by deciding to take action—if the plane can't fly, they're going to do everything they can to fix it before the next Japanese attack comes. *The Warriors* features a similar two-minute scene, which also comes after the death of their leader, Cleon; they scatter in the chaos, avoiding capture by both the other gangs and the police, and find themselves in a graveyard, where they take a moment to catch a breath. In the immediate aftermath of the assassination of Cyrus and the death of Cleon, they decide that they have to get to the subway and get back to Coney Island as quickly as possible. Hill's dialogue foregrounds Hawksian themes: leadership, which Swan assumes, and challenges to it, offered by Ajax; the necessity of sticking together; the formulation of a plan.

In *Air Force*, the scene at the plane's wreckage site begins when a Corporal comes out to the site to burn it on the Colonel's orders; Hawks starts in a wide shot, as the Corporal tramps through the jungle, with the Mary Ann visible through the trees. This framing continues the film's general trend, which is to align the fighting men with the plane itself, collapsing their individual identities into the service they perform aboard the aircraft—even denying many of the flyers names, referring to them instead only by their mechanical role. John Belton offers insight into how this process works: the film "reflects a tendency toward the integration of Hawks's characters with their environment. In *Air Force* this process is at its clearest: Hawks alternates close-ups of the individual crew members in the plane with long shots of the Mary Ann in flight. The men, in a sense, become the plane."[36] As the Corporal heads toward the wounded plane, the screen action travels leftward, with the Corporal and his crew, carrying gas cans to burn the Mary Ann, walking through the jungle while the camera pans left. Hawks uses another wide composition as Winocki (John Garfield) and White (Harry Carey) lift the propeller into position with a chain; the camera tilts down when White jumps off of the platform where he is standing, objecting to the

Corporal's announcement that they intend to burn the plane. In *The Warriors*, Hill begins the scene in the graveyard with a similar trajectory; a wide shot establishes the cemetery, bathed in darkness, and The Warriors run into the frame from the right in a series of wide shots that show them hustling for cover amongst the headstones. The graveyard imagery, with each of the gang members hiding among the stones, suggests that they are already dead men who just don't know it yet, which carries an echo of the Mary Ann in *Air Force*, rendered a shell of itself because of the damage it took during the firefight. The flight crew cannot resurrect the Pilot, but they can, if they're good enough, bring back the plane, which is their chance to save themselves from the incoming Japanese attack. If The Warriors can work together, they too may be able to save themselves and make it back to Coney Island alive.

The next movement of Hill's analogous scene in *The Warriors* shows the gang members unsteadily getting up from their hiding places after a helicopter passes overhead, searchlight shining down. Hill cuts much more frequently than Hawks, but that is largely because of the general acceleration in cutting speed, in keeping with David Bordwell's concept of "intensified continuity," in which the norms of continuity editing as constituted in classical filmmaking are largely still obeyed, just sped up.[37] Once The Warriors are standing and ready to regroup, Swan steps into a close-up; Hill cuts behind him to show the other Warriors walking towards him, with the implicit suggestion made by the framing that he is now ready to step into the leadership role in Cleon's absence. However, Hill does not use two- and three-shot framing in the initial moments of the conversation, as The Warriors trade information about what happened to Cleon and what to do next. Instead, he relies on shallow focus close-ups of the individual members, which isolate them in the frame. No one can quite agree on what happened or what to do—some want to wait for Cleon, and others want to get to the subway as quickly as they can. The isolated close-ups emphasize this lack of cohesion, a counterpoint to Hawks's strategy in *Air Force*.

Both scenes are built around conflict. In *Air Force*, the Mary Ann's crew must convince the skeptical Colonel, who has now joined the scene, to let them continue to harvest parts in an effort to salvage the plane. In a sophisticated contradiction, Hawks balances the frame through physical imbalance—the crew members stand on the left side of a medium shot, gathered together and staged in depth, while the Colonel, the representative of military authority who gives orders, and is not talked into them, stands on the right in profile—that expresses the power differential between the two opposing forces. In *The Warriors*, the conflict is over the direction of the gang, which Hill emphasizes through his use of close-ups, in which the characters stand alone. Cochise (David Harris) reminds them that the police will likely be after them, and Vermin (Terry Michos) worries that if the truce is over, "we're gonna have to bop our way back," a prospect that doesn't sit well with any of the group, save for Ajax (more than a little like *Air Force*'s Winocki), who steps forward to challenge Swan's leadership. "Who named you leader?" he wants to know, stepping into a wider shot taken from behind Ajax, out of focus, with Swan sharply defined in the shot's middle ground, that echoes the framing Hawks uses in *Air Force* as the Co-Pilot lobbies the Colonel to let them finish the plane. After another close-up on Ajax, into which Snow (Brian Tyler) can be seen stepping, Hill cuts to a wide composition in which Fox steps alongside Swan. Hill is subtly shaping the allegiances of the group, foregrounding the narrative stakes for each of the characters, whose survival depends on functioning together. The challenge comes to a head over a series of close-ups on Swan and Ajax, intercutting between the two—Snow still stands behind Ajax, though he is out of focus. The emphasis is clear; Swan must prove himself alone, equal to standing up to Ajax's challenge. The tension is defused when Hill cuts to one of the other members of the gang, Cowboy (Tom McKitterick), who tells Ajax to "lighten up." Hill initiates a rightward pan that reveals Vermin, who says, "Swan's war chief," then continues panning to reveal Cochise, who delivers an important credo: "We better stick together." The cut to Swan in close-up underlines his leadership—the group has chosen him. Another echo of the scene in *Air Force* comes when Rembrandt (Marcelino Sanchez) calls out from off screen because he sees the subway in the distance. A pair of wide shots show The Warriors hustling off to the train after Swan issues the order, "Let's move," the film's style now subordinated to his assertion of leadership. One last echo of *Air Force* comes in the scene's final shot, as The Warriors disappear out of frame through the graveyard in the distance, Rembrandt hustles back to the graveyard to tag a headstone at Swan's direction, a reminder of Cleon's desire to want everyone to know The Warriors were at the meeting. He hurries after the departing gang, shouting "Wait for me!" a similar momentary disruption in the group facilitated by the departure of the young gunner with the Colonel in *Air Force*, and Winocki and the Co-Pilot's concerned stare after him.

In filmmaking practice, much of this application of style is instinctual for a director, who follows the demands of character and narrative much more than any overt imitation of another filmmaker's style. Carroll is unconvinced by Hill's efforts, arguing that his work exists only on a foundation built by a superior filmmaker: "Hill's professionalism is different from Hawks's. Hill lacks the master's humor and sense of camaraderie. And yet without the critical hypostasization of Hawksian professionalism, Hill's professionalism would not be particularly comprehensible."[38] These analogous scenes from *Air Force* and *The Warriors* demonstrate that Hill is guided by the same collection of narrative and thematic instincts as Hawks—he manifests them through his choice of staging, shooting, and cutting. Because Hill is concerned with the internal dynamics of groups, as Hawks was throughout his career, he makes stylistic decisions that inevitably parallel those made by Hawks, but are perfectly comprehensible without intimate knowledge of Hawks's work. These visual strategies are so strongly reminiscent of Hawks that they may be direct allusions, but even more so, they are a representation of continuity with the reserved, austere, classical style that Hawks favored, well-suited to the themes shared between his films and Hill's. The classical approach to filmmaking, even in its intensified form, can subtly accommodate important narrative and thematic concerns through the seemingly simple uses of framing, camera movement, and cutting. It is easy to take the nuances of classical style, when applied in a sophisticated way by filmmakers like Hawks and Hill, for granted.

The Warriors and Sam Peckinpah

If Hawks's filmmaking is dominated by the simple efficiency of classical filmmaking, executed through careful orchestration of camera movement and framing, the staging of the actors, and the studious deployment of continuity editing, then Sam Peckinpah's movies are just as defined by their dynamic use of montage editing and slow motion inserts that vary the speed of the action. Though Hawks's antipathy for Peckinpah's films and technique was clear, Peckinpah was interested in a number of the same themes, narrative situations, and character types. Peckinpah's films offer a bleaker take on many of Hawks's preoccupations. In *The Wild Bunch*, a group of bounty hunters is trailing after Pike Bishop and his gang of outlaws at the behest of the railroad, under the reluctant leadership of Pike's former partner Deke Thornton (Robert Ryan), who is out of jail under the condition he help bring Pike in, dead or alive. When one of the bounty hunters, Coffer (Strother Martin), asks Deke what kind of man Pike is, Deke answers, "The best," a Hawksian response. On the other side of the narrative, Pike is primarily concerned with holding his Bunch together, asserting his leadership and reminding the other members of the importance of sticking to a code of honor. After the oldest member of the Bunch, Sykes (Edmond O'Brien), makes a mistake that sends the group's horses cascading down a slippery desert hill, Pike stops Tector (Ben Johnson) from punishing the old man by appealing to their shared sense of responsibility to the Bunch itself, which is a higher ideal. He shouts, "We're not gonna get rid of anybody! We're gonna stick together, just like it used to be! When you side with a man, you stay with him! And if you can't do that, you're like some animal, you're finished! *We're* finished! All of us!" Pike himself has repeatedly failed to live up to this code of honor, having fled out a window and leaving Deke behind to be caught by the law, information given in flashback.

Pike's words might likewise be seen as foreshadowing Cochise's reminder that The Warriors, too, had "better stick together." The Warriors, like the Bunch, represent an idea that goes beyond any one member—this is the impulse that Cleon speaks to, and Swan reminds Rembrandt of, to mark their presence at the meeting with a spraypainted "W," so people will "know we were there." *The Wild Bunch* also anticipates the challenge to Swan's leadership in its next moments, when Pike's stirrup snaps as he tries to climb onto his horse, sending him falling into the sand in a humiliating, if momentary, defeat for which he is mocked by Tector and his brother Lyle (Warren Oates), the Bunch's problem children, as is Ajax in *The Warriors*.

Peckinpah's westerns made the most lasting impact, which his many admirers see as specifically tied to his own biography and upbringing.[39] As a filmmaker, Peckinpah bore witness to, and some would say presided over, the decline of the western as a viable mainstream genre. The revisionist approach of many filmmakers coming to prominence in the 1960s and 1970s led to a series of westerns that deconstructed, rather than perpetuated, the mythology that the films of the classical studio period had helped to build. Many of these westerns, including *Soldier Blue* (1970, Nelson) and *Little Big Man* (1970, Penn), set out to turn the old heroes into violent aggressors, bringing their on-screen portrayal more in line with historical fact by casting white settlers as the villains who violently displaced the indigenous people who inhabited the West, instituting a genocide. Others, like *McCabe and Mrs. Miller* (1971, Altman) mocked the genre conventions of the old West by making its characters into clowns whose fates are ultimately irrelevant to the survival of civilization. Still others, like *Doc* (1971, Perry), changed the image of notable historical figures whose stories had been told on screen many times by imbuing them with contemporary political resonances. These cynical westerns are generally seen as responsible for driving the last nail in the genre's coffin, eventually reaching the point where, Steve Neale says, "By the late 1970s, the production of westerns in Hollywood had been in decline for over twenty years."[40]

Peckinpah's influence went well beyond westerns. Lee Clark Mitchell describes Peckinpah's innovations in *The Wild Bunch* as revealing the genre's long-held fascinations with violent action, made visible through Peckinpah's use of montage and slow motion:

> Especially at peak moments of violence, Peckinpah orchestrates fragments of scenes, intercutting them to suggest an incoherent immediacy—as in the slow-motion fall of an outlaw through a window, interrupted by nine other shots of random violence before he hits the ground.[41]

Though Mitchell is describing the use of this visual approach in a western, Peckinpah's style easily transferred to the action genre, which was beginning to take shape just as the western was entering its most accelerated phase of decline. One need look no further than Peckinpah's own film *The Getaway*, scripted by Hill. In one important scene, thief Doc McCoy (Steve McQueen) settles up with the man who bankrolled his latest robbery, Jack Benyon (Ben Johnson), in Benyon's living room. When Doc's wife Carol (Ali McGraw) suddenly appears behind Doc, and fires at Jack, the shooting takes place at normal speed. Benyon staggers backward, his chest riddled with bullets from Carol's gun, and trips over a coffee table; his tumble is captured in slow motion, his body flipping upside down as he goes lifeless. Peckinpah then cuts back to a new shot at regular speed, having briefly interrupted the narrative flow with a slow motion insert before returning to reality.

This tendency is something that those who associate Peckinpah with slow motion photography often paper over—Peckinpah was interested less in slow motion than in the jagged disruptions of slow motion inserts, which he used to interrupt the normal speed of action. He learned this from watching films by Akira Kurosawa, a filmmaker who, Hill says, Peckinpah "revered,"[42] an admiration they share. According to Jason Jacobs, Peckinpah's stylized use of slow motion inserts and montage editing helped bring the experience of a gunfight to the audience in a new way, which was revolutionary. The apocalyptic battle that concludes *The Wild Bunch* "captured—more precisely than anything before—the reality of gunfire as an excessive and bloody confusion, in which it is increasingly unclear who is shooting at whom and where the bullets are coming from."[43] With westerns on the decline, this new way of portraying screen violence, made increasingly possible by the abolition of the Production Code, was incredibly attractive to action filmmakers, who would take Peckinpah's general approach to screen violence and associate it with their genre as a stylistic convention.

Hill helped usher in this transition; his interest in and collaboration with Peckinpah on *The Getaway*, as well as his familiarity with the tradition of film westerns, made him ideally suited to adopt Peckinpah's approach in principle, but helped him avoid the trap that many other action filmmakers fall into—stylistic excess that cheapens the emotional impact of violence through exaggerated use of slow motion. Hill's grounding in the classical style of Hawks, with its narrative economy and visual efficiency, prevents his films from overindulging in the use of slow motion and montage editing. Hill's employment of Peckinpah-esque techniques would be a consistent feature throughout his work, but *The Warriors* offers an initial example of his use of slow motion and montage, neither of which he used in either of his first two features, *Hard Times* or *The Driver*.

The first use of slow motion in *The Warriors* comes during Cyrus's rally; Hill saves the slow motion insert for the moment when Luther pulls the trigger and assassinates the would-be gang leader. Hill creates an auditory cacophony, with the attendees whooping and hollering at one of Cyrus's pronouncements, which the slow motion insert then silences when the gunshot rings out. Luther, in a shot reminiscent of the one that closes *The Great Train Robbery* (1903, Porter), points his revolver directly into the camera lens and, as it pulls back, fires. Hill cuts to Cyrus atop the hustings, who is hit in slow motion and flies backward with a dramatic flail of the arms. Before Cyrus falls out of frame, Hill cuts back to a three-quarters composition of Luther, aiming the gun in normal speed. Hill then cuts back to a shot of Cyrus taken from below the platform, the gunshot echoing on the soundtrack to the exclusion of all other sounds, the crowd having fallen into a state of shock. Cyrus falls in slow motion, crashing through a floor of wooden planks. Then, the normal speed returns, alongside the soundtrack, as the collected members of the gangs realize what has happened and panic sets in. Hill has adopted Peckinpah's signature, which, again, is not the use of slow motion alone, but its intercutting with normal speed. John Saunders argues that this particular use of colliding images at different rates of speed "has the effect of exposing us to more information than we could absorb through conventional editing while retaining the immediacy of actual events."[44] In the way Hill uses both techniques here, the intent is well short of the chaotic deployment of multiple rates of speed in both the opening and closing gun battles of *The Wild Bunch*. Instead, Hill's use of slow motion, intercut with shots of normal speed, emphasize the singular act of violence instead of simulating the experience of being inside a chaotic melee. Another prominent use of the collision between slow motion and normal speed occurs later in the film when Fox, one of The Warriors, is tackled by a police officer in a subway station. Fox and the officer fight on the edge of the train platform, precariously close to the tracks; Hill cuts to a wide shot of the station, showing the rapid approach of an oncoming train. Next, he cuts to a shot in normal speed of Fox and the officer wrestling on the ground, and then, a shot in slow motion of the officer launching Fox onto the tracks. Just as most of his body disappears below the platform, Hill cuts to a shot of the subway train racing across the frame in normal speed, a juxtaposition which underlines the horrific violence of impact. Unlike Peckinpah's general tendency to display the horror of violence unvarnished, Hill cuts away, letting the violence of the edit achieve the effect instead of an explicit impact of the train car obliterating Fox's body.

The slow motion is not enough to create the intended emotional effect on its own, either in Peckinpah or in Hill's redeployment of his approach. Instead, the emotional effect is generated through collision, in the tradition of Eisensteinian montage. According to Paul Schrader, Peckinpah's efforts throughout *The Wild Bunch* succeed in "demonstrating Einstein's theory of collision montage even better than the master himself, whose assemblages always seemed more didactic than natural."[45] The effect in Peckinpah's work

Figure 2.2 The assassination of the politically minded gang leader Cyrus (Roger Hill) is shot in slow motion, a flourish in the moment of death that Walter Hill adapts from Sam Peckinpah's prodigious use of the technique to capture violence. *Source: Screenshot captured by author.*

is the achievement of simultaneity above all, which foregrounds the immediacy of violent events. Michael Bliss says that these rapid cuts between slow and normal speed do

> more than simply communicate a simultaneity of events; it also gives us a chance to ponder what the slow-motion photography suggests to us: that the manner in which abrupt or violent actions arc across time in the film is an approximation of the way that, when we are caught in the midst of striking events, these events seem to be taking place in slow motion.[46]

The impact of the train against Fox's body in *The Warriors* is never shown, but the edit contains the violence, aided by the high contrast between the slow motion shot of Fox being tossed onto the tracks and the normal speed shot of the rushing train.

Hill says that he was especially interested in exploring "Eisensteinian montage" throughout *The Warriors*, and specifically acknowledges its influence in the opening sequence, in which all the gangs of the city board subway trains headed for the Bronx for Cyrus's meeting.[47] Instead of showing the events in a linear fashion, Hill creates a montage that disrupts time and space; throughout the credits sequence, he eschews slow motion shots, but achieves Peckinpah's interest in simultaneity through editing that diverges wildly from the intensified continuity style he would use in scenes like the one in the graveyard after Cyrus's murder, which is built on a classical

Hawksian framework. It is impossible to imagine Hawks himself constructing something as elaborate as the first six minutes of *The Warriors*, but the jagged interruptions and quick shots, all unified by the sequence's visual refrain—a shot from the point of view of a subway train, racing along the tracks—are an extension of the same Eisensteinian approach taken by Peckinpah in *The Wild Bunch* and many of his subsequent films. In the opening sequence of *The Wild Bunch*, for instance, Peckinpah creates a much-discussed visual metaphor that features a group of children playing with a scorpion, which is surrounded by thousands of ants, which pick it apart. The images work on a literal level, to underline Peckinpah's sense that violence is inherent in all human beings, even children, but also a metaphorical level, to stand in as a signifier of the Bunch, who are riding into an ambush. Peckinpah goes a step further in *The Getaway*, disconnecting his interest in montage editing from the moment of violence and instead applying it, as Hill does in the opening of *The Warriors*, to the credits sequence. When *The Getaway* begins, Doc is incarcerated in a Texas jail, but is up for parole; Peckinpah emphasizes the repetitive nature of daily prison life with a series of images that deaden the soul, in which Doc's imprisonment is deliberately paralleled to the functioning of the machines in the prison workshop.

The Warriors begins with a long shot that follows the arrival of a subway train in the Coney Island station. The Warriors wait on the platform for the train to arrive, which they will board and take to the Bronx for Cyrus's meeting. After Cleon delivers his pep talk, concluding with "I think we'd better go have a look for ourself," the film's propulsive opening music track, "Theme from *The Warriors*," composed by Barry De Vorzon, begins. The score will unify the credits sequence's various images, which are about to splinter. Linearity is upheld momentarily, however, as a shot of the subway train's doors shows The Warriors, following Cleon, boarding it for their trip to the Bronx. All nine of the gang's members are visible in the frame when the doors hiss closed, sending them on their fateful journey. Because *The Warriors* is so shaped by mythic art forms, whether the mythology of Xenophon or the comic book style that inspired Hill, the opening sequence's montage suggests a kind of destiny, with the gang hurtling toward its fate, a theme supported by the consistent use of the train as an image; it is a symbol of travel and mobility, yes, but one defined by its fixed destination at the other end of the line. The train pulls away from the platform, and Hill cuts inside, where the gang members make the car their own—again, as in *Rio Bravo* and in *The Driver*, there are no civilians.

Hill creates the first moment of disruptive montage with an insert of a rushing train car, shown in disorienting close-up as it races by the frame, for just one second of screen time. Suddenly, the action has returned to the platform The Warriors have just left behind, where Swan talks to Cleon about the meeting they are about to attend. The first shot of the subway tunnels that will become the sequence's visual chorus appears next, followed by Hill's initial widening of the film's world, as he shows the first of many of the city's other gangs heading for the subway, descending down a long ramp in one of New York's many underground stations. He offers another insert of the rushing train, which gives way to another shot of another gang pushing through a station's turnstiles. He continues to rely on the inserts of the subway train rushing by as a disruptive transition, but gestures heavily towards conflict by alternating screen direction as each of the gangs enter the subway stations. One shot of a gang clad in camouflage jackets moves rightward, and in the next, the image begins on the harmoniously marching feet of another gang moving left. The implication is violence, a sensation created by the collision of these images of the gangs moving toward one another. The subway train itself, with its relentless race down the tracks ahead, suggests the inevitability of conflict. As the montage progresses, other shots emphasize the possibility of violence; in one, a gang member waiting on a train platform cracks his knuckles; in another, the subway turnstiles push towards the camera lens as each member of a gang slams through them, an almost three-dimensional assault; in another shot, Ajax plays speedbag with a subway standee handle, an image which directly precedes his hopeful confession to Cleon that they'll get to "waste a few heads." Despite the preponderance of imagery that foreshadows the powder keg of violence set to explode, it is also a sequence of tremendous harmony, as the various gangs from around the city move in rhythm towards their destination. Shots of the gangs, nine members of each, unarmed, unify the sequence and suggest a wider world of myth than that which the film itself will focus on; each of the gangs is like The Warriors, a manifestation of the line that closes *The Naked City* (1948, Dassin): "There are 8 million stories in the Naked City, and this has been one of them." Montage thus serves the mythic function of the story, as it does throughout *The Wild Bunch*; the film's closing montage, after the Bunch has been killed in the machine gun battle, features a series of dissolves that flashback to moments from earlier in the film, each member roaring with laughter. These images crossfade with a shot of the Bunch riding away from a Mexican village, their silhouettes drifting into the jungle ahead. The sequence no doubt intends to mythologize the Bunch, now dead and become legendary through a final act of violent self-sacrifice that reinforced their commitment to one another. In *The Warriors*, the opening montage serves a similar function, establishing myth from the beginning—Peckinpah ultimately decides that the Bunch is worthy of their mythic reputation, but Hill insists on it from the outset.

Though this use of montage is much more Peckinpah than Hawks, both directors share their reliance on a stock company of actors who appear in many of their films. Hawks and Peckinpah were hardly alone in this tendency, of course, as many directors have established a consistent identity at least in part through casting choices across a number of their films. Hawks used John Wayne, Walter Brennan, Cary Grant, Charles Coburn, and many others in several films of many different types (though Wayne appeared mostly in his westerns, with *Hatari!* a notable exception). Peckinpah's films are populated by a number of the same actors, including Warren Oates, L. Q. Jones, Strother Martin, Jason Robards, Ben Johnson, James Coburn, Kris Kristofferson, Slim Pickens, and Steve McQueen. Peckinpah specifically used many of these actors because of their impact in westerns. In Hill's directorial debut *Hard Times*, he borrows both Martin and Coburn from Peckinpah's stock company. Though neither would become one of Hill's regular collaborators, he begins to establish a company of actors of his own, including Felice Orlandi, Frank McCrae, and Edward Walsh, all of whom would later appear in Hill's works. Orlandi would play a police officer in *The Driver*, alongside Bruce Dern, a regular collaborator of Hill's. But it is in *The Warriors* that Hill really establishes a pair of important relationships with actors who would become integral players in his cinema: James Remar, who plays Ajax, and David Patrick Kelly, who plays Luther. Both would be essential creative relationships for Hill throughout his career.

According to Remar, Ajax "was written for a guy who was like, seven feet tall and three hundred pounds of muscle." This description does not describe the fairly slight Remar, who at the time of his audition for Hill and the producers, was just twenty-four years old and had shot only one small appearance in a feature film, the prison drama *On The Yard* (1978, Silver). Something about the character's as-written size told Remar that he had to make himself seem much bigger than he was, which led to a dramatic choice: while reading the scene in which Ajax is handcuffed to the park bench by the undercover policewoman after propositioning her, he "grabbed the corner of the table as I was doing the scene," and as he began reading his lines, he tapped into the adrenaline of the character and "picked the table up." Remar recalls that Hill told him during production that his boldness won him the role of Ajax: "I didn't have a choice. You picked the fuckin' table up!" Remar found the process of working with Hill on *The Warriors* and on their other collaborations (*The Long Riders*, *48 Hrs.*, and *Wild Bill*) to be incredibly rewarding, and rooted in his sense of professionalism, a Hawksian trait: "He truly embodied the essence of what it was to be a director, who is the man at the helm of the ship that you're just willing to do anything for." Throughout *The Warriors*, Remar brings an intensity to the role of Ajax that, despite his relatively early exit from the narrative at the hands of the policewoman, leaves a lasting impression. Though clearly the gang's most disruptive element, he is not the film's villain by any means; his challenge to Swan's authority is a natural sorting out of masculine intragroup hierarchy that is rooted in Ajax's sincere belief that his more combative approach is more likely to get the gang back home safely. When his challenge is put down by Swan and the other gang members agree, Ajax surrenders willingly, later serving ably during the fight with The Baseball Furies.

Remar credits Hill's direction with unlocking a kind of freedom in his performance, suggesting that the director's trust in such a young actor to create and collaborate on the character are typical of Hill's belief in his own material and sincere desire to get the best idea for the scene. Despite Remar's scant experience on screen, Hill "let me do my thing. He let me bring things to the character like extemporaneous lines and letting me behave . . . I would do things and they would stay in the movie." Remar's performance clearly interested Hill, taking Ajax, in Remar's words, from "somebody who was more of a minor player into an expanded position. I got billing right next to Michael Beck." Hill's "total confidence in his actors" is manifest during the fight with The Baseball Furies, when Ajax proves himself as one of the gang's best fighters. Remar recalls contributing to one of Ajax's key lines, when he looks at a Baseball Fury and says, "I'll shove that bat up your ass and turn you into a popsicle." He first said "lollipop" after observing the gang member in costume holding the bat, and Hill immediately liked the idea, suggesting "popsicle." This anecdote demonstrates Hill's organic approach to directing, working together with an actor he likes, to generate an interesting and specific moment rooted in character.[48] This line comes at the moment when Ajax is surrounded by the Furies; when the fight begins, Remar brings a tightly controlled intensity to Ajax's movements, bringing down the lead Fury with three quick blows, accelerated by Hill's cuts-on-impact. The propulsive musical score kicks in just as the Fury hits the ground, and Ajax begins to make quick work of the rest of them. Aided by the suddenly arriving Swan and Snow, Ajax more than holds his own, taking on the Furies individually—by contrast, Swan and Snow largely fight them in tandem. Ajax flips a Fury over his head and onto his back, and picks up a bat, quickly dispatching another. When the fight concludes, Ajax has, despite his malcontented challenge to Swan's leadership earlier in the film, proven himself; he and Swan share a nod of acknowledgment, each having developed more respect for one another in the fray. After his performance in the fight, Ajax is good enough in the eyes of his fellow Warriors—his fateful encounter with the policewoman a few scenes later shows he may not be. Hill clearly developed a close working relationship with Remar after this film that burgeoned during production, even leading him to believe that the film's narrative did the character a disservice. He regrets taking Ajax out of the story, thinking that "he should have been there at the end."[49] No doubt this impulse comes from his fondness for Remar as an actor, and the character that he created.

David Patrick Kelly, of course, is present at the end of the film as Luther, the film's chaotic force of nature who inaugurates the narrative action in his bizarre and little-motivated assassination of Cyrus. Kelly was performing on stage in Stephen Sondheim's *Working* when Hill came to see the production, and decided to audition the actor for Luther; *The Warriors* would feature Kelly's first screen role in a major production. To him, "the script seemed like a genre type of film, like a Roger Corman movie," which hardly dissuaded him—he was impressed with the attitude of the writing and the action that the story contained. Kelly believes that the film's genre feeling masked a kind of sophistication that "helped pave the way for Tarantino and people like that to come along because it brought together these different aspects: based on a novel, a very hard-hitting social realist novel by Sol Yurick and based on the classic by Xenophon. It brought these two worlds together," bridging the divide between the cinema of the art-house and the popular genre cinema of action and adventure. The actor observes that Hill's own persona is reflected in this dynamic, as a "football loving guy that he is who's also got his total intellectual side." He likens Hill's best work to the oft-quoted passage in Ernest Hemingway's *Death in the Afternoon* in which the novelist compares prose writing to an iceberg—much more exists below the surface than above it. Certainly this perspective informs the characterization of Luther in *The Warriors*, whose motivations for killing Cyrus are left mostly mysterious; he has a cryptic phone call with an unseen authority figure, to whom he apparently reports, but that relationship is left deliberately unexplored, and is only suggested partway through the film, well after the public assassination that incites the action. Though Kelly infuses Luther with a kind of unpredictable, manic energy, to assume that he kills Cyrus purely out of his own insanity fundamentally misreads the screenplay's control of narrative information and backstory.

Hill described the man on the phone as "the boss" to Kelly, which allowed him to inform his character's motivations for killing Cyrus with the presence of that authority figure, but didn't overdetermine them. Kelly suggests that Luther is also trying to prove himself in the criminal underworld by pulling off such a dramatic killing, an assassination that in Kelly's imagination was a complex conspiracy between "gangsters and politicos," suggesting a wider world beyond the film's narrative that nonetheless deepens its myth. Like Remar, Kelly describes Hill as a director who was willing to allow actors to bring their own ideas to their characters in order to serve the scene; as a filmmaker, he accommodated Kelly's extreme performance choices throughout the film, which also served the mythic tone of *The Warriors*. His background in experimental theatre led to the impulse that drives Luther's most famous moment in the film, which comes at the film's Coney Island climax. While The Warriors hide out on the boardwalk, Luther and his gang creep along in a rustbucket station wagon, on the prowl. Luther sits in the driver's seat, three empty beer bottles on his fingers. He clinks them together and screeches, over and over again, "Warriors, come out to play!" In Kelly's performance, each word takes on an almost mythic quality, as he stretches each syllable well past its breaking point, his entire head shaking with pent-up rage and violence. While they were preparing the shot, Hill instructed Kelly to find something to use to give the scene more life, and Kelly recalls that he initially picked up a trio of dead pigeons, but Hill encouraged him to use the bottles instead. "We tried to make music from it," Kelly says, paying attention to the ways in which scenic detail could be used to "memorialize the environment" in which they were shooting.[50] Though an undoubtedly mythic moment, the practicality of an actor sensitive to real, lived-in detail gives the scene a grounded quality that would shape many of Hill's films, which often bridge the divide between the mythic and the real.

This is the essence of the gap between Hawks and Peckinpah; each filmmaker is bound by the ambivalent relationship between myth and reality. Hawks's relentless focus on action, which was nearly always grounded in reality, belies the mythic approach he sometimes adopted (though that quality is more often associated with his contemporary John Ford). For his part, Peckinpah could not help relying on the mythic construction of his characters, despite his overt desire to situate his films' violence in an assaultive reality that refused to sanitize its impact. Many critics writing about Hawks celebrate his films' deceptively simple surfaces, which, like Hemingway's iceberg theory, conceal a deeper set of mature preoccupations. According to Peter John Dyer, "The durability of Hawks's films lies in the way that they have a mysterious life of their own going on under their familiar, facile surfaces."[51] By contrast, few would apply that standard to Peckinpah's films, which are characterized by their stylistic ostentatiousness, their dramatic use of self-conscious style that, in sharp distinction from Hawks, announces the director as an "artist," despite his most well-known work coming in the western genre. His formalist approach to style and deconstructive approach to narrative is perhaps best articulated by Stephen Prince, who suggests that "Peckinpah stripped the western genre of its fundamental, underlying myth of beneficent historical progress, and the violence here does not offer a ritual of cleansing and purgation. It registers personal dehumanization and social corruption in a parable of historical and existential loss. Through this cyclical narrative of betrayal and defeat, Peckinpah identified the paroxysms of violence through which history moves with a deadening of the spirit and the dawn of a dehumanizing era that is to be dreaded and feared."[52] This grand assessment of Peckinpah's work is a far cry from Hawks's self-assessment of his own films, where he wanted to do little more than "make some good scenes." Hawks's radically understated view of his own films' sophistication notwithstanding, there can be little doubt that he did not consider himself an "artist," but Peckinpah certainly did.

When Sam Peckinpah died in 1984, Michael Sragow offered a eulogy that acknowledged not only his achievements as a filmmaker, but the impact of his influence. Sragow was keenly aware of Hill's debt to Peckinpah, arguing that "the greatest lesson that Peckinpah imparted to his best students [. . .] was that 'action, if it's to work, must be rooted ruthlessly in character.'"[53] Though Sragow attributes this advice to Peckinpah, he might just as well have been speaking about Howard Hawks, who, despite his disdain for Peckinpah's work, could surely have agreed with him on that. Hill says that when conceiving of action sequences, it is difficult to generalize about design, because "they are particular to the narrative and character" demands of each individual story. In his estimation, his action sequences are "an extension of the characters," and he sees them as fundamentally tied to the "same principles that apply to any dramatic scene."[54] In *The Warriors*, as in the remainder of Hill's career, he demonstrates himself to be an assiduous student of both Hawks and Peckinpah; his work is at least in part a response to theirs, which, for some, may undermine its singularity of vision. As is the case with many filmmakers of Hill's generation, his films function on two levels: they are about their chosen subject matter, but they are also about cinema. Though Hill would certainly not confine himself to their influence alone, let Hawks and Peckinpah stand in as the ancestors of two traditions of filmmaking—the realist aesthetic championed by critic Andre Bazin and the montage approach of Sergei Eisenstein—that come together in Hill's work, tensions never fully reconciled, but always in negotiation.

NOTES

1. Howard Hawks, *Hawks on Hawks*, ed. Joseph McBride (University Press of Kentucky, 2013), 44.
2. Ibid, 194.
3. Peter Wollen, "Introduction," in *Howard Hawks: American Artist*, 4.
4. Andrew Sarris, "Howard Hawks," in *Howard Hawks: American Artist*, 104.
5. Jacques Rivette, "The Genius of Howard Hawks," in *Howard Hawks; American Artist*, 28.
6. Ibid.
7. Interview with the author, 5 February 2021.
8. Hawks, *Hawks on Hawks*, 100.
9. Interview with the author, 5 February 2021.
10. Ibid.
11. Rivette, 76.
12. Stephen Prince, *Savage Cinema*, 2.

13. Ibid, xiv.

14. Peckinpah scholar Paul Seydor makes this observation on the audio commentary for *Alfredo Garcia*, available on Blu-Ray from Kino Lorber.

15. Stephen Prince, "Introduction: Sam Peckinpah, Savage Poet of American Cinema," in *Sam Peckinpah's* The Wild Bunch, ed. Stephen Prince (Cambridge University Press, 1999), 2.

16. Wheeler Winston Dixon, "Re-Visioning the Western: Code, Myth, and Genre in Peckinpah's *The Wild Bunch*," in *Sam Peckinpah's The Wild Bunch*, 166.

17. Stephen Prince, *Classical Film Violence* (Rutgers University Press, 2003), 153.

18. Hawks, 81.

19. Prince, *Savage Cinema*, 48.

20. David Desser, "When We See The Ocean, We Figure We're Home: From Ritual to Romance in *The Warriors*," in *City That Never Sleeps*, ed. Murray Pomerance (Rutgers University Press, 2007), 132.

21. Manny Farber, "Howard Hawks," in *Focus on Howard Hawks*, ed. Joseph McBride (Prentice-Hall, 1972), 32.

22. Desser, 131.

23. Ibid, 124.

24. Ibid, 125.

25. Interview with the author, 5 February 2021.

26. Eric Lichtenfeld, *Action Speaks Louder*, 55.

27. Farber, 33.

28. Noel Carroll, "The Future of Allusion: Hollywood in the Seventies (And Beyond)," 68.

29. Lichtenfeld, 56.

30. Hawks, 31.

31. Henri Langlois, "The Modernity of Howard Hawks," in *Focus on Howard Hawks*, 67.

32. Ibid.

33. Ibid, 175.

34. Ibid, 102.

35. Andrew Sarris, "The World of Howard Hawks," in *Focus on Howard Hawks*, 50.

36. John Belton, "Hawks and Co.," in *Focus on Howard Hawks*, 100.

37. David Bordwell, "Intensified Continuity: Visual Style in Contemporary American Film," *Film Quarterly* 55, no. 3 (2002).

38. Carroll, 68.

39. Stephen Prince, *Savage Cinema*, xiv.

40. Steve Neale, "Westerns and Gangster Films since the 1970s," in *Genre and Contemporary Hollywood*, ed. Steven Neale (BFI, 2002), 27.

41. Lee Clark Mitchell, "Violence in the Film Western," in *Violence and American Cinema*, ed. J. David Slocum (Routledge, 2001), 186–187.

42. Interview with the author, 29 January 2021.

43. Jason Jacobs, "Gunfire," in *Action/Spectacle Cinema*, 11.

44. John Saunders, *The Western Genre: From Lordsburg to Big Whiskey* (Wallflower, 2001), 87.

45. Paul Schrader, "Sam Peckinpah Going to Mexico," in *Doing It Right: The Best Criticism on Sam Peckinpah's* The Wild Bunch (Southern Illinois University Press, 1994), 23.

46. Michael Bliss, "Introduction," in *Doing It Right: The Best Criticism on Sam Peckinpah's* The Wild Bunch, xix.

47. Interview with the author, 5 February 2021.

48. All of the quotes attributed to James Remar in this section come from an interview with the author, 26 January 2021.

49. Interview with the author, 12 March 2021.

50. All of the quotes and observations attributed to David Patrick Kelly in this section come from an interview with the author, 25 January 2021.

51. Peter John Dyer, "Sling the Lamps Low," in *Focus on Howard Hawks*, 81.

52. Prince, *Savage Cinema*, 145.

53. Michael Sragow, "Sam Peckinpah, 1925-1984," in *Doing It Right: The Best Criticism on Sam Peckinpah's* The Wild Bunch, 179.

54. Interview with the author, 12 March 2021.

Chapter 3

Soldiers of Misfortune

By the beginning of the 1980s, the period that has come to be known as New Hollywood was just about running out of time. Though many factors contributed to its decline, most histories of the era assign blame for its demise, at least as the last straw, to Michael Cimino's epic western *Heaven's Gate* (1980), a runaway train of a film production whose costs ballooned alongside its running time, nearly bankrupting United Artists, the studio that financed it. In *Heaven's Gate*'s failure, film historians have seen fit to make Cimino into a double murderer—not only is he responsible for the end of the New Hollywood era, but he also killed off the western as a viable film genre. Many of the substantial texts written about the western genre mention *Heaven's Gate*, almost always in the same context. John Cawelti is critical of the film: "Beginning in 1970, the western began a long decline that was accelerated by the disastrous failure of Michael Cimino's *Heaven's Gate* in 1980."[1] Jim Kitses calls the film "Michael Cimino's blockbuster failure."[2] And the British Film Institute states, "Michael Cimino may go down in history as The Man Who Killed the Western, in that this incredibly expensive box-office disaster effectively dissuaded the studios from investing in westerns in the '80s."[3] Walter Hill, with *The Long Riders*, also financed by United Artists, but admittedly a film of much smaller scope and scale, got in just under the wire.

Howard Hawks sums up the allure of the western with characteristic efficiency: "The western is the simplest form of drama—a gun, death."[4] With *The Long Riders*, Hill brings the story of the James Gang to the screen, as many filmmakers had done before. He grew up loving westerns as a kid, and so many of its myths, scenes, and characters made a lasting impression on him, which would define much of his cinema going forward.[5] *The Long Riders* is most notable for its casting, which uses sets of real brothers to portray the real-life brothers who made up the James Gang. Because Hill deeply internalizes the themes of male camaraderie central to the films of Hawks and Peckinpah, the presence of these brothers adds an extra-narrative dimension to scenes of compromised loyalties and frayed alliances that flesh out the performances of the actors.

In *The Long Riders*, the scope of Hill's execution of on-screen violence draws more heavily on the influence of Sam Peckinpah, especially in the chaotic Northfield Minnesota Raid sequence, which affords Hill the opportunity to restage the opening sequence of *The Wild Bunch*, complete with slow motion inserts and dramatic use of montage. Though the scale of *The Warriors* approached mythic heights, *The Long Riders* is a down-and-dirty film that demythologizes its outlaws, a vision in keeping with the other revisionist westerns of the New Hollywood period. And yet, Hill is steeped enough in the traditional westerns of the classical studio era that he prevents the film from becoming unrecognizable as a member of the genre. In *The Long Riders*, Hill continues to deepen his negotiation between the classical and the modernist sensibilities that shaped his cinematic worldview.

Hill's follow-up film, *Southern Comfort*, was released in 1981, and in its deeply disturbing vision of an American military misadventure in the backcountry of Louisiana, concludes the director's New Hollywood efforts before giving way to his more commercially minded films of the 1980s. *Southern Comfort* tells the story of a group of outgunned National Guardsmen who run afoul of Cajun fur trappers while running a routine training exercise in the Louisiana swamps. Its iconography, character types, and narrative structure have led many critics, and many of the film's stars, to interpret the movie as an allegory for the Vietnam War, an interpretation that Hill himself has often unconvincingly resisted—largely, it seems, out of fear that the allegorical reading will undermine the complexity of the film. If one indulges the allegory, which David Desser calls "clear, even obvious,"[6] it is easy to see *Southern Comfort* as a story of the war come home—it is conspicuously set in 1973, despite no overt narrative reason that it needs to be, the year which saw the end of major combat operations in Southeast Asia and brought many of the American servicemen stationed there back to the States. Substitute the fur trappers for the Viet Cong, with their superior knowledge of the terrain and ability to lead the Guardsmen into trap after trap; the Guardsmen are armed with rifles filled only with blank ammunition, a possible metaphor for the impotence of the American military. Whatever Hill's coy denials, the film's overriding imagery cannot help but resonate with the iconography of Vietnam, especially in the 1980s, which saw more direct confrontation of the war's political import.

Its allegory notwithstanding, *Southern Comfort* is undeniably a Walter Hill movie; its central premise, in which a leaderless group of men, plagued by infighting and failing to exhibit grace under pressure, must battle their way through hostile territory to reach safety, reworks *The Warriors*, just as Howard Hawks revisited his own narratives when he found something new in them he wanted to explore. As in *The Warriors*, Hill navigates the dividing line between classicism and modernism, relying on wide compositions that help him explore the group dynamics of the Guardsmen, but intermittently including slow motion inserts to accentuate moments of violence and relying on a striking use of colliding montage in the film's climactic sequence. Beyond all of these narrative and stylistic traits, *Southern Comfort* is a tense thriller that delivers what action films ought to provide—excitement, tension, and violence.

The New Hollywood era of the late 1960s and 1970s has developed into its own mythological epoch, with a series of well-worn cultural perceptions about how the era began, who the important directors of the period are, what its overriding concerns were, and especially, how it came to an end. This mythologizing is likely only to accelerate as many of its figures make their final films, their bodies of work settling into completion. Though Hill spent much of the early part of the New Hollywood period working exclusively as a screenwriter, the films he directed beginning in 1975 with *Hard Times* reveal someone working adjacent to, but not exactly within, the prevailing trends of the era. Though his debut film is set in the 1930s, as were many New Hollywood films, he does not interrogate the lovers-on-the-run narrative common to *Bonnie and Clyde* (1967, Penn), *Thieves Like Us* (1974, Altman), nor does he adopt the self-conscious manner of the screwball comedy, in the style of *Paper Moon* (1973, Bogdanovich). *The Driver* is far more forward looking, with its isolated noir-western anti-hero and visual aesthetic anticipating the turn towards stylization in the 1980s. So too is *The Warriors*, which exits the bankruptcy decade of New York in the 1970s, foreshadowing the post-apocalyptic science fiction future of John Carpenter's *Escape From New York* (1981). These are films that have their roots in the genres, style, and attitude of New Hollywood, but remain somewhat outside the tradition.

The Long Riders is an example of another of the overt interrogation of film genre that dominated New Hollywood; though many filmmakers undertook this project in a variety of genres, including noir, musicals, and the war film, the 1970s are strongly associated with the revisionist westerns that, according to Steve Neale, are "those which appeared to key in to an increasingly politicized counterculture; and those whose aesthetic characters keyed into contemporary, high-school, or college-educated notions of art."[7] Hill's vision for *The Long Riders* is undoubtedly shaped by the classical westerns of the studio era—including Henry King's *Jesse James* (1939) and Fritz Lang's sequel *The Return of Frank James* (1940)—but also shaped by the aesthetic choices of Sam Peckinpah, who arguably did more than any other director to usher in the revisionist approach to the genre that flourished in the 1970s. For all of Hill's admiration for Peckinpah, *The Wild Bunch* in particular, he is too loyal to the western's overriding ideas and iconography to throw away its classical traditions entirely; he could never make a film as openly deconstructive as *McCabe and Mrs. Miller* (1971, Altman), and certainly not as far into outright parody as *Blazing Saddles* (1974, Brooks). The result is *The Long Riders*, a film which maintains interest in the themes of the classical western, but infused with the stylistic immediacy in the modernist tradition of Peckinpah. Hill finds that the western remains a viable and necessary genre worth taking seriously; his revisions, such as they are, complicate and deepen the genre's themes.

Southern Comfort, too, has analogs in New Hollywood, taking its place alongside other films that, either directly or indirectly, engage with the Vietnam War. Whatever Hill's discomfort with the allegorical interpretation, *Southern Comfort*'s imagery demands to be read in the context of several other films made in the 1960s, 1970s, and 1980s on the subject of Vietnam. Even he acknowledges that this interpretation of the film is valid and obviously suggested by the film's narrative and stylistic constructed. To see *Southern Comfort* only in terms of Vietnam, however, is too reductive. In its portrayal of men lost in the backcountry of the American South, under threat by the local population, the film overlaps considerably with *Deliverance* (1972, Boorman) in its explorations of the nature of violence. The comparison was not lost on the studio that financed the film, 20th Century Fox, which foregrounded the analogy in its marketing push for *Southern Comfort*; over Hill's objections, the poster, which features the ghostly silhouette of a Guardsman, rifle slung over his back and knife drawn, standing knee deep in bayou swamp water, is headed by the warning, "Not since 'Deliverance' . . ." The ellipses invite the audience member to recall several of *Deliverance*'s most infamous scenes, implicitly suggesting that the nightmarish river journey of that film's four city boys will pale in comparison to the horrors on display in *Southern Comfort*. In the film, Hill draws upon the tradition of the Southern Gothic—Americans need not travel to Southeast Asia to find a war; they can have one in their own backyard.

Hill is both of the New Hollywood and apart from it. Generationally, he fits right in; temperamentally, the connection is a little more tenuous. Less self-consciously "artistic" than many of his contemporaries, Hill's comfort in the action genre and tendency to allow political or social commentary to remain subtext (even outright denying its presence in the case of *Southern Comfort*) shows a consistent awareness of the commercial demands of mainstream cinema that sometimes leads him to adhere to received genre conventions or implied audience demands. Hill's cinema is not reacting against the classicism of the studio era, but adopting its most essential characteristics and merging them with some of the New Hollywood's most adventurous stylistic qualities. *The Long Riders*, which sits alongside the revisionist westerns of the period, and *Southern Comfort*, which explores the heart of darkness through the American South, fit roughly into the New Hollywood period but remain difficult to categorize alongside other films made at the same time.

THE LONG RIDERS AND REVISIONIST WESTERNS

In Steve Neale's definition, revisionist westerns are "those which appeared to mock, reconfigure or renew the western's conventions in a cynical, disillusioned or parodically self-conscious way."[8] The self-conscious label, an assumption that many critics make about the life cycle of genres, has proven to be a contentious one. Tag Gallagher, for instance, has made the argument that self-conscious awareness of genre conventions in the western are visible even in *Stagecoach* (1939, Ford), which is often held up as the ur-example of the classical western.[9] Despite Gallagher's objections to "self-consciousness" as a defining characteristic of the revisionist western (objection noted and, I think, sustained), there is no denying that westerns after Peckinpah are different from those made in the classical era.

Several versions of the James Gang's story preceded *The Long Riders*—they demonstrate the trajectory from classical to revisionist. Though not the first cinematic adaptation of the life of the notorious outlaw, Henry King's 1939 film *Jesse James* in many respects sets the standard that subsequent iterations will follow. Alongside that year's other A-westerns, *Jesse James* contributes to a revitalization of the western genre; Barry Keith Grant calls *Stagecoach* "the first adult western,"[10] thanks to Ford's serious approach to the material, but King's film is similarly mature. *Jesse James* is an exemplar of the Hollywood studio era's classical style: As played by Tyrone Power, Jesse is a sympathetic, driven hero who is given ample psychological motivation for his outlaw ways, established in the film's first act, when a group of railroad thugs firebomb his home and kill his mother (Jane Darwell), for which he takes revenge. In King's film, Jesse is a family man wronged by the greedy forces of capital—its depiction of the railroad barons' avarice is in keeping with Ford's populist portrayal of the crooked banker in *Stagecoach*—who becomes a criminal because society lets him down. In the fateful scene where Jesse meets his maker at the hands of the coward Bob Ford (John Carradine), he has just resolved to reform, taking his wife Zee (Nancy Kelly) and their young son to California to leave the outlaw life behind, which makes Jesse into a tragic hero whose story is resolved with a rousing speech given at his grave, remembered as an honorable, if flawed man to whom history did not give a fair shake.[11]

Fritz Lang's sequel *The Return of Frank James* (1940) shifts focus to Frank (Henry Fonda, reprising his role), who helped anchor Jesse to a moral center in the first film, even though he too participated in the James Gang's activities. Frank is the only outlaw of note in King's film, as the other members of the Gang are little more than sketches, with the total erasure of the Younger brothers, even in the Northfield robbery sequence, where they were major historical participants. The sequel rationalizes Frank's quest for vengeance against the Ford brothers by rooting it in clear psychological motivation and shows his softer side by giving him a young sidekick, Clem (Jackie Cooper), and a love interest, a newspaper reporter, Eleanor (Gene Tierney). Frank doesn't actually kill either Ford brother—in a shootout with Charlie (Charles Tannen), the killer falls to his death when he slips off of a rock, and Clem delivers the fatal shot to Bob (John Carradine, back again) before dying himself. Though there are nominal gestures to the films' historical Midwestern settings (Liberty, the town where the main action takes place, is lined with greenery, and there are rolling green hills just outside it), the towns in both efforts are typical of backlot westerns in the studio era, situating them firmly within the diegetic world of genre, rather than the historical immediacy of Missouri and Minnesota. Lang's sequel takes the action west to Denver, where the landscape more overtly resembles other westerns—all dust and rock, beige and browns. These two James Gang films exemplify the classical approach to the material, in keeping with their production dates.

Sam Fuller's *I Shot Jesse James* (1949) and Nicholas Ray's *The True Story of Jesse James* (1957) are late-period classical films, made after World War II and infused with a psychological depth that characterizes many post-war Hollywood films, westerns included. Fuller's film contains no Northfield sequence because it centers the action on Bob Ford (John Ireland), who kills Jesse (Reed Hadley) in the first act. From there, Fuller's film shifts to the aftermath of Bob's legendary act of cowardice, as one of history's villains struggles to reckon with the legacy of his own assassination of the outlaw. Instead of a promised reward and widespread glory, Bob receives little but scorn from those who curse his name, and sing about his cowardly deed in folk songs. When Bob is killed in the film's final moments, he confesses to his love interest Cynthy (Barbara Britton), who finds his crime contemptible, that he is sorry for killing Jesse, the overriding sense is of a life wasted, and that Bob was a coward who was destroyed by the murder just as much as his victim. Fuller's approach revises King's portrayal of Jesse as a martyr made into a sacrifice by the vicissitudes of capital, finding instead little meaning in the deaths either of the outlaw or his killer. Hill will reference the title of Fuller's film in the final moment of *The Long Riders*, when his Bob announces, before he has pulled the trigger, as if writing his own place into history, that "I shot Jesse James."

Ray's non-linear approach to the James Gang's dissolution is rooted in 1950s melodrama, unsurprising for the man who directed *Rebel Without a Cause* (1955) and *Bigger Than Life* (1956); it also stars Robert Wagner as Jesse and Jeffrey Hunter as Frank, their teen idol screen presence outpacing Power and Fonda. John Carradine's appearance as the Reverend Bailey not only ties the film to its earlier iterations, but anticipates Hill's casting of the Carradine brothers as the Youngers in *The Long Riders*—the James Gang's appearances on screen are a Carradine family affair. Ray's flashback structure begins the action *in media res*, as the Northfield Raid descends into manic chaos, being made for the same studio, 20th Century Fox, it repurposes footage from the earlier film of the James boys crashing through the storefront window to escape the melee, and Jesse and Frank leaping with their horses from a cliff into a river below. This signifier of belatedness extends to a moment of high self-referentiality during the more extended Northfield sequence that occurs near the film's climax—after the nonlinear structure circles back around—when Jesse, shooting his way out of the ambush, spies a photographer on the balcony of a hotel snapping his picture. Jesse blows the photographer's camera to pieces and then takes off down the street. Ray's film continues this highly self-conscious approach into its final shot, also relying on the "Jesse James" ballad which Fuller's minstrel sang to Bob; Ray's minstrel sings the song to memorialize Jesse in the moments after he has been killed. The result is a Brechtian distancing effect, as the legend of Jesse James and his death at the hands of Bob Ford immediately cohere; the crowd of people stand still, listening to the minstrel's serenade as he strides through them towards the camera. Fuller's and Ray's approaches to the James Gang story reflect the deepening complexity of the late Classic Hollywood period, introducing psychological depth, moral ambiguity, and highly constructed artifice, all of which point the way to the western's revisionist turn in the 1960s.

Philip Kaufman's *The Great Northfield Minnesota Raid* is a proper revisionist western, with its sensibility firmly rooted in many of the countercultural positions of the late 1960s and early 1970s. Of *The Great Northfield Minnesota Raid*, John Saunders says, "While the film's relationship to earlier versions of the story is primarily subversive and satirical, it avoids crude overemphasis of other assaults on the genre."[12] Much of the film's tone is established by the faux-authoritative opening narration, which tells the story of the James Gang to the audience against the twang of a folksy banjo. The film's protagonist is Cole Younger (Cliff Robertson), who is given a shaggy beard and long hair, given to telling tall tales about how many times he has been shot and survived. Kaufman's overzealous Jesse (Robert Duvall) is an outlaw because of a deep-seated political commitment to continue the struggle of the Civil War. The Northfield Bank raid is ostensibly the purpose of the narrative, but Kaufman spends an extraordinary amount of time delaying it. When the raid finally does come, it offers little in the way of action spectacle, with some members of the James Gang cut down in comparatively bloodless ways, especially in the aftermath of *The Wild Bunch*. The film is rarely in a hurry to get anywhere, with extended sequences in which the Gang hangs out with prostitutes at a bordello just outside Northfield. The film never strives for the level of narrative or stylistic experimentation as *Easy Rider* (1969, Hopper), but it feels similarly directionless and loose. In this shaggy dog approach, Kaufman undermines the western's often relentless push toward narrative resolution, an economy of storytelling favored by its most well-known practitioners.

It would be wrong to call Hill's *The Long Riders* countercultural. So, is it revisionist? Not in the sense that *The Great Northfield Minnesota Raid* is, certainly. Unlike Kaufman's meandering approach, Hill's James Gang film moves forward in the Hawksian style. As to the film's self-consciousness, Hill says that he made sure to include a reference to as many of the previous film versions of the James Gang as he could, placing *The Long Riders* in conversation with not only revisionist westerns, but the classical versions as well.[13] The film's credits sequence features shots of the horizon, a grassy Missouri hill, as the James Gang's riders streak across the screen beneath the overhanging clouds. It is undoubtedly a Fordian image, which places the horizon line in the screen's upper third, but strikingly without the vistas of Monument Valley that became synonymous with Ford. In this sense, Hill's *The Long Riders* is revisionist, in that it locates the story not in the Old West of Hollywood, but in the Missouri grasslands and forests where the events actually took place—Hill calls it a "Midwestern."[14] Above all, Hill wanted to emphasize the roots of his characters, who were not cowboys, but the sons of farmers who grew up in a very traditional way tied to what Hill sees as essential to the western, America's "agrarian past."[15]

A title card announces the film's setting, "Missouri, after the Civil War . . . ," a valuable piece of historical context that sets up one of the film's core themes, associating the James Gang's outlaw ways with their time in combat. Many classical westerns, especially those made after World War II, foreground this psychological motivation; most famously, Ethan Edwards (John Wayne) in *The Searchers*, whose service in the Confederate army has led to his life as an outlaw before he rides up to the family ranch in the film's opening moments. Though Ethan's precise crimes are never outlined, the Reverend Captain Samuel Johnston Clayton (Ward Bond), also a local Marshal, says to him, "You fit a lot of descriptions." Hill encourages the association through juxtaposition, crashing immediately from the title card to Cole Younger (David Carradine), shooting off a rifle shot while on horseback in the middle of a bank robbery getaway. Most of the gang, with the exception of the hotheaded Ed Miller (Dennis Quaid), carries out the robbery with cold, professional efficiency; a shot of Cole firing his rifle at nothing in particular, totally expressionless, shows the detachment with which he approaches the job, shooting off rounds purely for crowd control. It is the kind of precise execution hardened in combat.

Throughout *The Long Riders*, Hill jumps at the chance to stage western action; the film features numerous gunfights and standoffs, many of which are aided by Peckinpah-esque stylistic interventions. In a scene where Pinkerton agents kill an innocent Younger cousin John (Kevin Brophy), Hill uses Peckinpah-style slow motion for the impact of the bullets—a shot of John taking one in the chest, and then the reverse, when John's shotgun goes off and the blast knocks the agent off his horse, sending him flying into the air. Hill cuts to two shots in normal speed, the first of Jim Younger (Keith Carradine) firing at the other agent, and then a shot of that agent starting his horse running, and then rejoins the first agent's fall, once again in slow motion, as he hits the ground, and then a slow-motion shot of John's body hitting the ground. In this deliberate invocation of Peckinpah's method of time-shifting montage, Hill achieves the same simultaneity; unlike the chaos of the opening and closing battles of *The Wild Bunch*, however, these acts of violence, like those uses of this style in *The Warriors*, are singular and personal. Hill underlines the emotion of the moment with a return to normal speed, where he offers a shot of Jim, still a-horseback, and then a subjective shot from his point of view looking down at John, gaping bullet wound open on his chest. Jim rides down the other agent and executes him, which Hill shoots in normal speed, lending the violence a coldness that befits the professional boundary Jim observes—"Now I gotta take him back to his family, dead," he complains, admonishing the Pinkerton before he kills him.

Hill juxtaposes regular speed and slow motion shots once again in the sequence where the James Gang rides down a pair of Pinkerton bounty hunters who participated in the firebombing of Jesse's house. Shot at night in the middle of town, the Gang members sit atop their horses, cocking their pistols and rifles while Jesse (James Keach) interrogates the two Pinkerton men, who stand in front of a pair of shop windows. The men insist they weren't there—they're lying—but Jesse has made up his mind, and starts the shooting himself, joined quickly by the other members of the Gang, which, as Saunders describes, "lifts them off their feet and backwards in slow motion through a shop window, in an elaborate montage of alternating shots of killers and victims."[16] Hill maintains a stark separation between the executed and their executioners; the murdered Pinkertons fly backward in slow motion, but all of the reverse shots of the Gang, close-ups of them firing down and out of frame, are in normal speed. It is an application of Peckinpah's principles, not a slavish imitation, because Hill's use of montage contains a separate idea. Throughout Peckinpah's work, Stephen Prince argues that a guiding principle is "the sudden intrusion of one or more slow motion details inserted or crosscut into the body of a sequence whose temporal rhythms are otherwise normal."[17] In photographing the human body in its moment of violent anguish, Peckinpah is exploring "the metaphysical paradox of the body's continued animate reactions during a moment of diminished or extinguished consciousness."[18] That is not quite what Hill's use of montage achieves in this scene. In its temporal bifurcation of killers and killed, Hill draws attention to the divergent fates of the two parties; for the men who have their lives snuffed out by the James Gang's fusillade of gunfire, the moment lasts an eternity, but for the men who pull their triggers, the moment is over in a flash. This constitutes a revision of the general attitude towards killing that dominates the classical western, in which the hero struggles with the consequences of taking a life. The execution of the Pinkertons in this moment in *The Long Riders* suggests the opposite—that it can become quite easy for the trained killer to move beyond the death he deals out.

While Kaufman's film ironically deemphasizes the Northfield Minnesota Raid, turning it into something of a comedy of errors, Hill eagerly takes the opportunity to largely restage the opening massacre of *The Wild Bunch*. Michael Bliss says that Peckinpah's battle is "without doubt one of the most brilliantly constructed, and violent, set pieces in motion pictures. By my count, there are 191 shots from the time that the railroad company clerk is pushed out of the building until Thornton tells his group to quit firing because the Bunch have 'cleared out'; these shots take up three minutes and forty five seconds of screen time."[19] The battle is based on several layers of misdirection; the Bunch, dressed in Army uniforms, ride into town past a temperance meeting being held by the town's mayor (Dub Taylor); Peckinpah reveals the presence of the bounty hunters, led by Deke Thornton (Robert Ryan), on top of the buildings, rifles at the ready. The battle lines seem clearly drawn—the bounty hunters are the outlaws, and they are going to ambush the Army. However, the film reverses all audience expectations when, inside the town's bank, the Army captain, who is really Pike Bishop (William Holden), the leader of the Bunch, throws the bank manager against a wall, draws his gun, and shouts "If they move, kill 'em!" an order that summons Peckinpah's directorial credit onto the screen. When the Bunch realizes that the bounty hunters are lying in wait for them, they decide that they'll have to shoot their way out. Pike pushes one of the bank employees out of the office and into the street as a decoy, and he is immediately shot to pieces by the bounty hunters. The battle is on, as the Bunch try to escape the town alive, just as the temperance meeting processes into the middle of the gunfight. From a stylistic perspective, says Prince, "these scenes in *The Wild Bunch* take what exists in the narrative as linear, separate lines of action (e.g., each member of the Bunch separately trying to escape the ambush, the bounty hunters picking their targets, and the panicked reactions of the pedestrians caught in the cross fire) and integrate them as a synthesized collage of activity."[20] It is this stylistic revisionism that "served Peckinpah's didactic intentions precisely because the elaborate stylizations it permitted were so decisively a rupture with previous screen traditions of representing violence and with the unremarkable visual presence of daily TV violence."[21]

By the time Hill gets around to restaging *The Wild Bunch*'s opening sequence during the Northfield robbery in *The Long Riders*, Peckinpah's use of montage and slow motion inserts is more than a decade old, the original political intent degraded considerably. Hill begins with a series of fateful, foreboding images—bereft of the narrative misdirection that characterizes the Bunch's Army disguises, though the Gang members all do wear the same signature tan duster that makes them easy to identify when the shooting breaks out—that culminate in the James Gang's arrival outside of town, where they pull their horses to a stop near the church's graveyard, its bells tolling ominously for them. Hill photographs each member of the Gang in his own close-up, recalling the visual approach he took to shooting a crucial moment in *The Warriors* at a moment of tension within the group; here, the James Gang is barely holding it together. The dialogue is marked by bickering and in-fighting, with the overriding sense that tensions between the Youngers and the James brothers are nearing a breaking point. Hill uses mise-en-scene to underline the impending doom, as Cole dismounts in front of the John Welsh Mortuary, which looms over his shoulder in the background. He stands between the sign for the funeral home and the sign for the bank the Gang is about to rob, an internal juxtaposition of commerce and violence. In each of the stories of the James Gang, the Northfield Minnesota Raid is unsuccessful—the time-locked safe thwarts their theft—but in *The Long Riders*, the robbery is a dismal failure, coming near the end of a long series of abject disasters for the group. When the bank manager tells Jesse that the vault can't be opened, he can't quite believe it; he hops the counter and repeats his instructions, as if insisting once more will do the trick. It's the end of the line. Jesse's pathetic attempts to shoot the lock off the safe door only add to the desperation.

The shootout begins similarly to the inciting incident in *The Wild Bunch*, with a customer, shot in the back, wandering out into the street and collapsing in the middle of town, in a deliberate echo of the bank manager offered up as a human sacrifice in Peckinpah's film. As a matter of staging, Hill creates a crossfire that recalls *The Wild Bunch*, with some Pinkerton agents on the roofs of the buildings, but many more in the streets. His first use of a slow motion insert, in keeping with the bifurcation he established in the storefront execution scene, comes when Jim is riddled with bullets and knocked from his horse. Hill cites Peckinpah overtly when he intercuts between several

Pinkertons and James Gang boys firing wildly and a man's fall from a roof—the shooters are all in normal speed and the falling man plummets in slow motion. Cole is also hit in slow motion, but one of the scene's most devastating impacts is when, in two successive slow motion medium close-ups, Jim is shot through the cheek, the bullet entering one side of his face and coming out the other. As the scene accelerates, however, Hill does not get bogged down in slow motion, opting instead for the action theatrics of the gunfight, escalating the cacophony of noise as bullets fly in all directions and the horses beat their hooves against the dirt. He uses it again, briefly, to mark the fallen members of the Gang, Chadwell (Edward Bunker), who is clotheslined by a tree branch, and Pitts (Tim Rossovich), who gains the distinct honor of having his foot catch in the horse's reins, dragging him through the street by his leg, in another citation not just of Peckinpah, but of the entire history of the western genre, for which this is a standard-issue stunt—it also appears in Ray's Northfield robbery, for instance. This stunt might play with a sense of winking irony, but it comes in the middle of a chaotic sequence of terrible violence and narrative stress, when subversion of generic tropes is about the farthest thing from the minds of both Hill and the audience.

The shootout climaxes as the Gang is faced with an impossible choice—trapped in the center of town, many more members are hit, including Clell Miller (Randy Quaid), who is gutshot, and Frank James (Stacy Keach), who is hit in the shoulder, alongside Cole and Jim, who are fighting their own

Figure 3.1 During the Northfield Bank robbery sequence in *The Long Riders* (1980), Hill exaggerates slow motion to an operatic degree, as in this dramatic shot when outlaw Jim Younger (Keith Carradine) takes a bullet through the cheek. *Source: Screenshot captured by author.*

serious injuries, and the Gang has nowhere to go. Many of these moments are seen through a giant window, lined with rectangular frames that separate the glass into square panes. The camera sits inside the building housing the window, looking out at the action on the street, as the James Gang rides in front of it. The window's shape, in one of the sequence's only self-conscious tricks, resembles a movie screen. When the James boys decide that they have no other options, Frank turns and leads the group of horses straight through the plate glass, which shatters in slow motion. In one shot, taken from inside the building, the horses charge directly at the camera, appearing to leap out of the movie screen; this stunt is borrowed from the Northfield sequence in King's *Jesse James*, and its staging encourages its referential quality. Hill, in a break with the stylistic unity he has preserved in his application of slow motion inserts, using them only for the impact of bullets on the victims of gunfire, shows the stunt in slow motion, first from the front, and then from the right side. This slow motion is intercut with images of Bob Younger (Robert Carradine) crying out in agony, who has been cut down by gunfire and did not make the leap through the glass—he, like some of the Gang's other fallen comrades, has been left behind. Though several subsequent shots return to normal speed, the overwhelming number of the remaining images appear in slow motion, including Jesse and Frank, now riding double, as their horse leaps over a low brick wall, and Cole, riding back to pick up Bob, and taking several shots in the process, his leg and shoulders exploding upon bullet impact.

In his dramatic acceleration of the use of slow motion, Hill tries something different from Peckinpah, who never used so many shots of slow motion in succession. As it intensifies, the Northfield sequence actually gets slower, which creates yet another disjunction through montage. The slow-motion shots come to dominate the scene, as Hill abandons the quick, contrastive cutting favored by Peckinpah in favor of something more operatic than balletic. The slow motion extends into the Gang's escape, as Hill's camera tracks alongside the battered riders as their horses gallop through the forest; no longer is the slow motion associated solely with the impact of violence on a body before it dies, but its lingering presence into the battle's aftermath suggests that finally, the violence of the Gang's past has caught up with them. From a formal perspective, however, this scene performs an important function; because Hill is one of the directors responsible for translating Peckinpah's experimental approach to screen violence into a classical form accepted into the nascent action genre, this scene plays a crucial role in demonstrating to other filmmakers how slow motion can be applied. Hill's deployment of slow motion in the Northfield sequence codifies its previous formal significance and associations and exponentially expands them to accommodate several other meanings.

Hill's use of slow motion does not have an explicitly political intent, which opens him up to charges of exploitation. By contrast, Peckinpah's approach to screen violence was intended, at least in *The Wild Bunch* and then in *Straw Dogs* (1971), to carry a politically confrontational charge. Tired of what he viewed as the complacency towards violence in the audiences of the late 1960s, especially in the context of the Vietnam War, Peckinpah wanted his films to serve as a shocking wake-up call to the effects of violence on real human bodies, which film style had sanitized for much of the medium's existence. But in choosing to represent violence in the heavily stylized manner he explored, Prince argues, he was inviting an unfortunate "contradiction between the aesthetic excitement it offers viewers through its montage editing and the moral revulsion toward violence which the narratives, characters, and dramatic situations often convey."[22] In Paul Schrader's view, *The Wild Bunch* manages to hold the line, striking the right balance:

> At the final level, the most difficult, Peckinpah goes beyond vicariousness to superfluity. We no longer want the violence, but it's still coming. Violence then can either become gratuitous or transcend itself. Peckinpah enjoys walking the thin line between destructive and constructive violence. For much of the film he allows the violence to verge on gratuity until, at one moment, it shifts gears and moves beyond itself.[23]

But, subsequent generations of filmmakers, Hill included, often divorced the aesthetic tools employed by Peckinpah from their original political intent, leaving only the stylization of violence behind. In Prince's estimation,

> Peckinpah's interest in violence was never prurient, and it was never conceived to stoke the extravagantly gory fantasies of its audience. But these characteristics are routine in the films of today's directors. Peckinpah's groundbreaking work clearly opened the door for their excesses, and many directors have consciously placed their work in reference to his to form an unfortunate and misguided stylistic tradition, one uniformed by the tortured moral complexity of his films.[24]

Though Hill's use of slow motion violence is not directly political, it is not entirely amoral, either. A close reading of the violence in *The Long Riders*, and especially the Northfield sequence, shows that Hill borrows the tradition of aestheticizing tools used by Peckinpah, but also expands the ways in which they can be used; he allows slow motion to travel beyond Peckinpah's inserts into total scenic dominance, coupled with a highly distorted soundtrack that makes a thunderous symphony of gunfire, beating hooves, broken glass, and the grunts of pain of his outlaw characters. The Northfield sequence does not abandon the "moral complexity," as Prince puts it, of violence, but elevates it to the level of myth. The conclusion of *The Wild Bunch* mythologizes the outlaws, sending them on to the great western graveyard that awaits them on the other side. In death, they become heroes, a mythic approach that contrasts with the demythologized violence of the opening and closing gun battles. Hill's adoption of slow motion throughout the Northfield sequence in *The Long Riders*, though it shares a surface-level relationship to Peckinpah's formal style, fundamentally reverses *The Wild Bunch*'s deployment of myth—Hill mythologizes the violence so that he can demythologize the Gang.

Two of the most important scenes in *The Long Riders* follow the chaos of the Northfield sequence, wherein Hill continues the theme of wrestling with violence that marked Fuller's James Gang film, which creates a contrast achieved through scenic juxtaposition. After the grandeur of the robbery's final section, dominated by Hill's exaggerated use of slow motion, the subsequent scene finds the Gang in a bloody mess in the woods, where they have retreated momentarily. Miller is gutshot and struggling to even open his canteen full of water; Jim, shot through the face, among other wounds, is shaking with pain; Cole took several shots in his efforts to save his brother Bob, who lies crying on the ground. Only the James brothers stand upright; Frank was hit in the shoulder, but Jesse escaped unscathed. Jesse tells Frank that they have to go—they can escape if they leave the shredded members of their crew behind. Frank is stunned at Jesse's lack of feeling for the Youngers and Clell, men who have been a part of their outfit since the war. Hill draws a marked contrast in a medium shot that accommodates all four of the injured, on the ground and leaning against a fallen tree, and the still-standing Jesse. "We gotta ride," he says. "You either stay here and die, or you come with us." A series of close-ups of the wounded offers different emotions: Jim is furious; Cole is detached; Bob is in tears; Clell is in agony. Jesse and Frank turn to go, which prompts Cole to struggle to his feet. "Frank," he says. "You're not leaving, are you?" This moment is where the use of the real brothers to play these teams of outlaws pays dividends. John Saunders suggests, with some skepticism, that the casting choice "might be expected to pay off in some indefinable way. In fact little fraternal warmth comes across; one is more struck by the distance between the characters."[25] The distance Saunders identifies is not a limitation of the film's use of real-life brothers, but creates productive moral complexity. Cole's appeal to Frank is defined by it: a Younger/Carradine asks a James/Keach to betray another James/Keach and side with the Youngers/Carradines. The James/Keach brother, even though he knows it's the right thing to do to stay with the Youngers/Carradines, can't do it. "I gotta stick with my brother, Cole," Frank says. He sides with Jesse, even though it betrays a man who, temperamentally at least, he is closer to. The aftermath of the violence, and Jesse's refusal to live with its consequences, fracture the group irrevocably—Cole pulls his gun on Frank and Jesse, and though he doesn't fire, he does declare their independence: "The Youngers don't need you," he snarls. "I like it better this way, Jesse. I get to see you run." He releases the hammer on his pistol, knowing at some deep level that the violent life he has lived is over for him now, and the James boys mount up and ride off. In the scene's final shots, Miller dies, and the three Younger brothers are left with their wounds, with Cole wondering, "Where the hell's Missouri?"

This scene is the comedown from the aesthetic opera of the Northfield sequence, which offers an extended exploration of the direct, immediate, emotional consequences of violence for the outlaw. Because Peckinpah's Wild Bunch all meet their fates more or less at once, they themselves never fully reckon with the violent lives they have lived; in this quiet, emotionally torturous scene in the woods outside Northfield, Jesse instigates, and Frank follows, a total abdication of the western code to which Peckinpah's characters aspire—"stick with a man or you're finished." Scenes like this call that code's very existence into question; these outlaws, when given the chance, look out for themselves and themselves alone. If *The Long Riders* is a revisionist western, it might be in this aggressive approach to the demythologizing of the western's codes of honor and loyalty, which, for all of Peckinpah's assaults on the genre's formal properties, he was still chasing.

The second scene that contributes to this dismantling of western codes comes in a Minnesota hospital where each of the Youngers is recovering from the wounds sustained during the Northfield raid. A reporter who has been closely following their exploits, Mr. Reddick (Felice Orlandi), is interviewing Bob from his sick bed. "You can say we was drove to it," Bob says, taking an active role in the shaping of his own myth. When the reporter wants to know what Bob means, he offers up his combat service as a motivating factor: "If it weren't for the war, we might have been something else." Bob has internalized the Civil War as a reason for his outlaw ways, even though, as Reddick points out, he was too young to fight; Bob acknowledges this, but says that his brothers did, and "we go everywhere together." *The Long Riders* foregrounds the James Gang's military service as a root cause of their violent ways, but Cole is much more fatalistic about the choices that led them to this moment, shot full of holes, lying in hospital beds awaiting a life sentence: "Aw, hell. We played a rough game. We lost." Even he, however, sees a connection. "I spent four years in the army. Eleven trying to get out of it." If Peckinpah's work was at least partially a way to harness his outrage about the Vietnam War, then still raging, then *The Long Riders* offers a way to reflect on the war's aftermath, some distance from the end of the conflict.

SOUTHERN COMFORT AND WAR

Sam Peckinpah made clear in interviews about *The Wild Bunch* that the film was intended to be a comment on the violence of the Vietnam War; however, he couched that violence in the western genre, as opposed to making a war film directly about the conflict: "The western is a universal frame within which it is possible to comment on today."[26] Director Robert Aldrich proved Peckinpah's point with *Ulzana's Raid* (1972), a western about a young cavalryman, Lieutenant DeBuin (Bruce Davison) who, with the help of a seasoned Indian scout, McIntosh (Burt Lancaster), leads a detachment of soldiers into Apache territory in search of the fearsome warrior Ulzana (Joaquin Martinez), only to find himself outmatched by the Apaches superior fighting skills. Aldrich and screenwriter Alan Sharp intended the film as a direct allegory for Vietnam, offering a nuanced take on both the vagaries of U.S. military outfits and the Apaches, though told from the point of view of the military officers. Douglas Pye holds the film in high esteem, calling it an "exemplary western, perhaps the most intelligent and rigorous of the 'seventies.'"[27]

Hill calls *Ulzana's Raid* "the best movie that is a metaphor for Vietnam."[28] Hill greatly admires Aldrich's films, including *Attack* (1956), another film set in a military context that features, like many of Hill's films, a complex dynamic among a group of men that leads to the breakdown in hierarchy. In *Attack*, set in the European theatre in 1944, Lt. Joe Costa (Jack Palance) is consumed by passionate hatred for the cowardly Captain Cooney (Eddie Albert), who is protected by superior officers because of his political connections; in taking this approach, Aldrich anticipates the contradictions and tensions that will drive many films made in the post-Vietnam era, including *Southern Comfort*. Hill observes that Aldrich's films are about "the corruption and hypocrisy within the institutions."[29] Critic Nick Pinkerton agrees, suggesting that *Ulzana's Raid*'s portrayal of an unsympathetic and conniving Cavalry brass echoes "the mismanaged military campaigns of Aldrich's World War II films," including *Attack*.[30] In Aldrich's films, "the boys in the office are always a known quantity in Aldrich and are never to be trusted."[31] Given Hill's admiration for *Ulzana's Raid* and *Attack*, *Southern Comfort*'s Vietnam allegory could be an exercise in that style. Hill's movie is something of a hybrid of both films, given *Attack*'s focus on the stresses of combat on unit cohesion, and the Vietnam context of *Ulzana's Raid*, transplanted to another time, another place. The Vietnam interpretation of *Southern Comfort* also coincides with films directly about the war made in the New Hollywood period and its aftermath. However, *Southern Comfort* exemplifies several other dimensions of New Hollywood filmmaking, especially when seen in the context of the film to which it was overtly compared by the studio that released it, *Deliverance*.

Hill's harnessing of the iconography of Vietnam is best seen in the tradition of *Ulzana's Raid*, a film he admires by a director he reveres. Throughout *Ulzana's Raid*, the young Lieutenant DeBuin is portrayed in such a way that gives rise to its themes. John Saunders articulates the connection: "a humane and sympathetic man, out of his depth in the circumstances, unable to understand the Apaches, helplessly holding up the rule book—helplessness in fact seems a principal motif in the film: there are no heroes or villains."[32] McIntosh is more experienced, but is killed at the end of the film because of a combination of bad luck and DeBuin's incompetence. To Pye, *Ulzana's Raid* "enforces a sense of institutional disintegration"[33] which likewise describes the general sensibility of *Southern Comfort*. Because Lt. Poole (Peter Coyote), the group's leader, is killed within the first twenty minutes of the film, the rest of the journey through the swamp is marked by infighting among the remaining men, with Sgt. Casper (Les Lannom) taking charge despite not commanding respect from the others. Spencer (Keith Carradine), the more natural leader, refuses the role until very late in the action, only taking charge after more than half of the men have been killed. In Hill's hands, the National Guard is a feckless organization populated by incompetents, psychos, and the insufficiently committed.

According to Pinkerton, Aldrich's film is "unstinting in its depiction of" violence perpetrated by the Apaches led by Ulzana, "though also quite comprehensive in showing the retributive violence by the U.S. Cavalry."[34] An early scene shows a group of Ulzana's warriors disemboweling a man and tossing his guts to each other; a later scene shows the Cavalrymen doing the same to a fallen Apache. Aldrich directly invites the comparison between the two, portraying the brutality of both sides as defining human qualities, not specific to the Apaches. As if speaking to the audience, McIntosh chides DeBuin: "you don't like to think of white men behavin' like Indians." Certainly not, especially when the film depicts its Apaches' violence so graphically; one of its more haunting images comes when the unit discovers the body of a white farmer, Rukeyser (Karl Swenson), with his genitals mutilated and the tail of his pet dog shoved into his mouth, a scene that Pinkerton argues has encouraged the allegorical reading of *Ulzana's Raid*.[35] The violation of the body is in keeping with the portrayal of Apaches and other Native tribes in many westerns, but equally resonant with the imagery of Vietnam. Oliver Stone's *Platoon* (1986), for instance, features a sequence in which an American soldier's body is put on display by the Viet Cong, his throat cut as a warning. *Southern Comfort* contains many similar images: the death of Cribbs (T. K. Carter), impaled by a booby trap made of tree branches, echoes the traps designed by Viet Cong guerillas. So too does the image of three dead men, Poole, Cribbs, and Reece (Fred Ward), their bodies exhumed by the trappers and tied together to taunt the remaining Guardsmen.

In each case, the "enemy," whether Aldrich's Apache, Stone's Viet Cong, or Hill's fur trappers, uses its superior command of the environment and willingness to mutilate the bodies of the invaders as ways of demonstrating authority; this violence is rooted in its theatricality. The Cajuns share a number of characteristics that echo the portrayal of the Viet Cong in a number of Vietnam films, in which, according to Brian J. Woodman, "the enemy often exhibits extraordinary endurance and power."[36] In their command of the land, and the way they seem constantly to be several steps ahead of the hapless Guardsmen, they resemble the common depiction of the VC as "an enemy of unbeatable Asian super-soldiers, an enemy of amazing, almost superhuman, willpower and wisdom."[37]

Ulzana's Raid, like many Vietnam films, is also concerned with the ineffectiveness of authority. Throughout the narrative, DeBuin is nominally in charge, but his inexperience leads him to yield to McIntosh, whose decisions really guides the troupe's maneuvers. This character type is common to westerns; Ford's *Fort Apache* (1948) situates it in Colonel Thursday (Henry Fonda), whose inexperience and arrogance form a tragic combination. However, the inexperienced officer is also a trope of many Vietnam films; in *Platoon*, young Lieutenant Wolfe (Mark Moses) defers to the battle-scarred Sergeant Barnes (Tom Berenger) at nearly every turn, but insists the orders should seem to come from him "in front of the men." These crises of leadership contribute to one of the major themes of *Southern Comfort*, which is the lack of unit cohesion brought about by the power vacuum, also reminiscent of *Attack*. Because the Guardsmen are totally unused to working together, they have no idea how to follow orders; Reece has brought live ammunition, which is against Guard regulations during maneuvers, and the film's inciting incident is the theft of the trappers' canoes, an act into which the cantankerous men browbeat the reluctant Poole. While *The Warriors* quickly codifies the leadership of Swan after the gang's leader Cleon is killed, the Guardsmen in *Southern Comfort* are not so eager to invest authority in his obvious parallel, Spencer. Throughout the film, Ian Murphy says, "all measure of solidarity is demolished by a combination of egocentric infighting and poor strategy."[38] Hill relies on two- and three-shots of the men during much of the film, consistently emphasizing the group over individuals. Whereas the wider compositions in *The Warriors* showed Swan gaining control over the gang, here, they allow space for competition. Reece and Stuckey (Lewis Smith) offer outright challenges to Casper, who has no control over them; Hardin (Powers Boothe), meanwhile, is new and therefore untrustworthy; Spencer obviously has contempt for Casper, but refuses to lead the group, instead reluctantly following even though he knows they are going in the wrong direction. In *Ulzana's Raid*, *Platoon*, and *Southern Comfort*, the chain of command conflicts mightily with the necessities of survival—the nominal leader of each unit is the least equipped to navigate the men through such an extreme situation.

After the decline of westerns is accelerated in the aftermath of widespread generic revisionism, their narrative constructions are displaced onto action films, which were newly ascendant and codify fully in the 1980s. As a result, westerns lost their ability to speak meaningfully to the Vietnam War, and action movies took up the mantle instead. A series of "behind enemy lines" films appears in the mid-1980s, in which the characters' objective is to rescue American prisoners-of-war left behind by the American government, including *Uncommon Valor* (1983, Kotcheff), *Missing in Action* (1984, Zito), and especially *Rambo: First Blood, Part II* (1985, Cosmatos). In sending an action hero or group action heroes back to Vietnam to rescue the POWs, these films allow the United States to fight the war all over again, and this time, as Rambo says, they "get to win." *Southern Comfort* precedes all of these films, and is not afforded the benefit of diegetic hindsight—it is set in 1973. *Southern Comfort* addresses Vietnam in a much more despairing, hopeless scenario than the redemptive narratives of subsequent 1980s action films, which offer national reclamation of pride that rectifies the country's defeat. In fact, *Southern Comfort*'s iconography directly anticipates the first Rambo film, *First Blood* (1982, Kotcheff), by one year. Rambo is a Vietnam veteran, trained as a ruthless killing machine, but comes home to an America that has largely forgotten him and veterans like him. Hassled by the police in the Pacific Northwest town he is passing through, the trauma of his torture at the hands of the Viet Cong awakens his violent tendencies, and he flees into the woods, pursued by the local police, led by Sheriff Will Teasle (Brian Dennehy). The police are hopelessly overmatched by Rambo's improvisatory skill, and he quickly makes mincemeat of them by turning the forest against them, leaving most of the officers terribly, but not fatally, wounded. In their abject humiliation at the hands of a craft enemy, the officers suffer the same fate as Hill's Guardsmen. Like the fur trappers in *Southern Comfort*, Rambo appears and then disappears into the forest seemingly at will, always maintaining the element of surprise, giving him a tremendous advantage over the officers, whose weaponry and unit cohesion are no help. Rambo picks them off one by one, hobbling them and weakening their numbers. The trappers in *Southern Comfort* follow the same strategy, even taunting the Guardsmen with an elaborate display of eight pelts, ostentatiously placed in the swamp to let them know what awaits them.

First Blood's Rambo/Stallone becomes virtually synonymous with the action cinema of the 1980s, but also the primary vehicle for mainstream cinema to explore the historical embarrassment of the Vietnam War. However, *First Blood* follows *Southern Comfort* in its restaging of the battles of the Vietnam War on American soil. So too do other action films of the decade, including *Aliens* (1986, Cameron), for which Hill served as a producer and collaborated on the story. James Cameron's portrayal of the Space Marines deliberately evokes Vietnam in the soldiers' costume design, their uniforms adorned with personalized messages and cartoon drawings that anticipate the "Born to Kill" scrawled on a soldier's helmet in *Full Metal Jacket* (1987, Kubrick). On the hostile planet, the aliens make quick work of most of the Marines, blending in with the environment in their nest in one action sequence, and staging a sneak attack from beneath the metal floor in another. The science-fiction action film *Predator* (1987, McTiernan), set in the jungles of Central America, is another film in the *Southern Comfort*-style, as a squad of elite commandos led by Dutch (Arnold Schwarzenegger) is picked off, one by one, by an alien monster who hunts them for sport, maintaining its cover by blending in with the environment and taking parts of their bodies as trophies. Though *Southern Comfort*'s overwhelmingly downbeat mood aligns it temperamentally with New Hollywood movies, its mixture of the iconography of Vietnam and violent action offers a model that subsequent filmmakers will imitate in their ideologically mixed approaches to the meaning of American defeat in Southeast Asia, filtered through mainstream action cinema.

Southern Comfort also contains a striking parallel to a moment of Eisensteinian montage in *Apocalypse Now* (1979, Coppola). In the final scenes of *Apocalypse Now*, Captain Willard (Martin Sheen), who has been sent upriver to kill the renegade Colonel Kurtz (Marlon Brando), creeps into Kurtz's compound under cover of darkness, while the Colonel's Montagnard army conducts a celebratory ritual slaughter of a caribou in the courtyard outside. Coppola intercuts shots of Willard, slashing at Kurtz with a blade, with the on-camera slaughter of the caribou, creating a brutal juxtaposition given extra heft by the unsimulated death of the animal. As Hardin and Spencer uneasily wait in the village at the end of *Southern Comfort*, a few of the townspeople bring in a pair of enormous hogs, awaiting slaughter in cages on the back of a pickup truck. Hardin also spies another group of townspeople throwing a pair of nooses over a crossbeam in the center of town. The film generates tension: are the nooses for Hardin and Spencer, or are they somehow going to be used for the pigs? In *Apocalypse Now*, Coppola's use of montage that parallels the death of Kurtz and the ritual slaughter of the caribou is highly mannered, foregrounding its metaphor through deliberate employment of Eisensteinian theory. In *Southern Comfort*, the metaphor is present, but it is rooted in the film's action. Hill includes striking, graphic close-ups of the pigs being shot, and then their throats being cut so they can be bled that anticipate the close quarters violence that is about to break out, as Hardin and Spencer's fears that they might still be in danger are realized. Because there are only blanks in Spencer's rifle—he empties his clip at one of the trappers at close range, but nothing happens—much of the violence left to come is done with blades. Hardin, shot and wounded on the ground, takes advantage of Spencer's show of force with the cacophony of blank rounds to plunge his knife into one trapper's groin; Hill cuts to a townsperson, roaring with delight in the other room, in keeping with the hoe-down music that has set the villagers to dancing, in another moment of juxtaposition that foregrounds the simultaneous shock and pleasure an audience member might take in seeing such a brutal act of violence. Spencer will, with Hardin's help, stab another trapper in close combat with his bayonet, before each of them flees into the woods, now certain that the nooses are meant for them.

Beyond Vietnam, *Southern Comfort* is also a gothic film that sends its characters into unfamiliar territory. Films set in Louisiana, according to Mathe Allain, tend to portray a state governed by its extremes, whether taking place in New Orleans or in the swamps; these films offer "Louisiana raised to the tenth power."[39] This similarity invited a number of comparisons at the time of the film's release to *Deliverance*, a connection encouraged in the studio's marketing push, despite Hill's discomfort with the association. In addition to the poster's tagline, the first line of the film's official trailer warns, against the image of a compass spinning, "It will show you as much about survival as *Deliverance*."[40] Based on the novel by James Dickey, *Deliverance* is about a group of four men, Lewis (Burt Reynolds), Ed (Jon Voight), Bobby (Ned Beatty), and Drew (Ronny Cox), who travel to Tennessee from Atlanta because they have heard that a particularly scenic river valley is set to be flooded by the building of a dam; while on the trip, a pair of woodsman rape Bobby, Lewis is severely injured, and Drew drowns. Ed kills a woodsman who may or may not have been one of their tormentors, and is subsequently haunted by nightmares of the violence on the river, even if he evades the law.

The similarities between *Southern Comfort* and *Deliverance* are obvious, but Murphy reminds us that "to lazily reduce Hill's film to '*Deliverance* in the bayou,' as so many critics have done, is to misread the varied historical traditions and contexts he draws on."[41] A close comparison of the two movies reveals similar preoccupations, but radically different areas of emphasis. Boorman's film slowly allows the menace and darkness that will soon consume his characters to creep in, while in Hill's film, the undercurrent of violence is present from the film's opening moments, given full life by Ry Cooder's moody, threatening score, which plays over the credits against foreboding shots of the bayou that emphasize its mystery. According to Allain, these images serve a crucial thematic purpose, in which "man's insignificance is emphasized by the credits, tucked in a corner so that the landscape occupies the full breadth of the screen."[42] The opening sequence of *Deliverance*, in which Drew plucks his guitar while one of the local boys does the same on a banjo, is one of its most oft-mentioned scenes, largely thanks to the song itself, "Dueling Banjos," arranged for the film by Eric

Weissberg and Steve Mandel. Drew and the local boy begin by trading chords on their respective instruments, but eventually play together, the banjo player eventually outpacing Drew. Despite the city boys' arrival in unfamiliar territory, the Dueling Banjos scene offers the possibility of understanding between urban and rural people, a hope that the film upholds for its first forty minutes. Then, the attack in the woods disrupts the narrative flow and sends *Deliverance* careening into horror and violence. *Southern Comfort* includes no equivalent scene, and its action gets going much more quickly—in keeping with Hill's Hawksian approach to accelerated narrative, the shot that kills Poole, rendered in a Peckinpah-style slow motion insert, comes just seventeen minutes into the film. *Deliverance* uses no slow motion, but does contain a highly surrealistic day-for-night scene when Ed climbs a rock wall, which anticipates *Southern Comfort*'s nightmarish vision of the landscape. In this way, both *Deliverance* and *Southern Comfort* can be seen to restage the conflict of Vietnam on American soil, with the land itself a hostile force that the intruders must overcome. As if the threat posed by the trappers weren't enough, the swamp itself is a constant danger; Hill emphasizes the connection between the trappers and the bayou when the homemade booby trap impales Cribbs, when quicksand takes Stuckey to his death, as well as in the disorienting sequence where the trees begin to fall into the knee deep water all around the surviving Guardsmen, sending them fleeing in all directions.

Deliverance and *Southern Comfort* are also both interested in the consequences of violence and contain extended scenes in which the characters wrestle with their moral responsibility for it. Ed has no desire to kill—his first attempt to use the bow on a deer early in the film, which ends with him missing his shot badly, foreshadows the later moment where he must shoot the woodsman—and is forced into the leadership role by Lewis's incapacitation. In removing the patriarchal Lewis from the narrative, unconscious and in severe pain from his broken leg, Boorman's film also carries the Hawksian danger device that Hill uses throughout his career. Hill eliminates the group's leader almost right away, upending all the decision-making power vested in military authority. In the absence of clear leadership, the moral certitude of violence is clouded. Though urged to take revenge for Drew's death by the delirious Lewis, Ed struggles with the responsibility entrusted to him and likely kills an innocent man. In *Southern Comfort*, the moral lines are blurred when Hardin intercedes on behalf of their hostage, the one-armed Trapper (Brion James), and kills his comrade Reece in a knife fight. The Guardsmen have also transgressed, moving through territory that belongs to the Cajuns—the one-armed Trapper, who finally reveals that he does speak English, tells Hardin and Spencer, "We live back in here. This is our home and nobody don't fuck with us." The ritualistic violence perpetrated against the Guardsmen by the Cajuns and their predilection for "rough justice" that marks Louisiana for Allain "as an ancient civilization, weighed down by age-old traditions, sophisticated and world-weary."[43]

Southern Comfort also maintains its commitment to the New Hollywood sensibility in the ambiguity of its ending. Spencer and Hardin have barely escaped from the small town which has turned out to be the home of the trappers who have been pursuing them; in this narrative development, *Southern Comfort* echoes *The Texas Chainsaw Massacre* (1974, Hooper), another nightmare vision of the threats posed to outsiders by rural America, in which the film's last survivor seeks refuge from the chainsaw-wielding maniac in the arms of a gas station owner, only to realize that he is the killer's father. As Spencer and Hardin rush back into the swamp, they hurry after a Guard helicopter that is obviously searching for their lost unit. The helicopter is one of the strongest visual symbols of the Vietnam War, made more salient after the "Ride of the Valkyries" sequence in *Apocalypse Now*. As in *The Long Riders*, Hill distorts the soundtrack, the whirring blades of the chopper crunching in auditory slow motion; the slowed audio soon joins the image, as he drifts the medium shot of the two men as they stagger towards the camera, Spencer propping up the injured Hardin, into slow motion, the auditory distortion of the blades reaching a fever pitch. The two men stare off-screen, looking at something; in the reverse, a truck is visible through the trees, turning in slow motion. A subsequent cut to the helicopter circling above, also in slow motion, is followed by a return to Spencer and Hardin, looking exhausted. Hill cuts to each of the three subjects—the truck, the helicopter, and the two men—once more, and in their two-shot, Spencer looks at Hardin in slow motion. The film's final shot is a cut around to the truck—it's a National Guard vehicle—the camera drifting in slow motion over the stenciling on the side, which reads, "USA," and then comes to rest on the white military star on the truck's door.

This moment of narrative ambiguity dramatically withholds resolution. As a survival film, *Southern Comfort* recalls the structure Hill used in *The Warriors*—there are even nine members of the Guard patrol, just as there were nine members of the gang—but *The Warriors* resolves neatly, with the gang's name cleared, the real assassin punished, and a sunny final image on the beach at Coney Island. In preserving the ambiguity and denying narrative resolution, Hill invites discomfort that comes with the unsettled conclusions of many other New Hollywood films, including *Deliverance*, which ends with Ed shrieking in bed after waking up from a nightmare in which he sees a dead man's hand rising slowly out of the lake that now covers the evidence of his crimes. In *Southern Comfort*, the lingering image of the truck's official markings, "USA" and the military star, may retroactively motivate Spencer's slow-motion glance at Hardin; the National Guard has arrived, but the two men, despite their anguish and exhaustion, do not rush out of the swamp to

Figure 3.2 In *Southern Comfort* (1981), the final surviving National Guardsmen, Spencer (Keith Carradine) and Hardin (Powers Boothe), flee their swamp-dwelling pursuers, but freeze at the sight of their would-be rescuers, the U.S. military, in the film's ambiguous conclusion. *Source: Screenshot captured by author.*

meet it. Their time in the bayou, in which a misunderstanding in the aftermath of their theft of the trappers' property leaves everyone in their unit dead but them, has totally upended their sense of the moral certitude of their country's military. This moment also recalls their previous race toward a truck, the one which carried them to the backwater town where they were nearly hanged and bled alongside the hogs. The experience has been so shattering, they have no sense of moral order—they are men without a country who, through the film's denial of narrative resolution, are left to wander the swamp forever. The final image of Spencer and Hardin in the film commemorates their uncertainty. In this way, Pye's observation about the conclusion of *Ulzana's Raid*, in which DeBuin's authority has been compromised, McIntosh has been killed, and Ulzana has been defeated, is resonant:

> The ending is very uncomfortable. The film makes a moral choice between the two races impossible, but at the same time offers no support for a position of comfortable disengagement from what is presented as an intractable situation: it attempts to confront rather than evade the problem of individual action in a context of military absurdity and moral collapse.[44]

With regard to *Ulzana's Raid*, Pye says the film's parallels to Vietnam are "worth noting, but should not distract from the integrity of the film as a western."[45] An overdetermined allegorical reading would inevitably reduce the salience of Aldrich's movie in the genre to which it more obviously belongs. This is undoubtedly what gives rise to Hill's anxiety about the Vietnam allegory being read into *Southern Comfort* and has led to his potentially disingenuous denials of it, which could reduce the complexity of the film to its metaphor. For their parts, Boothe, Carradine, and the rest of the cast have little such misgivings, openly discussing the film in relationship to its Vietnam subtext.[46] In Ian Murphy's view, *Southern Comfort* shows Hill "mobilizing the mechanics of genre cinema in order to stake a righteous claim to authorship."[47] The post–Civil War environment of *The Long Riders* likewise acknowledges the aftermath of Vietnam, but the film is rarely discussed in this context, instead typically seen as a Peckinpah-style western directed by one of his most fervent admirers. In both cases, the James Gang and the Guardsmen are soldiers who are ill-suited to the moment in which they find themselves, cut off from institutional support and left to fend for themselves in harsh survival situations. With respect to *Southern Comfort*, Murphy argues that "it is only by dismantling conventional models of male military heroism that Hill can voice a wider indictment of all government systems that are driven by a deep-rooted ethos of entitlement and a fatal condescension toward cultural difference."[48] The same insight might well apply to *The Long Riders*, which deconstructs western heroism by demythologizing the James Gang's outlaws both narratively and stylistically, through revisionist approaches to western conventions and slow motion. Close analysis of both *The Long Riders* and *Southern Comfort* reveals the films' director revising the technical virtuosity of Peckinpah's slow motion for his own purposes, and offering a deeply ambiguous approach to the Vietnam movie that fuse the action film to the post-war moment.

NOTES

1. John G. Cawelti, *The Six-Gun Mystique Sequel* (Bowling Green State University Popular Press, 1999), 2.
2. Jim Kitses, *Horizons West* (BFI, 2004), 5.
3. Quoted in Cawelti, 99.
4. Howard Hawks, *Hawks on Hawks*, 141.
5. Interview with the author, 26 February 2021.
6. David Desser, "When We See The Ocean, We Figure We're Home: From Ritual to Romance In The Warriors," 127.
7. Steve Neale, "Westerns and Gangster Films Since the 1970s," 29.
8. Ibid.
9. Tag Gallagher, "Shoot-Out at the Genre Corral: Problems in the "Evolution" of the Western," in *Film Genre Reader II*, ed. Barry Keith Grant (University of Texas Press, 1995), 252.

10. Grant, Barry Keith. "Introduction: Spokes in the Wheels," in *John Ford's Stagecoach*, ed. Barry Keith Grant (New York, Cambridge University Press, 2003), 2.

11. Conceptual application of the "classical" studio style in this paragraph is drawn, of course, from David Bordwell, Janet Staiger, and Kristin Thompson's foundational work *The Classical Hollywood Cinema*.

12. John Saunders, Western Films: From Lordsburg to Big Whiskey, 75.

13. Interview with the author, 26 February 2021.

14. Ibid.

15. Ibid.

16. Saunders, 76.

17. Stephen Prince, *Savage Cinema*, 62–63.

18. Ibid, 60.

19. Michael Bliss, "Introduction," *Doing It Right: The Best Criticism on Sam Peckinpah's* The Wild Bunch, xix.

20. Prince, 67.

21. Ibid, 49–50.

22. Ibid, 103.

23. Paul Schrader, "Sam Peckinpah Going to Mexico," 23.

24. Prince, 234.

25. Saunders, 75.

26. Quoted in Prince, 34.

27. Douglas Pye, "Ulzana's Raid," in *The Book of Westerns*, ed. Ian Cameron and Douglas Pye (Continuum, 1996), 263.

28. Interview with the author, 26 February 2021.

29. Ibid.

30. Nick Pinkerton, "Audio Commentary," *Ulzana's Raid* (1972, Aldrich), Kino Lorber, 2020, Blu-Ray.

31. Ibid.

32. Saunders, 102.

33. Pye, 266.

34. Pinkerton, "Audio Commentary."

35. Ibid.

36. Brian J. Woodman, "A Hollywood War of Wills: Cinematic Representation of Vietnamese Super-Soldiers and America's Defeat in the War," *Journal of Film and Video* 55, no. 2/3 (2003), 44.

37. Ibid.

38. Ian Murphy, "'Human Frailty Swallowed Whole': On Walter Hill's *Southern Comfort* (1981)," *Bright Lights Film Journal*, 31 October 2021. https://brightlightsfilm.com/human-frailty-swallowed-whole-on-walter-hills-southern-comfort-1981/.

39. Mathe Allain, "Glamour and Squalor: Louisiana on Film," *Louisiana History: The Journal of the Louisiana Historical Association* 27, no. 3 (1986), 231.

40. "Trailer for *Southern Comfort*," *Southern Comfort* Blu-Ray, Shout Factory, 2014.

41. Murphy.

42. Allain, 234.

43. Ibid, 236.
44. Pye, 268.
45. Ibid.
46. "The Making of *Southern Comfort*," *Southern Comfort* (1981, Hill), Shout Factory, 2014, Blu-Ray.
47. Murphy.
48. Murphy.

Chapter 4

Black and White

Though Walter Hill has been a defining figure of the action genre for many years, his lasting legacy will most likely be the success of *48 Hrs.* (1982), which pioneered a formula that many subsequent directors would replicate. Picking up on the popularity of the buddy movie, which proliferated in the 1970s New Hollywood period, Hill's film adds a racial component by pairing a white police officer, Jack Cates (Nick Nolte), with a Black convict, Reggie Hammond (Eddie Murphy), who work together to solve the murder of a cop and apprehend a dangerous criminal. Hill's film was not the first to offer a mixed-race pairing; by the time of *48 Hrs.*'s release, Richard Pryor and Gene Wilder had already made two of their four films together, *Silver Streak* (1976, Hiller) and *Stir Crazy* (1980, Poitier), which showed the comedic potential of a Black and white team. *48 Hrs.* situates the multiracial buddy pairing in the action genre, though Murphy's presence lends it a considerable amount of comedy. Its specific formula, with a mixed-race pair of heroes, has been endlessly repeated in the action-comedy hybrid, with the *Lethal Weapon* series, the *Rush Hour* films, and the *Fast and Furious* spin-off *Hobbs and Shaw* (2019, Leitch) just a few of the films that follow in the tradition established by *48 Hrs.* The film also led to a direct sequel of its own, Hill's *Another 48 Hrs.* (1990), which sees Cates and Hammond reteam to ferret out corruption in Cates's police department. Hill is quick to acknowledge the influence of *48 Hrs.* on other action films, but offers a crucial caveat that many directors miss the point: "they forget that these guys don't like each other."[1]

Beyond their impact on the action genre, the *48 Hrs.* films also reveal a crucial dimension of Hill's cinema, which is a consistent interest in Black characters that far outpaces that of any of his New Hollywood contemporaries. In general, Hill's films are more likely to feature Black actors in prominent roles than others of his generation; however, Hill's approach to casting does not merely tip his hat to the importance of diversity. A number of his films are concerned with experiences important to Black Americans. This is another thing that filmmakers inspired by the *48 Hrs.* pairing are content to leave behind: rather than simply pairing a white man and a Black man, Hill's movies openly confront the racial tensions produced by their uneasy partnerships of convenience. Far from following the expectation that these buddy films will harmoniously paper over the differences of the white and Black partners, thereby suggesting that racial peace is achievable for all Americans, the *48 Hrs.* movies are far more cautious about the possibility of reconciliation.

48 HRS., ITS SEQUEL, AND ROOTS IN GENRE

The two *48 Hrs.* films foreground crucial themes: racial conflict, the dividing line between cop and criminal, the tenuous nature of wealth, and especially how these societal problems complicate already uneasy relationships between white and Black men. Though their most direct antecedent is the buddy film of the New Hollywood period—*Butch Cassidy and the Sundance Kid* (1968, Hill), *Easy Rider* (1969, Hopper), *Scarecrow* (1973, Schatzberg), and *Thunderbolt and Lightfoot* (1974, Cimino) are just some of the most notable examples—the films also clearly call back to *The Defiant Ones* (1958), just one of many social problem films directed by Stanley Kramer. In it, a Black man and white man gradually come to respect and even like one another over the course of the film, thanks to their need to depend upon one another in order to survive. Critic Melvin Donalson argues that *The Defiant Ones* is "the ideal movie for the age of civil rights," which also establishes "the pattern of transforming hatred to respect and racial difference to racial blindness, while allowing for caring and trust within the confines of a heterosexual framework."[2] However, removing the racial dimension of the plot reveals its even deeper structure, which goes back to the Hollywood screwball comedies that proliferated during the Great Depression. While *The Defiant Ones* is often deathly serious, in the manner of Kramer's self-important pictures, both *48 Hrs.* and its sequel oscillate between thrilling action sequences and comedic patter between the interracial leads. The breezy tone, rooted in the conflict generated by the personality clash between Reggie and Jack, is closer to Frank Capra's *It Happened One Night* (1934) than Kramer's heavy pathos. The pivot point of Capra's film comes when the working class reporter Peter Warne (Clark Gable) and the runaway heiress Ellie Andrews (Claudette Colbert) have to pretend to be a bickering married couple in order to fool the police. The playacting works, and their romantic bond is really born in the aftermath, when they share a laugh over the trick they've played. This theatricality is equally important to *48 Hrs.*, as Reggie pretends to be a police officer in a redneck bar in the film's most memorable scene. Not only is it a showcase for Murphy's comedy, but the scene demonstrates to Jack that Reggie is a potentially worthy partner in the Hawksian sense: "You did a good job, Reggie," Cates says after Hammond exits the bar.

Hawks was one of the foremost practitioners of screwball comedy, with *Twentieth Century* (1934), *Bringing Up Baby* (1937), and especially *His Girl Friday* (1940) standing as landmarks of the cycle. *48 Hrs.* features a number of sequences of brutal violence resulting from gunplay, but Hill's fusion of action with comedy avoids the reckoning with violence that characterized *The Long Riders* and *Southern Comfort*, a signifier of the film's more mainstream entertainment aspirations. A gun battle between Jack, Ganz (James Remar), and Billy Bear (Sonny Landham) that leaves two cops dead, therefore, can immediately give way to an expository sequence that is directed much like the energetic screwball comedies of the 1930s and 1940s. Set in the police station directly after the shootout, Jack moves through the space of the precinct, asking questions and following up on leads. Hill stages the entirety of the sequence in one extended, choreographed shot; it is not a long take in the manner of the ostentatious opening of *Touch of Evil* (1958, Welles), but is much more workmanlike in its effect, the kind of shot present in any number of films by Otto Preminger and William Wyler, who created elaborate dances between the camera and the actors that never felt showy, but practical ways to cover the action of a scene without cutting. Hill recalls that the shot covered something like eleven pages of the screenplay; in the final film, it runs more than three minutes.[3] Throughout the extended take, Cates remains the shot's focal point, but Hill varies his position through changing the staging: early on, Cates is in the shot's background, with a wide composition; then, it tracks with him as he moves to the other side of the precinct's bullpen, moving closer; he steps into medium close-up as he confers with another cop; he moves back to the other side of the room near his desk, and back into a wide shot to talk with Kehoe (Brion James); then, he drags Kehoe to the evidence board on the right side of the room in medium close-up. Throughout, Hill establishes a busy, chaotic environment, as extras dressed in police uniforms repeatedly pass in front of the frame and otherwise fill out the background, with several pertinent and non-pertinent conversations happening at once. The scene offers important exposition, establishing Ganz's identity to the police and tying him to one off-screen murder, while also showing Cates's command of his job and the facts, which imbue him with a Hawksian professionalism. The scene overtly resembles the opening shots of *His Girl Friday*, in which Hawks introduces star reporter Hildy Johnson (Rosalind Russell) in the environment she makes her own—the bustling newsroom of the *Morning Post*. Hawks employs similar visual strategies, making liberal use of camera movement and busy staging to create a similarly chaotic space. Extras move in and out of the frame, ongoing conversations are interrupted as Hildy passes by with the camera tracking ahead of her, and the general impression is of a busy, living space teeming with energy. Though Hawks introduces Hildy in several shots, rather than Hill's use of an extended take in *48 Hrs.*, each establishes an accelerated pace. Hill's films generally feature short running times, but *48 Hrs.* moves more quickly than any of his previous efforts, a sense it shares with the energetic screwball comedies of a bygone era. Because *48 Hrs.* was so influential over a number of subsequent comedies, it can be easy to overlook the historical tradition to which it belongs.

In *His Girl Friday*, *It Happened One Night*, and other screwball comedies, the films conclude with a cessation of hostilities between the romantic partners. In *It Happened One Night*, the marriage between Peter and Ellie not only manages to reconcile their differences in personality but bridge a class divide between them—he the working class newspaperman and she the wealthy socialite, joined in matrimony as though they might solve the economic woes then ailing the country all by themselves. While the escapist Fred Astaire-Ginger Rogers RKO musicals of the 1930s successfully managed to keep the imagery of the Depression at bay, screwball comedies are shaped by them. In addition to *It Happened One Night*, the Depression figures prominently in Preston Sturges's *The Great McGinty* (1940) and *Sullivan's Travels* (1941), in which the writer-director's heroes experience the heights of wealth and the doldrums of poverty, bouncing between them seemingly at will. However, the screwball comedies largely aimed to offer a similarly light experience as the RKO musicals—indeed, this is the lesson that Sturges's John L. Sullivan (Joel McCrea), a film director who wants to make hard-hitting social dramas, comes to realize, as he experiences the joy of comedy while in prison for a crime he did not commit as his fellow inmates roar with laughter at a film screening. The result is a cycle of comedies that reflect the Depression-era context in which they were made, but are content to acknowledge, and not confront, its realities.

If the social message of the screwball comedies was vitiated substantially by the characters' wacky hijinks and uplifting conclusions, they cleansed the palate after such despairing dramas as *I Was a Fugitive From a Chain Gang* (1932, LeRoy), surely one of the bleakest films produced by a major studio during the classical era. Sturges's *Sullivan's Travels* is a comedic sendup of *Chain Gang*'s story, which sends World War I veteran James Allen (Paul Muni) to jail for a crime in which he was little more than a bystander; while incarcerated in Alabama, Allen is subject to harsh treatment by the guards and his fellow inmates, the film aiming to expose the deplorable conditions of prison work farms that dotted the American South, while also closely tying the character's downfall to his economic desperation. It is this tradition to which *The Defiant Ones* belongs, but its post-war release, in 1958, in the middle of an ongoing national battle over civil rights for Black Americans, allows it to foreground its social message more fully than did the screwball comedies. However, its ultimate outlook—that racial divisions can be healed, no matter the intransigence of prejudice—offers an optimism far beyond the defeated outrage of *Chain Gang*.

This was producer-director Stanley Kramer's approach in most of his 1950s and 1960s work: films of social immediacy, tempered by rays of hope. This particular blend of realism and optimism has earned Kramer a critical reputation as a filmmaker who was hopelessly naïve at best, but at worst, exemplifies the ambivalence of the white moderates to whom Martin Luther King Jr. addressed his famous "Letter from Birmingham Jail." The film's dual protagonists, escaped convicts Cullen (Sidney Poitier) and Joker (Tony Curtis) nearly come to blows while riding in the truck transporting a group of prisoners in the film's opening sequence, trading racist insults; once they escape after the truck carrying them turns over, they have to rely on one another because they remained chained together at the wrists, eventually achieving mutual respect. In the film's final scenes, Joker pursues the now-unchained Cullen into a swamp where he will almost surely die, desperately trying to save his friend's life. He catches Cullen, but when the two men have a chance to escape the posse chasing them by boarding a train, Joker falls—instead of riding the train to his own freedom, Cullen leaps off, unable to leave his friend behind. Donald Spoto suggests the film is not "the least bit homiletic" and "has a potent and timeless message."[4] On the other hand, writer and poet James Baldwin found this concluding note insultingly optimistic, recalling that Black audience members shouted at the screen at Poitier's character, "Get back on that train, you fool!" In Baldwin's estimation, the conclusion of *The Defiant Ones* is aimed more at white audiences, helping them to assuage their guilt: "The Black man jumps off the train in order to reassure white people, to make them know that they're not hated."[5]

Much of the criticism of *The Defiant Ones*' seeming lack of radical courage is situated in the screen persona of Poitier. Throughout his career, Donalson says, "In, various roles showing racial, class, and familial issues, Poitier personified the attributes deemed noble and exceptional for Black male characters, and by implication, the Black community."[6] The least charitable reading of Cullen's self-sacrifice at the end of *The Defiant Ones* is that it dramatizes the Black man's apparent embrace of his chains. Though Cullen and Joker are no longer tied together literally, the manacles remain in a metaphorical sense—when Joker falls, Cullen must go with him, and he subordinates his chance at freedom to the white man's needs. Donald Bogle is clearly sympathetic to Baldwin's reading of Cullen's final act, suggesting that for the mass white audience, Sidney Poitier was a Black man who had met their standards. His characters were tame; never did they act impulsively, nor were they threats to the system. They were amenable and pliant. And finally they were non-funky, almost sexless and sterile. In short, they were the perfect dream for white liberals anxious to have a colored man in for lunch or dinner.[7]

Bogle generalizes about the impact of Cullen's leap from the train on Black audiences, suggesting that at this moment, they became "consciously aware for the first time of the great tomism inherent in the Poitier character, indeed in the Poitier image."[8] In this sense, Poitier was a perfect embodiment of Kramer's liberalism, manifest in several of his films—alongside Poitier's other work in the 1950s and 1960s, *The Defiant Ones* made the actor into "a colorless Black" who "was fast becoming a national symbol of brotherly love."[9]

Crucially, Poitier's films accomplished this by making his characters as safe as possible, minimizing any potential threat or danger that they could possess. Poitier's characters were rarely violent, infrequently angry, and almost never sexual, all of which are responses to one of the early defining images of Black men on screen, the would-be rapist of a white woman in *Birth of a Nation* (1915, Griffith). This scene, in which a Black man (played by a white man in blackface) pursues a fair white maiden through the woods with lust in his eyes, is so influential that Bogle suggests "many of Hollywood's hangups and hesitations in presenting sensual Black men on screen resulted, in part, from the reactions to the Griffith spectacle."[10] Writing of Poitier's dock worker in the urban drama *Edge of the City* (1957, Ritt), Bogle finds the character brazenly, but unsurprisingly, neutered.[11] Allowing Poitier's characters to be sexual would have conflicted with the image that he presented on screen, which was as "one smart and refined young Negro, and middle-class America, Black and white, treasured him."[12] Ultimately, Poitier's carefully controlled image slowly introduced a Black star to American audiences, permitting individual moments of direct confrontation of racial issues, especially in a moment when those issues were being forced into the open through political dialogue, protest, and court decisions. However, these films are marked by their timidity—their depiction of a Black man was only able to move so far.

That changed dramatically in the 1960s and 1970s, with the arrival of Blaxploitation cinema and new, athletic stars whose defining characteristics were their violence, their anger, and their sexuality. The action cinema played a specific role in introducing Black heroes to dramatic situations beyond the earnest racial dramas associated with Poitier, a legacy that continues to this day—action is, by and large, the most integrated of mainstream genres.[13] Though Blaxploitation films like *Shaft* (1971, Parks) and *Superfly* (1972, Parks Jr.) were undoubtedly violent and featured Black heroes navigating the criminal underworld and doing battle with corrupt agents of the state and big business, these films were most radical in their depiction of Black men's sexuality. Bogle reminds us that this was a marked change from the 1950s and early 1960s, "when Poitier and [Harry] Belafonte, while considered sexually attractive, were rarely permitted to be sexually aggressive in their films, [and] audiences were ready for a sexual Black movie hero."[14] Bogle singles out football-star-turned-actor Jim Brown as a representative of this evolution in Black male screen persona. Though Brown made many types of films, his appearance in *The Dirty Dozen* (1967, Aldrich) led to several Blaxploitation movies of his own, including *Black Gunn* (1972, Hartford-Davis), *Slaughter* (1972, Starrett) and *Slaughter's Big Rip-Off* (1973, Douglas). Though not earnestly political in the tradition of Kramer's liberal dramas, these action films carried political import much as the screwball comedies did, through their simple acknowledgement of then present context and depiction of Black characters in new situations to which audiences (both white and Black) were unaccustomed. Bogle argues that "the Brown vehicles carried some political weight simply because there was a Black man up there on the screen, raising cain, strutting like a glorious prima donna, and sure to let everyone know that he could not care less whether he was liked or not."[15] The Blaxploitation action films of the 1970s were incredibly successful, but like many cycles, they eventually declined as audience interest waned. However, the continued presence of Black characters in mainstream action films, then beginning to cohere and move into their classical period in the 1980s, is a testament to their legacy.

48 Hrs., Another 48 Hrs., and the Legacy of Race

Hill's *48 Hrs.* is, in addition to its roots in the screwball comedy cycle, something of a hybrid made possible both by the socially liberal earnest dramas of Stanley Kramer (*The Defiant Ones* is the most obvious, but not the only model) and the Blaxploitation action pictures of the 1970s, many of which were produced outside the mainstream studio system. At the beginning of the 1980s, Bogle suggests, "For black Americans, it was a time to move fully into the system, rather than to remain outside it."[16] Because it features a multiracial pairing within a studio-produced film, *48 Hrs.* would no doubt be an example of what Bogle calls a "crossover film" that "had to have built-in devices to please white audiences. The first step towards making crossover movies was to strip the Black film of any raw political content."[17] The crossover appeal of *48 Hrs.* is also generated by the film's use of Murphy, then known to audiences of all races from his time on *Saturday Night Live*. In 1982, Murphy was, like Richard Pryor before him, a Black comedian with a substantial white following, which Tommy L.

Lott sees as part of a larger trend within American culture.[18] Murphy's star power would only expand after the success of *48 Hrs.*, which the actor then translated into an action-comedy franchise of his own with *Beverly Hills Cop* (1984, Brest) that clearly drew upon the formula established by Hill's movie, though it centered Murphy's Axel Foley as the police officer, not the convict.

Despite Murphy's appearances as both Reggie and Foley in films that were big box office draws, according to Ed Guerrero, "The 1980s saw a steady reduction of films with Black narratives and leading roles as Black actors found themselves increasingly pushed into the margins or background of the cinematic frame."[19] In 1981, the year before *48 Hrs.* was released, there were "6 Black-focused productions out of 240 releases. The situation bottomed out as the decade wore on, with Hollywood averaging about 6 or 7 Black-focused productions of varying sizes and budgets a year."[20] The presence of Murphy in *48 Hrs.* was cold comfort to critics like Guerrero, who saw his performance and the narrative more broadly in a similar light as Baldwin viewed *The Defiant Ones*. Guerrero argues that the 1980s were a time when harmful stereotypes once again reared their ugly heads, featuring "a disturbing resurfacing of images from Hollywood's pre–civil rights past, amounting to a cinematic style of appropriation and representation of African Americans that might be best described as 'neominstrelsy.'"[21] In his view, films like *48 Hrs.* "[deploy] a number of varied narrative and visual 'strategies of containment' to resubordinate the Black image, assigning it to a position of subservience or marginality in a given film and thus, symbolically or otherwise, upholding society's traditional racial hierarchy and relations of power."[22] Reggie's first appearance in the film, in his prison cell, listening to and loudly singing along to The Police's "Roxanne" on his Walkman, creates a dynamic in which "the white middle-middle class spectator is positioned to see someone they can reflexively feel superior to, a Black convict and an impulsive fool who is literally contained by society's walls and bars."[23] If Bogle saw Poitier as one of cinema's "toms," then Murphy's Hammond is no doubt one of its "coons,"[24] who "represents the loose, jivey, close to vulgar Black man, who does not threaten the white audience's feelings of superiority. Nor does he challenge (through insightful anger) racial attitudes."[25]

These same critics also express discomfort with the buddy film formula, which they argue relegates Reggie to the role of sidekick. Donalson suggests that the multiracial buddy film more or less preserves a longstanding tradition of mainstream cinema in which

> men of color in Hollywood features—with Black men being the most prevalent—have been juxtaposed with white male characters to accentuate and enhance the latter; in short, the characters of color have been rendered to make

white males appear more courageous, tolerant, heroic, intelligent, etc., in the narrative.[26]

Guerrero believes the buddy film to be a particularly insidious form "which reveals all the strategies by which the industry contains and controls the Black filmic image and conforms it to white expectations."[27] Through its narrative structure, the buddy film employs "a white 'buddy' as ideological chaperone to ensure its box office success,"[28] with *48 Hrs.* in particular placing the Black character "in the 'protective custody' of white authority."[29] Such subordination amounts to the "eradication of the Black point of view in these narratives; in all these films, the Black makes a sacrifice to solve problems the white man defines."[30] Bogle argues that this retrenched power dynamic is essential to the structure of the interracial buddy films, which "have usually held to one dictum: namely, that interracial buddies can be such only when the white buddy is in charge."[31] A mainstream product of the Hollywood system in the blockbuster era, *48 Hrs.* would seem to exemplify all of these critiques almost exactly—undoubtedly many of the interracial buddy films that come in its wake do.

Eddie Murphy doesn't see it that way. He says,

> The reason I blew up in films is because I'm the first African American—like the character in a movie, to go into the white world and take charge in the world. Because usually the Black character up until then, the Black character is the sidekick. The Black sidekick. My character shows up. In the first movie, it's written like the sidekick, but if you watch the movie, he's not the sidekick. He's the whole movie. Nick Nolte's going, "Now what are we gonna do, convict? What's our next move? Where do we go now? What happened now?" We go this way, we go that way. And they found that funny.[32]

Though Jack undoubtedly possesses the authority of the state, invested in him as a police officer, which sees him continue Reggie's incarceration into the streets as they pursue Ganz, Cates is totally in need of his character's help. Jack's narrative weakness, then, reverses the power dynamic, which contributes to the tension between the two characters throughout the film. Reggie is not totally in control—Jack frequently uses handcuffs to restrain him and holds other, less tangible threats of punishment over him. In this sense, Murphy is overstating how much narrative control Reggie has, but defends his character's agency.

Rather than depicting Jack as the consistent source of authoritative control and Reggie as its submissive victim, *48 Hrs.* dramatizes power struggle, rather than simply reflect static power relationships. To see Reggie as the sidekick requires seeing Cates as the hero; but Cates is not the film's sole hero, and neither is Reggie. *48 Hrs.* is a dual-protagonist film, but white star

Nick Nolte receives top billing, and appears first in the narrative, though only after the opening jailbreak sequence—Ganz and Billy Bear are introduced before either of the film's heroes. Reggie's obnoxious singing first creases Jack's ears at minute twenty-four, perhaps lending credence to Guerrero's suggestion that Murphy's Black convict is subordinated to Nolte's white cop. This dynamic would reverse in the sequel, with Murphy receiving top billing thanks to his massive success in the intervening years—Hill suggests he was likely "the biggest movie star in the world" when they made the sequel in 1990, the film's economic potential undoubtedly a motivating factor in its production.[33] Though Nolte's physical body appears on screen first in the shootout at the racetrack in *Another 48 Hrs.*, the biker antagonists look at Reggie's mugshot in the scene before, targeting him for assassination as revenge for the death of the first film's Ganz, a subtle suggestion that he, and not Jack, will be the focus of the narrative. However, Reggie's release from jail eventually draws him back into an investigation with Jack in which the two share the film's stage, navigating the power relationship between them over the course of the narrative. This misrepresentation is where traditional readings of *48 Hrs.* and *Another 48 Hrs.* fall short—they assume that Nolte, because he is white and Jack is a police officer, is the protagonist. Though Hill's films are not totally bereft of single protagonists, of his first six movies, only *The Driver* has one. The others are focused on small groups of men (*Hard Times*), the dynamics of a larger group (*The Warriors*, *The Long Riders*, and *Southern Comfort*), or in the case of *48 Hrs.*, a partnership. The film's real subject is the relationship between Jack and Reggie, and not the adventures of Jack and his Black sidekick.

Let me take a moment to acknowledge that these common readings of *48 Hrs.*, which I have started to critique, are all made by Black critics and academics, and as a white man, I feel a little uncomfortable challenging them. After all, if these interpretations are rooted in Black spectatorship, then I have to trust that they are genuine; they are no doubt persuasively argued, and shared by a number of other writers. Here is where I think some of these critics have made a mistake: they have dismissed the multiracial buddy film entirely, an overgeneralization that has scooped up the interesting films along with the formulaic ones. *48 Hrs.* and its sequel explore the racial tension between Jack and Reggie, with something concrete to say about the tenuous relationship they navigate throughout both pictures. These films are more insightful than the multiracial buddy films that would follow them because they do, in contrast to the way they and other entries in the genre have been seen, engage directly with political ideas. They achieve this because of Walter Hill's career-long privileging of Black characters in films that address, in often subtle but sometimes not-so-subtle ways, political ideas germane to those characters. Hill's own whiteness need not be determinative over the content of his films; in fact, considering only the work of Black directors essentializes the idea of Black cinema. In Tommy L. Lott's view, "biological criteria are neither necessary nor sufficient for the application of the concept of Black cinema."[34] In other words, the presence of a Black director does not create Black cinema any more than the absence of one prohibits it. Lott encourages audiences and critics alike to embrace nuance:

> Any definition that requires films to be made by Black filmmakers in order to be included in the category of Black cinema will simply not match the ambivalence engendered by having to place biological over cultural criteria in deciding questions of Black identity.[35]

Certainly Hill's identity as a white man shapes the films, just as it would if he were Black. This is not to say that Hill's race is immaterial, nor to ignore that as mainstream Hollywood product confined by the strictures of genre, they have little potential as radical texts. But as they stand, the two *48 Hrs.* films represent Black desire, wealth, authority, and refuse to allow for a complete, *The Defiant Ones*-style reconciliation of racial tension.

At least part of the objection to *48 Hrs.* stems from Murphy's depiction of Reggie as, at least at times, "negative image" of a Black man. These concerns are not unfounded. More than a century of simplistic depictions of Black characters on screen has understandably made critics and audiences alike hyper-attuned to the broad direction of individual representations. A dichotomy results—an image like Griffith's supersexed Black rapist hungering after a white woman in the forest is so shockingly offensive that it becomes a "negative" portrayal; a valorized vision of a Black superhero, King T'Challa (Chadwick Boseman) of *Black Panther* (2018, Coogler), who rules over a futuristic African society more advanced than any other nation on Earth, is a "positive" image. Like all dichotomies, however, such classification tends to erase nuances and subtleties, while infusing a (frequently justified!) moral dimension into interpretations of images. No doubt Griffith's negative images at least in part fueled horrific, racially motivated crimes in the Jim Crow South, and Coogler's positive images inspired Black youths around the globe to see themselves as superheroes as rarely, if ever, before. And yet, the positive/negative dichotomy simplifies too much—Hill tries to avoid this trap throughout both *48 Hrs.* films, working with the improvising Murphy to represent a character. Valerie Smith makes a convincing argument for the limitations of this perspective:

> Several problems exist with the positive/negative debate as it has been constituted. First, it focuses critical scrutiny on the ways in which African Americans have been represented in Hollywood cinema, often at the expense of analytical, theoretical, or historical work on the history of Black-directed

cinema. Second, it presupposes consensus about what a positive or negative (or authentic, for that matter) image actually is.[36]

More images exist between these two polar extremes and are not so easy to classify. The reflexive tendency to view with skepticism *48 Hrs.* and *Another 48 Hrs.*' portrayal of the relationship between Jack Cates and Reggie Hammond is certainly understandable, but judges too quickly.

The films have been criticized for offering a negative image of Black masculinity in its often crude portrayal of Reggie's sexually-charged motivation—while Jack escorts him around town during his furlough in the first film, Reggie keeps talking about how he needs to get "some trim." When Cates first takes Reggie to the police station where he works, Reggie impersonates an officer while talking to some prostitutes who have been brought in on a vice charge, openly flirting with them before Jack busts up the conversation. When the partners pay a visit to the women who are later revealed to be harboring Ganz and Billy Bear and Reggie spies an exercise show on the television through the window, in which a woman does aerobics in a skimpy outfit, he says, awestruck, "Man, TV has changed." Reggie visits a bar on his own after he is separated from Jack in a subway station shootout, and tries to pick up several women, who ignore him. He finally succeeds in dancing with one, Candy (Olivia Brown), but alienates her when he is too forthright: "It's 10:05. By 10:10, I want to be into some flesh," he tells her. Then, his attempt to pick her up, ham-fisted as it is, is frustrated by Jack's sudden arrival in the bar. To Melvin Donaldson, such "blatant sexual talk and sexual activity imbues Hammond with a prurient attitude that becomes a valorization of sexual stereotypes about black men."[37]

Reggie is a far cry from the desexualized Poitier, especially important in 1967s *Guess Who's Coming to Dinner*, another Stanley Kramer film defined by its serious-minded but ultimately rosy outlook, in which Poitier's elegant Black doctor intending to marry a wealthy white woman (Katharine Houghton) must first convince her old-fashioned but well-intentioned liberal parents (Spencer Tracy and Katharine Hepburn). However, Reggie's sexuality is mostly limited to the verbal—he does not go so far as the Blaxploitation heroes who preceded him to the screen by a decade, with their numerous dalliances with both white and Black women given extended visibility through montage set to soulful music. Though he does eventually sleep with Candy after the final shootout in the alley in which Jack saves his life and guns down Ganz, their sex takes place off-screen; he is shown leaving the apartment and promising Candy that he will see her when he gets out "in about six months." The Poitier-Kramer era social issue dramas prohibited Black characters from expressing nearly all sexual desire on screen out of fear of associating Poitier with the Griffith stereotype, by the 1960s infecting many Americans' perceptions of Black men in its various descendant forms; on the other end of the spectrum, the Blaxploitation directors, led by Melvin Van Peebles and his film *Sweet Sweetback's Baadasssss Song* (1971), Bogle argues, "reappropriated the old type and used it as a sign of political resistance."[38] *48 Hrs.* has no overt radical politics, as Van Peebles's film did—however, the mere adoption of a sexually driven Black character, without the conservatism of Poitier's roles, demonstrates how far the Blaxploitation films pushed the boundaries on what was acceptable on screen. By 1982, Reggie's sexual desire is not really a threat—instead, it is used for humor, with Murphy's confrontational reliance on sexually explicit dialogue a disarming tool that invites a white audience to lower its guard.[39]

While some critics found Reggie too sexual to the point of recalling Griffith's stereotypes, others argue that the absence of a stable sexual partner in Reggie's pre-prison life makes him too shallow, especially when contrasted to Jack, whose relationship with Elaine (Annette O'Toole) adds another dimension to his character beyond his role as a police officer. Bogle wonders, "Couldn't Reggie also have had a wife or girlfriend he had to leave behind? Might one not have known more about him if such were the case?"[40] Lamentations like this one overstate the degree to which a scene or two with an erstwhile lover would have shaded Reggie's character, but they also overstate the security and stability of Cates's relationship with Elaine. They appear in the same room in only one scene—albeit split in half by a brief cutaway to Ganz and Billy Bear—when Jack wakes up in her bed before rushing off on the police business that begins his pursuit of the criminals. Dialogue reveals that he doesn't let Elaine come to his house, but only visits hers; he doesn't open up to her about who he really is, but is content to maintain their mostly sexual relationship; and he deliberately antagonizes her through his obstinacy and taciturn behavior. They are not a happy couple, and Jack spends the rest of the film more or less ignoring her phone calls, cutting her off in mid-conversation to chase a lead, or breaking promises to come for dinner. One such frustrated discussion takes place over the phone, intercut with Reggie's attempts to solicit the prostitutes in the precinct. By *Another 48 Hrs.*, which takes place five years after the events of the first film, Elaine is gone entirely—Jack tells Reggie she left him. In her absence, Jack has thrown himself further into his work, the obsessive pursuit of the mysterious Iceman rendering him a departmental pariah, hated by Internal Affairs' Wilson (Kevin Tighe) and betrayed by officers Kehoe and Cruise (Ed O'Ross), who are supposed to be his friends. The sequel does not replace Elaine with another love interest for Jack, which allows space for the film to explore the relationship between himself and Reggie, now rekindled after a long absence. When Cates comes to visit with a new request for help on Reggie's penultimate day in prison, Reggie is the one who sounds like a jilted lover: "I ain't seen you in years, man. I thought you was my friend." Jack offers a weak apology before shifting the subject to business. "You and me's got another little job to do," he says. Throughout both films, neither character is really defined or shaded by their relationship with female characters: Reggie merely wants sexual release during his brief furlough from prison, and Jack's dismissive treatment of Elaine demonstrates his real concern for his job, not romance.

One of the subtle ways in which Hill and Murphy offer a sophisticated image of Reggie is through the choice of wardrobe. Wearing a gray suit with a white shirt and a thin black tie throughout both films, Reggie adopts the Poitier image of a middle-class, upwardly mobile Black man. Hill and Murphy do not dress Reggie in "street clothes," which would conform to a stereotype of an urban Black criminal seen in the vigilante films of the 1970s. The gray suit is understated, which helps the film avoid yet another stereotype, one promulgated by the Blaxploitation films, of a Black criminal decked out in brightly colored, ostentatious dress, jewelry, and otherwise accessorized. The outfit parodies the Black servant's finely tailored uniform, a stereotype that predominated throughout Classic Hollywood before Poitier (but continued after him). According to James A. Snead, "Chauffeurs, domestics, porters, jazz musicians, and other Blacks are marked by the Black/white codings in the contrast between their skins and white articles of clothing."[41] Reggie's gray, rather than Black and white, both acknowledges and revises that stereotype—Reggie takes great pride in the suit he wears, as he tells a number of people throughout both films, but it is a symbol of his own identity, not one imposed on him by a white power structure. It contrasts mightily with the denim prison uniform he wears in his first appearances in both *48 Hrs.* and the sequel. As in the film's treatment of Reggie's sexual desire, which represents a kind of middle ground between Poitier's sexlessness and the Blaxploitation hero's sexual voracity, the costuming synthesizes images of Black men on screen that grounds the character in reality. Reggie is not exclusively an icon of Blackness that will be acceptable to white audiences, nor is he exclusively an icon of Blackness that deliberately confronts white audiences through his transgressive qualities, but a bit of both. His sexually motivated dialogue is its own kind of transgression when it comes from a Black man who visually recalls the chaste Poitier through his dress.

Too much focus on Reggie's sexual desire, however, obscures the first film's real subject—Reggie's efforts to reclaim the $500,000 that has been sitting in the trunk of his car since Ganz double-crossed him and sent him to jail. Bogle's suggestion that Reggie might have benefited from a love interest to shade his character misreads the narrative at hand. Reggie's character is better served by his quest to retrieve his wealth. Throughout the narrative, Cates's objective is straightforward—his gun is used to kill a police officer during the hotel shootout with Ganz, and Jack wants to find him and bring him to justice. Reggie's objective is to help Cates find Ganz in order to protect his money, which Ganz wants and uses their former partner Luther (David Patrick Kelly) to obtain. Hill is infrequently interested in his characters' romantic lives (*Streets of Fire* and *Johnny Handsome* are notable exceptions), but he is often fascinated by their desire for wealth, a theme always present, but foregrounded in *Brewster's Millions*, *Trespass*, and *Undisputed*, all of which prominently feature Black characters. The pursuit of wealth is also central to both *48 Hrs.* films, as the same $500,000 is Reggie's motivation across each: he has hidden the money in his car and stashed it in a parking garage where Ganz cannot find it; Reggie becomes a more active participant in the narrative, approaching equal partnership, when Luther, who does know the location of the money, appears at the garage and takes it. During the subway shootout that follows, Hill reinforces each character's narrative motivation—Jack pursues cop-killers Ganz and Billy Bear when they retreat for the subway train, and Reggie races after the fleeing Luther, who carries the satchel with the half-million dollars inside. The money drives Reggie's participation in the narrative, and it is not Jack's to give him; it belongs to him before the narrative begins, and his agreeing to go along with Cates's pursuit of Ganz in the first place has less to do with Jack than it does with his own desire to protect his wealth.

Though the sequel repeats too many of the original film's story beats in an attempt to recapture its winning formula, *Another 48 Hrs.* offers a disheartening glimpse of Reggie's dream, hopelessly deferred by an extended jail sentence that has stretched his term by five years, a considerable distance from his promise to Candy that he will be back in six months. Jack promises at the end of the first film to hang on to Reggie's money, a pact which becomes a symbol of their partnership and at least mutual understanding and trust, if not love and friendship. When Jack arrives at the prison to solicit Reggie's help once again, Reggie rejects the offer: "When I get outta here, just give me my fuckin' money and walk away from me, all right? I played that cop shit once and it don't work. Have my money when I get out, please." Reggie does not see himself as Jack's buddy, especially given the officer's extended absence, all the while Reggie has been sitting in jail. Whatever trust they established at the end of the first film, however, is completely shattered when Jack suggests that the money no longer simply belongs to Reggie, but is instead, his to distribute: "Wait a minute, Reggie. You don't get it. You see, if you don't help me out on this one, I'm not ever gonna give you your money back." Reggie is incredulous, outraged that Jack has gone back on what he thought was a deal struck in honor: "I gave you that money in good faith because you told me I could fuckin' trust you. Now, you're gonna tell me that after all this shit, I can't have my money?" Jack, smirking, lords his authority over Reggie: "Now you got the picture, convict." Jack's use of the word "convict," his oft-used label in the first film, dehumanizes Reggie by identifying him with his incarceration, much as a prison ID number would. That he utters it here for the first time in the sequel, in a moment when he wants to demonstrate to Reggie his control of the Black man's wealth, is a striking comment on an entire history of the economic disenfranchisement of Black people in America. The story of *Another 48 Hrs.* is once again bifurcated: Jack is driven by his pursuit of the Iceman, which will expose the mastermind's corruption and clear his own name with Wilson, but Reggie is still fighting for the same goal, which is to get his hands on the money that belongs to him. While the white half of the partnership can move on to new business, the Black man has to keep working for the same objective because his wealth is never guaranteed.

Much of this relationship is negotiated through the power differential between Jack, as a police officer, and Reggie, as a prisoner. This hierarchy might seem to reinforce the societal power structure which it represents, with the white man in control and the Black man his subordinate, but the *48 Hrs.* films portray a *negotiation* of power between Jack and Reggie rather than a static order. Black characters are often used to round off a white character, rather than given an inner life of their own. As Snead points out, this narrative tendency is specifically bound up in power: "white male stars need Black butlers or sidekicks to make them seem more authoritatively manly."[42] The typical reading of *48 Hrs.* and *Another 48 Hrs.* that relegates Reggie to the role of sidekick invests narrative and institutional authority in Jack; however, Hill uses both films to undermine Jack's authority through privileging Reggie's point of view of him. Bogle argues that "one of the film's great shortcomings is that Reggie is seen almost exclusively from Cates's point of view without ever coming to know him in a full sense."[43] But this isn't true; from the first moment Jack meets Reggie in his prison cell in *48 Hrs.*, while Reggie is wailing "Roxanne," the editing and cinematography encourages identification with Reggie, not Jack. First off, his singing is heard on the soundtrack before the camera sees him; a long tracking shot moves back and to the right along the row of cells (in the first, a Confederate flag can be seen on the wall—more on those in a moment), as Jack is pulled along towards Reggie's cell by the sound of his voice. Though the image privileges Jack, looking up at him slightly as it tracks backward, the movement itself seems compelled by Reggie's voice. The first shot of Reggie is a waist-high medium from Jack's rough position, sitting in a recliner (which can't recline because of the cell's restrictions), seen through the bars of the cell door, which then slides open as if to reveal him. He wears sunglasses, singing into the air, presumably with his eyes closed—though this is not guaranteed—because Jack has to ask Reggie's cell mate if the singing convict is his man, going unacknowledged by Reggie himself. As Jack stands in the cell, the camera is at Reggie's level, a kind of modified over-the-shoulder that looks up at Jack, investing authority in all of Nolte's six-foot-plus frame. Remember, one of Guerrero's critiques of this scene in particular is that it invites the audience to see Reggie as "an impulsive fool" who "they can reflexively feel superior to."[44] For Guerrero, because Murphy's character is introduced in this comedic way—his falsetto imitation of Sting is blissfully ignorant of anyone else around him—the film "[treats] the white audience to the filmic pleasure of Blacks positioned as funny, subordinate, and useful tools in the narrative."[45] Reggie is undoubtedly associated visually with the prison cell's bars, but in this low-angle shot that aligns with his point of view, so is Jack—they loom behind him in diagonal angles like a gargoyle's wings, a static symbol of his reliance on the institutional authority vested in him by the carceral state. When Jack shouts into Reggie's Walkman and interrupts his singing, the film wastes no time in confirming Reggie's intelligence, just as defined a quality as his humor: "You got a name, cop?" is his first spoken line, revealing his ability to instantly recognize this white man, making a visual display of his authority, as a police officer. Notable too is the specific selection of a song by a band called The Police, a Murphy-generated improvisation which, according to Hill, was not cleared for publishing rights in advance, but was too good to abandon.[46] The combined use of Murphy's charismatic screen persona and careful cinematography embodies the film's negotiation of power. The camera constantly acknowledges the power differential between Jack and Reggie, but refuses to obey it; shots like the low angle looking up at Jack, but a shot which still includes Reggie, taken from his rough eye level, makes the police officer's authority over the Black man visible, while simultaneously encouraging skepticism.

Another 48 Hrs. further undermines Jack's authority as a police officer through its main narrative, which is his quest to expose and apprehend the Iceman, a criminal mastermind who has been bringing drugs into San Francisco. Even preceding the opening scenes, Jack is revealed to be on thin ice within the department, especially because he is being targeted himself for investigation by Wilson, the leader of the Internal Affairs unit. Cates thus spends most of the film on his back foot, growing increasingly desperate to prove his innocence and his worth as a police officer; this fundamental insecurity calls Jack's bravado in the scene with Reggie at the jail into question. He appears to need Reggie just as much as Reggie needs him, which inspires the provocation that concludes their reunion: he smashes the basketball he is holding into Jack's face and then sucker punches him. Hill cuts away before Cates returns the blows, denying Jack any equal agency. Though Jack is withholding his money, Reggie's power is increasing by virtue of his impending release from prison. Hammond no longer has to stand for Jack's taunts and

Figure 4.1 Through mise-en-scène and framing, *48 Hrs.* (1982) associates white police officer Jack Cates (Nick Nolte) with the oppressive architecture of the prison state he represents, filtering his authority through Black convict Reggie Hammond's (Eddie Murphy) skeptical gaze. *Source: Screenshot captured by author.*

belittling treatment, as he seems to sense the police officer's weakness. After his bus is crashed and an assassination attempt on Cates, Reggie agrees to help Jack in exchange for the return of his $500,000, but only after Jack uses his police authority to convince the local sheriff's deputies who discover the crash site to release Reggie into his custody. This is yet another moment of weakness by Jack, because he spins an elaborate fiction about Reggie's jail time; he tells the officer that Reggie is "a child molester" who is "involved in kiddie porn." That Jack has to resort to lies to continue his investigation reveals his desperation and devalues his moral authority as an officer of the law.

Reggie, of course, needs no such clarification, because he already knows well enough not to trust cops. He senses Jack's weakness; when Cates tries to put his arm around him in a gesture of faux-friendship, Reggie tosses it off and snaps,

> Get the fuck off me, man. I ain't no convict no more, I'm a free man. And you? You're about an inch away from where I was yesterday. You ain't runnin' jackshit, okay? Let me tell you somethin'. I ain't workin' for you, I don't like you, and I don't trust you.

One common critique of *Another 48 Hrs.* is that it offers little more than a retread of the first film, with nothing new to say.[47] Bogle perceives lack of character growth, wishing for "a more mature Hammond, who might have picked up a book in the prison library and learned something about the system that's incarcerated him. How different this might have been had Hammond been politicized and come out a firebrand."[48] But in performance, Murphy imbues the character with exactly this kind of anger; Hill is not typically the kind of screenwriter or director to include extended monologues where characters express didactic political messages in spoken language. Instead, the combination of Murphy's gestures and intonation carry Reggie's anger through the narrative, as the character finds the promises that were made to him have turned out to be lies. Hammond clearly derives some small pleasure from the precarious legal position in which Jack now finds himself, but his verbal taunts are shaped by political awareness. After Reggie suggests that they might pursue a lead with one of his prison contacts, he says, "Wouldn't be a bad idea for you to go to prison anyway, 'cause you might be spendin' some time there real soon, and I think it'd be a real good job for you to go get reacquainted with some of the brothers whose rights you violated." His dialogue reveals a deepened cynicism that outstrips the Reggie of five years previous, newly embittered by his extended prison sentence and betrayed by Jack's refusal to turn over his money. This jaundiced worldview leads Reggie, not Jack, to the conclusion that will ultimately reveal the Iceman's identity. While they stand over the body of one of the bikers in the morgue, shot to death by an unknown murderer, Reggie has a realization: "Jack. The Iceman's a cop." Cates doesn't want to hear it, his investigative abilities clouded by his personal loyalties to the ideal image of the job he does. He doesn't want to believe that a cop could be responsible for all the drugs, the mayhem, and the killings, or that a fellow officer would be willing to frame him for some of the crimes. It takes Reggie, who is skeptical of police authority, to make Jack see the truth. The sequel's rebalancing of the power differential between Reggie and Jack not only reverses some dimensions of the original *48 Hrs.*, but invests Reggie's narrative role with political motivations embedded in his point of view as a Black man.

The structure of many screwball comedies, including *It Happened One Night* and *His Girl Friday*, reveals how *48 Hrs.* and *Another 48 Hrs.* balance the narrative between two characters, telling a story about the relationship, rather than a single protagonist. Ellie is not Peter's antagonist in Capra's film, and neither is she his; the same is true of Hawks's picture, where Hildy and her erstwhile husband/editor Walter Burns (Cary Grant) bicker and argue, but ultimately share a common goal—to get the story for the paper and, though they won't admit it, reconcile their romantic relationship. Because both *48 Hrs.* and *Another 48 Hrs.* draw so heavily on screwball comedy structure, neither film forces an audience to choose between the two central characters, but invest themselves instead in the relationship they share. In screwball comedy, the trajectory of the romantic leads is from initial enmity to marital consummation. Reggie and Jack begin as enemies on opposite sides of the law, a fact underlined by their racial difference, and over the course of their time together—another narrative trope of the screwball comedy—they come to a seeming sense of mutual understanding that resembles something like friendship, a homosocial equivalent to marital consummation, for Hill, as always, rooted in Hawks. The conclusion of his *Red River* (1948) comes to mind, in which surrogate father and son Tom Dunson (John Wayne) and Matt Garth (Montgomery Clift) have a brutal fistfight, but stop when Tess Millay (Joanne Dru) fires a pistol to interrupt them and shouts, "Anybody with half a mind would know you two love each other!"

In *Red River*, but also in several other of Hawks's films, male characters prove their devotion to one another through physical action. Though undoubtedly harnessed in service of slapstick, the punches Jack and Reggie trade throughout *48 Hrs.* and its sequel are a physical manifestation of the film's primary concern—the negotiation of racial animus between Black and white men. Because the physical battle between Reggie and Jack is never settled, there is no moment of release at the end of either film, quite unlike the conclusion of *The Defiant Ones*, where Cullen makes his choice to return to prison with Joker, sacrificing his freedom. Throughout both *48 Hrs.* films, Jack and Reggie subject each other to physical and mental tests that are designed to force the other to prove himself; this is not the relationship of a master and servant, but of men fighting for equal treatment from one another. In the first film, this is primarily represented through Jack's continued reliance on racist language and epithets, steadily increasing in their biliousness until the film's midway point. In addition to the oft-repeated "convict," which becomes a kind of slur when Nolte utters it, filled with all the racially-imposed context that such a word creates, Jack calls Reggie "watermelon" and, in their first interaction in the prison corridor outside Hammond's cell, "boy." Bogle suggests that this flagrant use of dehumanizing language in a comedic film "makes racist jokes acceptable."[49] He suggests that throughout the first film, "the fact that Murphy's Reggie never becomes enraged or truly angry greatly neutralizes the inherent racism. The attitude of the scriptwriter is that America is now hip and sophisticated enough not to be bothered by racist remarks."[50] This critique ignores the fact that the first, and only, time that Jack calls Reggie a "nigger" immediately precedes an intensely physical fistfight between the two men. Irritated by Reggie's behavior, Jack tosses his gun and badge on the hood of his car while Reggie stands incredulous: "What? You gonna kick my ass, now?" he says. Jack says, "Let me explain one thing to you, nigger," and then sucker punches Reggie, who immediately responds by opening the car door into Jack's knees and then socking him in the jaw. The fistfight recalls *Red River*, but its racial context imbues it with a degree of menace. At this point, Reggie has more than proved his abilities as a partner, but Jack objects to the way he carries himself—the fight is clearly instigated by Jack, whose racist attitude and use of the word betrays his wounded ego. Reggie is a superior fighter, despite Jack's size, using his quickness to jab Cates with a collection of rights and lefts that send him staggering. The most striking thing about the scene is that Reggie fights back at all instead of trying to defuse the situation, despite being clearly aware that this man possesses the authority of the state, no matter if his badge is on his hip or lying on the hood of the car. His willingness to defend himself against a cop belies Bogle's assertion that "Reggie has no true sense of moral outrage."[51] The tension escalates when the fight is interrupted by the arrival of a squad car, with two uniformed police officers, guns drawn, aimed at Reggie and Jack. Cates is able to defuse the situation by leaning on his own police authority, and Reggie is savvy enough to know that his brawling partner's job is yet another get out of jail free card: he slips over to the car and settles inside, exhausted and in pain. After the cops leave, Jack seems to acknowledge that Reggie won the fight, but does so in the most petulant, pathetic way possible—he sucker punches Reggie once again, throwing a quick right above his eye before pulling the car out. Though the fistfight between the two men might suggest an evenly balanced scene between Jack and Reggie, the police officer is the aggressor and the dirty fighter.

In both *48 Hrs.* and *Another 48 Hrs.*, bar scenes are pivotal to the narrative; throughout Hill's work, bars are important spaces where his characters work out their differences through physical action. The most famous scene in *48 Hrs.* takes place in a redneck bar where Reggie, impersonating a police officer, interrogates the bartender about Billy Bear's whereabouts—the bar is one of his known hangouts. Before entering the bar, Jack and Reggie disagree over the best method to get information: Jack wants to take the lead, and so does Reggie, so they agree to bet on Reggie's success or failure. This arrangement sets up a Hawksian test—Will Reggie be good enough to win the bet? He will be aided in the effort by Jack's badge, which the officer cedes to him as a prop to convince the bar patrons of his authority. Some have seen Reggie's coopting of a police persona as disturbing, rather than comedic. For Guerrero, "the scene actually makes the argument that if Blacks were to attain institutional authority, and by implication social equality, they would behave as brutally to whites as they have been historically treated by them."[52] Though Guerrero's reading of the scene is undoubtedly motivated by its content, it denies Reggie's agency. Before stepping into the bar, Reggie takes Jack's badge and says, "You said bullshit and experience is all it takes, right? Well, come on in and experience some of my bullshit." Hammond's adoption of police authority is a performance—his ostentatious display of behavior that the patrons would come to expect from a police officer is a self-conscious parody.

The production design raises the specter of racial threat to Reggie with the first shot inside the bar—there is a smash cut to a redneck bar band, its cowboy-hatted fiddle player in the middle of a rousing solo. A wide shot of the smoky bar reveals not one, not two, but three Confederate flags hanging on the walls, with nary a Black face in sight. Hill offers a medium close-up of yet another Stars and Bars flag before tilting up to a topless dancer bouncing in a cowboy hat on top of it—this image powerfully invokes the racist stereotype propagated by *Birth of a Nation* and seen elsewhere, foregrounding the connection between the old Confederacy and its enforcement of its white women's virtue. The white men in the bar ogle the dancing girl without consequence, with one giving an obnoxious "Yeehaw!" as he looks on. A cut to Reggie, the lone Black man in this dangerous environment, shows him standing beneath another Confederate flag on the wall above his head. The combination of cinematography, sharp cutting, staging, and mise-en-scène establish a frightening subtext to the scene that, when it gives way to Reggie's humiliation of the rednecks in his performance of police authority, anticipates the cathartic violence of Quentin Tarantino's *Django Unchained* (2013), in which the former-slave-turned-gunfighter Django (Jamie Foxx) deals out brutal punishment to the slave traders and plantation owners who have held him and his wife Broomhilda (Kerry Washington) in bondage. The film also associates Jack with the racially threatening imagery of the bar—a cut to a profile shot of him and Reggie standing together positions another Confederate flag over his shoulder, and he says, "My kind of place. Always liked country boys." He turns to Reggie and grins: "They're sure as hell gonna like you," he says, before wandering into the crowd. While not acting in his official capacity as a police officer, Jack can easily blend in among the white patrons of the bar.

Reggie has no such luxury; to protect himself, he starts out trying to code switch: "Howdy," he says flatly, stepping between a man and a woman dancing—they seem surprised to see him. He tries another greeting: "How do?" he asks the Bartender (Peter Jason), who simply says, "Yeah?" Actor Jason's reserved affect expresses the Bartender's contempt for Reggie, obviously rooted in racial animus. When Reggie asks for a drink, the Bartender says, "Maybe you best have a Black Russian," spitting out the word "Black," making it a near bark. Reggie exaggeratedly laughs at the Bartender's remark, slapping the counter and trying to involve the man at the bar next to him, a defiant way of demonstrating to the barkeep that he has no intention of being bullied. He flips Jack's badge open—a close-up of Reggie's thumb covering Cates's picture identification is another acknowledgment of performance—and asks about Billy Bear, but gets the expected non-cooperation from the barman. "Look here," Reggie says, and then hurls his empty vodka glass against the mirror, shattering it into pieces in a thunderous crash that brings the music and revelry to a halt. At this point, the scene becomes a parodic recall of a similar scene in *The French Connection* (1971, Friedkin), in which that film's rogue cop "Popeye" Doyle (Gene Hackman)—who tells his partner "Never trust a nigger" early in the movie—rousts a bar filled with Black patrons. Reggie drops his performative amiability and switches gears, adopting a tough cop persona, yanking the Bartender towards him across the bar: "Fuckin' heard of him now, man?" he snarls. He releases the Bartender and steps into a wide shot in which Hill stages Hammond, surrounded by white men in flannel shirts and cowboy hats, imagery that suggests the terrifying moments before a lynching. Reggie, very much animated by a sense of moral outrage, tells them exactly what he thinks of them: "I never seen so many backwards-ass country fucks in my life. I'm sick just to be in here." With the sheer amount of Confederate flags and other icons that celebrate whiteness—a sign says "It takes a real man to be a cowboy"—and threaten his racial identity with violence, Reggie no doubt means it.

A patron who calls Reggie "nigger" gets a pair of punches in the mouth for his trouble. Far from being intimidated by the sea of white faces who stare at him—Reggie is truly all alone—he completely commands the space. In a Hawksian flourish, Jack is beginning to admire Reggie's professionalism when a man tries to run away, and Cates intercepts him: "Some of us citizens are behind you all the way, officer." Crucially, Cates's intervention is not necessary—the fleeing man confesses he is just on parole—to Reggie's control of the situation, which never slips for a moment. He adopts the

Figure 4.2 The pivotal scene in *48 Hrs.*, in which Reggie makes a spectacular public interrogation of a bar full of white country boys, foregrounds the film's racial politics; having challenged the white patrons, Reggie risks a racially-motivated reprisal. *Source: Screenshot captured by author.*

rhetoric of Black Nationalists, but in a parodic way that undoubtedly carries an element of truth: "I don't like white people," he announces, "And I hate rednecks. You people are rednecks. That means I'm enjoyin' this shit." Reggie's use of "you people" is itself an acknowledgment of racial offense, as he repurposes the language used against Black men to humiliate the white men he frisks for weapons. "What kind of cop are you?" asks one man. Reggie opens a switchblade he has just taken from the man's pocket and says, "You know what I am? I'm your worst fuckin' nightmare. A nigger with a badge. That means I got permission to kick your ass whenever I feel like it." This is the kind of line that likely gives Guerrero the impetus to read the scene for its masochistic potential for white spectators; however, Murphy's self-serious approach calls attention to his parodic performance of a cop. He doesn't say these things and behave this way because Reggie aspires to police authority—he does it because he has contempt for it. Finally, Reggie gets the Bartender to give him information about Billy Bear after he breaks some glasses and threatens the man's business, once again foregrounding the film's interest in the racial dimensions of wealth.

Reggie concludes his interrogation with one more parodic flourish, taking the Bartender's ten-gallon black hat from his head and snatching a toothpick off the bar. With the hat sitting on his head, Reggie says, "Well, look, Hoss. You start runnin' a respectable bidness, and I won't have to come in here and hassle you every night. Know what I mean?" Reggie's adoption of a country accent and deliberately folksy pronunciation—"bidness" for "business"—shows his knowledge of a certain kind of construction of white masculinity, which he seeks to dismantle through his parody of it. Hill repeats the rough positioning of Reggie's first exchange with the Bartender, though now switches the side from which he shoots, a reversal that underlines a change in scenic control, but the Bartender's contemptuous look remains the same. Reggie turns to the rest of the patrons and says, "And I want the rest of you cowboys to know somethin'. There's a new sheriff in town." He chews the toothpick exaggeratedly, and then, tossing off the hat and the accent with contempt that rivals the Bartender's racist dismissal of him, he says, in his normal voice, "And his name is Reggie Hammond. Y'all be cool. Right on." He strides out of the bar as the sea of white patrons part before him. The scene's humor undermines the image of whiteness that dominates the bar as a performed construction that can be parodied. Reggie isn't using the tools of traditional police authority—he's mocking them, but the white patrons are so used to seeing this construction of white male authority, they are stunned into obeying anyway, despite their perception of him as their racial inferior. The mise-en-scène and Murphy's performance of parody, especially of western conventions, makes the scene far more radical than others have given it credit for.

Much of *Another 48 Hrs.* is a reworking of the first film, but Hill reverses its narrative and character dynamics in crucial ways that further the relationship between Jack and Reggie. The second film likewise pivots around a midpoint scene in a bar; this time, however, the crowd is racially mixed, and the nightclub setting is bereft of the redneck bar's iconography. The substantial shift in political space reflects the rebalancing of the scales between Jack and Reggie in the sequel—Reggie does not have to overtly resist Jack's attempts to subjugate him through enforcement of the racial hierarchy, especially because Cates's own grasp on authority has become tenuous. The scene's objective is the same—Jack and Reggie are looking for clues—but the test dynamic is absent. Reggie need not prove himself to Jack, and so the two enter the space on more equal footing. They split up, with Jack resolving to talk to the barmaid (another reversal—in the first film, this was Reggie's responsibility), and Reggie heading into the crowd of patrons. Far from the rollicking hillbilly tune of the redneck bar, the band (all Black members) is playing a saxophone-driven, soul-infused rock tune, a synthesis of typically Black and white musical genres not unlike many of the songs that appear in Hill's *Streets of Fire*. When Cates asks the barmaid for information, she gives him attitude, and Hill reverses Reggie's interaction with another bartender—this time, when he asks for vodka, he gets a compliant "Sure!" a far cry from the first film's bartender contemptuous recommendation of a Black Russian. He hustles his way into retrieving a white man's wallet when it is lifted by a Black pickpocket, getting the mark to agree to surrendering half his money to Reggie in return for the wallet's recovery; this is yet another evolution from the bar scene in *48 Hrs.*, in which Reggie was acting at Jack's behest. Broke, Reggie is singularly concerned with improving his financial situation, yet again focusing his motivation on his wealth. When Reggie confronts the lady pickpocket in the women's bathroom, he starts working the other angle, trying to walk away with more money. While Reggie's motivation in the first film was two-fold—sex and securing his half-million dollars—the sequel's focus is almost entirely on his acquisition of wealth. Meanwhile, a group of white men dressed in trucker caps, cowboy hats, and flannel shirts, who resemble refugees from the redneck bar in the original *48 Hrs.*, intercept Jack and threaten him; Cates put one of them in jail, and he is none too happy about it. The dialogue encourages the moment's self-reflexivity: "People are always gettin' in barfights! It's a damn cliché! Happens all the time! You see it in the motion pictures," Jack shouts. Such self-aware commentary invites deliberate comparison with the bar scene in the previous film, but this time, a vision of Jack's racial resentments, those with whom he made common cause ("Always liked country boys," he told Reggie) have come back to haunt him. He starts the fight himself, breaking a bottle over the man's head, as if he knows little else to do but live up to the cliché he derides.

Bars are crucial spaces in both films even beyond these centerpiece scenes. After they are separated following the subway station shootout in *48 Hrs.*, Jack and Reggie reunite in another bar, across the street from Luther's hotel, where he is hiding out. This club is a visual and auditory counterpoint to the redneck bar—it is a sea of Black faces, dancing to songs performed by The Bus Boys, a Black rhythm and blues band. The set list includes "(The Boys Are) Back in Town," which becomes the de facto theme song for both *48 Hrs.* and *Another 48 Hrs.*, playing over the end credits for both films, and serving as the poster tagline for the sequel. Murphy would reuse the song in his own comedy special *Eddie Murphy: Delirious* (1983, Gowers)—The Bus Boys serve as his opening act, playing it in the theatre where he will perform, intercut with Eddie storming across America in his tour bus and a charter plane, a montage that shows the comedian beginning to conquer the country's entertainment landscape. If the redneck bar is Jack's space, then this bar belongs firmly to Reggie; it is also the site of the most important dialogue exchange between the two men in either film, in which Jack sheepishly apologizes, to an extent, for his racist treatment of Reggie since he got him out of jail. Knowing that Reggie, who has tailed Luther and called him to meet up, has saved him with the department, Cates is vulnerable. In a two-shot that balances the frame between the Black man and the white man, Jack stammers for a moment before slowly confessing, "Nigger. Watermelon. I didn't mean that stuff. I was just doin' my job. Keepin' you down." It is a striking admission. In this line of dialogue, the screenplay by Hill, Roger Spottiswoode, Larry Gross, and Steven E. DeSouza expresses the relationship between racism and police oppression of Black men; Cates sees his use of racist language as essential to maintaining the power structure he embodies as a police officer. And yet, Jack is unwilling, even in this revealing line, to admit real personal culpability, blaming his use of epithets on an institutional responsibility. Reggie is too smart to let him off the hook: "Yeah, well, doin' your job don't explain everything, Jack." The officer is quick to agree: "Yeah, you're right." Far from protesting that he is not a racist, Jack more or less admits it. Bogle is reluctant to give the film credit for this moment, saying that it is "a good piece of dialogue which, however, is quickly passed over as the movie moves on to another joke."[53] The moment of honesty between Reggie and Jack is indeed defused by the two men's laughter—they share a small laugh of recognition—but there is a lingering heaviness that has clarified their relationship. At least, after all their combat, both physical and verbal, they are able to tell each other the truth, which is that race will continue to divide them.

This moment helps *48 Hrs.* avoid the trap of *The Defiant Ones*. It refuses to ameliorate the racial conflict by suggesting that Jack has changed. His acknowledgement of the role that race plays in the justice system shows a self-conscious awareness of society's prejudices, but Reggie's refusal to forgive him completely forces him to confront his own racism. The white cop and the Black convict do not experience a moment of racial healing, but agree to disarm in the wake of an honest admission of the power dynamic between them. In the final moments of both films, Hill, Murphy, and Nolte root the racial conflict between Reggie and Jack in gesture. According to Laura Mulvey, "gesture is mime-like, a recognizable signal proffering a supplement to the verbal, reducing the abstraction of language to bodily, material expressiveness."[54] Because of its quiet efficiency, gesture is irresistible to a filmmaker like Hill, whose approach is defined by its balancing of austerity and excess. As employed by any director, "gesture hovers on the brink of meaning, suggesting but resisting and remaining closer to the ineffable than the fullness of language."[55] In both *48 Hrs.* films, Jack and Reggie engage in racial dialogue that some have seen as excessive, but Hill finds an austere approach in his deployment of physical gesture. Outside Candy's apartment at the end of the first film, Jack makes his promise to hold Reggie's half-million dollars until he gets out of jail in six months, an agreement between the two men which would seem to dramatize their now solidified trust. And yet, Hill creates a lingering doubt through his deployment of a signature Hawksian gesture—the lighting of a cigarette, so crucial to the director's *To Have and Have Not* (1944) and *The Big Sleep* (1946), two films in which lovers, on-screen and off-screen, Humphrey Bogart and Lauren Bacall, share an intimate connection when one lights the other's smoke with a burning match. While Hawks used this gesture to capture eroticism that the Production Code forbade, Hill repurposes it for an apparent symbol of racial détente. Trust now seemingly established, Jack waits a moment before starting the car: "Reggie," he says. "Can I have my lighter back?" With a knowing smile, Reggie gives him back the lighter, which he had slipped into his own pocket. Trust is still a tenuous commodity. One might think that *Another 48 Hrs.* would resolve this issue, but Hill once again revises the first film's ideas through a restaging of this moment. This time, Jack whispers to the injured Reggie, one of Jack's bullets in his shoulder and lying on a paramedic's gurney, that he lifted $500,000 from the Iceman and intimates that they will split it—"We'll talk about it at the hospital." Trust is once again seemingly established, but when the ambulance carts Reggie away, Jack reaches into his pocket for his cigarette lighter. It's gone, and Hill cuts to a smirking Reggie, holding the lighter open in the back of the ambulance. This time, Reggie has extracted a kind of collateral, which will ensure that Jack follows through on his promise. He will not be caught empty-handed again.

According to Bogle, the multiracial buddy films that *48 Hrs.* helped to inaugurate "have been wish-fulfillment fantasies for a nation that has repeatedly hoped to simplify its racial tensions."[56] Perhaps that is true of a film like *Lethal Weapon* (1987, Donner), in which the racial difference between the white Riggs (Mel Gibson) and Black Murtaugh (Danny Glover) is barely acknowledged, with the Black homebody eventually adopting the white, damaged loner into his own family. Their bond is sealed in the final image of the climactic fight scene, in which a beaten and battered Riggs, his white skin glistening in the nighttime rain, leans on a similarly injured and exposed Murtaugh, both men firing their guns into the camera lens in medium shot with the villain Joshua (Gary Busey) on the business ends of the barrels. The bond of violence seals the friendship between special agent Luke Hobbs (Dwayne Johnson) and British mercenary Owen Shaw (Jason Statham) in the *Fast & Furious Presents: Hobbs and Shaw*, as well, as the Samoan/Black Johnson/Hobbs and the white Shaw/Statham trade body blows with the Black villain Brixton (Idris Elba), similarly in the rain. Though these films allow their mixed-race heroes victory over their opponents, unlike the prison-bound Cullen and Joker in the final moments of *The Defiant Ones*, they do make good on the promise of racial harmony through their suppression of difference; subsumed into the narrative resolution, their differences are rarely framed through an overtly racial lens, which thus renders their disparate racial identities irrelevant. Subsequent generations of filmmakers learned a great deal from the success of *48 Hrs.* and its sequel, but have shown far less interest than Hill in using the mixed-race buddy film to explore the ramifications of its characters' racial differences. Of his mixture of comedy and action, Hill is fond of repeating a maxim that serves him well: "the jokes are funny but the bullets are real."[57] Though both *48 Hrs.* films are funny, the violence they depict is very much rooted in the everyday world; far from trivializing racial difference for the purposes of comedy, Hill never loses sight of the violence that racism can do, both on an interpersonal and societal level.

NOTES

1. Interview with the author, 26 January 2021.
2. Melvin Donalson, *Masculinity in the Interracial Buddy Film* (McFarland, 2006), 33.
3. Interview with the author.
4. Donald Spoto, *Stanley Kramer: Filmmaker* (Samuel French, 1978), 200.
5. James Baldwin, in *I Am Not Your Negro*, Dir. Raoul Peck.
6. Donalson, 31.
7. Donald Bogle, *Toms, Coons, Mulattoes, Mammies, and Bucks*, 5th Edition (Bloomsbury, 2016), 158.
8. Ibid, 164.
9. Ibid, 163.

10. Ibid, 13.
11. Ibid, 163.
12. Ibid, 158.
13. For more, see Yvonne Tasker, *Spectacular Bodies*, 32–35.
14. Ibid, 213.
15. Ibid, 201.
16. Ibid, 241.
17. Ibid, 233.
18. Tommy L. Lott, "A No-Theory Theory of Contemporary Black Cinema," in *Representing Blackness: Issues in Film and Video*, ed. Valerie Smith (Rutgers University Press, 1997), 88.
19. Ed Guerrero, *Framing Blackness: The African American Image in Film* (Temple University Press, 1993), 114.
20. Ibid, 120.
21. Ibid, 122.
22. Ibid, 125.
23. Ibid, 126.
24. Bogle's definition: "no-account roustabouts, those unreliable, crazy, lazy, subhuman creatures good for nothing more than eating watermelons, stealing chickens, shooting crap, or butchering the English language," 5.
25. Bogle, 254.
26. Donalson, 9.
27. Guerrero, 127.
28. Ibid, 128.
29. Ibid, 130.
30. Ibid, 131.
31. Bogle, 245.
32. Eddie Murphy, "Episode 1207 – Eddie Murphy," WTF with Marc Maron, 8 March 2021, http://www.wtfpod.com/podcast/episode-1207-eddie-murphy.
33. Interview with the author, 26 March 2021.
34. Lott, 85.
35. Ibid, 91.
36. Valerie Smith, "Introduction," in *Representing Blackness*, 3.
37. Donalson, 73.
38. Bogle, 13.
39. Manthia Diawara makes the argument that this is the entire purpose of *48 Hrs.* in "Black Spectatorship: Problems of Identification and Resistance," *Screen* 29, no. 4 (1988).
40. Ibid, 255.
41. James A. Snead, "Spectatorship and Capture in King Kong: The Guilty Look," in *Representing Blackness*, 28.
42. Ibid.
43. Bogle, 255.
44. Guerrero, 126.
45. Ibid.

46. Interview with the author.
47. Bogle, 363.
48. Ibid.
49. Bogle, 255.
50. Ibid.
51. Ibid.
52. Guerrero, 131.
53. Bogle, 255.
54. Laura Mulvey, "Cinematic Gesture: The Ghost in the Machine," in *Gesture and Film*, ed. Nicholas Chare and Liz Watkins (Routledge, 2017), 10.
55. Ibid.
56. Bogle, 245.
57. Interview with the author, 26 January 2021.

Chapter 5

Down These Streets of Fire

The buoyant sound of The Bus Boys' "(The Boys Are) Back in Town," which rolls over the end credits of Walter Hill's *48 Hrs.*, not only entrenched the film's point of view in Reggie Hammond, but signaled something of a shift in the director's filmmaking. The mood engendered by the song is a tonal leap from the understated, even staid conclusions of his debut *Hard Times* and his follow up *The Driver*, and a more joyful rock and roll tune than Joe Walsh's "In the City," which sent the wayward gang back home in *The Warriors*. The dark ambiguities of both of Hill's subsequent films, *The Long Riders* and *Southern Comfort*, carried through into those films' concluding musical notes, with composer Ry Cooder's folk and blues rhythms capturing the former film's wistfulness and the latter's sense of dread, neither relieved by the endings. The boogie-woogie beat of "(The Boys Are) Back in Town" at the end of *48 Hrs.* promises something new.

After the success of *48 Hrs.*, Hill had the freedom to make any movie he wanted—he would never get a chance like this again. His choice of follow up was an unlikely one, but a direction indicated by the final moments of his biggest hit to date. Having established a reputation as an action director, moving into the middle of the genre's most important decade, when its conventions and stars cohered into a recognizable form that would last for at least another thirty years, Hill did not immediately seek to recapture the success of *48 Hrs.* One of his stars, Murphy, was certainly interested in doing just that—in 1984, he would star in *Beverly Hills Cop*. Arnold Schwarzenegger was about to ignite his own superstardom with a menacing, dialogue-light turn in James Cameron's *The Terminator*. Hill's friend and contemporary John Milius offered a paranoid fever dream that imagined a Soviet invasion of the United States, *Red Dawn*, in which a group of teenagers band together to resist the country's new Communist overlords. In many ways, 1984 would prove to be one of the most important years for the action genre, not simply for the landmark films released that year, but because of the general trend those films represented: action movies starring white and Black actors alike were leavening their violence with comedy; they began to feature more and more hard-bodied stars whose physiques made them objects of desire and subjects of violence; and the genre increasingly gained a reputation as politically reactionary, with right-wing ideology driving the narratives and iconography that became the action film's stock in trade.

Despite being well-known as an action director, Hill's decision to make *Streets of Fire*, a film that David Desser calls "oddly unclassifiable,"[1] when the action genre was moving in its well-chronicled direction reveals a filmmaker who wanted to use the genre to explore his own ideas, rather than subordinate his vision to the demands of producers invested in mayhem, stars showing off their workout routines, or audiences eager to consume both; its commercial failure likewise reveals that he may have misread the cultural moment. Partially drawn from John Ford's *The Searchers*, and partially steeped in the heavy iconography of film noir, *Streets of Fire* is at its core a representative of the unlikeliest of genres for an action director to dabble in—the musical. Like many other films of the 1980s, it travels back to the 1950s, a decade it refuses to specify in the opening text that establishes its mythic setting—"Another Time, Another Place ... ," reads white block lettering on a black card—but one that informs every element of its mise-en-scène. But above all, *Streets of Fire* offers an invigorating testament to the healing power of rock and roll, which can offer a light in the darkness, a soundtrack of youth, and most powerfully, a chance at transcendence. At the height of Hill's clout in the industry, he made an unconventional choice that opened a narrative and stylistic door for him as an artist—the chance he took with *Streets of Fire* paved the way for the rest of the films he would make, allowing him to synthesize his admiration of westerns and noir films into an action cinema driven by his own vision. The action genre was heading in one direction, and Hill no doubt could have been successful on that path; that he chose not to take it was a fateful decision that led to increased willingness to experiment with different kinds of films, a burgeoning interest in the possibilities offered by film style, and a more personal vision. Its failure at the box office and with critics, however, almost certainly foreclosed opportunities. Had he immediately delivered a sequel to *48 Hrs.*, his career may have looked very different.

A ROCK 'N' ROLL FABLE

Part western, part noir, and all musical fairy-tale shot in comic-book style, *Streets of Fire* is a pastiche of a number of Hill's well-documented inspirations; however, its largely bloodless approach sanitizes the film's violence at the same time as the action genre is moving in an increasingly graphic and gory direction. Its sensibility deviates considerably from the spare approach of *Hard Times* and *The Driver*, the warlike brutality and abjection of *The Long Riders* and *Southern Comfort*, and the irreconcilable racial tensions of *48 Hrs*. In its iconography and heightened insularity, *Streets of Fire* is closest to *The Warriors*, but that film's nighttime odyssey is propelled by an unceasing sense of threat, a foreboding sense of doom which never comes to Hill's musical. It is unquestionably the most hopeful and optimistic of Hill's early films, and the one which foregrounds romance more considerably than any other, rooting its central character's dramatic motivation in his desire to reclaim lost love. It is, for Hill, something new—a reinvention.

The musical genre would seemingly make for uncharted territory for a director so heavily influenced by noir and western films, but such seemingly irreconcilable genres managing to coexist is not entirely without precedent. Made for MGM Studios' storied Arthur Freed unit, Vincente Minnelli's *The Band Wagon* (1953) is a high-profile example of noir's uneasy presence in musicals: it stars Fred Astaire as the very Astaire-like Tony Hunter, a musical star of stage and screen at something of a career crossroads. Feeling his age and worried that the song-and-dance style he personifies slipping away, he travels back to New York from California in hopes of reuniting with some old friends and putting a show together for Broadway that will remind audiences—and himself—that he still has something to offer. *The Band Wagon* concludes with a tour-de-force musical performance from Astaire's Tony and his ballet-trained dance partner Gabrielle Gerard (Cyd Charisse), which Minnelli stages as a film noir. Though the question of noir's identity remains one of film history's unsettled debates, Minnelli's adoption of the detective film's iconography and narrative tropes, complete with Charisse doing double duty as a blonde and brunette dancer who recall the femme fatale and her more wholesome doppelganger, is as good an argument as any for the increasing codification of noir into a full-fledged genre by 1953. Tony narrates in voice-over—a cinematic device completely at odds with the stage-bound diegetic circumstances of the conclusion of "The Band Wagon," the show in which Tony is performing—and moves from violent confrontation to lascivious encounter with one of Charisse's women. Minnelli offers expressionistic angles that distort the stage show's sets into urban nightmares; one portion of the number is shot in an empty subway platform suggested by the combination of mocked-up pillars and a forced perspective matte painting disappearing into the distance. When Tony and Gabrielle-as-femme-fatale dance together at the stage's apron, bright white lights flicker past them as though they were swinging each other in front of a hurtling train. The frame spins in circles at specific narrative moments common to noir, as when Tony is knocked unconscious by a mysterious stranger dressed all in black, the image swirling into mania. Elsewhere, Tony looks directly into the camera's lens, his eyes underlining his detective's confusion alongside the voice-over, two stylistic choices that exit from the narrative diegesis by inviting the film spectator, and not the constructed audience watching from the auditorium's house seats, into the story. The combination of the musical form and film noir offers both Minnelli and Astaire the opportunity to play with the possibility of reinvention; the film, and Astaire's star persona, almost literally become something else before our eyes.

In this scene, the musical form in which Minnelli often works adopts a theme common to noir films, many of which are about reinvention. Ordinary insurance salesman Walter Neff (Fred MacMurray) reinvents himself as a calculating killer in *Double Indemnity* (1944, Wilder); in *Dark Passage* (1947, Daves), escaped convict Vincent Parry (Humphrey Bogart) undergoes reconstructive plastic surgery that gives him a new face, the better to clear his name after being wrongfully accused of murdering his wife; the noir-infused boxing drama *The Set-Up* (1950, Wise) forces reinvention on its dead-end fighter Stoker Thompson (Robert Ryan) in its final moments after he wins a fixed fight, against the orders of the gangsters who have bet on him to lose, and shatter his hand in an alley as punishment. Noir is replete with self-deniers and self-adopters, characters who have little choice but to become someone else entirely in order to survive. At its core, noir suggests that the self is unstable, forever vulnerable to influence that could, in the darkest outcome that noir almost always foretells, lead to damnation.

Noir itself, of course, is notoriously unstable, its conventions and style infecting numerous film genres in the 1940s and 1950s. Raoul Walsh's *Pursued* (1947), a noir set in the west, stars Robert Mitchum as Jeb Rand, a boy adopted by the Callum family after his own parents are murdered when he is a boy. Rand is both himself and not, a member of the Callum family and likewise far outside it. Jeb's tenuous grasp on his sense of self might seem like the noir half of Walsh's hybrid, but westerns too feature a number of characters who seek to start over, people who literalize "Go West, young man" in remaking their identities and looking to become someone else. The adoption of monikers and nicknames allows western characters to hide themselves behind myth and legend, their reputations preceding them; we never learn the real name, for instance, of the hero of *Stagecoach* (1939, Ford), The Ringo Kid (John Wayne), despite knowing his motivation for revenge against the men who murdered his father and brother and framed him for the crime. His desire to get even has forced him to invent a new self, one that makes him an outlaw, forged by the crimes he has been accused of, but did not commit. While Ringo's nom de guerre helps him establish a reputation, other western heroes and anti-heroes are running away from something. In *Man of the West* (1958, Mann), Link Jones (Gary Cooper) has left behind a life of crime and violence, starting again as an upstanding citizen entrusted by his fellow townspeople to travel by train to hire a schoolteacher for their children. Though Link has suppressed his violence, burying it underneath a reinvented self, it roars back when he is reunited with his cruel, monstrous stepfather Dock Tobin (Lee J. Cobb), a brutal, sadistic outlaw who taught Link how to rob and kill. The West offers the hope of reinvention to many of the genre's protagonists, but as in noir, the self is just as hard to leave behind as it is to create.

Streets of Fire shares a title with a song by Bruce Springsteen, a track which appears on his album *Darkness on the Edge of Town*, released in 1978. For his part, Hill says that he is "a great admirer of Springsteen."[2] Hill says he did not intentionally lift Springsteen's title for his film,[3] but its title does echo those of the rock and roll juvenile films that of the 1950s which, according to David Ehrenstein and Bill Reed,

> held out the promise of lurid thrills, for example: *Hot Rod Rumble*, *Motorcycle Gang*, *Reform School Girl*, *Riot in Juvenile Prison*, and *Explosive Generation*. It would seem as if almost no possible combination of words that connoted speed, sex and anarchy eluded the producers of these stormy double-bill features.[4]

Hill's *Streets of Fire* and Springsteen's reveal how two distinctly American artists rely on similar conventions common to the film western and noir to express something universal about the complex relationship between the individual and the community. Both Springsteen and Hill situate their shot at reinvention on their respective streets of fire.

Hill's *Streets of Fire* is a riff on *The Searchers*, in which biker gang leader Raven (Willem Dafoe) kidnaps rock star Ellen Aim (Diane Lane), and Tom Cody (Michael Pare), the crusading hero at its center, determined to rescue Ellen, his former lover, from Raven's clutches. Many filmmakers who were coming to cinematic prominence at the same time as Hill also cite *The Searchers* as an influence. Steven Spielberg, George Lucas, John Milius, Martin Scorsese, and especially Paul Schrader have all declared their love for Ford's film. Scorsese's *Taxi Driver* (1976), written by Schrader, is partially lifted from it, as is Schrader's own 1979 film *Hardcore*. Of *The Searchers*, Schrader says the Ethan Edwards (John Wayne) character illustrates "the frailty of the great American hero, the psychological instability of the pioneer."[5] Regarding the film's famous final shot, he says,

> At the end of the movie he walks away and the door closes on him; he has returned the lost child to the home but he can't enter. It also has resonances

of Moses, who struggled through the desert and was not allowed to enter the Promised Land—it has great traditional resonances.[6]

Though *The Searchers* is an incredibly rich film, one of its central concerns is the limits of Ethan's ability to sufficiently reinvent himself. Schrader's invocation of the Moses story shows how much Ethan's racism and violence have excluded him from the community—he cannot enter the home, and is left, like the dead Comanche warrior whose eyes he shoots out, "to wander forever between the winds."

In *Streets of Fire*, Tom Cody returns from life as a mercenary outside of The Richmond neighborhood in the film's first act. Actor Michael Pare got the part of Cody in Hill's rock and roll fantasy after his performance in *Eddie and the Cruisers* (1983, Davidson), in which he portrayed a mythic rock star who got his start on the Jersey Shore, and whose sound is very much indebted to Springsteen. That film's most well-known track, "On the Dark Side," has a fluttering Bo Diddley guitar sound, not unlike the one Springsteen had used on *Born to Run*'s "She's the One." Like the protagonists of many Springsteen songs, and even the songwriter himself, Pare's performances in this period typify the wounded American man who wants to prove his worth but struggles to self-actualize, owing to a combination of social forces and his own failures. In *Streets of Fire*, Tom Cody is a man driven by clear purpose, like Ethan Edwards before him—rescue Ellen Aim. And yet, the character's journey is undercut by inner sadness, which he carries silently. Cody's body moves with physical power—he beats up threatening street gang members, he's a crack shot with a rifle, and he overcomes Raven in their showdown, a sledgehammer street fight. But Cody's heart drifts away, pulled somewhere else by an uneasy sense that this time, this place, this life, isn't quite right. His immediate purpose is to be the blunt instrument who can bring Ellen back to her screaming fans, but his greater purpose remains elusive.

Streets of Fire depicts a world of alienated characters, centralized in the anti-hero Tom Cody, a searcher in the John Wayne-Ethan Edwards sense, driven by the pursuit of a specific goal, but ultimately unfulfilled by accomplishing that goal. Of the Edwards character, historian Glenn Frankel says, "The mission is accomplished, but there is no place for the avenger in the new civilization he has helped forge."[7] Both westerns and films noir, the twin sources that drive Hill's movie, share the alienated, searching central character as a part of their respective generic legacies. In westerns, the cowboy heroes—like Wayne's Edwards, or Alan Ladd's Shane, or The Magnificent Seven—are good with a gun, come to settle the town by ridding the space of its outlaw element through purgative violence. He is a tool, used until his work is completed, and then rejected by the civil society he has created. In noir, the equivalent character is the private investigator working outside the strictures of traditional law and order. According to Borde and Chaumeton,

> The private eye had been the standard character of 1940s film noir [. . .] he moved around in a twilight world, on the borderline of legality. Accepting of dubious clients, mixed up in suspect affairs, he symbolized the rottenness that inevitably from contact with crime. Yet at the same time he played the scapegoat's role, he stomached all the wrongdoing so that the police might remain above suspicion. In that sense, he was American cinema's alibi, and it interposed his pervasive myth between spectator and society.[8]

Once again, the character is excluded from civil society because of his anti-social behavior. Variations in both genres exist, of course, and not all western heroes or noir detectives fit this pattern. Some western heroes and noir detectives are born exiles, others become exiles, and some have it thrust upon them. But many westerns and many films noir are about the individual man separated from civil society. Indeed, the western and noir characters most likely to find themselves on the outside looking in are those who try to reinvent themselves most conspicuously.

Westerns and films noir both suggest that conflict must be resolved in the streets. In westerns, it is the town square. In noir, it is the mean streets of America's cities at night, where betrayal and murder lurk around every corner. As the men at the centers of westerns and films noir discover, the violence of their respective worlds will not allow them to rejoin polite society at the conclusions of their narratives. Though Borde and Chaumeton would undoubtedly find ironic distance in *Streets of Fire*, owing to its 1984 release date and Hill's knowing adoption of noir tropes, the film itself really is an earnest, genuine article. *Streets of Fire* wants its audience and its characters to believe in the transcendent power of rock and roll. It presents a noir world of ruined urban space, pockmarked by decay, rain-soaked pavement, and almost endless night. Its characters spit tough-guy patter ripped straight out of 1940s noir films. The small ray of light shining through the darkness is music, especially represented by heroine Ellen Aim and her band, The Attackers. Hill's streets of fire are, like in Springsteen's song, spaces of conflict. The rescue of Ellen, led by Cody, plays out in the alley in front of The Battery, Raven's headquarters. The final conflict between Cody and Raven takes place in the streets of The Richmond, beneath the elevated train tracks that block out the sun. The battle of brute strength between the two men is a western showdown on noir streets.

Hill centralizes these noir and western tropes in Cody. He is a military veteran ("I liked shooting the guns, but I didn't win no medal," he tells driver McCoy (Amy Madigan), who also describes herself as a "soldier." So is Ethan Edwards, having served in the Civil War on the Confederate side, and Ethan has spent the post-war years wandering the west, seemingly involved in outlawry and generally dubious activities, and "fits a lot of descriptions." His reintegration into polite society has been difficult, to say the least. Ironically, Ethan's roughness, obsession, and brutality make him an effective pursuer of Debbie, but also prevent him from reentering the home at the film's conclusion. The growing civility of the west will leave Ethan behind, just as the Jorgensons (now taking care of Debbie) close the door on him. Veterans of foreign wars also figure prominently in noir films, many of which feature central characters traumatized by their service abroad and experiencing difficulty reintegrating into civil, stateside society. Mark Osteen argues "Noir veterans' healing or reintegration could occur after they were broken down and rebuilt," but he raises a critical question: "Into what sort of world were they reborn?"[9] Ethan and noir protagonists both find themselves at odds with the broader culture's accepted rules and norms; throughout the narrative of *The Searchers* and numerous noir films, the protagonists navigate these worlds with great difficulty, frequently stumbling through them and lashing out violently, which only escalates their isolation.

Like Ethan Edwards, Tom Cody returns to the narrative setting of *Streets of Fire* after a mysterious absence, having chosen exile after his breakup with Ellen. He shares the western hero's preference for working alone, only reluctantly accepting the companionship of Ellen's manager Billy Fish (Rick Moranis) and mechanic McCoy in the rescue attempt. Cody is filled with intense longing—as he plans his assault on Raven's hideout, he spies Ellen through a window, tied to a bed, followed by his reaction in close-up. As Cody looks down the barrel of his repeating rifle, a mournful twang of Ry Cooder's guitar cries for the hero's wounded heart, as he sees Ellen for the first time since they parted before the narrative began. This too has parallels in *The Searchers*, which suggests the forbidden love between Ethan and his sister-in-law Martha, a relationship never consummated, never acknowledged in dialogue, and only shown subtly through staging by director Ford. The source of their pain is different, but the result is the same—a character in self-imposed exile as a result of his feeling of loss.

After Cody rescues Ellen, they bicker and argue over their breakup, clashing in the way that only two people desperately in love can. Upon their return to The Richmond, Cody and Ellen even briefly rekindle their relationship, embracing an everlasting kiss in the rain beneath the elevated train tracks that loom over the street, but it is not to be. After he has successfully returned her to The Richmond and defended the town from Raven's goons in a knockdown street sledgehammer fight, Cody feels his purpose has dried up. The man of action no longer feels necessary once the action concludes. Cody knows his purpose, telling his sister early in the film, "They always hire bums like me for jobs like this," before setting off after Ellen. Cody has developed

Figure 5.1 The alienated anti-hero Tom Cody (Michael Pare) in *Streets of Fire* (1984) combines the mythic figures at the center of westerns and noir traditions—the lonely man of violence, cowboy, or detective, who serve their narrative and societal purpose, then end up alone. *Source: Screenshot captured by author.*

a sense of his own disconnection from the world; he sees himself as having very limited value, ripe for exploitation by others, and has no illusions about how his story ends. Before he leaves Ellen's victorious, celebratory concert after her rescue, he tells Fish, "She loves me, but she needs you." Fish, the talent manager, can provide everything that Ellen wants for her music career, and the fact that she loves Cody is immaterial. Love doesn't buy happiness, fame, or success on the rock and roll stage. On his way out the door, Cody runs into Ellen, and offers a softer version of the same sentiment he expressed to Fish. She knows he's leaving, and he explains himself:

> Look, I know you're gonna be going places with your music and stuff and . . . and I'm not the kind of guy to be carrying your guitars along for you. But if you ever need me for something . . . I'll be there.

The one thing Cody can define for himself is who gets to use him. He gains what little agency he has by deciding where and when he is willing to participate in the community. In Cody's sacrifice, he rejects community because he believes it can only flourish without him, but also carries the deep desire to be included.

These irreconcilable differences lead to his reluctant exile, with the surface nobility of the strong, silent type undercut by the deep longing in his soul. In *Streets of Fire*, a rock and roll show is the ultimate communal space, where multiple souls join together as one, and Cody decides he does not belong there. If rock and roll is the only source of hope for a better future that the film offers, then Cody's departure during the final concert is his Ethan Edwards moment. Cody is no rock and roll man. That is what ultimately separates him from the community in Hill's film. Ellen Aim takes the stage to sing the film's anthemic final song, "Tonight Is What It Means to Be Young," the message of which is living for the moment—"one last chance to make it real,"[10] as Springsteen sings in "Thunder Road." This is cinematic transcendence through the power of community; for the other characters in the story, rock and roll can break the dead-end cycle of generic alienation in westerns and films noir. The hero, however, is still alienated. Like the 1950s rock and roll musicals to which *Streets of Fire* is indebted, its final concert offers what Thomas Doherty calls a "subcultural function as a ritual occasion for the congregation,"[11] both in the diegetic crowd and in the moviehouse's audience.

This final concert is especially resonant given the fact that according to Walter Hill, in a making-of-the-movie documentary included on Shout Factory's special edition Blu-ray, "Tonight Is What It Means to Be Young" was not the original choice for the final song. It was Springsteen's "Streets of Fire," which they shot Ellen performing.[12] It was apparently Springsteen's last-minute reluctance to let someone else sing his song that forced the production to commission "Tonight" and reshoot the sequence. The final version of the film works better without it. Springsteen's "Streets of Fire" is a dark, brooding ballad shot through with the fury of its protagonist and songwriter. This is where the film and the song diverge—the film is about the possibility of escape that rock and roll offers, which is a theme essential to Springsteen, but not in his "Streets of Fire." The song is about the narrator's desire to fight back against the world he feels has done him wrong, and go down swinging if necessary. And yet, the film's ultimate conclusion is one that Springsteen shares. In fact, the final moments of Hill's *Streets of Fire*, though they do not contain an actual Springsteen song, capture the experience of the artist in concert—community, brought together by its members' shared passion for music, collectively experiencing transcendence in the present moment, however fleeting. The film and the song, united by their titles, offer both of Springsteen's major ideas: alienation of the individual by an unfair, unjust world, and the path to that individual's redemption through shared experience.

The conclusion of *Streets of Fire* also bridges the films Hill made both before and after. Its fusion of the conventions of westerns and noir go beyond simple reference, but instead reveal how much they share; in this way, *Streets of Fire* extends the examination of noir and western hero types that Hill began in *The Driver*, and foreshadows the more overt negotiation between those genres in *Extreme Prejudice*, *Red Heat*, *Johnny Handsome*, *Wild Bill*, and *Last Man Standing*. Beyond revealing the director's increasingly secure command of genre conventions, *Streets of Fire* also has an open heart—it is the most flagrantly emotional of Hill's films. Despite Cody's decision to choose exile at the end of the film, Hill does not quite go so far as to send him off alone, like Ford's Ethan Edwards. While the concert rages inside the theatre, Cody joins McCoy outside, the two friends driving away together on more certain ground than Jack Cates and Reggie Hammond, who also drive into the night at the end of *48 Hrs*. While their racial differences reached a kind of truce, but not resolution, one of the most powerful ideas suggested by the conclusion of *Streets of Fire* is that music provides the possibility for the transcendence of difference. Ellen and her band The Attackers are joined on stage by the Black doo-wop group The Sorels, singing together in an inspiring vision of integration. Hill's refusal to isolate Cody completely and his more hopeful, aspirational depiction of race relations make *Streets of Fire* the most emotionally uplifting film of his career.

MUSIC, MUSICALS, AND ACTION CINEMA

While *Streets of Fire* is indebted to both westerns and noir, it is also a musical. Hill's appropriation of the musical form represents a stylistic evolution that will clear the way for increasing experimentation with cinematography, editing, music, and sound. As Minnelli's adoption of noir style in the musical number that concludes *The Band Wagon* reveals, the intrusion of an unwelcome genre's iconography can lead to creative inspiration. In Hill's case, the musical genre's intrusion into noir and westerns, where he is usually more comfortable, is the key to a stylistic breakthrough.

Minnelli's film offers an unlikely narrative parallel to *Streets of Fire*, while likewise anticipating the opening of *The Searchers*. Like *Streets of Fire*, *The Band Wagon* dramatizes a journey of individual characters driven by their own desires towards something more communal. Tony's first song in the film is "By Myself," in which he not-so-convincingly sings about how comfortable he is on his own; Astaire's performance, especially in light of his missing partner, Ginger Rogers, with whom his screen persona is most often associated, imbues the song's lyrics with a countercurrent of sadness. His alienation is further underlined in the subsequent reunion with Lily (Nanette Fabray) and Lester (Oscar Levant), when the trio walks along 42nd Street, now unfamiliar to him after so many years away. Minnelli's camera captures Tony's dislocation in a scene in a penny arcade that has been built in place of a theatre where he previously worked as a dancer, in which Astaire wanders from game to game, both overwhelmed and saddened by the change in environment. Minnelli keeps the camera fluid, moving smoothly through the space, but constantly interrupts the mise-en-scène as gamers and tourists crash into the frame, a deft revision of the common situation in which audiences are used to seeing Astaire, who typically masters the physical space of an otherwise empty frame in dance, either alone or with Rogers. There is no room for Tony to move.

Though their structural similarities are evident,[13] the musical genre shares a fundamental characteristic with the action film in that it privileges the body in motion. According to Jennifer M. Bean,

> The most notable characteristic of the action cinema is its dynamic tempo: rapid editing at once articulates and accelerates the breathtaking pace of the stunting human body. It is also true that the body takes primacy over voice in the genre, that the action film "speaks" through visual spectacle, that spectacle, in fact, takes precedence over narrative meaning.[14]

By contrast, the musical is characterized by its long takes; many of Astaire's most famous on-screen moments, for instance, like his dance on the ceiling in *Royal Wedding* (1951, Donen), come in extended single shots. Extreme close-ups and staccato editing in the action film, especially when they come in the context of physical altercations like fistfights and gun battles, emphasize the punch of impact. The floating long take of the musical matches its dancers' elegance, privileging the highly rehearsed, but seemingly spontaneous rush of emotion harnessed by the subjects' bodies. And yet, despite the opposition in style—the rapid editing of the action cinema and the fluid long takes of the musical genre—the goal, which is to provide a kind of visual spectacle, is undeniably similar.

These seemingly oppositional genres have even begun to borrow from one another's stylistic identities. Aided by digital technology, action films have increasingly experimented with long takes for their action sequences. The centerpiece of David Leitch's espionage thriller *Atomic Blonde* (2017) finds the spy Lorraine (Charlize Theron) fighting off henchmen in the stairwell of a French hotel, its edits stitched together digitally to create the appearance of a continuous take that recalls the fluid motion of the Astaire films. On the other hand, a breakdancing and hip-hop dance musical like *Step Up* (2006, Fletcher) cedes the visual space to editing; the climactic dance sequence, though it takes place on a stage before an audience like much of *The Band Wagon* and its fellow backstage musicals, is cut rhythmically, with each edit driven by the propulsive beat of the song. Though action films tend to privilege editing and musicals tend to privilege longer takes, those stylistic barriers have begun to break down, with certain filmmakers seeking to leap across these dividing lines in order to explore the possibilities offered by the other. In each, however, music itself is the bridge, which unifies the edits of the action film and lends its action sequences their intensity, but also matches the swoop and glide of the fluid camera in the musical.

Streets of Fire is one of the very few examples of an action-musical hybrid, and thus offers a test case in the manipulation of these various stylistic possibilities. Throughout the first six films of Walter Hill's career, his visual style is dominated by a couple of defining characteristics: largely stable compositions that hold close-ups in reserve, often privileging several characters at once, visible in *Hard Times* and *The Driver*; a manipulation of slow motion that begins in the tradition of Sam Peckinpah's use of inserts but eventually gives way to a more singular approach specific to Hill himself, especially in *The Long Riders*; and a reliance on continuity editing only occasionally interrupted by montage in targeted sequences, like the opening of *The Warriors* or the final scenes of *Southern Comfort*. His seventh feature, *Streets of Fire* is notably devoid of slow motion—as Hill uses it in *The Long Riders*, *Southern Comfort*, and *48 Hrs.*, it comes in moments of intense violence that foregrounds the bodily impact of bullets on his characters. Because *Streets of Fire* deliberately reduces the stakes of its violence—there is hardly a drop of blood in the whole movie, and no one is killed—slow motion, as Hill uses it throughout his career, is incompatible with the comic book, fairy-tale style. For those who accuse Hill of Peckinpah plagiarism and see his use of slow motion in some films as an overreliance on the technique, *Streets of Fire* offers a challenge.

The other reason that Hill avoids slow motion in *Streets of Fire* is because the film moves forward at a relentless pace; running only ninety minutes, Hill creates a film that feels like a three-and-a-half-minute rock and roll song. After the Universal Studios logo fades to black, a crashing guitar riff hits the soundtrack; its percussive, circular chords announce the film's tone from the beginning, the musical sound echoing the revving engine of a muscle car or a motorcycle, both 1950s icons that appear prominently throughout the film. As soon as the title card reading "STREETS OF FIRE" hits the screen, a drumbeat begins, driving the song even harder. When the film comes up from black, Hill uses a greasy wipe transition, accompanied by a mechanical sound that likewise furthers the automotive imagery, as if the film's engine is roaring to life. The film's first shot, like many musicals, privileges the feet of the concertgoers who are flooding into The Richmond's theatre, hurrying inside to see Ellen Aim's show. From here, Hill offers a collage of images that establish The Richmond's central space beneath the elevated train tracks, as well as its smaller locations, like Reva's Diner and inside the theatre where Ellen's band is getting ready to perform. The cuts are extremely quick—shots that mostly last no longer than a second or two—and interrupt action, breaking it into pieces. Reva (Deborah Van Valkenburgh) begins to check her hair in a mirror in one shot, and then six shots later, after cuts to the flickering neon marquee outside and flocks of teenagers heading inside, among other things, Reva finishes primping and steps out of the frame. Above all, there is a sense of efficiency, an attempt to use these images to capture in visual poetry the kind of aesthetic breeziness that defines rock and roll lyrics. It is a use of montage that calls back to the urban milieu of *The Warriors*, in which Hill and his editors (led by regular collaborator Freeman Davies) similarly explored temporal and geographic disunity; recall that the general design of the credits sequence oscillated between four basic elements: shots of The Warriors on the subway platform in Coney Island; shots of the gang members on the train itself; various images of other gangs boarding the subway around the city; and shots in the tunnels from the point of view of the train as it hurtles through the Manhattan underground. All the gangs are headed for the meeting with Cyrus, but the montage induces a sense of fate that foreshadows his assassination and The Warriors' persecution. In *Streets of Fire*, the rock and roll aesthetic of the montage captures the excitement of the moments before a concert begins, with the nervous anticipation of the possibility of transcendence buzzing through a humming venue. It does so by establishing its editing language, creating a kind of harmony with the music, the film's dominant stylistic virtue in the opening sequence.

The song Ellen and The Attackers play, "Nowhere Fast," is actually performed by the band Fire, Inc., and has a definably 1980s sound. Ellen herself echoes Bonnie Tyler, whose hits "Total Eclipse of the Heart" and "Holding Out for a Hero" were recorded in 1983. The stage where she sings with her backing band, who are all dressed in David Byrne-like matching gray suits,[15] is bathed in darkness but broken up by intense, colored lighting. A red spotlight shines down on her when she takes her place at the microphone but crashes to blue when she kicks into the chorus. Throughout, Hill oscillates between close-ups of Ellen, looking up at her from a low angle to elevate her to the mythic, shots of the adoring crowd clapping in rhythm, and crane shots that privilege the entirety of the musical performance, with Ellen and her band working in harmony. The visual design of the film's fantasy concert is in keeping with the rapid expansion of rock and roll films that began in the late 1960s, which both brought about and were made possible by technological developments in the cinematic apparatus. According to Ehrenstein and Reed,

> For filmmakers these new rock spectacles provided an exciting challenge. Technical streamlining allowed cameramen to blend in unobtrusively with concert attendees. At their anonymous perches, camera operators had at their disposal perfected zoom lenses that could show performers either microscope-close or landscape-distant in a fraction of a second. Film stock had advanced to

the point where once-needed mega-watt overkill was no longer mandatory for proper lighting.[16]

Hill shoots Ellen's concert as though it were real, lending the show-within-the-film a sense of verisimilitude that makes *Streets of Fire* part concert movie, in addition to its other generic referents. The prevalence of neon and the driving intensity of "Nowhere Fast" situate the film firmly in its moment of release, but a countervailing force comes through juxtaposition outside the theatre—a blast from the past, Raven's band of leather-clad bikers, creeps slowly into The Richmond beneath its elevated tracks. The sudden intrusion of the gang destabilizes the film's sense of iconographic stability, making good on its promise to deliver a story set in "Another Time, Another Place." Hill's epigraph undoubtedly recalls the similar phrase that begins each of the films in the *Star Wars* saga, "A long time ago in a galaxy far away," but does so in keeping with his typically terse, direct screenwriting voice. His reduction of the *Star Wars* text to four words, given a kind of internal rhyme through the repetition of the word "another," announces the rock and roll style through lyrical efficiency.

The bikers materialize out of the 1950s, seemingly crashing through a time warp from movies like *The Wild One* (1954, Benedek), which stars Marlon Brando as a motorcycle roughneck who, when asked what he's rebelling against, replies, "Whaddya got?" In its adoption of this particular iconography, *Streets of Fire* associates itself with what Thomas Doherty calls "the teenpic," a series of movies made in the 1950s that focused on juvenile delinquency and street racing, and signaled a sea change in the way films were marketed, as Hollywood took notice of the teenage movie-going audience for the first time.[17] Crucial to the development of the teenpic in the 1950s was the shared sense of identity that united teenagers in the 1950s, which Doherty suggests was a new American phenomenon.[18] One of the forces that united these teenagers was rock and roll, which became the defining sound of youth culture thanks to the success of Elvis Presley and others, but was immensely profitable for record labels and, eventually, film studios.[19] The release of *Blackboard Jungle* (1955, Brooks) accelerated this trend—its opening credits are accompanied by the toe-tapping rhythm of "Rock Around the Clock," by Bill Haley and His Comets, which signaled a kind of sea change in American cinema that would pave the way for filmmakers who used rock and roll songs as soundtrack, substituting for musical score. This pairing of narrative subject matter with rock and roll cemented what Ehrenstein and Reed call "rock's reputation as an anarchic social force inextricably linked to violence" through its suggestion "that juvenile delinquency is being aided and abetted by the sound of 'Rock Around the Clock.'"[20] The film's opening, with the music blasting over an image of a classroom's blackboard, its all-capital letters credits fading in and out, anticipates Hill's use of white text-on-black screen in *Streets of Fire*. Its first images after the credits feature the neighborhood's elevated train, and its second shot begins under the tracks, from behind the film's idealistic teacher, Richard Dadier (Glenn Ford), as he orients himself to his new surroundings. "Rock Around the Clock" continues, but becomes diegetic music filtering into the space over a radio, as he steps toward the school where he is about to begin working, the camera trailing behind him just as it will the concertgoers in *Streets of Fire*. In *Blackboard Jungle*, Brooks establishes the school as the place where the film's young people congregate, but suggests it is a kind of prison—Dadier comes face to face with a wrought iron fence that resembles a penitentiary; in Hill's film, the theatre where Ellen is about to perform is a space of liberation, not incarceration.

According to Doherty, "Throughout *Blackboard Jungle* was a real sense that the terms of the social contract between the young and old had changed. On film at least, the relationship had never been so frightening, ambivalent, or antagonistic."[21] Brooks's film stages a conflict between Dadier, who represents adult authority, and the juvenile delinquents he teaches, many of whom are dangerous and have no interest in reforming. Hill's film removes adult authority entirely, with the entire core cast made up of actors under thirty. Though he includes a common trope of the teen pics identified by Doherty, a "mediating agent, often a sympathetic cop,"[22] in the form of Black police officer Ed Price (Richard Lawson), whose presence neatly reverses the racial dynamic between Dadier and one of his most troublesome students, Gregory Miller (Sidney Poitier), his role is to mediate between The Richmond's residents and Raven's Battery bikers; before the sledgehammer fight between Cody and Raven, however, Price's police authority, never strong to begin with, is removed entirely, and he cedes the battleground to Cody with an encouraging "Kick his ass" that abdicates his supposed neutrality. Because there is little police authority to speak of and seemingly no adults to supervise—in *Streets of Fire*, they are just as absent as the civilians in *The Driver* and *The Warriors*—the entire cast is made up of juvenile delinquents. In the 1950s, Doherty says the teen pics were populated by "rejectionist, 'alienated' groups such as delinquent gangs, bohemians, social cliques, and sects religious and political,"[23] which certainly describes the characters in *Streets of Fire*. Raven's bikers are a roving gang who bring chaos and mayhem with them wherever they go, as in the melee that disrupts Ellen's gig and results in her kidnapping. The Richmond is hardly a sanctified space, however; it is not the picturesque suburban image of 1950s America, nor is it the sanitized small town that Brando's gang shatters in *The Wild One*. The Richmond, like The Battery where Raven lives, is a slum; *Streets of Fire* does not dramatize a dichotomy between civilization and wilderness, as Jim Kitses argues is common to many westerns,[24] but stages a battle between one urban wilderness and another.

Raven embodies what Doherty calls "the image of the urban juvenile as a switchblade-brandishing menace"[25] that dominated teen pics and the popular imagination alike, as during the 1950s, the "soaring teenage crime rate put the 'problem of juvenile delinquency' high on the national agenda."[26] Dressed in black leather and with sculpted hair shaped into a pair of points that look like Satan's horns, Raven is a nightmare vision of the juvenile delinquent. The lighting and cinematography introduce him slowly, with a pair of images that cast him in silhouette, flanked by a pair of fellow bikers, as he moves through the unsuspecting crowd. Though the stage is flashing with neon lights from Ellen's rock and roll show, the light seems unable to penetrate Raven's shots, remaining shrouded in darkness. As Ellen's song reaches a crescendo, she begins to twirl and move to the music like a woman possessed, which Hill and editor Freeman Davies (et al.) capture in a series of jump cuts that reflect the style of then contemporary music videos, a hallmark of the 1980s. The reverse shot of Raven, still standing in the darkness, is marked by its absolute stillness—a tightly framed close-up of Raven watching, the barest outline of Willem Dafoe's then little known visage barely visible, slowly comes into view as a white light shines on his face. An icon of the 1950s has roared into this definably 1980s space, come to disrupt it by dragging it back into the past; in a decade marked by a number of films gripped by nostalgia, which lovingly render the 1950s as a simpler, better time, *Streets of Fire* presents it as a potential threat. Sound underlines the moment at which Raven's transfixed gaze transforms into violence with a non-diegetic roar of a motorcycle engine, ignited by the gang leader's simple shout: "Now!"

The fight between the bikers and the band, as well as some of the concert-goers who try to step in, is the first moment of violence in the film, but sets the template for how Hill will stylize his combat. Having established ground rules for himself—no blood and no death—Hill might seem to be in a bind, presenting violence that ultimately has no consequences, which at least in spirit might violate his general approach when making *48 Hrs.*: "the jokes are funny but the bullets are real."[27] In order to make the punches and kicks land harder, Hill often pairs the impact with a second, non-diegetic sound that creates a sonic ripple; Raven's second Greer (Lee Ving) takes a big pair of swings at would-be rescuer Clyde (Bill Paxton), and in addition to the punch sound effect, a metallic echo rings out. In a film full of engines, electric guitars, and subway trains, the violence between human beings becomes almost mechanical, a mythic distillation of the rough-and-ready teen pic's soundtrack: fast cars and fast music. Though all of Hill's previous films, save *The Warriors*, might be readily described as realistic, *Streets of Fire* moves far into expressionism, offering a more coherent and confident deployment of the stylistic elements of cinema than present in *The Warriors*.

The mechanical sound of an electric guitar—an original, Bo Diddley-inspired flutter performed by composer Ry Cooder—overlaps with the images of the moving gears of a typewriter, as Reva writes to Tom to tell him to come back to The Richmond. In a reversal of the opening montage of *The Warriors*, one man (he is completely alone in the train car) rides the subway to get back home, not leave it; this time, however, Hill doesn't just cut between the sputtering typewriter and the approaching elevated train, but overlaps the images in dissolve, lending the sequence a lyrical mood that contrasts with the menace of the similar montage in *The Warriors*. Cooder's score lends each image a propulsive drive, not only punctuating each cut, but guiding the movement of the actors in the frame. When Tom enters Reva's diner, he seems to float in on the wind—there is something of the western hero in his costume, a tan duster that recalls the James Gang's outfits during the fateful Northfield Minnesota Raid in *The Long Riders*, but a musical star's grace in his unhurried movements. With the film's sonic expressionism firmly established with the film's violence in its opening sequence, it now merges with the editing, as Tom fends off a gang of delinquents much less imposing than Raven's bikers, but, in keeping with the tradition of the western hero, does it all by himself. First, he takes a butterfly switchblade away from the gang's leader in one swipe, and then smacks him around, during which the cutting accelerates, each smack coinciding with an edit that lends the violence a kind of musical rhythm in keeping with Cooder's Bo Diddley-flutter, a la the guitarist's "Mona." A Chuck Berry winding riff (think "Johnny B. Goode") begins over a freeze frame of one of the gang, and the second part of the fight begins, with each moment of impact—Tom wields a coat rack—punctuated by a drumbeat and culminating in one of the gang sailing through Reva's plate glass window, as Cody makes quick work of the interlopers and sends them on their way.

In the film's first fifteen minutes, Hill establishes a variety of expressionistic choices that are unified by their ability to enhance *Streets of Fire*'s rock and roll sensibility; the elements of cinematic style transform the film into a rock and roll song. Thus far, the film's soundtrack, a collaboration between composer Cooder and music supervisor and rock producer Jimmy Iovine, has also drawn upon four rock and roll traditions, featuring a kind of California surf rock chug, a 1980s-style power ballad, a Bo Diddley flutter, and a Chuck Berry swirl. In its unification of these styles, the film offers itself as yet another by showcasing the medium's ability to adopt the conventions of rock and roll music. The film associates Raven's gang, The Bombers, with yet another of these musical traditions, ceding the space to The Blasters, a rockabilly punk group founded in Los Angeles, who portray The Battery's house band, performing "One Bad Stud" to an eager audience of barroom bikers. As in the film's opening, it privileges The Blasters' performance, just one way that *Streets of Fire* adopts the conventions of the musical genre. The film is as much a vehicle for these performances as it is a narrative; it is a celebration of the various traditions of rock and roll that come together. The Richmond has its own musical sound, The Battery has its own, and so too will The Sorels, whose bus Tom and company will board, and have their own doo-wop and Motown vibe. The film's extended privileging of The Blasters, Ellen's band The Attackers, and The Sorels does not place these musical traditions in opposition to one another, a critique leveled at a contemporary musical like *La La Land* (2016, Chazelle), which treads into somewhat uncomfortable racial territory by making its white pianist Sebastian (Ryan Gosling) into the guardian of the spirit of jazz, in stark contrast to the pop sensibility of Black singer and bandleader Keith (John Legend). In Hill's *Streets of Fire*, all the musical traditions he presents are worth appreciating.

Rock and roll becomes the motivating device for much of Hill's stylistic approach throughout the film, but the film is most effective when it unifies the action cinema's moments of spectacular violence with the sensibility of the musical genre. Yvonne Yasker helpfully articulates the ways in which the action film is often dismissed as style over substance: "For some, the narrative of contemporary action is all but subsumed within the spectacular staging of action sequences employing star bodies, special effects, artful editing and percussive music."[28] *Streets of Fire* is no ordinary action film—it is literally about the relationship between violence and music, dramatized through its stylistic fusion of music, editing, and narrative action. According to James Buhler and Mark Durrand, "Music is an efficient medium for organizing cinekinetic powers and attuning bodies to them so that we come to feel the affective dimensions of the particular cinematic universe, how it moves and how bodies move within it, from the experience of these themes."[29] Though *Blackboard Jungle* is often credited with inspiring the shift towards more rock and roll songs in cinema, the New Hollywood period accelerated this trend considerably. This increased use of rock and roll music as soundtrack coincided with the cohering of the action genre, setting a template for action films that would increasingly associate the two—rock and roll and action films working together. Look no further than the electric guitar-driven musical score of *Lethal Weapon* (1987, Donner), performed by Michael Kamen and guitarist Eric Clapton; likewise, the Nicolas Cage action thriller *Con Air* (1997, West) features a rock score with ample noisy stadium-rock shredding by Yes's Trevor Rabin. A number of rock songs have also appeared in the action film as "needle drops": the Kenny Loggins song "Danger Zone" that propels the fighter pilot action in *Top Gun* (1986, Scott); George Thorogood's "Bad to the Bone" as the theme song for the leather-clad, sunglasses-wearing Terminator (Arnold Schwarzenegger) in *T2: Judgment Day* (1991, Cameron); and the hyper-controlled use of "Bellbottoms" by the Jon Spencer Blues Explosion in *Baby Driver* (2017), directed by ardent Hill admirer Edgar Wright, borrowing not only its narrative premise from *The Driver* but the general stylistic sensibility of *Streets of Fire*.

According to Amanda Howell, "Rock 'n' roll offered a challenge to Hollywood that was both aesthetic and social, in its difference from the orchestral scores that constituted quality film entertainment and in its controversial connection to new youth subcultures."[30] In other words, as a musical style, rock and roll harnessed the rebellion of young people— "Rock Around the Clock" aligns the audience's sensibility with the delinquents, not the staid teacher, whatever the narrative itself has to say. Howell suggests that rock and roll was scary: "In part because of its mixed heritage of race, class, and region, and in part due to some incidents of violence following rock 'n' roll shows, rock 'n' roll became firmly yoked to juvenile delinquency in the popular imagination."[31] *Streets of Fire* depicts a world where the delinquents, and thus rock and roll, have won out—the absence of adult authority has ceded the narrative space to the young. Rock and roll, however, is not a symbol of their destruction, but the only thing saving them from oblivion. Ellen Aim is an aspirational figure, someone who has defined herself by rock and roll and as a result, has managed to not only transcend The Richmond, the slum in which she was reared, but offer transcendence back to those who remain. Subsequent to *Streets of Fire*, Hill only intermittently uses rock and roll music as score, and no film of his is as suffused with its sensibility, even including the blues drama *Crossroads*. Michael Baumgartner argues that in most action films, music "is immediate, direct, and intuitive, triggering our most elemental fight-or-flight instincts consistent with real-world encounters with threat, menace, and fear."[32] *Streets of Fire* does not simply use rock and roll as either score or needle drops, but internalizes the properties of rock and roll itself.

Contrast the use of music throughout *Streets of Fire* with Lalo Schifrin's score for *Bullitt*. The famous car chase in *Bullitt*, which Hill had a hand in shaping and elaborated upon in *The Driver*, is partially scored by Schifrin's smoky barroom jazz. The first portion of the chase during Bullitt's cat-and-mouse game with the car following him, is given healthy underscoring. Before the action accelerates into a full-blown chase, the music helps establish suspense. Baumgartner reads it like this: "Schifrin enhances the action of this segment of the chase with a drawn-out blues that lingers for an extended period on a tonic pedal point before the standard blues pattern reveals itself toward the end of the cue."[33] The purpose of the score is to define the mood of the chase; because *Bullitt* offers one of the first modern car chases, its narrative beats are not yet well-defined, and the music helps to add a suspenseful mood to what amounts to little more than a series of intercut images of Bullitt and his pursuers. Baumgartner argues that this kind of non-diegetic score, which is "direct and explicit in terms of its narrative function," is best thought of as what he calls "music of immediacy,"[34] a style common to action cinema, where the role of the musical score is to propel the action forward by accelerating the emotions engendered by the images and editing. In *Bullitt*,

> Schifrin's straightforward score assumes the function of music of immediacy: music that does not contain any meaning beyond its most basic associations. It is conceived for the sole purpose of heightening narrative suspense in an unambiguous, descriptive and direct fashion.[35]

When the chase accelerates to a point where its narrative stakes become clearer, Yates abandons Schifrin's score entirely, instead relying on the roar of Bullitt's engine and the squeal of his tires to fill the soundtrack. The novelty of the action sequence in *Bullitt* demonstrates Baumgartner's thesis effectively—because the car chase is just coming into its own, it needs no music to accelerate the emotions of the images, editing, and narrative circumstances. Tellingly, William Friedkin does not use music in the car chase in *The French Connection* (1971), either.

Hill's adoption of music throughout *Streets of Fire* goes far beyond Baumgartner's "music of immediacy," suffusing the entirety of the film's narrative and style in a way that more fully reflects the musical genre. However, *Streets of Fire* does not separate the musical sequences and the narrative sequences into discrete elements, as many film musicals do— because the film hybridizes action cinema and the musical, it uses rock and roll as score and centralizes it in performance. Though the film's numerous musical performances introduce the conventions of the musical into the action cinema, its violent sequences send the transmission the other way. The action sequences in *Streets of Fire* are driven by a percussive beat that seemingly aligns with the way scenes of violence are shot and edited in other action films, but it has more stylistic coherence. During Cody's rescue of Ellen from The Battery, a similar audiovisual strategy in the brief skirmish between Tom and the poser gang in Reva's diner recurs, as the cutting accelerates and timed to percussive drumbeats of the musical score, paralleled with bodily impact. Just as Astaire's tap shoes hit the stage in a rhythmic beat, or his punctuated swaying of his arms accentuate the melody, Cody's dispatching of Raven's Bombers is tied to music. Cody fires his rifle, and in the next shot, the cut and the score's beat coincides with the explosion of a motorcycle. When Cody breaks into the hideout and kicks in the door of the room where Ellen is being held captive, the pace of editing accelerates the action by stripping out unnecessary motion—he kicks in the door, she sees him, he flutters open the butterfly knife, he steps forward, a close-up of the knife hitting the ropes that bind Ellen's wrists, and suddenly, they're running through the hallway outside the room. The brutally efficient approach to the editing offers seven cuts in four seconds, but the accelerated pace is not simply for the sake of quick cutting; for one thing, the sequence never loses spatial orientation, keeping constant control of screen direction, and he lets each shot linger just long enough to maintain visual clarity, aided by specific choice of framing. Everything unnecessary has been stripped out, telling a miniature story—Tom finds and frees Ellen—in as rhythmic and propulsive a way as possible, underscored by Cooder's chugging blues guitar. In the alley outside The Bombers' warehouse, Cody stays behind to fend off the bikers while Ellen, McCoy, and Fish can escape; Hill applies the same approach to editing, cutting on each impact of the butt of Cody's rifle against the bikers' jaws. Hill and Davies experimented with this style of editing in the alley fight between Jack and Reggie in *48 Hrs.*, cutting on each punch landing, but didn't go quite so far, remaining bound by the reality of that film's narrative. *Streets of Fire* willingly sacrifices continuity of action in favor of a kind of rhythmic jump cut that, in keeping with the film's rock and roll sensibility, keeps driving forward.

Midway through *West Side Story* (1961, Wise and Robbins), a switchblade fight between Jets leader Riff (Russ Tamblyn) and Sharks leader Bernardo (George Chakiris) escalates the narrative tension—both men are killed, Riff by Bernardo and then Bernardo by Tony (Richard Beymer). The scene is a kind of ballet, with Riff and Bernardo lunging at one another in time with the orchestral strings that ring out on the soundtrack. Wise stays wide for much of the action, only shooting Bernardo's fatal stabbing in a medium over-the-shoulder, privileging Tony's reaction to the killing. The climactic sledgehammer fight between Raven and Tom in *Streets of Fire* is no doubt indebted to the narrative circumstances of *West Side Story*, but Hill's staging of the scene—a duel between two men, a standoff undertaken before an audience of onlookers—is a narrative trope that appears throughout his work. The final bareknuckle boxing match in *Hard Times* plays out before several gamblers; there is a knife fight in a bar in *The Long Riders*, with the two men holding a scarf between their teeth to keep them together; two Guardsmen fight with knives in *Southern Comfort*; the climax of *Crossroads* features a duel between guitarists; childhood friends, now enemies, stage a count-to-ten turn-and-draw in *Extreme Prejudice* that is interrupted before it can be completed; another boxing match concludes *Undisputed*, while a crowd of prisoners roars its approval and disapproval; the last moments of *Bullet To The Head* bring a hitman face-to-face with the man who killed his partner, each man brandishing an axe. *West Side Story*'s ritualistic depiction of violence anticipates a trend throughout Hill's work, as his male characters often prove that they are "good enough" in direct competition with their equal.

Another trope of musical films is the shot that follows the completion of a musical performance—the cut to an audience, furiously applauding, which performs a diegetic function, bringing the scene (and sometimes the entire film) to a close, but also an extra-diegetic function, acting as a vicarious representation of the cinema audience's desire to clap for the display of musical bravado that the film has just captured, despite the absence of live performers in the moviehouse. Whether audience members literally join in the applause, these images of the audience reacting to the musical number in *The Band Wagon* embody their satisfaction. The knife fight in *West Side Story* includes the trope of the audience, despite its distance from the backstage musical, because the standoff between Bernardo and Riff is staged before a group of their fellow gang members; in this construction, the film also picks up on another pair of famous on-screen juvenile delinquent standoffs in *Rebel Without a Cause* (1955, Ray). Both the knife fight outside the Griffith Observatory and the drag race "chickee run" are conducted before an audience of teenagers, holding their collective breath in anticipation in some moments and cheering the boys on in others. The sledgehammer fight between Tom and Raven takes place in a public space, beneath the elevated tracks of The Richmond, with each man surrounded by backup: Raven's Bombers look on, brandishing shotguns and other weapons, as do the denizens of the neighborhood. The Bombers ride into the sound of Cooder's adaptation of Link Wray's "Rumble," another example of the film's catalog of rock and roll traditions. When Tom's friend Clyde arrives with his fellow Richmonders, balancing the scales against the fearsome bikers, Cooder's quick-picking blues hits the soundtrack, and the sledgehammer fight begins.

As Cody and Raven swing at one another, their hammers clinking and crossing in a rhythmic symphony of wood-on-wood and metal-on-metal, the editing follows the same pattern, cutting directly to moments of impact, creating a kind of musical jump cut that accelerates the action. Hill says that this cutting pattern also evokes a "comic book style" that reflects the way individual panels capture the action in still frames, the motion simulated by the spaces between the isolated images, and largely supplied by the reader.[36] Each impact is aided by sound, which joins individual shots and aligns with the jarring, but never disorienting, edits: Raven swings his hammer down in one shot, and Tom blocks it with his handle; without the camera showing Raven's readjustment, in the next shot, he elbows Tom in the face, the crunch motivating the next cut; in it, Raven swings his hammer with an exaggerated whoosh, as Tom ducks out of the way; then, a cut to a swish pan of the crowd that whips by (and recalls the similar inserts of the subway train in *The Warriors*) without focusing on a single subject; and then, another shot of Raven swinging his hammer wildly with whooshing sound effects. The sounds, images, and edits work together to create a musical sequence of impact and near-misses, a rock and roll dance of drumbeats and cymbal crashes built out of the world itself—hammers thunk against concrete, shatter glass, clang into the elevated tracks' pillars, and crunch into a parked car. When the two men abandon their hammers in favor of their fists, there is a series of similar jump cuts, all taken from behind Cody and focusing on Raven, as he levies a combination of punches, each given their own shot. The music escalates, reaching a rock and roll high as Raven staggers back; The Richmond's residents start to cheer, as though a song were about to end, the final winding down of a band in live concert performance bringing a track to its drum-out conclusion. Tom walks up to the reeling Raven and gives him a soft shove, sending the biker to the ground, defeated, as Cooder's blues guitar riffs out, the crowd going into an appreciative frenzy.

The conclusion of the fight sequence gives way to the film's final concert, a transition bridged through editing that aligns violence and rock and roll using the language of cinema. The standoff is now over and Raven beaten, a tense moment between the bikers and The Richmond's teenagers comes in a series of three rhythmic cuts as the Richmonders cock their rifles in unison. Greer, now left to command The Bombers, takes three steps—another beat—and then disbands the gang: "Let's get outta here!" he shouts. The bikers roar out of town, and the soundtrack introduces one of the film's final songs, Winston

Figure 5.2 The climactic sledgehammer fight between Cody and Biker Raven (Willem Dafoe) features the film's total commitment to rock and roll aesthetic, with its edits carefully timed to coincide with the rhythmic blows dealt by the metal sledgehammers. *Source: Screenshot captured by author.*

Ford's "I Can Dream About You," performed in the movie by The Sorels, through its drumbeat; a cut to The Sorels, dancing in the dark on stage inside the theatre, begins the transition to the concert, but the film cuts back to the defeated Bombers hauling the unconscious Raven onto a jeep and heading out of The Richmond, each cut accompanying a drumbeat of the soul track—Raven's abandoned bike; The Sorels dancing in unison; a shot of the blazing neon marquee; a poster advertising Ellen Aim and The Attackers. Though Hill says he initially "wanted to end the film with 'I Can Dream About You,'"[37] the conventions of the musical genre allow for the double conclusion, with Ellen's subsequent performance of "Tonight Is What It Means to Be Young" a dramatic reclamation of a musical tradition, unapologetic in its defense of the power of rock and roll to bridge racial and class divides.

Streets of Fire fuses its action violence with the rhythm of rock and roll, a manifestation of the film's subject matter that acts as a passionate embodiment of the music itself. The spirit of rock and roll suffuses *Streets of Fire* because it appears in its every frame. It is the guiding principle that shapes the film's narrative, through its reliance on the iconography of rock and roll juvenile delinquent films, shared noir and western imagery, but also its style, in Hill's careful attention to the rhythms of editing and integration of sound effects and music that cover the breadth of rock and roll's history as a genre. For Hill, it is an artistic breakthrough that concludes the first phase of his career and ignites a more varied approach to cinematic style, narrative, and genre, which will characterize his cinema going forward. The transcendence of the film's final moments in the concert hall in this respect offer a parallel to the director's own transcendence—the musical genre liberates Hill from the action film. When he returns to it, he will bring a new point of view.

NOTES

1. David Desser, "When We See The Ocean, We Figure We're Home: From Ritual to Romance in The Warriors," 134.
2. Interview with the author, 26 January 2021.
3. Ibid.
4. David Ehrenstein and Bill Reed, *Rock on Film*, Delilah Books, 1982, 43.
5. Paul Schrader, *Schrader on Schrader & Other Writings: Revised Edition*. Ed. Kevin Jackson (Faber and Faber, 2004), 155.
6. Ibid.
7. Glenn Frankel, *The Searchers: The Making of an American Legend* (Bloomsbury, 2013), 309.
8. Borde and Chaumeton, 158.

9. Osteen, *Nightmare Alley: Film Noir and the American Dream* (Johns Hopkins University Press, 2013), 105.

10. Springsteen, "Thunder Road."

11. Thomas Doherty, *Teenagers and Teenpics: The Juvenilization of American Movies in the 1950s* (Temple University Press, 2002), 78.

12. Walter Hill, *Shotguns and Six-Strings: The Making of a Rock 'N' Roll Fable*, on *Streets of Fire* Blu-Ray, Shout Factory, 2014.

13. James Buhler and Mark Durrand, "Preface," in *Music in Action Film: Sounds Like Action!*, ed. James Buhler and Mark Durrand (Routledge, 2021), xviii.

14. Jennifer M. Bean, "Trauma Thrills: Notes on Early Action Cinema," in *Action and Adventure Cinema*, 17.

15. *Stop Making Sense*, the Talking Heads concert film directed by Jonathan Demme, premiered just a few months before *Streets of Fire* in 1984, and was drawn from the band's 1983 tour.

16. Ehrenstein and Reed, 76.

17. Doherty, 2.

18. Ibid, 35.

19. Ibid, 46.

20. Ehrenstein and Reed, 65.

21. Doherty, 58.

22. Ibid, 88.

23. Ibid, 37.

24. See his book *Horizons West*, 12.

25. Doherty, 40.

26. Ibid.

27. Interview with the author, 26 January 2021.

28. Yvonne Tasker, "Introduction," in *Action and Adventure Cinema*, 6.

29. Buhler and Durrand, xix.

30. Amanda Howell, *Popular Film Music and Masculinity in Action: A Different Tune* (Routledge, 2015), 38.

31. Ibid, 23.

32. Michael Baumgartner, "Underscoring Chased Heroes and Robbing Villains: Music of Immediacy in New Hollywood Action Thrillers of the late 1960s and 1970s," in *Music in Action Film: Sounds Like Action!*, 102.

33. Ibid, 105.

34. Ibid, 102.

35. Ibid, 107.

36. Interview with the author, 5 March 2021.

37. Ibid.

Chapter 6

Black versus White

The opening shot of the premiere episode of HBO's *Tales From the Crypt*, Walter Hill's "The Man Who Was Death," is taken from a low angle looking up at a Black man seated in a tightly framed prison cell, iron bars cluttering the frame in a collage of parallel and perpendicular lines. For pure composition's sake, it is one of the busiest tableaux of Hill's career as a director up to that point; though usually given to a restrained visual style indebted to the cool efficiency of Howard Hawks and Raoul Walsh, the generic shift to ironic horror of "The Man Who Was Death" cements a shift in visual approach that was unlocked by *Streets of Fire*—there, the introduction of the musical genre freed Hill to experiment with montage and sound as rarely before. This is not to say that Hill's visual style was simple or undeveloped; instead, he prized austerity as a stylistic value. *Streets of Fire* represents a pivot point that led to increased exploration of other methods; the results are plainly visible in the opening shot of "The Man Who Was Death," more German Expressionism than Classic Hollywood.

The Black man sitting in the cell is Charley Ledbetter (J. W. Smith), and a voice-over narration, equal parts macabre and cheerful, says that Charley is awaiting execution at midnight. The narration is performed by the star of "The Man Who Was Death," actor William Sadler, who portrays Niles Talbot, the state's executioner, who flips the switch on the electric chair every time the phone call announcing the governor's last-minute reprieve doesn't ring. After a cut into Charley in a medium close-up, which contains a stark shadow pattern of the bars cast across the wall behind him, Hill returns to the low angle that began the scene, dollying the camera slowly back, raking the extreme angle even more sharply as a reverend reads a prayer outside the cell and a pair of guards come to take Charley to his execution over his increasingly frantic objections. As soon as Charley is hustled out of frame, the camera continues to dolly back and finally tilts up dramatically as Talbot steps into the shot, looming over the frame like a gargoyle. A wide-angle lens on the camera, the image floats up to Talbot's head and shoulders, and Sadler looks directly into the lens, a smug grin on his face as he says, "I guess right about now old Charlie's startin' to think pretty serious about that valley of death." The effect is highly distorted, with the intersecting shadows of prison bars turning the ceiling into a nightmarish geometric pattern. Sadler's face is half in shadow, and he is barely backlit by a pair of hanging lamps, all while Charley's panicked screams drift over the soundtrack; Ry Cooder's carousel score takes on an undercurrent of heaping menace.

In a few moments, Talbot will throw the switch and send Charley to his state-sponsored great reward; throughout the episode, Talbot continues to address the audience directly, a confessional, conspiratorial secret between himself and the television viewer. The executioner likes his job, which makes it especially difficult when the death penalty is outlawed in the state of California and his position is eliminated; bereft, Talbot takes it upon himself to mete out justice on his own, electrocuting criminals he catches in the act. His crime spree is so horrible that it inspires a dramatic policy reversal, and he is apprehended by the police and becomes the first prisoner put to death in the electric chair he once operated; in his final moments, Talbot's swagger leaves him and he more overtly resembles the panicking, terrified Charley, who is certain that the governor will pardon him at any moment, a phone call that never comes. In Hill's hands, the episode is a stylistic playground: it marks the first appearance of Hill's use of wide-angle lenses in close-up, which would become common in his next several films; its direct-address narration is playful and menacing; its interplay of light and shadow creates a highly expressionistic world that not only sets the tone for the series, but lingers well into Hill's other work.

"It took a week to shoot it," says Sadler.[1] He describes a highly improvisational and creative set that played into Hill's general tendency to move fast and shoot quickly. For one of Talbot's first big monologues to camera, which appears in the final cut of the episode on a bridge above one of Los Angeles's many highways, Sadler recalls a snap decision: "We all pile in a van with Walter, and stop in the middle of this overpass above of the 405, jump out, set up the camera, and do one of the monologues with the highway going behind us. We didn't have permits. We didn't have anything. It was, 'All right, Bill, go!' Which is sort of his style, this guerilla thing. It was great."[2] For all of the efficiency of the run-and-gun production, the florid language that Talbot uses is a far cry from the austerity of *The Driver*. When Hill forms a partnership with an actor he respects, their creative language expands greatly—Sadler recalls Hill writing new pages for lines for him to say in between takes and on lunch breaks, his inspiration unlocked by the actor's command of the character. "He'd say, 'Bill, read this!' And I'd read it, and we'd both laugh, and an hour later, we're filming it."[3] In general, Hill prefers direct, but specific, lines of dialogue, and has since he began writing for the screen. Sadler thinks of him as a writer most of all: "He was a writer before he was an editor, before he was a director. He could put words in this character's mouth. I brought the character, and he said, 'Oh, I can write for that.'"[4]

In contrast to the austerity of many of Hill's other films as a writer and as a director, "The Man Who Was Death" offers an example of his exploration of a different extreme—a highly expressionistic approach to language, character, narrative, and above all, cinematic style. After the failure of *Streets of Fire*, Hill continued to explore other areas of cinema: the screwball comedy *Brewster's Millions* and the blues drama *Crossroads*, to mixed results. Before he returned to the action genre, they offered a glimpse of another kind of filmmaker, with a softer side, yet one still concerned with issues of wealth and race, which first overtly surfaced in *48 Hrs.* By contrast, Hill's debut *Hard Times*, a bareknuckle boxing film set in the Great Depression, shows a different kind of filmmaker—austere in visual style and in his writing; the highly expressionistic late feature *Undisputed*, another boxing film set in a maximum security federal penitentiary, is its opposite. *Hard Times* and *Undisputed*, made nearly thirty years apart, feature white and Black protagonists, respectively, with each fighting to maintain control over wealth and reputation; *Brewster's Millions* and *Crossroads* are likewise concerned with these issues of ownership, as the Black protagonist of the former suddenly inherits a ridiculous fortune from a long-lost white relative, and the uneasy blues partnership of the latter negotiates cultural propriety over a musical form that has both united and split white and Black musicians.

These disparate threads come together in *Trespass*, an updated take on *Treasure of the Sierra Madre* (1948, Huston) set in East St. Louis, which pits a pair of white Arkansas firefighters against a gang of Black drug dealers, with each staking an important claim to a seemingly worthless, but deceptively valuable, piece of territory: an abandoned warehouse that may contain buried gold. This collection of films, with its totalized balance of Black and white protagonists, explores the racial strife that divides Americans; in Hill's work, this strife is specifically tied to issues of ownership, wealth, and legacy, which are highly contested in *Hard Times*, *Undisputed*, *Brewster's Millions*, *Crossroads*, and *Trespass*. These films complicate the examination of these themes in the *48 Hrs.* movies, revealing the director's nearly career-long fascination with them.

Chapter 6

"LET'S BOX"

In the final scene of *Hard Times*, the charismatic hustler Speed (James Coburn) stands in a trainyard with his partner Poe (Strother Martin) and their bareknuckle boxer Chaney (Charles Bronson); they've come to the end of their relationship and, feeling the bittersweet emotions of parting, Speed says, "We've gotta say something." He wants to mark the occasion, to verbalize what these men have meant to each other throughout their association, which has been equal parts trying and remunerative. Chaney offers something less than half a smile, in keeping with his reserved manner, and walks off into the night, bound for northern parts unknown. The moment goes undescribed in dialogue, the connection between the three of them severed unceremoniously; however, in the absence of commemoration, the moment achieves greater poignancy. What good would words do? What would they mark? What could they say that a look couldn't? Speed, Poe, and Chaney already know. They don't need to say a word.

Hard Times also begins in a trainyard, the period setting of the 1930s instantly recognizable from the twangy score by Barry De Vorzon and the Depression-era imagery. The screenplay is credited to Hill, alongside Bryan Gindoff and Bruce Henstell, who also received story credit. Hill says that the main idea for the film was rooted in a story told to him by his paternal grandfather, "a wildcat oil guy" and "a driller" who "ended up with a couple of his own wells."[5] It was during his grandfather's time running a drilling crew that, while working on a job in the middle of nowhere and living in an ad hoc camp built to house the crew members, the regular boxing and gambling events that the workers held on Sundays was interrupted by the arrival of a strange man who rode into camp on the back of a work truck. After watching the half-organized boxing match, the stranger said, "Tell you what. You give me a place to sleep and feed me, and I'll fight, you can bet on me, and we'll split the winnings." Hill says that the stranger did not ask to be a part of the drilling crew, and would spend his idle hours mostly sitting around and reading, but come Sunday, "he would knock the shit out of whoever it was the other camp brought over." So the story goes, the stranger "did this for three or four weeks," making the workers who bet on him a tremendous amount of money, "and then they woke up one day, and he was gone." He never revealed his real name or anything about his background. Hill says, "My grandfather always assumed he was in trouble with the law. It was a reasonable hideout, he built up his resources and then moved on."[6] The inspiration for *Hard Times* is obvious—Bronson's Chaney is the stranger, with Hill keeping the mysterious nature of the character from his grandfather's story, along with, of course, the driving force of the film narrative: the money.

Despite his prolific career as a director, Hill considers himself "a writer first."[7] He began his screenwriting career with a pair of screenplays for *The Getaway* and *Hickey & Boggs*, both of which were released in 1972. Hill's arrival in the movie business coincides with the major shifts away from the remnants of the old studio system and toward the experimentation of New Hollywood; though these changes have been well documented by many writers, a great deal of the major figures of the period have tended to be its directors and actors, whose contributions to the New Hollywood cinema overlap with the simultaneous proliferation in film theory of auteurist and performance-based analysis. There has been less attention to the major shifts in New Hollywood in screenwriting practice—not only freed from the shackles of the Production Code, which allowed the creation of different kinds of images on screen, screenwriters working in the New Hollywood period were also able to situate their stories in profound ambiguity. Gone is the requirement to portray police in a positive light: enter Ernest Tidyman's screenplay for *The French Connection* (1971, Friedkin), which features a maniacal, racist, obsessive detective who mistakenly guns down a federal agent in the film's final moments and shows not even the slightest hint of remorse. Characters need not be punished for their misdeeds by death or law: the psychotic cabbie in Paul Schrader's screenplay for *Taxi Driver* (1976, Scorsese) is not only not punished for his killing spree at the end of the film, he is hailed by the newspapers as a hero and left to drive the streets of New York, a time bomb whose fuse has been relit. Characters likewise no longer required clear motivations: in Frank Pierson's screenplay for *Dog Day Afternoon* (1975, Lumet), a bank robber explains his reason for the attempted heist in obvious terms ("It's a bank. They got money here."), but really it is to pay for a sex change operation for his husband, who wants to become a woman. These three examples, culled from the screenplays for some of the most important films of the period, reveal how dramatically the New Hollywood screenwriters moved beyond the norms and conventions that dominated throughout the studio era, even as it began its decline in the 1950s.

Hill describes a sense of discontent with the conventions of screenwriting and both a strategic and tactical level—not only did he want to use the form to tell different kinds of stories, but he also wanted to tell them differently, and specifically expresses a desire to elevate the quality beyond that of the commonly held maxim that the script itself is little more than a blueprint: "I do believe they're a form of literature." He definitely knew what he didn't want to do, which he learned from reading screenplays that "always seemed to be mechanical. The dialogue seemed to be to be written in a very trite way." He offers an observation shared with him by the novelist, cultural critic, and sometimes screenwriter Gore Vidal, who pointed out over dinner that lines of dialogue too often seemed overtly directed at the characters: "Well, let me tell you, Tom," Hill says, laughing. At the time he was beginning his career, "there was still an enormous amount of that kind of writing." Screenwriting has changed for the better in his estimation, but Hill credits his generation of writers with shepherding that into being: "it was mainly because of a lot of people breaking the mold back in the '70s. You really can't emphasize enough how much that period changed things, and changed the point of view of those in control."[8]

The screenplay for *Hard Times* begins with a pair of epigraphs, a practice that dominates throughout Hill's writing career; his epigraphs always frame the remainder of the screenplays to follow, but the two that lead the *Hard Times* script might be taken to sum up the entirety of his filmography. They say: "After all, characters are best explained through their behavior," an oft-repeated maxim which he credits as an "Old Welsh saying," and in a kind of translation into stateside vernacular, "Talk's cheap," which he calls an "Old American saying."[9] Juxtaposing the two proverbs resonates with the film's themes—each epigraph says more or less the same thing, but their difference in tone pits the old world against the new world in anticipation of the bareknuckle boxing that will dominate *Hard Times*. The first page of the screenplay announces a specifically American viewpoint, a pithy two-word maxim that, by virtue of its indirection, suggests the value of action over language, but also situates that worldview in the context of monetary worth. The actual execution of the screenplay itself takes "Talk's cheap" as its guiding principle. Throughout, Hill's stage directions are brutally efficient, with specific images suggested through carefully selected description and precise verbs chosen to both move narrative and reveal character. The opening scene of *Hard Times*, as Chaney rides into Baton Rouge aboard a freight train, features this passage of setting detail: "TRAIN. [indent] Blast of steam. [indent] Cars slam against their couplings as the engine continues to decelerate."[10] There is a Hemingway-esque approach to the specificity of detail, with careful attention to the cinematic medium's stylistic conventions. The "blast of steam" suggests a sound effect that places the story in the authentic mechanism of the world; the "cars slam against their couplings" also manifest in the finished film through sound. Hill's written description of Chaney standing aboard the train, "the city of Baton Rouge sliding before him"[11] is given visual life in the film with a shot taken from behind Chaney as the location seems to slip past, gliding to the left side of the image.

The sparse approach to cinematic language reveals Hill's interest in direct images: he is always seeking the most efficient, workmanlike way to describe his setting details, but in so doing, achieves a kind of poetry in specificity. The same approach defines the characters' lines, which Hill suggests has long been his goal: "I always wanted to write terse dialogue."[12] The first official meeting between Speed and Chaney in the oyster bar, which comes after Chaney has observed Speed's fighter take a beating, not only recalls the story Hill tells about his grandfather's encounter with the mysterious fighter in the oil fields, but shows his written commitment to direct language. Speed notices Chaney sitting in the oyster bar and says, "You can start anytime, pal." The other man responds as directly as possible: "Chaney," he simply says. Another screenwriter might have included supporting language; it's easy to imagine the alternatives: "The name's Chaney"; "They call me Chaney"; "I'm Chaney." Hill doesn't include any—he trusts the simplicity, which reveals his character's reflexive instinct never to say more than he has to. The scene itself gets right down to business, with Speed hitting back: "So what," he says, a simple two words that suggests an entire attitude. The pair of words, somehow equally dismissive (you are not currently important to me, they say) and inviting (persuade me you are important to me), dramatize Speed's simultaneous disinterest and curiosity. Chaney quickly dispels any mystery by cutting directly to the chase: "We can make some money." He offers no preamble, no introduction, no small talk. He goes straight to business. The loquacious Speed respects the stoic Chaney's forthrightness: "Right. I'm all ears, friend," he replies.[13] This five-line exchange of dialogue appears largely unchanged in the finished film—Hill has allowed Coburn to eliminate two words from his first line, which the actor reads as "Start anytime, pal," making the line even more direct. Coburn also adds a "Well" before "I'm all ears, friend," which simply eases the transition between "Right" and the next sentence, but adds no real meaning.

This scene reveals a general trend that characterizes the dialogue throughout *Hard Times*—an emphasis on transaction. The general principles of Aristotelean drama foreground the transactional nature of dialogue; playwright and screenwriter David Mamet, known for his signature approach to spoken language, articulates his modern application of this approach as "What does the character want? What happens if he doesn't get it? And why now?"[14] Mamet's three questions say something to a degree universal about the nature of drama—that scenes use characters to move the overall narrative forward, especially in the theatre, which relies so heavily on dialogue to communicate all three. In *Hard Times*, these principles are taken to an extreme, as Hill's characters mostly participate in dialogue for the purposes of exchange; most of its scenes center on gambling, compensation, wealth, debt, costs, and speculation. Chaney's eventual agreement to partner with Speed on a regular basis is a financial negotiation, wherein Chaney takes a hard line, demanding 60 percent of the winnings; Speed's introduction of Poe hinges on Chaney's assent to give the erstwhile doctor a 10 percent cut; Speed's visit to gambler Chick Gandil (Michael McGuire) at a bathhouse sees the gambler and fight manager engaged in not one, but two transactions simultaneously, balancing his interests in a poker game with his laying out terms to Speed; later, Gandil's attempt to buy the rights to Chaney are undertaken in a matter-of-fact way, as he slides 5,000 dollars in an envelope across the table to Speed, certain that the other man will accept; Chaney's refusal to be bought leads Gandil to buy another fighter instead, setting up the final match for Speed's life. This is a small sampling of the film's scenes, but their consistency of theme reveals Hill's single-minded focus on the construction of a film gathered around rates of exchange. Chaney, Speed, Poe, Gandil, and all the film's other assorted gamblers, loan sharks, creditors, and fighters have their price—each scene finds them working toward it. Most individual scenes in *Hard Times* advance a specific goal, presenting a negotiation between two opposing parties who, whether through money or the violence of the bareknuckle boxing ring, work out the figures. In many boxing films, the physical body and money are incompatible, a zero-sum exchange that dictates the sacrifice of one in order to secure the other, which often results in destitution.

This conflict is also the subject of *Undisputed*, which saw Hill return to the boxing film more than twenty-five years after his directorial debut. Hill cowrote the film with frequent collaborator and co-producer David Giler; as its inspiration, Hill mentions the immediacy of *The China Syndrome* (1979, Bridges), which actually predated the nuclear accident at Three Mile Island by nine days, but nevertheless tapped into a rich vein of audience interest thanks to the historical moment.[15] Hill and Giler's desire to tell a story with contemporary resonance got them discussing the imprisonment of boxer Mike Tyson on rape charges, a case that sent the fighter to jail for three years in the prime of his career. Essentially, the idea for *Undisputed* came down to: "if you juxtaposed Mike Tyson being dropped into prison, where Sonny

Figure 6.1 Nearly every scene in Walter Hill's directorial debut, *Hard Times* (1975), is about commerce; small-time hustler Speed (James Coburn) tries to force a delinquent debtor to pay after his fighter Chaney (Charles Bronson) won a bareknuckle boxing match. *Source: Screenshot captured by author.*

Liston was the reigning tough guy."[16] Shot in the empty cell blocks of a real prison located outside Las Vegas, *Undisputed* offers a racial counterpoint to the ideas of wealth raised by *Hard Times*.

The film's Liston character is Monroe Hutchen (Wesley Snipes), the champion boxer with an undefeated record in Sweetwater Prison's special fight program; the film opens with his defeat of the Great White Supremacist Hope from another prison, a victory that is then followed by the TV appearance of *Undisputed*'s Tyson, George "Iceman" Chambers (Ving Rhames). From a directorial standpoint, *Undisputed* is a far cry from the austerity of *Hard Times*, which resonates with the images of The Great Depression during which it is set. Though they run a nearly identical ninety-three minutes, *Hard Times* is quiet and reserved, taking a cue from its central character Chaney; as played by Bronson, the hitter never says more than he has to and never raises his voice. By contrast, *Undisputed* is loud, fast, and frenetic in its pace, made up of short scenes that accelerate the narrative forward at a relentless pitch. *Hard Times* walks leisurely, but *Undisputed* sprints. The film's visual design favors busy, contested compositions that foreground the conflict between the characters: especially when Monroe and Chambers share a scene, Hill and cinematographer Lloyd Ahern tend to shoot over the shoulder of one fighter or the other to dramatize their struggle for dominance of the prison hierarchy. The camera is also highly mobile, featuring an extended Steadicam long take in the run-up to the final match that covers the entirety of the ring MC Marvin Bonds's (Ed Lover) introductions of the two men to the roaring crowd. Freeman Davies edits quickly, the cuts coming faster and more furiously than in the laidback *Hard Times*; he also uses crossfading consistently, overlaying images on top of one another that create yet another conflict, as the eye fights between two competing sets of visuals. The film also features heavily interventionist narrational strategies throughout, vacillating between color photography and black and white, while offering introductions of many of the prisoners; the effect produces a kind of mug shot, with a freeze frame in black and white, complete with superimposed text that gives each character's name, the crimes for which they were convicted, and the sentence they are serving. While *Hard Times* features De Vorzon's folky score that evokes the Depression, *Undisputed*'s soundtrack is full of numerous rap and hip-hop cuts, including "Souljas" and the pre-fight spin on the United States' National Anthem, both performed by Master P, who appears in a small role.

Working with Giler as his co-writer, Hill creates a film that, like *Hard Times* before it, positions its characters as men with something to gain and something to lose. What makes *Undisputed* distinct, of course, is that it focuses on two Black characters, making the film something of an outlier in the Hollywood of 2002, and even, to a certain degree, the Hollywood of 2022. Donald Bogle sums up the general state of Black characters in the

American movie business thusly: "Those who green light movies—enabling them to go into production—generally do not want a movie to be too black."[17] In their screenplay's foregrounding of two Black protagonists, who fight against one another for dominance of the environment they inhabit, Hill and Giler largely exclude hegemonic whiteness; neither Monroe nor Chambers fight for the approval of Meyer Lansky-inspired gangster Mendy Ripstein (Peter Falk), the other Mafiosi, or the prison's authority figures, but fight to find out, in the Hawksian sense, which of them is the best, a conflict raised by the film's title. As in *Hard Times*, however, money is also a significant factor: Chambers wants to secure his release from prison so he can get back in the ring and reclaim his title from a man he sees as a usurper, but the money is primarily his manager Yank's (Dayton Callie) concern. Monroe, on the other hand, cannot secure his release from prison and has no money on the line—he is incarcerated for murder and has no chance at parole—but can solidify his reputation as a superb boxer by defeating The Iceman, a fighter who outweighs him considerably. The disconnect between the Black fighters, who struggle for dominance primarily vested in their names, and the power structure around them, who place bets on the outcome, raises a central criticism of athletics in the United States: that powerful white owners profit by the physical labor of mostly Black and Latino men, whose bodies are bought and sold through commercial exchange.

Wesley Snipes's characterization of Monroe echoes the quiet, businesslike demeanor of Chaney in *Hard Times*. While in solitary confinement after the initial mess hall dustup with Chambers, Monroe meditatively builds a Japanese Buddhist Temple out of toothpicks, methodically gluing them together into a structure seemingly from nothing more than memory. When one of the prison's brass, Darlene Early (Amy Aquino), comes to interview Monroe, she apologizes for his time in solitary, but he doesn't seem to mind it: "It's okay in here," he tells her. "It's all a prison. I live inside my head." His specific task, gluing together a structure out of toothpicks, also recalls a similar preoccupation of Doc McCoy (Steve McQueen) in Hill's screenplay for *The Getaway*; likewise incarcerated at the outset of Peckinpah's film, McCoy passes the time by fashioning a bridge out of toothpicks. The film's credits sequence dramatizes McCoy's rejection for parole, with Peckinpah's montage editing capturing the deadening mundanity of prison life through emphasis on the mechanical operation of the jailhouse workshop where Doc spends his days. At one key moment after he is rejected, Doc sits in his cell gluing together his toothpick bridge, but suddenly turns white hot with rage, smashing it in fury. McCoy will soon suggest his wife Carol (Ali McGraw) visit a powerful man with influence over the parole board in an effort to secure his release, with the knowledge that Carol may have to sleep with the power broker in order to do it. His desperation contrasts mightily with Monroe's, whose work on his toothpick sculpture (he will spend the final moments of the film, when Chambers wins his televised match with the titleholder and regains his belt, gluing together a bridge identical to Doc's) correlates with the inner peace he has found. The screenplay for *The Getaway* portrays Doc as incapable of tolerating another day of his incarceration, but the depiction of Monroe offers the opposite—Hutchen can take it.

Throughout the scene with Early, Hutchen offers a defense of his own psychiatric makeup, which is the polar opposite of Chambers's yawning insecurities and performative bravado. Hutchen's outlook is more circumspect, without the driving need to be the champion:

> He's a fighter, I'm a fighter. If I'm better on that day, I win. That's just the way it goes. Someday every fighter loses. Sooner or later, somebody comes along and they got your ticket. Too old, just wasn't your day, whatever the reason is . . . in the end, everybody gets beat. Most you can hope for is that you stay on top awhile. Be the best.

By contrast, the volatile Chambers spends his first moments on screen trying to prove that he deserves his fearsome reputation as a worthy fighter. The few glimpses the film offers of Chambers's pre-incarceration time as a boxer take place at a press conference, in which he confidently asserts his supremacy over his next likely opponent, but also situates fighting, as do the boxers in *Hard Times*, in its financial context: "If the money's right, bring on Montel," The Iceman tells a reporter. When another suggests that the forthcoming match between Chambers and a challenger could net $300 million, Chambers's manager Yank offers a smug reply: "My guess is you're a few million short." The loss of his title, the loss of his financial remuneration, and the loss of his reputation make Chambers into an even more dangerous, desperate character; the rape accusations made against him by Tawnee Rawlins (Rose Rollins), are credible enough to get him convicted. Chambers defends himself throughout the film, insisting upon his innocence, but Hill and Giler's script carefully avoids taking sides; footage from a television interview with Rawlins show her clearly dealing with a kind of post-traumatic stress, tearfully relaying her side of the story, but does not spend a meaningful amount of time privileging her point of view—she appears only in the news broadcast. And yet, the film offers the opportunity to believe her, despite the male-oriented setting that places Chambers's version of events at its center—even though *Undisputed* dramatizes The Iceman's time behind bars and efforts to reclaim his title and reputation, it refuses to exonerate him for the crime he may have committed. The Iceman is far from the "respectability" image of Black athletes represented by Michael Jordan, Derek Jeter, and others, with Hill and Giler's script leaning heavily into Tyson's heel persona, which allows the film to critique various constructions of Black masculinity. According to Joshua Wright, "respectability countered negative stereotypes that held down the Black race. As a result, pioneering Black athletes were expected to conduct themselves with class. However, for some Black leaders, respectable behavior was not sufficient. They expected them to use their lofty platforms for the improvement of the African American community."[18] Chambers's eventual victory after his release is laden with irony, which prevents him from ascending to the respectability pantheon alongside Jordan and others. Not only is he not the undisputed champion (Monroe wins their match), but he is also possibly guilty of the crime for which he was serving time.

Hard Times and *Undisputed* both offer two kinds of scenes: negotiations (over rules, money, or power) and fights (both in the boxing ring and outside it). Midway through *Hard Times*, after Speed and company have secured enough money to set up a match between Chaney and Jim Henry (Robert Tessier), Gandil's bald brawler, the two men meet in an empty factory and trade blows before a screaming crowd in an improvised ring: a square of hard concrete surrounded by chain link fencing. Throughout *Hard Times*, the fights take place in a series of these kinds of spaces—a back alley, a dock, a lakefront field, an empty warehouse—that makes good on the itinerant iconography of The Great Depression, established in the film's opening and closing moments in the trainyard as Chaney arrives and departs. While Chaney and Henry exchange punches inside the steel cage, the crowd roars and rattles the fencing, each of the men with money riding on the outcome. The scene's staging exaggerates the fundamental principles of sport, which offers a display of the physical body for the entertainment of others; of all sports, boxing is the most extreme example. In *Undisputed*, Chambers makes this explicit when he tells the reporter Jim Lampley that "people play baseball. I'm a gladiator." In *Hard Times*, the camera occupies two separate vantage points: it steps inside the cage as Chaney and Henry box, lending part of the match an immersive feeling, but also stays outside the cage from a variety of points of view (extreme high angles looking down on the two men, shots through the fencing), which emphasizes spectatorship. In general, shots from inside the ring that feature the fighters and shots from outside that adopt the perspective of the crowd define the fight scenes in most boxing movies; the latter approach is an adaptation of a boxing film convention—instead of shooting through the ring's ropes, the camera's framing suggests that these working class men are trapped inside a cage that they cannot escape. The only way out is to prove themselves capable of horrific violence, acts undertaken for compensation.

The floating boxing matches of *Hard Times* turn working class spaces into improvised arenas where capital and violence meet. The prison setting of *Undisputed* takes the metaphor expressed by the cage match fight between

Chaney and Henry and universalizes it. As Monroe says to Early during their interview, "It's all a prison." The organized fights in Sweetwater Prison take place in the facility's converted gymnasium, which features an enormous cage with vertical bars lined with barbed wire at the top. As in *Hard Times*, an audience watches from all around the cage, but in *Undisputed*, the spectators are seated in bleachers, a formalized, professionalized systemization of the class dynamics that were a reflection of improvisation in the earlier film. Because both of the film's protagonists, as well as many of the supporting characters, are Black, the heavy emphasis on imagery of incarceration gives *Undisputed* an added racial dimension to the class politics it carries on from *Hard Times*. According to Ed Guerrero, "Mainstream commercial cinema of the 1980s concentrated on manipulating the audience's response and assent to its reassuring mediations of dominant social and political values," a dynamic that he applies especially to the decade's depiction of Black people.[19] Released in 2002—though hardly the halcyon days of Black representation on screen—*Undisputed* offers a critique of the white-controlled power structure that uses the Black body for its own amusement. Nearly all the film's authority figures are white. Ripstein is racially white, but as a Jewish prisoner, he occupies a kind of middle space; certainly he is powerful, but ultimately a prisoner just like the others in that his freedoms have been restricted, his identity subordinated to the carceral state.

Neither Monroe nor The Iceman are free. They are the playthings of a white power structure that seeks to use them for entertainment. As Chaney, Speed, and the other gamblers in *Hard Times* are trapped by the necessities of market capitalism, a critique accelerated by the film's Depression-era setting, the prisoners of *Undisputed* are double-bound: held in poverty by

Figure 6.2 The final boxing match in the prison-set *Undisputed* (2002) between Monroe Hutchen (Wesley Snipes) and George "Iceman" Chambers (Ving Rhames) takes place in a giant cage, a setting that literalizes the film's themes of exploitation and incarceration. *Source: Screenshot captured by author.*

their exclusion from society and by their race. Chambers's release from prison at the end of the film, which allows him to reenter the professional ring and fight the new champion for the title, seems like freedom. Certainly by contrast to Hutchen, who remains in his cell, Chambers is free to fight, earn money, and thereby restore a piece of his reputation by regaining the championship belt. However, the film's compounded ironies—Chambers didn't win, he is celebrated despite his crimes—suggest that little has really changed for him. As a prisoner, he fought to earn his freedom, but ultimately had to prove himself to others in order to secure it; as a free man, he still fights to earn their approval. That Monroe wins the prison match, but it does not earn him his freedom—it was never even at stake—offers yet another irony that speaks to the treacherous path walked by Black men in America, especially once they become cogs in the penitentiary machine. The film's portrayal of the interrelationship between the prison system and capital, with Black men's bodies as their most highly traded commodity, resonates with what Michelle Alexander calls "The New Jim Crow," a thesis that suggests the United States' institutionalization of Black men in an era of mass incarceration extends the legacy of slavery and the segregated south.[20] The repeated images throughout *Undisputed* of Hutchen and Chambers fighting behind bars provide a visual representation of the conditions under which Black men labor in America; much of the final fight is shot from inside the cage, but features far more shots from outside it than the similar sequence in *Hard Times*, emphasizing the thematic resonance provided by prison bars. Through the camera's lens, the prison becomes a microcosm of America: "It's all a prison," indeed.

Though they are separated by more than a quarter century and represent two vastly different stylistic approaches, the austere *Hard Times* and the brazen *Undisputed* demonstrate how Hill's work is suffused with political and racial ideas. *Hard Times* is set in the 1930s and focuses on the middle-aged Chaney, Speed, and Poe, men who have waged a lifelong battle against capital. Sometimes they win, sometimes they lose, but above all, the precarity they navigate takes its toll; to survive in America, they must fight, but each time they step in the ring, they earn more than a few permanent scars. The film's weariness is written all over the faces of Bronson, Coburn, and Martin, and its ponderous pace and quiet austerity stand in marked contrast to the 1930s-set *Bonnie and Clyde*, which announces its New Wave forebears through jagged montage editing. *Hard Times* is also notable for what isn't here—there are never any Peckinpah-esque flourishes of slow motion during the boxing scenes, despite Hill's prior work with the director and admiration of his films.

Undisputed features a return to the subject matter of *Hard Times*, but reveals how much Hill's visual style has changed; far beyond the enforced austerity of his debut, *Undisputed* is fast-paced and intense, but notable also for a kind of reservation of its own. Though the film is set in a prison, Hill resists the clichés of the genre: there is no escape subplot, nor does it openly confront the issue of rape, either as a plot device to humiliate his characters or as a ham-fisted joke, as is often the case in masculinist genres. The absence of these clichés makes *Undisputed* a lean, fleet interrogation of power dynamics among its characters, infused with racial consciousness; the film has much to say about the relationship among sports, capital, and incarceration, specifically concerning Black men.

GENERATIONAL WEALTH

After the financial failure of *Streets of Fire*, Hill's work moved in a different direction, as he stepped far away from the action films with which he was associated. Though *Streets of Fire*'s experimentation with genre hybridity and formal expressionism undoubtedly produced a creative breakthrough for Hill's art, its failure to find an audience left him feeling somewhat adrift. He responded by making two films that seem like outliers in his filmography. He says, "I saw that film as kind of coming at the end of a cycle. I thought that the next few movies I did, I was kind of in a sense taking some time off."[21] The direction of both, neither of them action films, seems a little listless, as if Hill himself is fighting against his own disinterest. The first was *Brewster's Millions*, a throwback screwball comedy inspired by a story that had been brought to the screen twice before. Hill's version, made in 1985, was the first to feature a Black actor in the role of Montgomery Brewster, with comedian Richard Pryor bringing his characteristic blend of manic energy and acerbic wit to the role. The mere presence of a Black man in the film, spending money like a drunken sailor, adds a racial dimension to the story that resonates powerfully against a prevailing sentiment in American culture in the 1980s that demonized so-called welfare queens for the dual sin of being poor and needing help.

Crossroads, Hill's follow-up to *Brewster's Millions*, is another apparent outlier; it also features no meaningful action or violence, but is a quiet, character-driven drama that shares a tonal similarity with *Hard Times*. A road movie focused on the legacy of blues music, the film is, like *Brewster's Millions*, not as much of a departure as it may seem on its surface. Both *Brewster's Millions* and *Crossroads* are concerned with ownership, wealth, and who gets to control it. *Brewster's Millions* literalizes this concept through the spend-a-fortune-get-a-fortune conceit of the narrative; the film's images of piles of money sitting in a bank vault, rapidly dwindling in montage, concretize a common theme in which the bankroll remains frustratingly out of reach: Reggie's half-million in a duffel bag, stuck in his car in a parking garage in *48 Hrs.*, or the promise of a windfall on the other side of a Chaney victory in *Hard Times*, or trapped behind a time-locked safe in Northfield, Minnesota in *The Long Riders*. In *Crossroads*, the wealth is cultural; the film's old bluesman, now wasting away spiritually in a New York City nursing home, has little more than his memories of youthful artistic virtuosity. His journey south to the Mississippi Delta, the birthplace of the blues, with his energetic white companion, is one of rediscovery of generational wealth—not financial, but racial.

Richard Pryor's appearance in *Brewster's Millions* is a logical extension of Hill's casting of Eddie Murphy in his first screen role in *48 Hrs.*, if less funny in the end result. Hill saw Pryor's potential to evoke the screen presence of William Powell, while costar John "Candy would take care of the broad comedy."[22] Pryor's confessional, confrontational, often incendiary standup comedy gave him a volatile, if often hilarious, reputation, that was only rarely matched in his film performances. His screen persona is more associated with the mixed-race buddy comedies he made with Gene Wilder—*Silver Streak* (1976, Hiller), *Stir Crazy* (1980, Poitier), *See No Evil, Hear No Evil* (1989, Hiller), and *Another You* (1991, Philips)—the first two of which, in their own way, anticipate what Hill does with Nolte and Murphy in the *48 Hrs.* films. Critic Ed Guerrero was skeptical of the Wilder/Pryor pairings, as he was of Murphy's work with Hill.[23] Of the comedies Pryor made with Wilder, *Silver Streak* is the most widely discussed, largely thanks to a scene in which, the two men, who are on the run from a crook who wants them dead, fashion an elaborate ploy to slip past the villain by painting Wilder's character in blackface; Pryor's Grover not only paints Wilder's face, but coaches him through the process of adopting cultural, performative Blackness that will help the subterfuge be more convincing. Donald Bogle argues that Pryor's presence throughout the film is essential to its success because he makes the film's world his own.[24] Bogle's assertion that Pryor's character moves through the white world without subordinating himself to them resonates with Murphy's belief about the success of *48 Hrs.*, in which Reggie not only openly challenges Jack's authority, but dictates the terms of their time together because he has information the cop doesn't.[25]

Throughout *Brewster's Millions*, Pryor's character performs a similar function. Brewster's chaotic approach to spending money, especially because he is a Black, poverty-stricken minor league baseball pitcher suddenly given $30 million to waste, exposes the entire class structure of the United States, rooted in white supremacy going back to the country's original sin of slavery, as illegitimate. Like Reggie Hammond before him, Brewster is suddenly set loose in a white man's world and upends it. Marking Pryor's transition into the middle phase of his career that includes *Brewster's Millions*, where the comic appears alongside mostly white people, Bogle generalizes: "it was also distressing for Pryor's fans to see the man who had once spoken for America's underclass now removed entirely from that class structure and often surrounded by white co-stars."[26] The world of wealth and privilege as presented in *Brewster's Millions*, but also in many American films, is one built on an immobile order, where procedure, manners, and hierarchy rule the day, ultimately perpetuating the unequal distribution of wealth. Brewster's sudden intrusion into the New York hoi polloi doesn't remove Pryor from the class structure, as Bogle suggests; his arrival heightens its contradictions. Albert Johnson sees both Pryor and Murphy in this light, with their chaotic intrusion into white space a foundational feature of their comedy: "Each actor represents an odd mixture of rebel-against-society, the Black man outrageously confronting social restrictions, and the vaudeville comic brought up to date."[27]

Pryor's comic persona is, according to Johnson, built on contradictions.[28] In *Brewster's Millions*, Pryor manifests this dichotomy throughout the narrative in performative choices, seemingly set adrift by a screenplay credited to Herschel Weingrod and Timothy Harris that is light on humor. Brewster's task, to waste more money than he has ever imagined at any point in his life so that he can secure an even greater fortune, is fundamentally contradictory, which informs Pryor's every movement and line reading. Charging out of the conference room where he has just seen the film starring his Uncle Rupert (Hume Cronyn, who is white!), and having agreed to the terms of the deal, Brewster is riven by his competing emotions. He races up to his best friend and catcher Spike (John Candy) and hugs him, then pulls back, reminding himself of the restraint necessary to win the money—he can't reveal the terms of the deal to anyone around him, even Spike. He talks a mile a minute, each line made up of a series of contradictions: "I'm gonna be a little crazy for a while, but I'm not crazy, but people are gonna think I'm crazy!" he shouts, despite his seeming effort to stop himself from shouting. Pryor's physicality bears evidence of the "nervous gestures and darting glances" that Johnson identifies,[29] as he constantly adjusts his feet, moves his arms wildly, and passes back and forth between direct eye contact with Spike and looking around the room at other people, as though he has no idea how to move his body or control his emotions. And yet, his choices are dictated by the need to do just that—control himself, keep quiet, and conceal the truth. He can't hide his exuberance in the following scenes in the bank vault, where he lays eyes on three piles of money—each made up of $10 million—for the first time, and then manically declines the bank manager's offer of interest on his fortune, which he knows will increase his wealth beyond the terms of the arrangement set out by his uncle's estate. When Angela objects that he will be leaving money on the table, Brewster utters a line drenched in irony: "Just because I'm rich doesn't mean I should take advantage of people!" The white, presumably wealthy bank manager, eager to grant Brewster an interest-free account, agrees with him immediately.

This populist sensibility is in the tradition of the late 1930s and early 1940s films of director Frank Capra, whose everymen heroes brought a healthy dose of good, old-fashioned common sense to bear against institutions of wealth and power. With *Brewster's Millions*, Hill saw the film as an opportunity to create a "comedic drama" in the mode of the films, like Capra's, that were popular in the 1930s and 1940s; in his estimation, the story of the film is very much indebted to Capra's films.[30] Hill did his usual amount of rewriting, specifically in adding the baseball narrative, which forms the basis of Brewster's character arc.[31] The presence of the baseball story grounds Brewster not only in a very specific slice of Americana, but also in Capra's *Meet John Doe* (1941) where Gary Cooper plays washed-up baseball player Long John Willoughby. Like Brewster, he wants to get his baseball career back after suffering a debilitating elbow injury, and he agrees to become a populist mouthpiece in exchange for financial help with a reparative surgery. Hill pays homage to *Meet John Doe* by restaging one of its hero's idle scenes in a luxury hotel, as both Willoughby and Brewster throw pitches from a makeshift mound; in both scenes, the working class baseball player transgresses the finely controlled spaces of wealth and power in New York City by transforming the lavish suite into a playground that reiterates their individualism. According to Ray Carney, "Capra's films gradually make imaginative space for energies of idealism and feeling that potentially bring into question all mere political, social, and practical arrangements."[32] *Brewster's Millions* includes a racial dimension that eluded Capra, given the context in which he was making films.

That context also produced the screwball comedy, many of which directly engage with the class issues of the decade spurred by the Depression. This modern update of the screwball formula, with its inclusion of a specifically racialized assault on the class structure, also revises the romantic narrative by giving Brewster a Black love interest in the accountant Angela. As in Capra's populist pictures, the initiated Angela acts as the guide for the fish out of water Brewster; both romantic leads, however, are Black, an unthinkable prospect in the late 1930s, but even still rare in the mid-1980s. Hill's casting of Lonette McKee as Angela is quietly transgressive, as he situates two Black actors inside the traditional screwball comedy narrative; she spends much of the film mystified by Brewster's profligacy and, charged with tallying up his receipts, lets her contempt for his carelessness build. The screenplay also gives Angela the most overt selection of class-conscious dialogue; in a confrontation in Brewster's hotel room after he has spent nearly all of his remaining fortune, she objects passionately to his seeming indifference to wasting his last $38,000 on a party: "How dare you. That's more money than a lot of hardworking people earn in a year. You better get your values together, because you're gonna need 'em," she says, storming out of Brewster's hotel room. Though Angela has herself sought to enter the world of wealth and privilege as a paralegal working for the law firm representing Brewster, she has not lost her working class roots—she knows that wealth is hard to come by, and takes great offense at Brewster's carelessness with his. They are only reunited in the film's final moments when they work together to outwit the crooked lawyers, including Angela's white fiancé, and protect Brewster's fortune from their attempt to swindle him; the too-abrupt conclusion of the movie nonetheless evokes the screwball comedy, with the intertwined financial stakes and romantic stakes of the narrative now settled. Its image of two Black characters, given space inside a narrative structure which they have rarely been permitted to enter, in which they secure wealth and romantic love, is exceedingly rare in mainstream Hollywood comedy of the 1980s, but remains so in contemporary cinema.

Hill's addition of Brewster's baseball aspirations also points the way forward to *Undisputed* in its depiction of Black athleticism as a vehicle for obtaining wealth. Unfortunately for Brewster, his dreams of baseball glory are little more than an illusion; he spends much of the early part of the film wearing a Chicago Cubs jersey, an old, beaten-up reminder of the brief moment he spent with that organization during his major league callup. The Cubs, of course, before their World Series victory in 2016 ended a championship drought that lasted more than a century, had a reputation as baseball's "loveable losers" who were always expected to come up short. Hill's choice to make Brewster a former Cubs pitcher, as opposed to the New York Yankees, a franchise associated with consistent success, is another of the film's sly acknowledgements of a history of racial inequity in the United States. Brewster is wearing this Cubs jersey in jail at the beginning of the film when his irascible minor league manager Charley (Jerry Orbach) comes to tell him that the team has decided to cut ties with both Brewster and Spike rather than pay their bail. He tells them that the team is going younger, focusing more on college draftees: "Look at this way, Brewster. You're lucky. You got to be a pro ballplayer for fifteen years. That's a lot more than most people get." Charley's wisdom anticipates what Monroe will tell the prison official Early during his solitary confinement interview in *Undisputed*, and tellingly comes in the same setting—behind bars, which come to signify the ways in which capital makes prisoners of all Americans, but especially Black men. Brewster himself comes around to this way of thinking after surrendering the grand slam to the Yankees in the exhibition game he organizes. Dejected, he returns to the locker room and sits in silence, wrestling with the ramifications of failure and the end of the line. He internalizes and repeats a variation of Charley's wisdom, however, to Angela in the hotel room before their argument: "It happens to everyone, sooner or later. It's the nature of the game." As a director, Hill seems more comfortable with Brewster's pathos than in the scenes built around broad comedy, which results in a strangely melancholic tone.

Brewster comes to understand what *Undisputed*'s Monroe already knows, and what The Iceman fears: because an athlete's body eventually betrays him, his ability to accumulate and then secure wealth is transient—especially for Black men. Aging is likewise the subject of *Crossroads*, with the athleticism of Brewster, *Hard Times*'s Chaney, and the twin boxers of *Undisputed* transferred to blues music. Like *48 Hrs.*, *Crossroads* sits uneasily with a number of critics, who find its narrative of Black bluesman Willie Brown (Joe Seneca) and his young, white traveling companion-cum-protégé Eugene Martino (Ralph Macchio) too accommodating of a white character's point of view, which, in their estimation, comes at the expense of the Black man and the cultural tradition he represents. According to Ed Guerrero, Hill "does well enough with the cultural ambience of the blues idiom; however, the moment at which Black culture is subordinated and, so to speak, put in its place, arrives in the film's narrative resolution."[33] Bogle is more charitable to *Crossroads* than to the *48 Hrs.* films, calling it "an intriguing but misbegotten study."[34] Some critics have dismissed *Crossroads* as what Adam Gussow calls "a southern-fried interracial buddy flick,"[35] an obvious attack given Hill's *48 Hrs.*, but Gussow defends the film against accusations that it "distorts its Black cultural materials in an egregious way, giving full flower to white blues romanticism."[36]

Like *Brewster's Millions*, *Crossroads* fits uneasily into the rest of Hill's filmography. Willie is fighting to save his soul from Scratch (Robert Judd), and the white Eugene is, like Willie before him, seeking an opportunity to define himself through blues music. The film belongs to Willie and Eugene both, mimicking the parallel structures of many of Hill's other films, including both *48 Hrs.* movies, *Southern Comfort*, and several of his partner movies (*Red Heat*, *Bullet to the Head*). Hill stages two important sequences in racially segregated bars, with Eugene and teen runaway Frances (Jami Gertz) cut loose in a redneck bar in the tradition of Torchy's in *48 Hrs.*, and the Black bar where Eugene joins Willie on stage an echo of the bar where Reggie hears Jack's apology. Its musical focus is also a logical continuation of the subject matter of *Streets of Fire*, though *Crossroads* is less overtly indebted to comic book style; it has a spare, workmanlike approach that not only takes Hill back to *Hard Times*, but mimics the austerity of blues music itself. Ry Cooder's musical score, for instance, is largely confined to the acoustic guitar, which echoes the Robert Johnson-era Delta blues music that drives much of the story, with the film "going electric" during the final duel between Eugene and Jack Butler (Steve Vai). Despite *Crossroads*'s relative stylistic reservation, it repeatedly mixes color film stock with sepia-toned flashbacks and dream sequences, which Hill would use as a major stylistic tool in many of his post-1990 films. *Crossroads* also contains some of the most surrealistic imagery of Hill's career to that point, culminating in a highly expressionistic nightmare late in the film. Willie tosses and turns in bed, and in black and white, sees Scratch's assistant (Joe Morton) open a door more than double his size (he reaches up to turn the knob), and stalk toward him down the hallway. The forced perspective effect created by the image becomes more confrontational as Scratch's assistant walks closer to the camera, looking directly into the lens as he warns Willie that, in an echo of Robert Johnson's track, "hellhounds are on your trail." The film rapidly cuts between the direct address close-up of Scratch's assistant and Willie himself, also looking into the lens in terror, an editing pattern that goes far beyond the rhythmic functionality of the action sequences in *Streets of Fire*. Here, the editing dramatizes the hypnotic, mystical hold that Scratch and his minions have over Willie—there is an inevitability to the oscillation, as if Willie cannot look away from the assistant, no matter how hard he wants to.

Thematically, *Crossroads* carries on the consistent preoccupation with wealth that defines much of Hill's work; though wealth in *Hard Times*, the *48 Hrs.* films, and *Brewster's Millions* is financial, *Crossroads* shares more with *Undisputed* in that the wealth its characters are trying to secure is less tangible. Both Monroe and The Iceman fought for reputation, and in *Crossroads*, Willie and Eugene negotiate over the legacy of the blues itself. Willie, the aging blues man who knows he is reaching the end of the line, decides to help Eugene take up the cause by carrying the music forward. In this formulation, the Black character possesses secret knowledge that the white character desires; not only does Eugene want Willie to help him find a missing Robert Johnson song, he also seeks instruction in the blues itself. Willie obliges by forcing Eugene to "hobo" through much of the South, cuts him loose in the redneck bar, and nurses him through heartbreak after Frances leaves without saying goodbye. This dynamic is the crux of most critical objections to the film—they see the drama subordinating the Black man's knowledge of the blues to the white man's adoption of it. This critique echoes anxieties raised by the commonly told story of the blues as a musical genre: beginning in the Mississippi Delta and developing out of slave spirituals, the blues evades mainstream penetration with white audiences even in its subsequent incarnation as a Chicago-driven, electric guitar and harmonica-powered style—that is, until a collection of white, mostly British musicians cover the songs on their early records and thereby launder the blues for white listeners. The British Invasion bands move on from directly recording cover versions of old blues tracks by Muddy Waters, Howlin' Wolf, and others, and more deeply merge their rock and roll aesthetic with blues riffs and wailing harmonicas. On The Rolling Stones' 1969 album *Let It Bleed*, they covered a newly rediscovered Robert Johnson song called "Love in Vain," a musical event that gets mentioned in *Crossroads*, when Eugene tells Willie that he wants to unearth the missing Robert Johnson song so he might cover it, as The Stones did.

The popularity of blues music, as interpreted by British Invasion rock stars, has led to accusations of cultural appropriation and, in some extreme cases, outright theft. Willie gives voice to this concern when he meets Eugene's delusions of Stones-inspired grandeur, "Just one more white boy rippin' off our music." Eugene objects, insisting that "we'd be giving it to the whole world." Willie is unconvinced, telling Eugene, "You don't deserve it. No mileage." Eugene is merely seventeen, and studies at Julliard—he has no life experience and is insulated from the sense of struggle and pain that the blues is meant to capture. In Willie's estimation, Black men own the blues, and the musical form becomes one more thing that white men have taken from them. Some critics have suggested that *Crossroads* acts as another site of cultural theft, dramatizing the process of white men's appropriation of a Black genre. Hill's other films offer a framework for reading *Crossroads* not as a dramatization of cultural appropriation, but as negotiation and transaction. As in *Hard Times*, the *48 Hrs.* films, and *Undisputed*, among others, Hill's characters negotiate their worth with their enemies, whether their opposition is economic, racial, or hierarchical. As in *48 Hrs.*, Willie and Eugene's trip to Mississippi is a business arrangement in which each character receives something in exchange: Willie gets a jailbreak and a ride South, and Eugene gets an education in the blues that he can't learn at Julliard. The film's "crossroads" are not merely evocative of the Robert Johnson legend, but the site of cultural and economic exchange where Willie and Eugene agree not only to trade with one another, but work together to save their souls from Scratch. Adam Gussow argues that this dynamic speaks to

> a specific mid-1980s moment when an increasingly mainstreamed American blues scene was struggling to navigate a racial crisis that was also an ethical and aesthetic crisis. The crossroads, in this sense, wasn't about devil-sponsored black magic, but about aging black blues masters and the younger men who would succeed them. As the face of the blues trended increasingly white, who owed what to whom? What were the music's core values, and what sort of transmission process would ensure that they remained vital?[37]

The film suggests that knowledge of history provides a possible answer to these questions. With a script by John Fusco, the film features a consistent awareness of the history of the blues as a musical form, represented by his staging of the fabled Robert Johnson deal-with-the-devil, a pseudo-origin story for the blues. *Crossroads* also features contributions from composer Ry Cooder, one of Hill's most important creative partners, who worked with Hill on eleven separate creative projects, beginning with his folky score for *The Long Riders* that established the Midwestern setting, carrying forward into the menacing guitar twang of *Southern Comfort*, and blossoming into a full-fledged partnership on *Streets of Fire*, where Cooder's music drives many of the sequences dramatically and stylistically. The American Cooder played on The Stones' version of "Love in Vain," and participated in a Stones-related side project (Mick Jagger, drummer Charlie Watts, and bassist Bill Wyman), the 1972 album *Jamming With Edward!*, which features six blues cuts, including "Blow With Ry." Though white, Cooder is steeped in blues music, which he has played throughout his career both as a session musician and film composer. When Eugene plays guitar in *Crossroads*, it's Cooder's overdubbing. Christopher J. Smith sees Cooder's contributions as essential to the film's approach to the blues, which is less interested in the heaviness of "mileage" and more so in the foot-stomping, head-nodding rhythm it creates: the film "portray[s] the reckless joy that the film seeks to find in the blues experience: music, dance, and a kind of gloomy celebration as the obverse of popular history's sense of the Delta's grinding daytime oppression."[38]

 The racial dynamics of the story were not lost on Hill when the screenplay came to him, with Ralph Macchio, fresh off *The Karate Kid* (1984, Avildsen), attached to star as Eugene. Though he liked Macchio as an actor, Hill suggested to the studio that the story "makes a lot more sense if you use a young Black man trying to stay in touch with the cultural origins of music that he's interested in."[39] The studio balked, Hill was forced to compromise, and the film went forward with Macchio as Eugene and, as is the case with *48 Hrs.*, became a story of negotiation between Hill's white and Black protagonists over ownership, power, and wealth. Upon reflection, Hill thinks that the movie is more interesting because of the racial disparity between Eugene and Willie; his initial concerns over a white character entering the world of the blues "made the movie smaller," but perhaps "more obviously honest."[40] The scene of Willie and Eugene, Black man and white man, playing the blues together on stage in the barn in front of Scratch's discerning audience, echoes the aspirational conclusion of *Streets of Fire*, with its images of an integrated tradition of musical form that transcends not just race, but offers a near-utopian vision of society. The duel sequence in *Crossroads* synthesizes the combat of the sledgehammer fight with the climactic musical numbers that follow it. Hill almost completely eschews dialogue for the duration of the sequence, which runs nearly ten minutes of screen time—in Scratch's barn, the instruments do the talking.

 Though the film's surface "buddy" structure has raised the hackles of a number of critics disinclined to read films that carry even a hint of *48 Hrs.*

charitably, the duel has received a substantial amount of attention for its apparent sidelining of Willie and Eugene's victory in the duel, which comes when he falls back on his classical guitar training at Julliard, playing Niccolo Paganini's "Caprice #5," which Jack Butler fails to mimic effectively. Ed Guerrero, though kinder to *Crossroads* than either of the *48 Hrs.* films, argues that the film's conclusion uses blues music and then summarily discards it.[41] Though complimentary of the film's embrace of the joy that the blues can bring, Christopher J. Smith sees the duel's resolution as one of its limitations.[42] But the duel portrays Butler's skill with the guitar as merely technical, rather than legitimately earned. Gussow describes Butler as "saddled not just with soulless machine-gun technique, but with a fey affect and a burlesque style that veer cartoonishly away from anything resembling established blues practice for signifying deep and earnestly conveyed emotion."[43] As in Hill's other duels, the audience is a crucial player; Eugene and Butler attempt to best one another with their guitars, but each plays for the approval of Scratch and his assembled spectators. The racial makeup of the crowd—entirely Black—speaks to Hill's conscious effort to mitigate the presence of his white protagonist. Only through proving himself to the Black crowd can Eugene protect his soul. The scene restages Eugene's performance in the Black bar earlier in the film; rejected from the white redneck bar, where his Long Island accent makes him as unwelcome as a Black man might be, he seeks refuge in the Black bar. He eventually earns the adulation of the crowd by accompanying Willie in a performance of "Willie Brown Blues," cowritten by Cooder and actor Joe Seneca, that gets the whole joint rocking. In both the Black bar and in Scratch's barn, Black audiences withhold their approval of white men until those white men prove themselves capable of capturing something honest. Though Eugene returns to the classical tradition of Paganini to defeat Butler, eschewing the blues, the myth of Paganini's Robert Johnson-esque deal with the devil expresses a kind of musical continuity between his classicism and the blues tradition. Music, like wealth, can be passed from generation to generation. Eugene, though white, earns the right to play the blues not by replacing Willie and other Black bluesmen, but by carrying forward their legacy with full knowledge of its origins.

"The duel is *good*," says Hill.[44] Like *Brewster's Millions*, *Crossroads* sits more comfortably inside Hill's filmography than it might seem at first glance. It is also a quieter, more contemplative film than the three-minute record approach of *Streets of Fire* or the occasionally inert screwball humor of *Brewster's Millions*, an austere throwback to the mood of *Hard Times*. Hill confesses that something about the film's script spoke to him when he received it. When he started circling the project, his father, whom he was quite close to, was sick with Parkinson's disease, and "it was clear that he was not going to last too much longer." Hill credits his father with instilling in him a lifelong admiration for music, and had "a great appreciation for jazz."[45] The story of *Crossroads*, with an older man trying to settle unfinished business while shepherding a younger man through his musical education, no doubt resonated with a filmmaker who was on the cusp of losing the man who had done the same for him.

LOOTERS

When the verdict in the trial of the four Los Angeles officers who had been videotaped severely beating Black motorist Rodney King was announced on Wednesday, April 29th, 1992, Walter Hill was in an ADR session with actor and rapper Ice-T, who had starred in Hill's latest film, then called "Looters," with a screenplay by Bob Gale and Robert Zemeckis. Of the Rodney King beating, Bogle argues that "no incident proved more disturbing or indicative of a country still beset by racial conflicts."[46] When Hill, Ice-T, and the sound engineers heard the verdict had been announced, Hill recalls, "Ice looked over at me and said, 'Don't go south of Pico tonight." When the film was more or less finished, Hill remembers a preview screening that made the audience very uncomfortable; he is frank about what the cause was: "the confrontation between Black and white. And it scared the studio to death."[47] In yet another compromise enforced by the studio, the film would be called *Trespass* after Universal balked at the original title in the aftermath of the Los Angeles riots, and coincides with a country living through a racial reckoning. It also offers the most intense distillation of Hill's career-long interest in the struggle for wealth waged between Black and white Americans. With a Hawksian premise that carries claustrophobic echoes of *Rio Bravo*, *Trespass* walks in the footsteps of *Treasure of the Sierra Madre* in its depiction of Americans' desperate chase for gold.

Trespass appears alongside several other films in what has most often been called the "hood film" cycle. Made up of a collection of films made in the early 1990s that focus primarily on the lives of young Black men who confront the challenges of urban life in America, including drugs and gangs, the hood cycle features the largest sustained group of Hollywood films by Black directors since the Blaxploitation period. Steve Neale argues that the hood films are a logical successor to the Blaxploitation films, given their urban settings and focus on crime.[48] For Valerie Smith, the hood films "reinscribed the conventions associated with their 1970s counterparts," the Blaxploitation films.[49] In particular, the hood films' focus on Black men often carries forth the images that became dominant during the Blaxploitation period, which include, according to Yvonne Tasker, "constructing the Black hero as a powerful figure, but also as hyper-(hetero)sexual and as very much part of an urban culture."⁵⁰ The hood films present their Black male heroes as inextricably tied to their environments: in some of the hood films, these heroes seek to control their surroundings by rising through the criminal underworld, and in others, the difficult circumstances of "ghetto life" threaten their lives and livelihoods, becoming overly determinative and foreclosing the possibility of "getting out." Ed Guerrero attributes the proliferation of these hood films to "a climate of long-muted Black frustration and anger over the worsening political and economic conditions that African Americans continue to endure in the nation's decaying urban centers."⁵¹ As was true of Blaxploitation films, the hood films are largely inconceivable without their urban settings (South Central Los Angeles, New York City, and more), cementing a connection in the cultural imagination between Black people and cities. Valerie Smith argues that they are inextricably linked:

> The idea of the urban has become virtually synonymous with notions of Blackness and blight in public discourse; markers of drug and gang culture, rather than those of indigenous or vernacular Black culture, have circulated and been read increasingly as signs of racial (and geographic) authenticity.⁵²

Many of the Blaxploitation films were directed by Black men, though not all; by the time of the hood cycle, nearly all of the films are directed by Black filmmakers, with predominantly Black crews. Hill's *Trespass* is basically the only hood film that is directed by a white man. Despite the presence of Ice-T and Ice Cube, who each appeared in a number of other canonically recognized hood films, *Trespass* has gained little critical attention. The narrative standoff that drives *Trespass* is not exclusively concerned with an "authentic" portrayal of the urban lives of Black men, but uses the action film genre to stage a race war in microcosm, depicting a battle between white rednecks and Black gangsters, each of whom are simply trying to find economic security in a deindustrialized America that ignores the travails of working people, regardless of their race. Hill sees the film's white firefighters and Black gangsters in primarily historical terms, more or less permanently locked out of wealth and power: "These are groups that have been in this country for three hundred years. The pure redneck and now urban Black but clearly with agricultural roots in the South."⁵³ The film interrogates the historical legacy of poverty, afflicting both working-class white people and the Black descendants of former slaves and refugees of Jim Crow, and lends a combustible temper to the screenplay's update of *Treasure of the Sierra Madre*, one of the most important of all American films, in which Humphrey Bogart stars as Fred C. Dobbs, an itinerant down-and-outer living in Mexico. He is introduced begging passersby for money so he can eat: "Stake a fellow American to a meal?" he pleads, filling his voice with shame, downcast eyes afraid to look his mark in the face. Partnered in poverty with fellow American

Curtin (Tim Holt), Dobbs gets the idea to dig for gold after overhearing an old man, Howard (Walter Huston), bragging about his previous finds during a night in a sweaty flophouse.

In *Trespass*, fireman Vince (Bill Paxton) tells Bradlee (Art Evans), the Black man living in the warehouse where he has come looking for gold, "We're just lookin' to get ahead like everybody else," a neat encapsulation of the zero-sum philosophy that governs wealth distribution in America. Vince is the film's Curtin, and his partner Don (William Sadler) is its Dobbs, driven by bitter resentments and insecurities, with an ex-wife he wants to keep from knowing about his share of the gold that he and Vince have traveled to East St. Louis to find. The film's locations in Atlanta, Georgia and Memphis, Tennessee, feature devastated factories and warehouses that chronicle the early stages of American deindustrialization. East St. Louis was a canary in the country's economic coal mine, and its Black residents, personified in the film by the gangsters who rule the territory where the warehouse still stands, were left to choke on the gas. King James (Ice-T), the leader, eschews the gangster label, repeatedly insisting that he is "a businessman." For much of *Trespass*, King James and fellow "businessmen" don't even know that they're fighting for hidden gold; they're simply trying to eliminate a potential threat, as Vince and Don have witnessed their murder of a rival gang leader. The disparity in knowledge that propels the film's standoff, with Vince and Don trapped in a single room on the fifth floor with James's brother Lucky (De'voreaux White) as a hostage, reveals how its Black gangsters see their environment. It has been so totally stripped of worth, so utterly left to ruin, that they do not consider that it could hold anything of value; James knows that building wealth requires violence in America, and he and his gang are starting from nothing. They have inherited nothing, have no generational wealth to pass down. His lieutenant Savon (Ice Cube) knows it, too—he sees James as weak and is eager to take over himself, yet another manifestation of the zero-sum idea that Vince uses to motivate his search for the gold. Both King James and Savon understand that wealth and power are conferred upon them by their control of territory in urban space, which William Covey attributes to Black men's exclusion from white spaces: "If the African American male could not be the CEO of a major corporation, he was able to be the 'king' of his neighborhood."[54] This dynamic is literalized in King James's self-adopted sobriquet, a declaration of his wealth and power. The narrative of *Trespass* seems to take place in isolation, with all innocent bystanders removed from the playing space—the result is an ironic vision of James's kingdom, which is made up of little more than some empty warehouses, broken windows, and piles of twisted scrap metal.

Though the abandoned factory initially does not yield the hidden gold, Don and Vince eventually discover it stashed in the ceiling. Trapped inside the building and surrounded by King James's men, they have no choice but to search for a way out. Don's increasing paranoia and greed deliberately parallel Dobbs's in *The Treasure of the Sierra Madre*, but Hill's film adds a dimension of racial resentment to Don's anger and terror. When Vince discovers heroin on Lucky's belt, Don bitterly says, "That figures." Don is equally offended by the presence of Bradlee; it is his space, because he has claimed it, where Vince and Don trespass. In an echo of Dobbs's pleas of poverty south of the border, Don complains about his own disadvantaged economic position—a mortgage on a house now occupied solely by his ex-wife, an apartment he now inhabits, and "taxes that get higher every fuckin' year just so that guys like him can keep eatin' without doin' any work." Bradlee becomes the familiar object of derision for embittered white working-class men. Bradlee, however, is the film's Howard—its conscience, its street-wise sage, and ultimately, its victor. *Trespass* likewise maps the fates of its major characters onto their equivalents in *The Treasure of the Sierra Madre*, with Don killed by King James in a shootout, and Vince and Bradlee both allowed to escape with their lives. However, the fate of the gold is quite different: in Huston's film, irony and wind send the gold dust, which looks more or less like ordinary sand in its unrefined form, scattered back to the mountains whence it came. In Hill's, Bradlee makes off with the gold, a sudden injection of wealth made possible by his willingness to invoke the threat of racially motivated reprisal against Vince; while Vince has made it out of the warehouse, set ablaze by Savon and the other gangsters, Bradlee warns him that he'd better get out of there "before them niggas catch you." Vince, though certainly more noble than Don, flees back to Arkansas and presumably, the safety afforded to him by whiteness. Vince has left without the wealth he sought, but keeps his life. Bradlee, who lived in the same room with the gold for years without knowing it was just above his head, laughs and carries the bag off into the night. He receives the same boon as Brewster, who secures his wealth and Angela, and *Crossroads*'s Willie Brown, who earns back his soul from Scratch with Eugene's help, free to continue his pursuit of the blues when the two set off for Chicago in the film's final scene.

Hill's films often stage negotiations over wealth and power between Black men and white society, whether represented by police officer Jack Cates in the *48 Hrs.* films, the law firm in *Brewster's Millions*, or the largely white authority figures of Sweetwater Prison in *Undisputed*. *Trespass* raises the stakes of these negotiations considerably, placing its Black gangsters and white firefighters in a life-and-death battle for control of the gold hidden in the warehouse's ceiling. While several of Hill's other films suggest the possibility of resolution, when the Black character can outwit (Reggie), outhustle (Brewster), or outplay (Monroe and The Iceman, Willie Brown) white authority, *Trespass* is far more apocalyptic in its outlook—it concludes with most of the Black gangsters shooting one another to death, along with the killing of Don, in the fiery warehouse. As a genre film, *Trespass* is largely free from the demands of authenticity that shape so many of the other hood films that surround it. It is under little obligation to present urban Black life "as it really is" (perhaps an impossible task for a white director, anyway), clearing the way for a more mythic approach that recalls *The Warriors* and *Southern Comfort*, which each exaggerated their characters' environments for larger thematic purpose. Hill has often had a skeptical vision of racial reconciliation, but *Trespass* sees him at his most cynical on the subject.

Stylistically, *Trespass* bears evidence of Hill's post–*Streets of Fire* interest in film form, but his choices are infused with racial import. As *Crossroads* mixed color film stock with sepia-toned flashbacks and dream sequences, Hill *Trespass* features grainy video footage integrated into the narrative. The film opens on videotape, a handheld camera capturing the murder for which King James and his men will seek revenge on the warehouse roof; it is also diegetically motivated, as Video (T. E. Russell), one of King James's gang, shoots their exploits for posterity. A number of their scenes are shot on videotape, as King James struggles to maintain his authority in the face of challenges from Savon, another echo of the unstable leadership of *The Warriors*. Hill's use of video footage originated in a news article that he read in which a gang had been convicted of criminal activity partially on the basis of evidence that they themselves had created—video of their misdeeds. Though cinematographer Lloyd Ahern (working with Hill as director of photography for the first of many subsequent

Figure 6.3 The claustrophobic thriller *Trespass* (1992) stages a race war in microcosm. White Arkansas firefighter Don (William Sadler) holds Black gangster Lucky (De'voreaux White) hostage while he and his partner Vince (Bill Paxton) search an empty warehouse for gold. *Source: Screenshot captured by author.*

collaborations) and the editors were skeptical, Hill insisted that the video footage itself should appear in the film, and entire scenes should be constructed around it.[55] That film form should rhyme so forcefully with then-contemporary social events—the video footage of the beating of Rodney King—makes *Trespass* a vital example of the hood film cycle because, as in the actual criminal case, it dramatizes America of 1992 as a racial powder keg. Though in Hill's words the decision to use the footage was "a historical accident" that "nobody ever believes was done before Rodney King," its presence in *Trespass* makes it one of the first cinematic intersection of Blackness and amateur video; technological developments that led to the ubiquity of cell phone cameras in the 2010s saw not only a rise in visibility of police violence against unarmed Black men, but also in cinematic depictions of it through techniques articulated in *Trespass*. Films as varied as *Fruitvale Station* (2013, Coogler), *The Hate U Give* (2018, Tillman Jr.), *Monsters and Men* (2018, Green), and *Spiral: From the Book of Saw* (2021, Bousman) all feature the use of video footage of a police killing of a Black man as a crucial plot element, oscillating between the film image and the diegetically-created video of the assault.

Both as a screenwriter and as a director working from other writers' scripts, Walter Hill shows a consistent interest in the relationship between wealth and race. He is attracted to characters who fight on that battlefield. In Hill's films, the Black characters struggle to prove they are good enough in a country that has historically been hostile to them. As a screenwriter, his work is grounded thematically in issues of wealth, class, race, and history, shaped by a distinctly American point of view that is reserved but specific. *Trespass*'s William Sadler says Hill has "an economy of words both as a writer and as a director. He could say things in as few words as possible, but often with a kind of gallows humor,"[56] a sensibility clearly evident from his directorial debut, *Hard Times*. A vision of the past, the Great Depression, as filtered through a reflective imagination that avoids the trappings of nostalgia while acknowledging the simplicity of the slower pace of life of a bygone era, the screenplay for *Hard Times* establishes a template that will define much of Hill's filmography, despite his later, experimentation with genre and expressionistic style. As Sadler sees it, Hill's work shows that he is "a student of the westerns. He always feels like a man out of place and time."[57]

NOTES

1. William Sadler, interview with the author, 22 February 2021.
2. Ibid.
3. Ibid.
4. Ibid.

5. Walter Hill, interview with the author, 5 February 2021.
6. Ibid.
7. Walter Hill, interview with the author, 26 January 2021.
8. Hill, interview with the author, 5 February 2021.
9. Walter Hill, Screenplay for *Hard Times*, front material.
10. Ibid, 1.
11. Ibid.
12. Interview with the author, 5 February 2021.
13. Hill, screenplay for *Hard Times*, 7.
14. David Mamet, *On Directing Film*, Penguin Books, 1991, xv.
15. Hill, interview with the author, 7 May 2021.
16. Ibid.
17. Donald Bogle, *Toms, Coons, Mulattoes, Mammies, and Bucks*, 400.
18. Joshua Wright, "Be Like Mike?: The Black Athlete's Dilemma," *Spectrum: A Journal on Black Men* 4, no. 2 (2016), 8.
19. Ed Guerrero, *Framing Blackness: The African American Image in Film*, 116.
20. Michelle Alexander, *The New Jim Crow* (New Press, 2010).
21. Hill, interview with the author, 5 March 2021.
22. Interview with the author, 5 March 2021.
23. Guerrero, 126.
24. Bogle, 238.
25. I quoted Murphy's framing of Reggie's function in the narrative of *48 Hrs.*, shared with Marc Maron on the WTF Podcast, in Chapter 4.
26. Bogle, 253.
27. Albert Johnson, "Moods Indigo: A Long View," *Film Quarterly* 44, no. 2 (1990), 13.
28. Ibid, 14.
29. Ibid.
30. Interview with the author, 5 March 2021.
31. Ibid.
32. Ray Carney, *American Vision: The Films of Frank Capra* (Wesleyan University Press, 1986), 4.
33. Guerrero, 134.
34. Bogle, 262.
35. Adam Gussow, "'I Got a Big White Fella From Memphis Made a Deal With Me;' Black Men, White Boys, and the Anxieties of Blues Postmodernity in Walter Hill's *Crossroads* (1986)," *Arkansas Review: A Journal of Delta Studies* 46, no. 2 (August 2015), 85.
36. Ibid, 86.
37. Ibid, 100.
38. Christopher J. Smith, "Papa Legba and the Liminal Spaces of the Blues: Roots Music in Deep South Film," in *American Cinema and the Southern Imaginary*, ed. Deborah E. Barker and Kathryn McKee (University of Georgia Press, 2011), 322.
39. Interview with the author, 5 March 2021.
40. Ibid.

41. Guerrero, 134.
42. Smith, 323.
43. Gussow, 90.
44. Interview with the author, 5 March 2021.
45. Ibid.
46. Bogle, 294.
47. Interview with the author, 26 March 2021.
48. Steve Neale, "Westerns and Gangster Films since the 1970s," in Genre and Contemporary Hollywood, 39.
49. Valerie Smith, "Introduction," in *Representing Blackness*, 3.
50. Yvonne Tasker, *Spectacular Bodies*, 37.
51. Guerrero, 159.
52. Smith, 2–3.
53. Interview with the author, 26 March 2021.
54. William Covey, "The Genre Don't Know Where It Came From: African American Neo-Noir Since the 1960s," *Journal of Film and Video* 55, no. 2/3 (2003), 64.
55. Interview with the author, 26 March 2021.
56. Interview with the author, 22 February 2021.
57. Ibid.

Chapter 7

Last Men Standing

Early in *Undisputed*, the newly incarcerated heavyweight champion George "The Iceman" Chambers (Ving Rhames) asks his cellmate Mingo Pace (Wes Studi), "Since we gonna be stuck together, what you in here for?" Mingo, still tentative about the new arrival, cautiously warns Chambers that questions like this are impolitic in prison: "You know, champ, I don't mean to be telling you what to do or anything, but it's not considered polite to ask why we're here. Kind of a violation of the ethics, you know? The code." Mingo's carefully worded instructions to Chambers, as written by Walter Hill and David Giler, embody an observation of the director's about the code of the West: "In the American West, you were never supposed to ask somebody, when you met a stranger, where they were from. Because the assumption was that in many cases, they were running from something. In many cases, the law."[1] The dusty, wind-blown, sun-drenched prison yard likewise lends the scene a kind of western flair; so too does the name of the facility, dubbed "Sweetwater" in the film, a moniker shared by western towns throughout the genre. Though a prison-set boxing film featuring a hip-hop soundtrack, *Undisputed* demonstrates how thoroughly the conventions, iconography, themes, and mythos of the western genre suffuse Hill's work. Even in the most unlikely places, the western animates his films.

Though the creative success of *The Long Riders* in 1980 would cement Hill's reputation as a filmmaker, Hill would not make another traditional western until 1993's *Geronimo: An American Legend*. As if unleashed from the action genre in which he most often works, Hill made more westerns: *Wild Bill* in 1995, then *Last Man Standing* in 1996, directing the pilot for HBO's *Deadwood* in 2004, and then the television miniseries *Broken Trail* for AMC in 2006. Ironically, Hill comes to prominence as a filmmaker at the moment when westerns were beginning a so-far irreversible decline, in defiance of prevailing economic trends in the movie business. He admires the genre perhaps more than any other director of his New Hollywood generation and has presided over its transition into the action film. According to Eric Lichtenfeld, the heroes of classic westerns, and especially their highly skilled gunfighters "would be urban vigilantes. Mythologically, the filmmakers align urban vigilantism with western heroism and individuality."[2] Though not a vigilante in the same mold as the architect-turned-killer in *Death Wish* (1974, Winner), *48 Hrs.*'s Jack Cates steps outside the law to bring the criminal Albert Ganz to justice. In the final shootout sequence, Jack approaches Ganz in an alley while the villain holds Jack's partner, the convict Reggie Hammond hostage. The gunfight at high noon, a convention of so many westerns, is transplanted to the back alleys of San Francisco's Chinatown. Jack in stands in silhouette, framed in a long shot that aligns the officer, his gun held at his right thigh, with the environment—like the gunfighter of the western, this man uses the pistol to negotiate between his surroundings and those who would challenge it. With steely reserve, Jack approaches Ganz, and flatly says, "You're not gonna make it." Jack quick draws, a sudden movement underlined by a smash cut that interrupts Ganz's lines of dialogue, and a thunderous gunshot that echoes through the alley. Ganz charges Jack, who cuts him down, the villain's death captured in slow motion. The long silence that follows, stretching across a series of images—a reaction shot of the shaken Reggie, Ganz's lifeless, bullet-riddled body, and the emotionless Jack in close-up, his hair lightly blowing in the wind—offers a moment of reflection that seems to transform the alley into a quiet western thoroughfare, which violence, for the moment at least, has preserved.

Nearly all of Hill's films are built on a western foundation; he explains the appeal of the genre thusly:

> I think the best thing about westerns for me is that you're just telling stories that are very primal, and that kind of hearken back. I always say that western film reference shouldn't always be so much about westerns themselves, but how they fit into a much larger, Old Testament tradition. And when you're making a western, a great degree, you're walking around in Old Testament kind of storytelling.[3]

No one understood this better, of course, than the deeply Catholic John Ford, whose westerns reverberate through cinema history. Though their mythological function is well-articulated by numerous genre theorists, westerns also perform a historical role, depicting another time, another place in mythological terms. The 164-minute epic *How the West Was Won* (1962), which brought together frequent western directors Ford, Henry Hathaway, and George Marshall for five stories, offers a paean to the genre's historical authority, asserting its authenticity through its commitment to fifty years of

American lore. Intoning over sweeping shots of the American West in the film's final moments, narrator Spencer Tracy offers this historical homily:

> The west that was won by its pioneers, settlers, adventurers is long gone now. Yet it is theirs forever, for they left tracks in history that will never be eroded by wind or rain—
> never plowed under by tractors, never buried in a compost of events. Out of the hard simplicity of their lives, out of their vitality, of their hopes and sorrows, grew legends of courage and pride to inspire their children and their children's children. From soil enriched by their blood, out of their fever to explore and build, came lakes where once there were burning deserts—came the goods of the earth; mine and wheat fields, orchards and great lumber mills. All the sinews of a growing country. Out of their rude settlements, their trading posts came cities to rank among the great ones of the world. All the heritage of a people free to dream, free to act, free to mold their own destiny.

Though the epic *Heaven's Gate* (1980, Cimino), based on the historical Johnson County War and one of the most revisionist of so-called revisionist westerns, is often wrongly blamed with bringing about both the end of the genre and the New Hollywood period, it offers a countermyth to films like *How the West Was Won*, telling a story of cruel, capitalist predation that, when perpetrated by the powerful, crushes the poor, working people, immigrants, and anyone who dares deviate from America's present, but rarely acknowledged, class hierarchy. In exaggerating and dramatizing history to serve a cynical myth, rather than a hopeful one, director Michael Cimino ran afoul of the traditional path blazed by the western. Then contemporary history also likely contributed to its catastrophic box office failure; Jeanine Basinger blames the divisive Vietnam War.[4]

The westerns of Walter Hill collect several of the genre's varying traditions. Though undoubtedly informed by the history of the American West, both real and mythological, Hill's films are also a continuation of the several manifestations of the western genre's evolution, and, in contrast to the pure revisionists who are his rough contemporaries (Altman, Cimino, Penn), blend a classical and revisionist approach. As in *The Long Riders*, Hill's other westerns both uphold and revise the genre's conventions. *Geronimo: An American Legend* offers a grounded, ensemble approach to the Apache Wars that neither centralizes the Indian nor the Indian Fighter; *Wild Bill* is a deeply personal, psychologically tortured examination of a real-life figure that recalls the heroes of Anthony Mann, each reckoning with a history of violence; the miniseries *Broken Trail* stages a cattle drive (though the livestock are horses), foregrounding issues of capital and ownership; and *Last Man Standing*, Hill's adaptation of Kurosawa's *Yojimbo* (1961), transplants the story of the samurai and Sergio Leone's gunfighter to the Texas border in the Prohibition era, fusing western iconography with that of the gangster film to produce a distinctly American take on the material that hearkens back to Dashiell Hammett's source novel. Hill's westerns foreground his career-long interest in the genre's themes and conventions, which populate his many films; his work in the western genre not only interrogates its history but its mythological representation of American history.

THE GERONIMO WAR

Perhaps no Native American historical figure has been more represented on screen than Geronimo, a Chiricahua Apache warrior who waged a violent campaign in the American Southwest against the American cavalry before he was eventually displaced to Florida, where he lived on a reservation until his death in 1909. His threatening presence is invoked in *Stagecoach*, but he is given no characterization; he is seemingly the basis for Massai (Burt Lancaster) in *Apache* (1954, Aldrich) the last holdout against forced displacement; he likewise inspires the titular Apache of *Ulzana's Raid*, his violence unvarnished but given narrative justification in his vengeance for the brutality perpetrated upon his people and family by the cavalry. According to Michael Walker, Geronimo was

> the most notoriously hostile and intransigent of the Native American leaders resisting White oppression, and cinematically, in a whole series of subsequent westerns, right up to the present. Indeed, Geronimo has captured the imagination of filmmakers over the years far more effectively than Cochise, a comment on the dominant view in westerns of the Native American: the title of the latest film about him—*Geronimo: An American Legend* (Walter Hill, 1994)—emphasizing the potency of his image.[5]

The film's title does suggest the centralizing of Geronimo, but it was not Hill's preferred name—he wanted to call the film "The Geronimo War," in an effort to declare the film's epic scope, which would tell the story of the violence that pitted the U.S. Cavalry against Geronimo's Chiricahua through a historical frame, but was overruled by Columbia, the studio financing the film.[6]

Geronimo fuses the sensibility of the Indian western, which in its 1950s form sought to centralize the plight of the Indian by lamenting his martyrdom, with the Cavalry westerns of John Ford—chiefly, *Fort Apache* (1948), *She Wore a Yellow Ribbon* (1949), and *Rio Grande* (1950), which generally embrace the imperialist framework of Manifest Destiny that displaced indigenous people. Throughout Ford's cavalry westerns, the Indians are less individuated characters and more representative of an idea; for Ford, they are an obstacle to the construction of a peaceful, harmonious society. In Ford's *My Darling Clementine* (1946), Wyatt Earp (Henry Fonda), just arrived in Tombstone, exiles the drunken Indian Charlie (Charles Stevens), yelling "Get out of town, you drunken Indian!", clearing the way for Earp's adoption of the Marshal's badge and eventual slaying of the villainous cattle rustlers, the Clantons, which makes Tombstone safe for churches, schools, and the white Clementine (Cathy Downs) of the title, who will presumably safeguard both in his absence. Though scenes of this general ideological import are common in Ford, this moment in *My Darling Clementine* encapsulates Richard Maltby's observation that "in the confrontation between savagery and civilization which is at the heart of the frontier myth, the 'Indian' has been cast as the savage."[7] Indian Charlie, whose drunken unruliness makes the streets unsafe—he is wildly firing off a gun when Wyatt gets the drop on him—must be expelled.

Because the symbolic Indian is often little more than a reflection of white culture, most Indian westerns feature a white protagonist who witnesses or aids the Indian character. *Broken Arrow* (1950, Daves), for instance, focuses on the journey of the white Tom Jeffords (James Stewart), whose friendship with Cochise (Jeff Chandler) is the primary vehicle through which spectators achieve empathy for the Apache chief. Armando Jose Prats sees in this narrative structure a general tendency to render the Indian invisible, which is central to the western genre's creation of history: "The Hollywood western never produced an Indian antagonist more memorable, or more familiar, than the one whom we never quite see."[8] Ford's *Stagecoach* (1939) features a thrilling chase through Monument Valley, as the titular conveyance is set upon by a horde of trilling Indians; Geronimo and his band of Apache warriors are introduced like ghosts, appearing out of thin air and waiting to strike the coach at its most vulnerable moment. The Apaches are given no spoken lines—they exist merely as a threat of violence, death, rape, and mutilation, a menace inseparable from the land itself. The Indian westerns of the 1950s aimed to correct these images by deepening characterization and offering sympathy in place of terror.[9] For Prats, the Indian western "deploys its strategies and methodologies, its historical claims and cultural assumptions, in order to transform its figure of the Indian into the many forms that leave only the Indian's trace."[10] The result is that the Indian is more an idea than a real person or a representation of a historical figure, even in the Indian westerns. The character "Geronimo" in particular exemplifies this trend early on in Ford's *Stagecoach*, in which "the mere name Geronimo stands for savage menace itself," and despite being "disconnected alike from action or intention—nonetheless ripples through the first scene to strike terror in the hearts of the white characters."[11] By the time of the Indian westerns like *Broken Arrow* and *Apache*, however, "revisionism may render the Indian noble where myth rendered him savage, but the one is no less a distillation of dubious origin and ambiguous motive than is the other."[12] The filtration of the Indian through the white character's point of view parallels the approach taken by other social problem dramas of the 1950s, including those that focus on racial conflict; the Indian westerns at least in part offer a thinly veiled allegory for the brewing fights over civil rights. This is also the approach taken by *Dances With Wolves* (1990, Costner), in which Cavalryman Lieutenant John Dunbar (Kevin Costner) comes to understand the Sioux people by living with them; its title makes the point, as "Dances With Wolves" is the name given to Dunbar by the Sioux people, emphasizing the white protagonist as the person to whom the film really belongs.

As many mistakenly view Cates as the protagonist of *48 Hrs.*, with Reggie relegated to the buddy/sidekick role, the formal structure of *Geronimo* invites a similar misreading. The studio-imposed title partially contributes to the confusion—because the film bears the Apache warrior's name, it seems to promise a biopic, in contrast to Hill's intention to tell something more akin to a war story that examines multiple players in the military campaign. However, the cards for several other performers precede "and Wes Studi as Geronimo" in the film's credits sequence. And though Jason Patric is billed first, it would be difficult to call his mercurial Lt. Gatewood the film's protagonist; General Crook (Gene Hackman) exits the narrative early upon his resignation from the Cavalry; Scout Al Sieber (Robert Duvall) is wounded midway through and then killed before the final rendezvous; Geronimo's presence is likewise fleeting, moving in and out of the narrative as both legend and character, which sometimes keeps him frustratingly remote; Lt. Britton Davis (Matt Damon) offers the film's voice-over narration, but is too passive and inexperienced to truly be its main character. The film's point of view is fractured; it withholds identification with a single character in favor of telling a broader, historically minded story about the entirety of the U.S. Cavalry's campaign against Geronimo. Thus, the film's focus is constantly shifting from one character to another, with Davis's voice-over as the anchor point.

As a technique, voice-over in the Indian western has earned considerable criticism as a formal embodiment of the subgenre's limited point of view. *Dances With Wolves* also uses voice-over, in which Dunbar relays his increasing sympathy for the Sioux people. Of the elderly Ten Bears (Floyd "Red Crow" Westerman), Dunbar says in voice-over,

> I pushed him as far as I could to move the camp. But in the end, he only smiled and talked of simple pleasures. He reminded me that at his age, a good fire was better than anything. Ten Bears was an extraordinary man.

The narration situates Ten Bears's character in relationship to Dunbar's personal growth; it centers what Dunbar learns from Ten Bears, reminding him to focus on "simple pleasures," wisdom that presumably helps him in the undefined present, when he narrates. According to Prats, films like *Dances With Wolves* "deploy the white character's voiceover in order to praise the virtues of both the natives and the lone white man who, having befriended them, comes to admire them and, at times, becomes 'one of them.'"[13] The temporal space of narration is also significant, as Dunbar survives, while the indigenous people don't. These Indian westerns complete the erasure of the Indian from the historical narrative, because the "voiceover almost invariably adopts the past tense and thus already presupposes the Indian's disappearance."[14] Because Dunbar adopts the name "Dances With Wolves," the film can be said to dramatize the white hero's replacement of the Indian; the Sioux will be eliminated by history, with only sensitive and understanding white men left to carry forward their memory.

Geronimo may seem to follow the same trajectory, grounding the narrative in the white officer Davis's voice-over narration, which opens, appears throughout, and closes the film. Many Indian westerns preach understanding, which can be built between tolerant white men and noble Indians; in *Geronimo*, the struggle animates the drama rather than the progression to an already agreed-upon, didactic conclusion. Thus, the point of view conferred upon a white man by Davis's voice-over narration conflicts with the film's first visible icon: Geronimo's accusatory stare, roaring out of the long-dead past, is aimed directly at the audience in an audaciously confrontational image. A parlay between Crook and Geronimo midway through embodies the conflict that the film seeks to dramatize. Sitting at Geronimo's level, Crook says, "The army's the best friend the Chiricahua ever had. You know it, and I know it." Unconvinced by Crook's certainty, Geronimo replies: "With all this land, why is there no room for the Apache? Why does the White-Eye want all land?" Crook has no answer—he wipes his sweating brow and looks away. The two men, who do share a respectful understanding, occupy irreconcilable positions: Crook sees the army's gestures as magnanimous and noble, but Geronimo's instinctive understanding of the imperialist credo of Manifest Destiny imbues him with the scene's moral authority. Though Crook's basic respect for Geronimo distinguishes him from the unapologetically duplicitous General Miles (Kevin Tighe) who will replace him, he is hamstrung by his military service; because he believes he has acted nobly, he cannot conceive that the army itself has failed to do so. The scene is propelled by its ideological contradictions, not its clarity, animated by characters who struggle against one another, each believing themselves to be right. Throughout Hill's work, point of view is contested, often shared among groups of characters rather than grounded in one protagonist; the dual protagonist structure of the *48 Hrs.*

movies, *Southern Comfort*, and the partner films like *Red Heat* and *Bullet to the Head*, along with the group focus of *The Warriors*, *The Long Riders*, and *Trespass* reveal a director who is often driven by a Hawksian interest in how people work together—more often in Hill's films, how they fail to do so.

Geronimo is much closer to Hill's dual-protagonist and group films than an Indian western like *Dances With Wolves*, where Dunbar is the central focus; though Davis narrates the film, he is not its protagonist. His character's inexperience and naiveté recall a consistent type who appears in the Indian western, including the young Lieutenant DeBuin (Bruce Davison) in *Ulzana's Raid*. Davis has humility and respect for Geronimo and the Chiricahua, unlike another of his cinematic forebears, Col. Owen Thursday (Henry Fonda) in *Fort Apache*, a Custer-figure whose contempt for the Chiricahua not only alienates him from many of the men under his command, but leads to a slaughter in which he loses his own life, obviously modeled on the Battle of Little Big Horn. The film's conclusion is notable for the rewriting of Thursday's actions, portrayed as foolhardy and reckless, into heroism by his subordinate, Lt. Kirby York (John Wayne), who disagreed vehemently with his superior; when reporters gathered in York's office at the fort in the film's final scenes ask York to confirm Thursday's heroic actions, he immediately replies, "Correct in every detail!" though he, and the audience, know better. However, Ford plays the scene straight, closing the gap between the reality of Thursday's foolish stand against the Apache and the myth that has been crafted out of it; York has told lies in service of the Cavalry's greater mission, which is to make the West safe for building "civilization," a paradise not unlike the one that comes to Tombstone at the end of *My Darling Clementine*. The final images of *Fort Apache*, in which the fort's women stand on the ramparts and watch their men ride out in a column, attempt to resolve the ironic contradictions raised by York's knowing lie; his fiction about Thursday's "honorable" death motivates the continued waging of the campaign against the Chiricahua.

Inevitably, a film like *Geronimo* must contend with the titanic legacy of Ford's westerns; its shooting locations in Monument Valley firmly situate the film in Ford Country, and the images of Cavalrymen fighting with Apache warriors in the rocky desert amongst the mesas and buttes echo Ford's cavalry westerns in particular. As in many of his other films, Ford's Irish roots led him to examine the ways in which the Cavalry serves as a melting pot in which immigrants of various backgrounds can learn to get along. In *Fort Apache*, a drunken brawl amongst the Cavalrymen led by the Irish Sergeant Mulcahy (Victor McLaglen) ultimately whips the new recruits into shape; in *She Wore a Yellow Ribbon*, the wounds of the Civil War are healed when former Yankee Captain Nathan Brittles (John Wayne) and the erstwhile Confederate Sergeant Tyree (Ben Johnson) agree that Robert E. Lee ought to be included among a group of great Americans; *Rio Grande* even attempts to integrate the unit's Navajo scout, Son of Many Mules, into the American experiment when he is decorated alongside several of the Cavalry's troopers who distinguish themselves during the battle against the Apache across the Southern border in Mexico. Taken together, Jim Kitses argues that "the overarching theme of the trilogy's films is the question of leadership's proper sphere, the relationship of authority and its boundaries, the dialectics of ends and means."[15] *Geronimo* balances the point of view scales, paying attention to Geronimo's methods of and motivations for waging war against the Cavalrymen; in addition to his critique of Crook's execution of the Manifest Destiny idea, Geronimo resists the military's efforts to make the Chiricahua into corn farmers, especially given the inhospitable desert conditions that make growing a sufficient crop impossible. He tolerates the limitations of the reservation until the Cavalry's unforgivable execution of Apache holy man The Dreamer, who wants the soldiers to leave because, subtitles inform us, "the dead chiefs will not rise if you are here." Ultimately, the Cavalry's unwillingness to understand the Apaches' way of life leads to chaos, as the military unit misinterprets The Dreamer's prayer as a threat, and they open fire.

Revisionist westerns have a confrontational, often deconstructive agenda; weary of the myths offered by classical westerns, the revisionists seek to replace them with their opposite. Where classic westerns offered resolution, revisionist westerns supply mostly irresolution; if the classicists believed in the American story, the revisionists saw it as a fraud. Though Hill's westerns belong to the era of the revisionist western, he believes in the genre too much to let his films drift openly into such flagrant cynicism. Instead, his westerns intensify the experience of classic westerns, or they offer a dramatic corrective rooted in history. This is much the approach that he takes in *Geronimo*, which cannot truly be called a revisionist take on Ford's Cavalry westerns, but both an intensification of and corrective to their most basic assumptions. Hill's references to Ford's westerns do not offer a replacement myth, as revisionist westerns do, but gesture more overtly towards lived history. When Ford's Cavalrymen gather in formation at their forts, he often uses the scenes for cornball humor. In *Geronimo*, the Cavalrymen assemble in formation to watch Geronimo ride into the fort at San Carlos on his horse, having tentatively agreed to surrender. In voice-over, Davis comments on the ceremony of the event, a preoccupation of Ford's, introducing an element of self-conscious theatricality and pageantry that lends the momentary surrender of the Apache warrior a historical significance which Davis calls "no small event." Later, the gathered Cavalrymen also line up in formation to bear witness to the execution of three Apache as retribution for Geronimo's killing of a group of miners. As in the conclusion of *Fort Apache*, the

Cavalrymen are joined by their wives, mothers, and children, who all gather to watch the hanging in a morbid counterpoint to the ritualistic dance that symbolizes white society's building of the West in *Fort Apache*. Their final words, shouted in their own language, are shared with the spectator through subtitling, but withheld from the gathered soldiers and their families, who do not speak it, another way in which Hill deliberately creates tension through fractured point of view. In showing the hanging of the three Apache as a community spectacle, Hill includes what Ford often leaves out—that white society's conquest of the American West came at a terrible cost.

Geronimo is also replete with references to Ford's *The Searchers*, which, though not a cavalry western, is one of the director's most significant explorations of relations between white society and Indians. The film's Comanche chief Scar (Henry Brandon) evokes the historical Geronimo, but his violence is more personal than political. After the crucial offscreen sequence in *The Searchers* where Scar's Comanches raid the Edwards ranch, kill most of its residents, and abduct young Debbie (Lana Wood, then Natalie Wood), crazed and racist Uncle Ethan sets out to find her, accompanied by a group of deputies. While riding in pursuit of Scar, the white men ride through a shallow valley surrounded by sand dunes; suddenly, the Comanche appear on either side of them, with Ethan cautioning the men to ride slowly so as not to draw an attack. Knowing the assault is coming either way, the white men make a break for it, and the chase is on; Ford carefully builds tension by placing the Comanche on the hill and the white men in the valley, just as he did when he reveals Geronimo watching over the passing buggy in *Stagecoach*. In *Geronimo*, the attack never comes; instead, a single Apache warrior rides ahead to challenge Gatewood alone, who trots his horse out to meet him. Only when the Apache fires his pistol into the air and charges does Gatewood defend himself, using his horse as a barricade and firing from behind it. In substituting a scene of one-on-one combat for the attacking column of Indians, Hill invites reconsideration of the dividing lines by revising the genre's images; first, there is a familiar scenic setup, then a corrective that centralizes the conflict in the actions of individuals. Neither the Apache warriors nor the Cavalry act as a unit, but give way to the whims of individual members who choose to fight—though Gatewood seems willing to give the Chiricahua warrior a chance to turn back until the last possible moment.

Gatewood is similar in characterization to *Fort Apache*'s York; he respects and knows the Apache and shares an understanding with Geronimo, reluctant to use force. When the quartet of trackers happen upon the Yaqui massacre south of the border, Gatewood is sickened to the point of rage, demanding that scout Chato (Steve Reevis) lead them in the direction of the bounty hunters. Though Gatewood turns to violence against Apache as a last resort, his eagerness to punish the bounty hunters is evident in his contempt for their brutal methods. When their leader, Schoonover (Stephen McHattie) threatens Chato, Gatewood defends the Apache scout by putting his own life on the line, inciting the gunfight that will claim Sieber's life. Gatewood shoots first, blasting Schoonover in the throat before the villain has a chance to draw his gun, a sudden act of vengeance imbued with personal hatred. After the dust settles and Sieber lies bleeding to death against the bar, he says, "I never thought I'd get killed tryin' to save an Apache." Sieber respects the Apache, but mostly sees their violence; "Save the last bullet for yourself," he tells Davis, "'cause you don't want to get taken alive," repeating a common maxim in the western genre that appears both in dialogue and in scenes, as in the gambler Hatfield's (John Carradine) pistol creeping into the frame against the head of Lucy Mallory (Louise Platt) in *Stagecoach*, or the sudden, graphic suicide of a Cavalryman set upon by Chiricahua in *Ulzana's Raid*. Gatewood, on the other hand, sees their humanity. In this respect, he is more like *Broken Arrow*'s Tom Jeffords or *Dances With Wolves*'s Dunbar, but he is under no illusions about becoming one of the Apache himself; Gatewood's humane treatment of the Apache does not sanctify him, but makes him an outlier among the military's power structure. Crook and Sieber claim to respect the Chiricahua, but not enough to overcome either the mission or their prejudices against them. Gatewood, on the other hand, does not believe in the military campaign, and plays his part in it reluctantly. As Sieber contemptuously tells Gatewood, "You don't love who you're fighting for, and you don't hate who you're fighting against."

Gatewood's misanthropy leads to his exile at the end of the film, like *The Searchers*'s Ethan, unable to enter the home after securing Debbie's return. While Ethan's exile is punishment for his antisocial, racist, maniacal behavior throughout the seven-year pursuit of Debbie, Gatewood's sin is his recognition of the Apaches' basic humanity. After securing Geronimo's surrender, Gatewood is given an obscure post by General Miles, whose offer of land to the Apaches if they lay down their arms is cynical: "I don't believe the government intends to keep this promise," Gatewood tells Miles, who reminds him that his only job is to make the offer. Davis describes Gatewood's fate in voice-over, a long shot watching his horse "ride away," as in the chorus of the song that concludes *The Searchers*. Once Gatewood's horse exits the frame (traveling in the same direction, screen right, as Ethan at the end of Ford's film), the action shifts to the outpost at San Carlos, an over-the-shoulder shot of Davis standing on the porch of the General's office. The next shot comes from inside the office, shooting through the doorway with the mesas of Monument Valley looming in the sun-streaked background. This image deliberately recalls the opening and closing images of *The Searchers*, which begins and ends inside the darkness of the homestead, looking out onto Monument Valley in the distance. The final shot of *The Searchers*, in which Ethan stands alone outside the home and the community which has left him behind, laments the incompatibility of such a brutal man with the changing culture of the American West. The composition of the shot evokes *The Searchers*, but the military's Apache scouts stand in Ethan's place; in this scene, the Cavalry will enact its final humiliation of the Chiricahua who served in the military, tracking and interpreting their fellow Apache, regarded as traitors to their people, by stripping them of their ranks and sentencing them to exile in Florida, where they will live on the reservation with Geronimo. For their sacrifice, the military rewards them with further subjugation, a betrayal of a litany of promises. *Geronimo*'s reversal of *The Searchers* in this moment shifts identification: instead of mourning Ethan's exile, it bears witness to what was taken from the Apache.

The stripping of Chato's rank and taking of his weapon is the most impactful moment of the scene; in close-up, Chato tells the faceless officer who grabs his rifle, "This is not right. I'm Sergeant Chato. The scout." The officer, in an echo of Crook's inability to answer Geronimo's challenge of his unquestioning pursuit of Manifest Destiny, does not say a word. He, like Crook, carries out his orders without larger consideration of the morality (or lack thereof) of his actions. As elsewhere in *Geronimo*, the scene's point of view is contested; there are over-the-shoulder shots of Davis, watching the humiliation of the scouts, which completes his journey of disillusionment with the army, but the camera also lingers on the stunned Chato while the officers continue to collect other Apaches' weapons. Chato enumerates his regrets to Geronimo in their final scene together, riding in the train car that ferries them to Florida: "You were right to fight the White-Eye," Chato

Figure 7.1 One of the many references to *The Searchers* (1956, Ford) in Hill's *Geronimo: An American Legend* (1993) comes at a moment of historical shame for the U.S. Cavalry, as they strip Apache scouts of their ranks and discharge them from service. *Source*: Screenshot captured by author.

says. "Everything they said to me was a lie." In *Fort Apache*, lies serve the Cavalry's agenda, with Thursday's foolishness rewritten as heroism to motivate the remaining men to continue the fight against the Apache; *Geronimo* is disgusted with such lies, tracing their destructive ramifications on the few noble members of the military and the Chiricahua alike. If Ford's films ultimately affirm that the lie, reframed as "the legend" in *The Man Who Shot Liberty Valance* (1962), created the conditions for American ideals to take root in the West, then Hill's *Geronimo* looks unflinchingly at the consequences of that lie. It is this rage that radiates from Geronimo in the film's opening credits, staring out of the past, directly into the camera lens with a potent reminder of the lies that history has told about the fate of the Chiricahua.

MANN'S MAN

After Geronimo goes to live on the Turkey Creek reservation, Gatewood comes to visit him. Dissatisfied with reservation life, not only due to its harsh, unforgiving conditions, but personally, Geronimo says, "I am not good farmer, Gatewood." The film cuts from Geronimo's close-up to a series of black-and-white images that recall the quick montage of Willie Brown's nightmare in *Crossroads*: Geronimo's horse rushes across the desert; feathered headdresses flit through the frame; a hand brandishing a pistol fires into a man's back; a woman cries, and the camera darts up to the accusatory glance of Geronimo, staring into the camera once again, as his still image does in the film's opening credits. The black-and-white images suggest Geronimo's existence has been shaped irrevocably by the violence done to him and by him. In rejecting his new life as a farmer, he recalls the moments of terror that shaped him, the violence done to his family that he repaid in kind. The violent Geronimo of the flashback stares not only at the audience, but at the reluctantly pacified Geronimo of the present. Hill's use of black-and-white in this brief moment in *Geronimo* not only recalls his use of video footage in *Trespass*, but anticipates his blending of the two techniques throughout *Wild Bill*. While the historical action of his biopic of James Butler "Wild Bill" Hickok (Jeff Bridges) moves forward inexorably toward his killing at the hands of Jack McCall (David Arquette), the film flashes back to black-and-white video footage that marks the gunfighter's history of violence. Drawn from a play by author Thomas Babe called "Fathers and Sons," along with a few elements from Pete Dexter's novel *Deadwood*, Hill's version of *Wild Bill* gave the director a chance to explore a historical figure who had always interested him: "of the legends of the West, he's the one who's really closest to the real, who lives up to the legend."[16] Throughout

Wild Bill, Hill engages in two seemingly contradictory efforts: to reinforce the myth of Hickok, while simultaneously deconstructing it.

Wild Bill is also notable for its more overtly autobiographical implications, a stark change of pace for a director whose filmography is usually more opaque; Hill contends that his "ideas are usually a little more disguised," but in *Wild Bill*, "there is a deeper ongoing psychological concern than I usually am comfortable with."[17] In Hill's estimation, the film is much more "an essay or a meditation"[18] than a straightforward narrative. If so, what is he meditating on? During the making of Hill's neo-noir *Johnny Handsome* (1989), actor Lance Henriksen turned to the director during a break and, seeking guidance on his performance, asked him about the dark glasses he was always wearing. According to Henriksen, Hill said, "I have astigmatism and bright light really hurts my eyes." Henriksen was embarrassed to have asked.[19] Hill's habit of wearing dark glasses was a product of consistent eye troubles that led to a series of operations, Hill says.[20] Needless to say, the difficulty of eye problems would pose a near-existential threat not only to a film director's career, but his or her very identity, in which the eyes are essential to imagining, composing, and evaluating shots. So too, of course, does the western gunfighter; after the film's cold open, which begins at Hickok's funeral, Hickok is introduced squinting in a handheld mirror, preparing to perform a trick shot, picking off a shot glass from its resting place on top of a bulldog's head, firing over his own shoulder. This early image establishes a number of the film's thematic concerns and visual tropes, centering the relationship between vision and gunfire. Hickok is literally framing a reflective image of the clueless bulldog, a visual that recalls the work of a film director. He completes the shot (without killing the dog) and is cheered by the saloon patrons as "A Walter Hill Film" appears on the screen.

Hill's primary concern throughout his career in action has been in staging sequences of violence that propel the narrative forward. Though *Wild Bill* contains a number of action sequences of gun violence (many of them in its first act, offered as a sort of extended montage), its primary concern is the ramifications of that violence on Hickok as a character. Hill says, "I wanted to show how he had become a prisoner of the legend."[21] To this end, he relied on a mixture of historical fact and exaggeration: "My intention with Hickok was to use factual" incidents, but there is some "enlargement of the factual" throughout the film.[22] In navigating the complexity of a historical figure whose exploits have contributed to the western genre, the most mythical of all Hollywood products, *Wild Bill* presents "the statement of the legend and the debunking of the legend simultaneously."[23] Hill is preceded in this effort by the western films of Anthony Mann starring James Stewart, many of which were similar meditations on the history of violence that Stewart's characters must come to terms with throughout the film. In the Mann westerns, Stewart's characters are haunted by their pasts and torn apart by the violence they must commit. According to Jim Kitses,

> As if possessed, these men push ahead completely at the mercy of forces within themselves. Whether demonic or divine, the vessels of a vision or a disturbance, they have little hope of the settled relationships within which most men live. Typically, they are driven to sacrifice or reject the complex ties of family and society; often, they are usurpers.[24]

As played by Stewart, these dark heroes represented a deeper, more complex manifestation of the western sheriff or gunfighter, who wrestled with the consequences of his actions. According to Dennis Bingham, "Stewart's performances in the Mann westerns undermine the power of the western protagonist."[25] In these films, Douglas Pye argues Stewart plays "men trapped within and struggling to escape a narrow, stifling, traditional definition of masculinity,"[26] as they struggle to navigate "a nightmare of psychological trauma, violence and hysteria."[27]

These assessments of Mann's films might equally apply to *Wild Bill*, which introduces the character by way of a series of violent confrontations between Hickok and various challengers, all of whom are mercilessly gunned down. Mann's *The Man From Laramie* finds Stewart's Will Lockhart on a quest for retributive vengeance, as he hunts the man responsible for his brother's death; killed in a raid by Apaches bearing repeating rifles sold to them by a white man, Lockhart is driven by the violence that has shaped his past. Hints about his backstory reveal him to be, like Hickok, a former Union soldier who knows how to handle a gun. During his investigation, Lockhart finds himself at odds with Dave Waggoman (Alex Nicol), the volatile son of cattle baron Alec (Donald Crisp), and during a shootout, a bullet from Lockhart's gun catches his opponent in the hand. Dave's ranch hands grab Lockhart and hold him still while he fires a bullet through Lockhart's palm at point blank range, a direct manifestation of cyclical violence. Slights, humiliations, and melodramatic contests over women motivate Hickok's gunfights in *Wild Bill*; he punishes several men for the crime of touching his hat, a violation of his personal honor, and his killing of Dave Tutt (Robert Knott), rooted in history,[28] comes after the man has stolen his watch and taken up with his former lover Susannah Moore (Diane Lane). Both *The Man From Laramie* and *Wild Bill* explicitly connect violent reprisal to a man's loss of public face. Early in Mann's film, Lockhart is humiliated for the first time by Dave, whose men burn his wagons, kill his mules, and drag him by lasso through the raging flames, an embarrassment which begins Lockhart's conflict with the Waggomans. In *Wild Bill*, a wheelchair-bound Will Plummer (Bruce Dern) calls out Hickok to avenge the loss of his legs, which occurred years before during a gunfight (again a dispute over a woman) in which Plummer's horse crushed them. When Hickok, who is busy at cards, finally decides to shoot it out with Plummer, he has himself tied to his chair and carried out; ostensibly a gesture made to level the playing field, Hickok's surliness turns it instead into a mockery of the man's disability. Not only is Hickok not apologetic nor sympathetic to Plummer, his arrogance makes a seemingly noble gesture a further provocation.

The Man From Laramie is likewise concerned with issues of sight. Alec Waggoman, the cattle patriarch, is slowly losing his vision, a limitation exposed when he attempts to make amends for Dave's assault on Lockhart's wagons, and passes him bills in the wrong denomination. Alec has also been unable to keep a close eye on his ranch's accounting, handled instead by his trusted ranch hand Vic Hansbro (Arthur Kennedy), who has surreptitiously been selling the repeating rifles to the Apache behind Alec's back. He literally cannot see the evidence of Vic's treachery, which becomes clearer when the ranch hand turns against him openly and pushes him from his horse, sending Alec tumbling down the mountainside. The fall is not fatal, but pushes Alec into full blindness, whereupon he points Lockhart to Vic's guilt in the death of his brother. The historical Hickok suffered from "ophthalmia" that was treated by doctors in the Black Hills of South Dakota, with mixed success. According to Jon Tuska, his ability to see "was for a time entirely destroyed, was partly restored, but he never again regained his perfect vision."[29] In *Wild Bill*, Hill stages a historical gunfight in which Hickok, while serving as marshal in Abilene, Kansas, accidentally shoots his own deputy through the heart[30]; in the middle of a gun battle, a medium-shot is framed over Hickok's shoulder, and an approaching man calls out "Bill!", and Hickok turns and quickly fires without really seeing the supposed attacker. He looks back in front of him, and the gunfight is over, a voice calling from the gathered crowd, "You just shot your own deputy." Hickok's inability or unwillingness to see has humiliated him in front of the townspeople he is charged with protecting. He clears the street with a threat of violence—"I see one sumbitch on the street, I'll kill him"—and then weeps over the body. An immediately subsequent interlude featuring Hickok's poor theatrical debut in Buffalo Bill Cody's (Keith Carradine) Wild West show ends with the gunfighter breaking character to urge the spotlight operator to turn the lamp off in the middle of the performance, because it could "damn near blind a feller." A slow dissolve to a close-up of Hickok's eye, during a doctor's examination of his condition, once again aligns the loss of sight with humiliation—Cody's audience laughs uproariously at Hickok's ineptitude as an actor.

The doctor diagnoses Hickok as having glaucoma, a product of "too much proximity to infected females." When he delivers the news that the gunfighter's eyesight is in irrevocable but erratic decline, Bridges appears in

Figure 7.2 The slyly autobiographical *Wild Bill* (1995), in which gunfighter Wild Bill Hickok (Jeff Bridges) reckons with a history of violence while dealing with the impending loss of his eyesight, which director Walter Hill emphasizes through a highlight on Bill's eyes. *Source: Screenshot captured by author.*

silhouette, a band of shadow over his eyes. Hickok has a different diagnosis: "I expect just too much time staring at the prairie sun." His refusal to accept the reality of his condition is yet another instance of his inability to see himself clearly. He likewise cannot see the purity of Calamity Jane's (Ellen Barkin) love for him, routinely dismissing her overtures; even their one on-screen moment of intimacy is interrupted by McCall's pistol against his ear—once again, Hickok has been unable to see what's coming for him. He is typically at a loss, unable to understand, much less articulate, the direction his life has taken him. In the morning after an opium hangover, he confides in a Chinese woman who brings him soup: "Maybe you can help me. Where the hell did things go wrong? This kid, Miss Jane, trouble with my eyes." After a pause, he looks at the woman listening to him, and realizes she doesn't speak English: "You don't understand a blessed word I'm saying, do you?" As in the scene of his introduction, holding the mirror up to perform the trick shot over his shoulder, he cannot really see himself—he tries, but fails. His vision only becomes truly clear in moments of violence. After a lengthy sequence in the Number 10 saloon when McCall and a band of hired guns hold him hostage and then decide not to kill him, Hickok straps on a pair of guns and prepares to settle the score. He steps toward the saloon door, stopping in a beam of narrow light that forms a horizontal highlight across his brow, his blue eyes glimmering. In soft focus, his friend Charley Prince (John Hurt) asks him,

"How are the eyes, Bill?" Hickok, refusing to overpromise, says, "You never can tell. Comes and goes." He strides out to finish the job, heading down the street for the barn where the mercenaries are gathering their horses to ride out of town. In a high crane shot, Hickok walks alone down the middle of the street—an unmistakable allusion to *High Noon* (1952, Zinnemann) that achieves Hill's stated intention to simultaneously present and deconstruct the myth of the gunfighter. Hickok is the film's hero, but he is profoundly flawed, a disturbing predilection for violence and personal cantankerousness leavened by Bridges's fundamental integrity and decency as a screen performer. He is a murderer, a card sharp, and a brute—not the noble lawman taking on a gang of killers all by himself, as Gary Cooper does in *High Noon*. The history of the West, and the western, is alive for interpretation in Hill's work; as *The Long Riders* showed, followed by *Geronimo* and the others, Hill is neither classicist nor revisionist, but negotiates between the two.

Another of Hill's references to a classic western demonstrates this tendency. Midway through *Wild Bill*, Hickok takes a seat on the porch of the Number 10 saloon where he will shortly meet his end, leaning carefully back in a wooden chair with his foot planted on the upright pillar that holds the awning aloft; it is an unmistakable echo of a famous image from *My Darling Clementine,* in which Wyatt Earp performs the same gesture, framed in a nearly identical medium shot that places its subject nearly in silhouette against the western backdrop. The reference to *My Darling Clementine*, according to Hill, "didn't start that way." He saw Bridges put his foot on the pillar and lean back, and Hill says, "I knew where I was."[31] The context of the scene, when contrasted with Ford's film, reveals another of the film's revisions of classic westerns; instead of Fonda's noble lawman on the way to making Tombstone safe for the blessings of civilization, Wild Bill, notorious gunfighter and man of violence, lords over the town in which he will meet his bloody, ignominious fate. However, the scene also foregrounds the film's other thematic concern—Hickok uses a magnifying glass to scour the newspaper, a gestural reminder of his declining vision. It is Hickok's inability to see the traitorous McCall for who he really is—a threat that must be taken seriously—that leads to his death, when the young man shoots him from behind. The film itself looks away at that moment; McCall approaches the camera and raises the gun into the wide angle lens in close-up, and pulls the trigger, followed by a cut to the screaming Calamity Jane. Hickok's fear that he will be shot in the head like President Lincoln, expressed to McCall when he and his band of mercenaries first get the drop on Hickok in the Number 10, comes true. He cannot see the end coming; one last time, his eyes fail him. Of *Wild Bill*, Hill says, "It is one of my favorites, if not my very favorite film."[32]

TAKE 'EM TO WYOMING

The temporal setting of Hill's AMC miniseries *Broken Trail*—1898—places it astride the ending of the era of the American West and the beginning of the twentieth century. Working from a script originally been conceived as a two-hour feature by Alan Geoffrion, who had previously written the western drama *Open Range* (2003, Costner), Hill was recruited to shepherd the project for a cable television network interested in making a move into original productions. Before the AMC network developed a reputation for daring, interesting television shows, the channel had mostly shown old movies. Hill says that their audience's familiarity with the western led to their interest in developing *Broken Trail* as a miniseries instead of a two-hour feature.[33] Because the story was originally around 105 pages (in Hill's recollection), AMC's request to expand it to three hours over two nights led to a certain number of challenges, including Hill's contribution of a handful of scenes.[34] *Broken Trail* follows an aging cowboy named Prentice Ritter (Robert Duvall) and his estranged nephew Tom Harte (Thomas Haden Church) as they drive a herd of horses from Oregon to Wyoming in search of a windfall payout that will allow them to establish their own stakes instead of working for wages. Along the way, the cowboys see their ranks grow as they are joined by a violinist, Heck Gilpin (Scott Cooper), and eventually a group of five Chinese women who are being sold into prostitution by the disgusting Billy Fender (James Russo). The film chronicles their journey to Wyoming, complications growing as Harte kills Fender after he robs their party and leaves the Chinese women in their charge, and then finding themselves pursued by the outlaw Big Ears Bob (Chris Mulkey) on assignment from the prostitutes' jilted buyer.

The slowly paced *Broken Trail* is a story in the tradition of cattle drive westerns like *Red River* (1948, Hawks) in which relationships between traveling companions along the trail are forged and ultimately tested by the difficult task of making such a long and arduous journey. The cattle drive, and ownership of livestock more broadly, is a defining convention of the western; the lasting impact of the range story centralizes issues of capital in a country where such pursuits are often highly fraught for the individual enterpriser. *Red River*, Robert Sklar argues,

> is a film about the issues of empire. It is a film about the territorial expansion of one society by the usurpation of land from others, and the consequences arising therefrom—in the relations between men and women, in the relations between men and other men, in the social compact that binds people together for a common purpose. And these human themes, important as they are, are subordinate to even more fundamental issues of economic survival, of commodity production, above all of the need to find a market for one's goods.[35]

Hawks has no monopoly on these themes. Cattle westerns place individuals in conflict with larger economic forces that define the American experiment. In some films, those characters gain dominion over the capital by protecting their herds of cattle from natural and unnatural dangers, securing a legacy of generational wealth for years to come; in others, they are crushed by capital, robbed blind by thieves, set upon by sudden storms or fires, and left on the outside looking in. That film's classicism no doubt infuses *Broken Trail*, but so too does the revisionism of a western like *The Outlaw Josey Wales* (1976, Eastwood), which features a similar traveling party that grows in number as the vengeance-driven hero Josey Wales (Clint Eastwood) builds a community on wagon wheels, taking in the destitute and the wounded in a show of benevolence that counteracts his tendency toward brutal violence. *Broken Trail* is more lyrical than either film; Hawks's film offers an incisive exploration of different modes of leadership, while Eastwood's picture is characterized by intermittent gunfights that draw on his work with Sergio Leone. *Broken Trail* is the longest single film of Hill's career; most of Hill's films settle around 100 minutes (with several much shorter than that), so excess of 180 minutes is a considerable departure for a filmmaker whose narrative efficiency is usually paramount, and at some points, the film gets stuck, trapped by its airtime-mandated duration. It is easy to sense that there is a leaner story aching to get out.

Its lyricism appears in small moments, such as a vignette during which Tom discovers one of the horses has broken its leg and puts it down with a pistol shot. A scene like this is certainly not an undiscovered territory, a variation appearing in numerous westerns both on the page and on the screen. As ever, the genre is enlivened by individual filmmakers' specific execution of its tropes and conventions. In this version, the scene takes on a mournful, elegiac mood as Hill and editors Freeman Davies and Phil Norden cut between Tom, the horse, Prentice, and the Chinese women who look on as Tom prepares the horse for its final breaths. Wide shots of the herd of horses galloping emphasize the mobility of the collective; the lame horse first appears over Tom's shoulder in the background, having fallen back from the group. Lloyd Ahern's camera racks focus on the horse standing alone in the tall grass, and then Davies cuts to a shot of the horses galloping, panning along with them. Tom rides into the next shot, away from the camera, and looks over his shoulder, when he finally notices that one of the animals has fallen behind. He rides back to the struggling straggler and sees its broken leg. He (and the audience) knows what comes next, and he hops down from his own horse to take a closer look. He grabs a rope from his saddle and tenderly ties it around the horse's neck and mouth, improvising a muzzle that will allow him to grab hold of the animal. His hands linger on the horse's snout, Tom silently providing comfort. The film cuts away to the other members of the party, who notice that Tom has stopped, and he stands with his pistol drawn and aimed at the horse's forehead, shown in a wide shot. There is a close-up of the horse with the barrel of the gun resting on its head, and then a cut to a corresponding close-up of Tom, who pulls the trigger. Hill inserts a flash of white (shades of *Geronimo* and *Wild Bill*) to coincide with the sonic boom of the pistol shot, and the tenderness of the moment is shattered by the reality of violence. The horse shrieks in pain and falls back, and the Chinese women cry out in horror. The camera lingers past the occurrence of violence to reckon with the aftermath. The killing concludes quickly, but its effects ripple into the following moments, a heavy silence hanging over reaction shots of the confused women and the grim acknowledgement on Prentice's face. He, no doubt, has had to put a horse down and knows the pain.

As usual in cattle westerns, moments like this offer brief interludes from the journey of the drive. In *Red River*, tensions between Dunson and Matt spawn a battle over the best way to lead their men. According to Robert B. Pippin, its subjects are "the charismatic nature of authority, the psychological glue in various sorts of social bonds, and psychic costs of unique forms of social cooperation and sacrifice demanded by modern societies."[36] *Broken Trail*'s horse drive gives Tom and Prentice the opportunity to rebuild their tenuous family bond, stretched thin by Tom's alienation from his mother. Her death brings Prentice to Oregon in the first place, ashamed that she has excised her son from her will and left her estate to Prentice instead. To restore their relationship, they enter into a cooperative agreement grounded in economic venture, as in *Red River*, in which Sklar says "themes of contract and compact are central."[37] Prentice offers Tom a chance to earn the inheritance that he has been denied, with Prentice stepping into the parental role abdicated by Tom's deceased mother. For Hawks's Tom and Matt, Sklar argues,

> The cattle drive is not simply a way to earn a living, it is their opportunity to accumulate capital, to qualify for full participation in the rewards of the new capitalist era. Their need for solidarity, for an effective working compact, is no abstract or sentimental thing, it is essential for their economic advancement.[38]

Hill's Prentice and Tom, as in *Southern Comfort*, *48 Hrs.*, *Trespass*, and others, must work together to secure wealth that can only be achieved cooperatively. As Prentice sees it, the horse drive allows himself and Tom a chance to write their own future. He tells Tom, who is reluctant to make the commitment, "The truth is, you're as loose as ashes in the wind." He speaks with the authority of a man who knows that life, just as he recognizes the pain Tom feels in the killing of the horse. Ownership means freedom from a life of wages and backbreaking labor, on the other side of which is a life of old age and a diminished body.

While *Red River* primarily dramatizes the contest for control of the group between Dunson and Matt, *Broken Trail* expands its definition of community as more join it. *Red River*'s ancillary characters are marginalized in the film's final moments, as Dunson and Matt first fight one another, and then make up, before its final image of a "D" and "M" bisected by the Red River, the father's proposed insignia for their shared brand drawn in the dirt, seals their bond. In *The Outlaw Josey Wales*, by contrast, the broken hero not only retains his humanity during his quest for vengeance, but strengthens it by adding members to his traveling party, including a Cherokee wise man and the blonde Laura Lee (Sondra Locke), who becomes his romantic partner after he rescues her from a rape attempt. Though obviously a man of violence, Josey chooses to negotiate with the Comanche chief Ten Bears (Will Sampson) while staying on land claimed by his tribe. "I'm just giving you life, and you're giving me life," Wales tells the Comanche leader. "I'm saying that men can live together without butchering one another." His pitch is successful and echoed at a moment in *Broken Trail* when, deep into the horse drive, Prentice and the others are waylaid by a group of Crow Indians, who demand a tax for their passage through Crow land under threat of violence. Though the Crow insists upon two horses, Prentice refuses, much to the consternation of Heck, who translates. Prentice is reluctant to use violence himself, however, and successfully defuses the tension when he hands the Crow leader a small figurine of a horse, which he has whittled out of wood, and says, "Two horses." The Crow man appreciates Prentice's sense of humor, and takes one colt along with the figurine. Josey's predilection for violence gives way in his negotiation with Ten Bears to the realization that it is not always necessary for survival; Prentice, standing on the precipice of the twentieth century, sees violence increasingly as a relic of the past. Tom feels this, too—his hanging of the treacherous Billy Fender for robbing them is an act of frontier justice that takes place nearly a decade after the metaphorical closing of the frontier.[39]

The western form makes violence nearly inevitable, however. Prentice engages in a little frontier justice of his own, gunning down the notorious Smallpox Bob (Shaun Johnston), an outlaw infamous for supplying indigenous people with infected blankets. Prentice and Tom are inclined to complete their sale of the horses in Wyoming without a showdown with Big Ears, but the outlaw will not allow it, partially because his erstwhile lover Nola (Greta Scacchi) has joined Tom and Prentice's band. Hill's visual sensitivity to the abuse suffered by *Broken Trail*'s female characters, Nola and the Chinese women, adds a gendered dimension to his consistent interest in the aftermath of violence that is scarcely present in his many other, male-dominated films.[40] Nola has long suffered Big Ears's wrath, a story she shares with Prentice during an intimate conversation by the water one night.

Fender's craven, dehumanizing treatment of the Chinese women makes him the film's most despicable character—his off-screen rape of Ye Fung (Olivia Cheng) leads her to later commit suicide by throwing herself in the path of the oncoming herd. As in many westerns, deaths of the members of the traveling community are mourned and they are ritualistically buried; both Ye Fung and earlier, Mai Ling (Caroline Chan), who succumbs to disease. Violent death brought about by harsh conditions of life in the West, many of which are perpetuated by those who serve the demands of capital, is a threat to the solidarity of the community that forms along the trail.

Ownership and wealth are again important themes, as the herd of horses is consistently paralleled with the group of Chinese women. Fender sees them as little more than cattle, as does saloon operator Big Rump Kate (Rusty Schwimmer), who wants the prostitutes she has paid for. Prentice, Tom, and Heck recognize the women's humanity, despite the language barrier between them, which is eased somewhat with the arrival of yet another traveling companion, the Chinese man Lung Hay (Donald Fong), who speaks English. When Lung Hay earns a crack on the head, the community binds together to sew his wound shut. The community built through shared enterprise and cooperation, driving the herd across the trail, restores and heals itself; a community populated by cutthroats, roughnecks, and slave traders, is hardly a community at all. The final gun battle, as Big Ears and his mercenaries assault the farmhouse where Prentice, Tom, and the others have come to stay temporarily after making the deal for the horses, places these two communities in opposition to one another. Big Ears and his men exert power through violence. Though Prentice and Tom shoot back to defend themselves, they put their guns down at the end of the film, choosing the cooperative community that heals, rather than inflicts, pain. Big Ears and his men lie dead at the end of *Broken Trail*, the gunfight featuring several instances of slow motion, mostly reserved for the shots of men falling after the bullets make impact on their bodies. Soaring violin music accompanies the shootout, lending the scene an elegiac tone that likewise dominated the scene when Tom executes the horse (although music is conspicuously absent at that moment, preventing it from becoming maudlin). When Tom fires at the last outlaw fleeing on horseback, there is a sense of *Broken Trail* capturing the West's last gunfight, the final purging of the violent outlaws from the land. The staging of Tom's final shot, fired from his pistol and matched by one of Hill's white flashes, yet again echoes *My Darling Clementine*—Hill adapts the stunt that concludes the shootout at Ford's OK Corral, in which the treacherous Old Man Clanton (Walter Brennan) is picked off of his horse by Morgan Earp (Ward Bond) at a distance. The violence of the OK Corral clears the way for the schoolhouse, the church, and the other blessings of civilization to come to Tombstone. Tom's purgative violence at the end of

Broken Trail allows him to join in marriage with Sun Foy (Gwendoline Yeo), the Chinese women's matriarchal figure, with whom he builds a trusting relationship along the trail. Prentice, too, softens along the way: his fatherly protection of Ging Wa (Valerie Tian), the youngest of the girls who walks with a limp, along with his courtly but unconsummated relationship with Nola reveal a man eager to move into a life beyond violence. As in many cattle drive westerns, violence interrupts the progress of the journey. *Broken Trail* hopes that, for its characters at least, violence will no longer be required to preserve community.

LAST MEN STANDING

Pulp writer Dashiell Hammett's story "Nightmare Town," originally published in 1924, begins thusly: "A Ford—whitened by desert travel until it was almost indistinguishable from the dust-clouds that swirled around it—came down Izzard's Main Street. Like the dust, it came swiftly, erratically, zigzagging the breadth of the roadway."[41] A nearly identical image brings wayward gunfighter John Smith (Bruce Willis) to the town of Jericho in *Last Man Standing*; riding through the desert, kicking up dust behind him, Smith brings his two automatics, short-brimmed fedora, and cynically detached attitude to a nearly abandoned West Texas burg torn apart by two warring gangs. As in many of Hill's films, the town is nearly entirely bereft of non-combatants—everyone in Jericho has a role to play in the coming slaughter, on one side or the other. Though the parallels to Hammett's lesser-known "Nightmare Town" are obvious, *Last Man Standing* is part of the long lineage of films drawn from the author's subsequent novel *Red Harvest* (1926), in which his longest-running character, The Continental Op, makes mincemeat of the factions battling for control of a town dubbed "Poisonville" by playing them against one another through manipulation, double-dealing, and misdirection. Hammett describes Poisonville in characteristically caustic prose:

> The city wasn't pretty. Most of its builders had gone in for gaudiness. Maybe they had been successful at first. Since then the smelters whose brick stacks stuck up tall against a gloomy mountain to the south had yellow-smoked everything into uniform dinginess. The result was an ugly city of forty thousand people, set in an ugly notch between two ugly mountains that had been all dirtied up by mining. Spread over this was a grimy sky that looked as if it had come out of the smelters' stacks.[42]

Hill's Jericho is far less populated; Smith rumbles past a sign that lists the number of inhabitants at 57, a hand-painted downward revision that marks the gangs' takeover.

The bad town is a long-running theme of westerns, but Hammett's pulp style brought the convention into the Prohibition era. In Akira Kurosawa's samurai classic *Yojimbo* in 1961, his itchy ronin Sanjuro (Toshiro Mifune), wandering the Japanese countryside, stumbles across a similarly bad town, and makes it his business to purge it of its nefarious factions. Often regarded as the most "western" (in a geographical and cultural sense) of Japanese directors, Kurosawa's samurai films both adopted the visual and thematic conventions of many American westerns and subsequently influenced many more. Most famously, there are the remakes; one of the most notable is Leone's *A Fistful of Dollars* (1964), which lifts substantially from *Yojimbo*, often times shot-for-shot. More than the literal translations and remakes of his films, however, Kurosawa's approach to violent action left a stylistic mark on cinema; it is Kurosawa's form that influenced Peckinpah, Leone, and others. Stephen Prince sees Peckinpah's overt citation of Kurosawa's cinema in shaping his own work as essential to a dialectical relationship between their films.[43] Peckinpah's work, innovative and influential though it may be, is built on Kurosawa's use of slow motion, intercutting, and manipulation of the moving camera. Prince argues that Kurosawa "wrote the textbook for modern movie violence, and in this regard, he altered the face of contemporary film."[44] Though he made no westerns of his own, Kurosawa is among the most important of all western filmmakers because of his creation of a cinematic language that western directors could use; his work translates Ford's classicism into Peckinpah's modernism.

Kurosawa never officially acknowledged that *Yojimbo* was inspired by *Red Harvest*, but David Desser argues that "it is strongly reminiscent in plot and setting" of Hammett's work.[45] Thanks to Kurosawa's adaptation, *Red Harvest* has garnered a profoundly international profile; *Yojimbo* would serve as the direct inspiration for Leone's *A Fistful of Dollars*, in which Eastwood's mercenary, like Sanjuro and The Continental Op, cleans up a bad town by playing its unsavory elements against one another. Joel and Ethan Coen took a turn with Hammett's story in their 1920s-set gangster movie *Miller's Crossing* (1990), with actor Gabriel Byrne's Irish brogue and the bevy of Italian gangsters lending the film old country flavor. Each of the films feature a version of a sequence from *Red Harvest* in which one faction of gangsters burns the other out of its hideout, and then shoots them down one by one as they emerge, choking from the smoke.

Hill's *Last Man Standing* features the same sequence, but the credits point to Kurosawa's *Yojimbo* as the source of the film's story. Though the film is often referred to as a remake of *Yojimbo*, Hill prefers to think of it as an "adaptation."[46] Hill is an admirer of Kurosawa's work, sharing with the Japanese master an affinity for Hollywood westerns. Stephen Prince argues that Kurosawa's samurai films have much in common with westerns, including their "men of violence who are defined in terms of their weapons," but is careful to acknowledge that the Japanese historical periods in which the samurai films take place inevitably infuse them with different thematic concerns than American westerns of the post–Civil War period.[47] The historical resonances of the Prohibition era and the American gangster film offer yet another distinction from both the samurai and the western genres; *Last Man Standing* closes the historical loop by returning to the milieu of Hammett's original novel. Hill's interest in westerns makes *Last Man Standing* a hybrid of various systems of interlocking American film genre iconography, as he marks the passage of time between the western and the gangster/noir film.

To achieve this, Hill, who also wrote the screenplay, extends the end-of-an-era 1913 setting of *The Wild Bunch* to the 1920s, showing the gangsters that would replace the Old West outlaws in the mythic American imagination. One of Hill's adaptations of Kurosawa literalizes this transition; in *Yojimbo*, Sanjuro's arrival in the bad town is marked by a blackly comic episode in which a dog shuffles down the street, a severed human hand hanging from its jaws. In *Last Man Standing*, instead of a dog bearing a human hand, Smith peers out the window of his dusty rustbucket and sees a white horse, lying dead in the town square, its body teeming with flies. Not only does the dead horse signify the passing of the torch to the gangster, in his 1920s sedan with running boards made to bear a Thompson-wielding hoodlum, but it Americanizes the ideas suggested by Kurosawa's Japanese original. Above all, Hill is an American filmmaker who is, throughout his work, concerned with the historical mythology of the country of his birth, and *Last Man Standing* adapts the international baggage of *Yojimbo* and, to a lesser extent, *A Fistful of Dollars*, by bringing the story home to America. After Smith has decided to join the Italian gangster family, he eats dinner with them at their hotel; named the Sweetwater (another fusion of gangster and western iconography), the gangsters sit at a long table, full of platters heaped with spaghetti, metal boats of tomato sauce, and jugs of wine. Hill begins the shot of the table and its chowing gangsters at one end, a delightfully parodic image that recalls Norman Rockwell's 1943 painting "Freedom From Want," in which an all-American family prepares to settle in for a wholesome Thanksgiving dinner. Ford's westerns feature a number of similarly framed shots, taken from a vantage at the end of a long dinner table while his families prepare to break bread together—*The Searchers* offers one such example at the Edwards homestead before the Comanche attack, shortly after Ethan's arrival.

Hill's major deviation from the sword-wielding samurai of *Yojimbo* to *Last Man Standing* is the gun violence, which is without question the most exaggerated and stylized of any of his action films and stands in distinction

Figure 7.3 As lone gunman John Smith (Bruce Willis) rolls into the dead town of Jericho by automobile in *Last Man Standing* (1996), a dead horse greets him, a symbol of the film's blending of the iconography of westerns and film noir. *Source: Screenshot captured by author.*

to his typical commitment to slightly heightened realism. When gangsters working for one of the rival families bust up Smith's car, he retaliates by shooting their leader dead in a fusillade of bullets from a pair of automatic pistols. The man sails backward, the impact of the bullets pushing him through the hideout's open doors, down the stairs, and rolling over into the dusty street outside. Hill says that this dramatic, over-the-top impact started as an accident when the stunt crew overcranked the harness that yanks an actor backward to simulate a gun blast, but, the more he considered it, the more he liked the idea of the exaggeration, which he says fit into the film's tone as "a dark fairy tale."[48] The on-set improvisation then characterized and shaped the violence for the rest of the film, and *Last Man Standing* features some of the most impressive stunt and action work of Hill's career, shepherded by longtime collaborator Allan Graf, who served as stunt coordinator and appears in a small role in the film, as he did for Hill many times, first as a train station security guard in *The Driver*. The violence also seems to rhyme with another international influence, however, which is Smith's dual-pistol wielding recalls then contemporary Hong Kong action films by director John Woo. Akin to the gunfights in Woo's *The Killer* (1989) and *Hard Boiled* (1992), Smith's explosive performances with his two pistols leave the saloons and hotel rooms where the action scenes take place riddled with holes, not to mention the gangsters he perforates. Woo's gangsters, hitmen, and cops needed not be accurate with their bullets—they made up for it in sheer volume, spraying the fighting space with gunfire that made quick work of their less skilled opponents, and drew out their cat-and-mouse battles with their equals. David Bordwell identifies the success of sequences in Woo's films and other Hong Kong action films as dependent upon their acceleration and deceleration of action, "alternating the swift movements of each one's pistol hands with long periods of immobility."[49] During a hotel gunfight in *Last Man Standing*, when a pair of gangsters interrupt Smith's sexual encounter with a prostitute, he rolls out of bed, naked, and grabs his pistols from the table, hitting the wooden floor and starting to fire in one continuous movement. His bullets riddle the first attacker off screen right, and then a momentary pause in the action (filled sonically by the prostitute's screaming) precedes the resumption of the gunfire, as Smith turns (still nude, still on the ground) to fire in the other direction, off screen left, at the second man. He too hits the ground, and Smith gets up, charging into the hallway, using the prostitute as his hostage. The explosive, chaotic action of the gunfire—some fifty bullets are shot in about fifteen seconds—is nonetheless controlled through momentary lulls in the violence.

Leone's westerns earned considerable criticism not only for their stylistic approach to the gunfights, but their apparent separation of any moral judgment from the violent behavior of their characters. Eastwood's hero is a near-nihilist, dealing in death for less than noble reasons. It is a world of fallen people, craven and monstrous, who exploit and punish one another with no regard for human life. In a number of Leone's films, violence becomes the only unifying force; *A Fistful of Dollars* takes place in what Lee Clark Mitchell calls "a ghost town [. . .] leaving the professional heroes and villains to operate in an uncanny social vacuum."[50] In the spaghetti westerns, combined with the films of Peckinpah, cinematic violence, once practiced inside a defined perimeter of morality, has broken loose from morality. See this concern from Devin McKinney, that film violence "seems to come equipped with its own escape hatch, its own assurance that involvement can be avoided."[51] The Leone westerns allow screen violence to be understood ironically, detaching spectators from its moral consequences through aesthetic and thematic portrayal; the same critiques were then leveled at Peckinpah, despite his oft-stated artistic intentions to use the gunfights in *The Wild Bunch* to make a political statement that made violence *more* immediate to his audiences, not less.

In *Yojimbo*, the gun is a terrifying symbol of the modern world, wielded by Unosuke (Tatsuya Nakadai), Sanjuro's most serious nemesis. Unosuke carries a pistol for which he has developed a fetishistic attraction, stroking and purring to it. When Sanjuro's blade finally bests him, Unosuke dies reaching for the gun, asking to be reunited with it in death. It's a ruse, and the treacherous villain tries to aim the gun at Sanjuro; he succumbs to his wounds and dies firing an impotent shot into the mud. Because the American setting of *Last Man Standing* represents not only a historical but cultural evolution from the feudal Japan of *Yojimbo*, Hill is forced to dramatically reconsider the Unosuke character in his adaptation. Enter Hickey (Christopher Walken), the Irish gang's most fearsome enforcer, who has a reputation for brutally effective violence, a product of a childhood in which he murdered his own father and burned down the orphanage where he was sent to live. Hickey's face is lined with scars, and Walken speaks in a throaty rattle that seems like another vestige of Hammett's *Red Harvest*, which features a gangster called "Whisper" Thaler, whom the Op describes as having "no emotion in his hoarse whispering voice, only a shade of annoyance."[52] Because all of the characters in *Last Man Standing* have guns, Hickey is distinguished by his sheer sadism and cunning. In a scene set in a Mexican cantina, Hickey baits a Texas Ranger into pulling a gun on him by tossing aside his Thompson, which he has just used to plug a room full of Federales, and then turning away. "Bet you're the kind of guy who'd shoot an unarmed man in the back," Hickey says, and then urges the Ranger to "make your move." When the Ranger goes for his gun, Hickey pulls his own pistol from concealment and blows the hapless officer away. His duplicity and ruthlessness are matched only by Smith's. When Hickey tries the same trick at the end of the film, Smith sees through the ruse and fires first, sending Hickey careening to the dust with a hole in his chest. Smith is far less honorable than Sanjuro; though similarly peripatetic—each decides on a direction that leads them into town randomly at the outset of their respective films—Smith is not clearing Jericho of its villains so that a more wholesome, respectable life may return. He just thinks, as he says in voice-over at the film's end, "They were all better off dead."

The sheer volume of the chaotic violence has led some critics to see in *Last Man Standing* a kind of nihilism. According to Ron Wilson, "it fails to engender any sympathy for its characters, and instead becomes little more than a series of violent set pieces."[53] Though the violence is highly stylized in *Last Man Standing*, the film still contains Hill's characteristic interest in the consequences of killing, though they are fewer and farther between than in earlier films. Smith's execution of the gangster who busted his car is the closest to some of the violence of Hill's early films, including a Peckinpah-esque use of intercut slow-motion to track the gangster's harness-aided trip down the stairs to the dusty street. However, slow motion is scarcely found elsewhere in *Last Man Standing*; instead, Hill follows up a number of action sequences with shots of gangsters' bloody, bullet-pierced bodies lying in a pile of debris. When the bullets fly, only some hit their intended targets, others slamming into whiskey glasses and decks of cards and lamps and hats and tables and chairs, another hallmark of Woo's gunfights. Such heavy stylization can mask the film's interest in the effects of such nihilistic violence; the film moves so quickly and is so loud, these small grace notes can tend to get lost.

Last Man Standing's fusion of the western with the gangster film shows that despite the changing of the generic guard, the violence is a constant. In

America, violence is power, and the film's gangsters know no other way of life. After the Irish gang, led by Doyle (David Patrick Kelly), has eliminated its Italian rivals, there is little left for them to do, which leads them to the burned out roadhouse on the edge of town where Smith hides. The Doyle gang has rubbed out the Italians, and Smith has returned the favor by shooting his way through Doyle's hideout, killing most of his men. At the roadhouse in the film's final scene, Doyle pleads for the violence to stop, offering Smith a chance to let bygones be bygones and join the gang in running the town. Of course, there is nothing left of the town to rule. All the decent people have left, and Sheriff Galt (Bruce Dern) declares his intention to pull out, as well. Even the undertaker, Galt says, is packing up to leave—surely he knows that his business is about to dry up, with all the gangsters dead and no one left to attend, nor pay for, the funerals. The rival factions have ensured a kind of mutually assured destruction, wiping each other out and taking the town's lifeblood with them. For actor David Patrick Kelly, Doyle's inability to manifest a business empire after the bloodshed is a powerful evocation of historian Francis Fukuyama's book *The End of History and the Last Man* (1992), written in the afterglow of the collapse of the Soviet Union and the end of the Cold War, with American democratic supremacy supposedly firmly established, all enemies vanquished. Having read Fukuyama's book, Kelly improvised Doyle's final lines: "We don't need the guns," he says. "We won this war! We're survivors! We won! We won!" Made in the 1990s, with geopolitical great power conflict seemingly resolved, *Last Man Standing*'s very title seemingly evokes a metaphorical United States; Kelly sees Doyle's victory over the Italian gangsters as a historical parallel, but his character's naïve grandiosity—that the town's history has ended with his triumph—is undercut by the subsequent return of violence. A moment later, he's gunned down by Smith's bartender friend Joe (William Sanderson), whom Doyle has held hostage and had tortured, but Smith has freed. The world Doyle sought to control is nothing more than a smoking ruin, and he joins it in death, as did his Italian rivals. In the aftermath of war, Kelly says, "It's hard to tell if anybody ever really wins."[54]

Smith, the amoral free agent, the dealer in death, comes closest. But, he is unmoored, disconnected from any larger ideology or relationship to society. He has no close friends, no romantic attachments, and, seemingly, little purpose. "It ended about the same place it started. On the road to Mexico," Smith says in voice-over as he hops into his car, nursing a bullet wound. "I was just as broke as when I arrived. But something would turn up. Always does." He rumbles into the dusty desert, presumably headed off to begin the cycle anew. Perpetual violence, without end, gives the lie to the image of Wyatt Earp in *My Darling Clementine*, making Tombstone safe for civilization to flourish. As in *Wild Bill*, Hill references the iconic shot of

Fonda resting his foot on the pillar and rocking gently back in his chair in *Last Man Standing*. Hickok's use of a magnifying glass to read the newspaper was a reminder of his declining vision, a signifier of his limitations; in *Last Man Standing*, Smith cuts slices of an apple with a knife while he waits for something to happen in the bad town in which he finds himself. Smith makes his living through violence, keeping himself fed with the twin tools of his trade, holstered underneath each arm, ready to roar to life at the slightest provocation.

Westerns themselves began their accelerated decline at the exact moment that Hill started to make more of them. Many of his films of the 1990s are westerns, revealing a filmmaker with a growing attachment to another time, another place. As the industry changed around him, Hill's interest in westerns seemed only to distance him from the prevailing trends—towards fantasy, science fiction, spectacle, and eventually, at the end of the decade, comic book superheroes. The generic iconography of *Last Man Standing*, however, is just as much indebted to the visual language of film noir as it is the western, its hybridity a testament to genre conventions' malleability. Though Hill's interest in westerns seemed to put him at odds with the direction of the American film industry, his fascination with the conventions of noir were right at home in the 1980s and beyond.

NOTES

1. Walter Hill, interview with the author, 23 April 2021.
2. Eric Lichtenfeld, *Action Speaks Louder*, 23.
3. Walter Hill, interview with the author, 26 February 2021.
4. Jeanine Basinger, 1986, quoted in Yvonne Tasker, *Spectacular Bodies*, 68.
5. Michael Walker, "The Westerns of Delmer Daves," in *The Book of Westerns*, 127.
6. Walter Hill, interview with the author, 26 March 2021.
7. Richard Maltby, "A Better Sense of History: John Ford and the Indians," in *The Book of Westerns*, 46.
8. Armando Jose Prats, *Invisible Natives: Myth & Identity in the American Western* (Cornell University Press, 2002), 23.
9. Throughout this chapter, I use the term "Indian" to refer to the cinematic idea. Indigenous people of the United States are not monolithic, and there are vast differences between the various tribes; when I say "Indian," I mean the cinematic construct, which itself exemplifies the ways in which the medium papers over such differences—see Ford's casting of Navajo people to play Apaches in a number of his Monument Valley Westerns.
10. Prats, 4.
11. Ibid, 36–37.

12. Ibid, 143.
13. Ibid, 12.
14. Ibid, 143.
15. Jim Kitses, *Horizons West*, 77–78.
16. Walter Hill, interview with the author, 9 April 2021.
17. Ibid.
18. Ibid.
19. Lance Henriksen, interview with the author, 2 February 2021.
20. Walter Hill, interview with the author, 9 April 2021.
21. Ibid.
22. Ibid.
23. Ibid.
24. Kitses, 139.
25. Dennis Bingham, *Acting Male* (Rutgers University Press, 1993), 57.
26. Douglas Pye, "The Collapse of Fantasy: Masculinity in the Westerns of Anthony Mann," in *The Book of Westerns*, 172.
27. Ibid, 170.
28. For the details, see Jon Tuska, *The American West in Film* (University of Nebraska Press, 1988), 170.
29. Ibid, 172.
30. More on this from Tuska, 173.
31. Interview with the author, 26 March 2021.
32. Interview with the author, 9 April 2021.
33. Walter Hill, interview with the author, 4 June 2021.
34. Ibid.
35. Robert Sklar, "Empire to the West: *Red River*," in *Howard Hawks: American Artist*, 153.
36. Robert B. Pippin, *Hollywood Westerns and American Myth: The Importance of Howard Hawks and John Ford for Political Philosophy* (Yale University Press, 2010), 13–14.
37. Sklar, 153.
38. Ibid, 160.
39. Frederick Jackson Turner made this declaration in his 1893 thesis, "The Significance of the Frontier in American History," dating the "closing of the frontier" to 1890.
40. *The Assignment* is a notable exception to this. See Chapter 8.
41. Dashiell Hammett, "Nightmare Town," *Nightmare Town* (First Vintage Crime/Black Lizard Edition, 2000), 3.
42. Hammett, *Red Harvest* (Vintage Crime/Black Lizard Books Edition, 1992), 3–4.
43. Stephen Prince, "Genre and Violence in the Work of Kurosawa and Peckinpah," in *Action and Adventure Cinema*, 331–332.
44. Ibid, 339.
45. David Desser, "Toward a Structural Analysis of the Postwar Samurai Film," *Quarterly Review of Film Studies* (Winter 1983), 33.
46. Interview with the author, 9 April 2021.

47. Stephen Prince, *The Warrior's Camera: The Cinema of Akira Kurosawa*, Revised and Expanded Edition (Princeton University Press, 1991), 14–15.

48. Interview with the author, 12 March 2021.

49. David Bordwell, "Aesthetics in Action: *Kungfu*, Gunplay, and Cinematic Expressivity," 81.

50. Lee Clark Mitchell, *Westerns: Making the Man in Fiction and Film*, 228.

51. Devin McKinney, "Violence: The Strong and the Weak," in *Screening Violence*, 108.

52. Hammett, *Red Harvest*, 53.

53. Ron Wilson, "The Left-Handed Form of Human Endeavor: Crime Films during the 1990s," in *Film Genre 2000*, ed. Wheeler Winston Dixon (SUNY Press, 2000), 153.

54. David Patrick Kelly, interview with the author, 25 January 2021.

Chapter 8

Partners in Crime

Though the shootout that ends *48 Hrs.* undoubtedly transplants the conventions of the western gunfight to the back alleys of San Francisco, its more specific location carries substantial resonances of film noir. The city itself is synonymous with noir, notably the setting of Dashiell Hammett's novel *The Maltese Falcon* (1929) and its most celebrated film adaptation. Albert Ganz has chosen to hide out in Chinatown, and uneasy partners Jack Cates and Reggie Hammond have tracked him there. In Chinatown, Cates restores order, killing Ganz, avenging the murdered cops, and clears the way for détente with Hammond. Walter Hill's restorative conclusion—though the film's racial tensions remained unresolved—in effect rewrites the ending of the most influential and oft-imitated of the New Hollywood neo-noir films, *Chinatown* (1974, Polanksi). According to Richard T. Jameson,

> *Chinatown is* the past, that country of guilty legend which, one way or another, the best films noirs describe. Everyone of consequence in the film doubles back upon himself in some way, repeating prior mistakes, even causing them to be repeated against the best of conscious intentions.[1]

The film's downbeat ending, in which the private detective J. J. Gittes (Jack Nicholson) loses it all, encapsulates the feeling of noir more fully than most of the films made in its first cycle. The noir films of the 1940s and 1950s were, as a result of the Production Code, forced to punish their anti-heroes' transgressions with incarceration or death. By 1974, New Hollywood filmmakers were under no such obligation to assuage the ideological misgivings their films might engender in audiences. Hill's career-long reliance on the western genre predetermines the outcome of *48 Hrs.* It is more western than noir, but the sense of place achieved in the final shootout in the back alleys of Chinatown reveals the importance of noir to his filmography. In Hill's work, it is possible to see the manifestation of Eric Lichtenfeld's suggestion that "the western and *film noir* may indeed be the positive/negative images of each other, but the action film reconciles them."[2]

Hill's *Last Man Standing* is a hybrid work that imagines a dusty western town nearly abandoned, save for the noir-steeped gangsters who fight for control within its borders. Hill's exercises in neo-noir are sharply defined by their sensitivity to physical place, an essential dimension of classic film noir. Though shooting on location has been an important part of filmmaking since the very beginning, the ascendancy of the Hollywood studio system, which favored controlled environments above all else, forced location shooting into the background for much of the first twenty years of sound filmmaking. World War II changed that, of course, and the influence of Italian Neorealism and improvements in technology that made cameras lighter and sound recording more flexible led to a post-war boom in location work. Because noir's classical period (1941–1958[3]) coincided with and was accelerated by this increased awareness of space, whether it be on location or through careful manipulation of studio sets through lighting, shadow, and design, noir becomes among the most geographical of film genres. According to R. Barton Palmer, noir was inextricable from place from the very beginning.[4] A definition of noir may continue to prove elusive to critics, but what is true is that from the era predating the critically recognized beginnings of noir to the heavily self-conscious neo-noir period, filmmakers have been attracted to stories of human darkness, and wrap those stories in expressionistic design. When Walter Hill does noir, he uses place to evoke violence, danger, cruelty, and loss.

From his directorial debut *Hard Times*, Hill's work has mostly relied on location shooting; The Richmond neighborhood in *Streets of Fire* is a notable exception, its massive elevated train tracks constructed on the street scene backlot at Universal Studios. But even the set of *Streets of Fire* is designed to look as much like a location as possible. Its wet pavement, rusted metal pylons, and cracked concrete are hard to distinguish from The Battery, which was shot on location in Los Angeles, or the numerous other sequences shot on the streets of Chicago. Hill returned to Chicago for 1988's *Red Heat*, a cop thriller that pairs Windy City detective Art Ridzik (James Belushi) with Moscow import Ivan Danko (Arnold Schwarzenegger) as each looks to avenge his dead partner and bring a notorious Russian drug dealer to justice. Though much of the action is set stateside, the film's first act takes place in Moscow, with Budapest doubling for the Russian capitol city in all but a few shots, secured guerilla style by the director, a camera operator, and the star. *Bullet to the Head* (2012) revives the dead partner device, set in New Orleans, where much of *Hard Times* had been shot. Its climactic fight was even shot about a hundred feet from the site of one of *Hard Times*'s bareknuckle boxing matches.[5] The sweaty New Orleans night likewise suffuses *Johnny Handsome* (1989), which stars Mickey Rourke as the titular gangster, ironically given a sobriquet that sends up his monstrous looks, changed to Rourke's more familiar visage by a prison doctor eager to give the convict a chance to mend his violent ways.[6] Hammett's back alley San Francisco is the setting for another of Hill's noir efforts, *The Assignment* (2016), which also features a violent criminal living two lives divided by surgical intervention. In each of these noir films, Hill explores themes common to the style—the limits of trust, the pain of betrayal, the loss of the self, the inevitability of fate, the indifference of institutions—by grounding them in use of physical space.

BRUTE FORCES

When private detective Sam Spade (Humphrey Bogart) explains why he has decided to turn in femme fatale Brigid O'Shaughnessy (Mary Astor) in *The Maltese Falcon* (1941, Huston), he offers this as one reason: "When a man's partner is killed, he's supposed to do something about it. It doesn't make any difference what you thought of him. He was your partner and you're supposed to do something about it." Brigid was the one who gunned his partner down, and though Spade has unknowingly pursued her, he cannot let her transgression go unpunished. He is bound by a code, not unlike that of the western lawman, which says that professional loyalty means something and is to be upheld. Though the narrative device of the dead partner almost certainly precedes *The Maltese Falcon*, action films of the 1970s and beyond use it freely, just one way in which they reveal their roots in film noir. *Red Heat* and *Bullet to the Head* rely on the same narrative setup. In *Red Heat*'s first act, Danko's partner is killed in Moscow by drug dealer Viktor Rosta (Ed O'Ross); after Danko has traveled to Chicago in pursuit, Ridzik's partner Gallagher (Richard Bright) is killed by Rosta's men. If partnerships between cops are a kind of marriage, then both Danko and Ridzik are widowed, and left to marry each other, learning to bridge the cultural divide between them and work together to bring down Rosta. The same thing happens on opposite sides of the law in *Bullet to the Head*; mob hitman Jimmy Bobo (Sylvester Stallone) and his partner Louis (Jon Seda) fulfill a contract on Hank Greely (Holt McCallany), who turns out to be a disgraced former police officer, the ex-partner of Washington, D.C., cop Taylor Kwon (Sung Kang). When mob enforcer Keegan (Jason Momoa) kills Louis, Jimmy vows revenge, and reluctantly partners with Kwon, who comes to New Orleans looking for the guys who ordered the hit on Greely. In both *Red Heat* and *Bullet to the Head*, the reluctant partners reach a kind of mutual respect earned through performance in the Hawksian tradition—each man shows the other that he is dependable, worthy of trust, and can be relied on as a partner.

Red Heat's attention to location begins immediately with the film's first image, a shot looking up at a group of bulbous Muscovite towers from beneath a bridge, its shadowy archway stretched across the top of the frame. The sky is gray. The trees are dead, their branches reaching into the shot like bony fingers. The absence of color briefly makes it seem as though *Red Heat* will be in black and white—Walter Hill's directorial credit, in a Cyrillic font lined with red, breaks that illusion. But the image of a city in near black and white, with its attendant suggestions of death and violence, announces *Red Heat*'s noir intentions. This is a dead place, the opening shot demonstrating Imogen Sara Smith's assertion that the city in a noir film "is a necropolis: its tremendous energies are destructive rather than creative."[7] A smash cut to a burning oven, flames raging inside, creates a dynamic contrast that opposes the icy Moscow winter with the steaming heat of a Russian bathhouse, where Danko will begin his search for Rosta with a bare-skinned fight first inside the sauna and then in the snowy field outside its walls. *Bullet to the Head* likewise opens with a noir flourish, cycling backwards from a narrative midpoint in which Jimmy draws a gun on a police officer in a car and pulls the trigger, another scene that takes place under a bridge. Its first images are of an elevated train squealing across its tracks in black and white, and then cuts to a tracking shot, spying Kwon standing against a steel pylon through a chain link fence. The cluttered frame recalls the imagery of noir, with the steel beams' sharp angles, steel gray against the washed-out white background, forming a geometric urban prison of light and shadow. It then transitions to the hotel room where he and Louis will gun down the stripped-to-the-waist Greely.

Instead of playing into the Schwarzenegger's burgeoning reputation as a superhuman action star, *Red Heat*'s screenplay by Hill, Harry Kleiner, and Troy Kennedy-Martin, refuses to supply him with winking one-liners or quips, and though the sheer size of his physical frame is hard to deny, the film largely keeps his body grounded in the realm of the possible. Danko is a professional, not an ubermensch.[8] In one Moscow-set scene, Danko finds Rosta in one of Hill's ubiquitous bars and, as his characters often do, must prove himself worthy of the crowd's attention. He upends one of Rosta's thugs, who charges him, and seems about to, with typical Schwarzeneggerian flourish, smash the man's leg at the knee joint to a sickening crunch and a cry of pain. He does indeed bring his fist down on the man's knee, but harmlessly pulls off a wooden prosthesis, from which he extracts a pouch of cocaine. The chiseled star's presence in one of Hill's partner stories makes *Red Heat* something of an outlier in his filmography, in which he is almost always a man apart; here, he cares enough about his dead Russian partner to travel to

America to find his killer, and comes to care enough about his brash, boorish new American partner that he saves his life and bestows upon him a gift in parting at the film's end. "We're police officers, not politicians," Danko tells Ridzik at the airport just before he boards the plane back to Russia. "It's okay to like each other." Danko's acknowledgment that the professional respect and personal bond developed between himself and Ridzik is more meaningful that the divides that shaped the previous three-plus decades of geopolitical history. In contrast to the conclusion of *Rocky IV* (1985, Stallone), in which Rocky (Sylvester Stallone) defeats the Soviet fighter Ivan Drago (Dolph Lundgren) to avenge the death of Apollo Creed (Carl Weathers), and in the process seems to win the Cold War all by himself, *Red Heat* is aware of the limitations of its characters. Ridzik and Danko have developed an understanding, but their appreciation for one another won't have a meaningful impact on the larger ideological divide between the United States and the Soviet Union.

Schwarzenegger's characters are not typically given to limitations, but one of the larger themes of *Red Heat* is the limitations of ideology. Its characters confront the ineffectiveness of their ideals, a theme that echoes the sense of disillusionment that pervades film noir. During the search for Rosta, Ridzik and Danko visit Joliet Correctional Facility to see Abdul Elijah (Brent Jennings), the leader of a Black radical gang that deals drugs in the United States as a way of taking vengeance on a country that has forsaken his people. Danko makes him an offer—give up Rosta and keep the cocaine for himself, to which Elijah laughs and says, "You're trying to make me compromise my principles." His cool detachment betrays his cynicism; the ideological justifications he makes for his life of crime are little more than rationalizations. When Danko asks Elijah what political offense has landed him in jail, he smirks and responds, with winking self-awareness, "I robbed a bank." Rosta delivers the film's biggest attack on the terror wrought by ideology; justifying his crimes to Danko, he says, "Any country that can survive Stalin can certainly handle a little dope." In a discussion of the politics of noir films *The Asphalt Jungle* (1950) and *The Prowler* (1952), Reynolds Humphries argues that the films reveal the degree to which "crime has become the norm within the system set up by the 'liberal consensus'" that came to dominate the United States in the aftermath of World War II.[9] Humphries' assertion would imbue Rosta's cynical but market-conscious insistence that his cocaine will bring Moscow its "first taste of freedom" with the awareness that the liberal consensus of the United States, and the crime it brings, is about to spread to the entire world with the oncoming collapse of the Soviet Union. *Red Heat*'s setting during the early years of Perestroika means that both Rosta and Danko are aware of the changing of the guard— the Soviet way of life as constituted since the October Revolution of 1917 is not long for the geopolitical world.

Bullet to the Head forces both Jimmy and Kwon into a similarly compromised position. In voice-over after the opening scene, Bobo explains why he pulled the trigger: "The guy I just saved is a cop. That's not the usual way I do things, but sometimes you gotta abandon your principles and do what's right." Jimmy the hitman is forced to trust his new partner, a police officer, despite standing on opposite sides of the law—*48 Hrs.* again. Some of the mistrust between Jimmy and Kwon is cultural, as the Italian-American gangster chafes against the Korean-American cop. In Hill's estimation, *Bullet to the Head* is "essentially centered on a debate about codes of honor, the ethical standards of the killer and the policeman, and their nearly complete lack of understanding of each other's point of view."[10] Bobo is the temperamental if not legal equivalent of the world-weary Cates, while Kwon is the young, hip analog for Reggie; the formulaic structure of the screenplay written by Alessandro Camon (based on a graphic novel) shows the degree to which Hill's own formula for *48 Hrs.* has been internalized by other writers. Though Jimmy's racialized barbs against his new partner are less venomous than Jack's for Reggie (Kwon anticipates Jimmy making an "Asians can't drive" joke), their primary point of opposition is age. Jimmy is played by the sixty-six-year-old Stallone, and his alienation from Kwon is at least partially rooted in the digital divide. Kwon uses his police connections to run quick checks on criminals which leads him and Jimmy to their location; he also effortlessly navigates the incriminating contents of a flash drive, the film's MacGuffin, while Jimmy looks on mystified. *Red Heat*'s MacGuffin is a key to a storage locker that Danko takes off of Rosta; a visit to Ridzik's estranged brother-in-law, a locksmith, reveals its location. In both cases, the combined efforts of the two partners yields the results they need. As in many noir investigative narratives that feature detectives, the stories of both *Red Heat* and *Bullet to the Head* send their characters into the nighttime cities they inhabit, a two-headed "knight errant," as Raymond Durgnat called the private eyes of film noir.[11]

According to Durgnat, the private eye films place their heroes in opposition to the traditional institutions of law and order from which they have been exiled: "the insistence on city corruption is countered by the trust in private enterprise."[12] Though Danko and Ridzik are both police officers, they are positioned as outsiders, something no doubt framed by Hill's own belief that "institutions of authority, I think, should always be looked at with skepticism."[13] Danko is a loyal servant in Moscow, but stateside, his Russian police uniform and thick accent mark him as a foreigner; Ridzik, on the other hand, is a loudmouth who, his captain Lou (Peter Boyle) says, is "a good cop and a total expert at fucking up." He is likewise held in contempt by Lt. Stobbs (Laurence Fishburne), his by-the-book colleague, who thinks little of Ridzik's seat-of-the-pants approach to policework. Their alienation from the police hierarchy makes them functionally outsiders, semi-private operatives running their own case away from the prying eyes of their superiors. Their independence, however, is abetted by the political maneuvering of Lou, who sees a way to take credit for their potential successes and wash his hands of their possible failures: "Departmentally," he says to Stobbs, "I got no downside here." In *Bullet to the Head*, Kwon's attachment to the police power structure grows increasingly more tenuous as they reveal their corruption; many of the New Orleans cops are on the payroll of the film's wealthy puppet-master, Robert Morel (Adewale Akinnuoye-Agbaje), leaving Kwon cut off from the official system that might protect him. Jimmy too is separated from the gangland organization to which he belongs; after the hit on Greely, Keegan kills Louis and comes for him next, a confrontation in the tight quarters of a honky tonk men's room that he barely escapes. The brawl between Keegan and Jimmy in the bathroom echoes a similar fight in a classic noir, *The Narrow Margin* (1952, Fleischer), in which a tough cop played by Charles McGraw, protecting a witness against the mob on a train, fends off a would-be assassin in a similar setting. Fleischer's shaky, handheld camerawork and tight close-ups, complete with the damage to the environment—a mirror is shattered, sinks bumped, leather seats streaked with sweat—anticipates the private combat in *Bullet to the Head*.

Two sequences of violence in *Red Heat* and *Bullet to the Head* also seem to exist in the lineage of a pair of classic confrontation in film noir, a famous scene in Anthony Mann's *T-Men* (1947), in which a man is murdered in a steam room, an example of the director's tendency to use what Jeanine Basinger identifies as "spatial distortions of all types" in his noir films.[14] This time, McGraw plays the assassin, stepping into the misty, dimly lit sauna wrapped in a towel and sits across from his soon-to-be victim, played by Wallace Ford. In a low-angle shot looking up into the steam, illuminated by a beam of rectangular light piercing the closed door, McGraw prevents Ford from leaving. McGraw steps out, kills the lights, and cranks the steam, suffocating Ford inside. Don Siegel's San Francisco-set *The Lineup* (1958) features a similar steam-room scene in which Eli Wallach's hired assassin bumps off a con man while both men wear towels. In both scenes, place adds a layer of menace to the threat of violence; in *T-Men*, Ford's cries of agony are drowned out beneath the hissing steam, his body disappearing entirely through the fog, while in *The Lineup*, the victim goes silent after Wallach shoots him, his bloodied hand drifting into the frame in front of his eyes, barely visible in the cloud. *Red Heat*'s opening sends the loincloth-wearing Danko into a Russian steam room on the hunt for information about Rosta. As in *T-Men*, shafts of light beam in through small windows, clouds of steam swirling about the room. This is no private affair, however—Danko strides through the crowd of Herculean men lifting weights and nude sirens bathing in the pool. Danko's first appearance is pure noir—a hissing cloud of steam floats up from the floor and he passes through it, and a beam of light, his body half in shadow. The geometric pattern of the stained-glass window on the wall is shattered when Danko sends a suspect flying through it to the wintry field outside, where their battle continues, near-nude bodies framed against a chiaroscuro landscape of snow and dead forest.

Bullet to the Head features a similar sequence in the tradition of *T-Men* and *The Lineup*, in which Kwon and Jimmy track potential suspect Ronnie Earl (Brian Van Holt) to a Turkish bath where he is getting a massage. Jimmy enters in his underwear with a towel wrapped around his shoulders, carrying with him only a pistol. The cavernous space is sparsely lit, with deep shadows against the gray walls fluttered by the shimmering light of the pool. A wide shot of Jimmy talking to Ronnie, who is pushing himself up from the massage table, features a bright shaft of unsourced light, clouds of steam rising off the surface of the water. Ronnie reveals his own treachery, but Jimmy's gun jams, and the two men fight hand-to-hand, skin on skin, slamming each other against the stone walls of the bathhouse. As in the tight quarters fight in *The Narrow Margin*, they smash the environment around them. Jimmy gets a gun and fires, and as in *The Lineup*, the victim sees his own blood. In the thick clouds of steam in *T-Men* and *The Lineup*, the violence is somewhat obscured—the final shot of the equivalent scene of *Bullet to the Head* is taken from Ronnie's point of view beneath the surface of the pool, as an out-of-focus, rippling Jimmy tosses the gun into the water and steps out of frame. This approach to violence is common in classic noir—specificity of place makes those violent episodes more memorable than they might be otherwise, investing each killing with a level of detail that seems organically tied to the environment. The space becomes a violent tool of the assassin, used against his opponent and playing a role in his death.

Both *Red Heat* and *Bullet to the Head* force their characters to cross borders. In order to catch Rosta, Danko must become a Chicago cop, and Ridzik must become a Russian one; to bring down the corrupt New Orleans power structure, Kwon must embrace the gangster Jimmy's contempt for the law, while Jimmy must learn to trust a police officer. According to Eric Lott, "Film noir is a cinematic mode defined by its border crossings. In it people fall from grace into the deep shadows new film technologies had recently made possible."[15] Hill's partner films pose a difficult dilemma for their dual protagonists: they must decide how much of themselves to surrender to the partnership, and how much of themselves they will retain. Ridzik makes a dramatic show of repeatedly reminding Danko that in America, suspects are given their Miranda rights, which entitles them to a lawyer and protections from police brutality. And yet, when the two men question a suspect, Ridzik plants heroin in the man's pocket as a means of persuading him to talk; when his dubious method proves fruitless, Danko steps in and breaks the man's fingers, which yields results. Ridzik's commitment to Miranda and the rule of law, however, is little more than a fig leaf, an official creed to be discarded when it stands in the way of accomplishing a goal. Kwon has a similarly tenuous relationship with the law; during Jimmy's fight with Ronnie, his gun misfires because Kwon has surreptitiously removed the firing pin, ensuring that he can't use it. However, while Jimmy and Keegan do battle in the axe fight (an echo of the sledgehammer fight between Tom Cody and Raven in *Streets of Fire*), Kwon puts two bullets in the back of Keegan's head, hardly what officers might refer to as "a clean shoot."

Most societal infrastructure in both *Red Heat* and *Bullet to the Head* is either on the verge of collapse or, at the very least, cannot be counted on. Many noir films in the classic period manifest this theme through their visual design. According to Robert Porfirio, "The *mise-en-scène* of film noir reinforced the vulnerability of its heroes" through its emphasis on his "entrapment."[16] The shadows that create the image of prison bars, for instance, turn the environment the characters inhabit against them, making the world seem treacherous, the hand of fate pointing its finger at them. Systems of ideology, like communism and capitalism, don't have much utility for individuals operating within them in *Red Heat*; sometimes Danko's approach wins out, and sometimes Ridzik's does. The final shootout between Danko and Rosta, however, is another of Hill's hybrids of westerns and noir films, despite Ridzik's insistence that Danko's showdown with his nemesis is "all very Russian." Next to a nearly derailed freight train, Rosta and Danko step towards each other at night, bright highlights on their faces, clouds of

Figure 8.1 The noir-steeped climactic gunfight of the Chicago-set *Red Heat* (1988), in which Russian cop Ivan Danko (Arnold Schwarzenegger) marches towards his standoff with the drug dealer who killed his partner in a trainyard. *Source: Screenshot captured by author.*

steam from the locomotive billowing around them. Danko raises his weapon, Dirty Harry's .44 Magnum, a signature American weapon, and fires at Rosta, killing him. Images of American cinema—Clint Eastwood, westerns, noir films, *Chinatown*, Hill's own *48 Hrs.*—merge with Danko's enactment of Russian honor, a blood feud with Rosta that has traveled halfway around the world to resolve itself. In *Bullet to the Head*, Kwon's practical execution of Keegan robs Jimmy of the killing blow, turning the villain's death into a tag-team affair. Jimmy repays the favor by putting a bullet in Kwon's shoulder to create enough time for him to escape the approaching squad cars. However, the two men's rivalry does not preclude a final meeting in the bar where they first met, in which Kwon promises Jimmy that, if he breaks the law again, he'll do everything he can to bring him down. Citing Ethan Edwards in *The Searchers*, Jimmy says, "That'll be the day," and swaggers out of the bar. In voice-over, his attitude bears more than a hint of fatalism: "Nobody lives forever," he says, then drives away in his new car. Unlike in classic noir, the criminal is allowed to escape, but there is a sense that his time is running out—whatever uneasy partnership Jimmy formed with Kwon has run its course. As in noir, the structures that divide individuals remain in place; whatever personal relationship Jimmy and Kwon have developed, their allegiance to their opposing sides of the law makes them enemies. In the noir city, they have little choice.

DARK PASSAGES

According to Imogen Sara Smith,

> the force driving noir stories is the urge to escape: from the past, from the law, from the ordinary, from poverty, from constricting relationships, from the limitations of the self. Noir found its fullest expression in America because the American psyche harbors a passion for independence.[17]

The cautious explorations of other cultures undertaken by Hill's noir partners in *Red Heat* and *Bullet to the Head* reveal their unconscious desire to escape. The capitalist American cop Ridzik subordinates his highly individualistic identity to work with Danko, a partner who represents a communist authoritarian state; Ridzik is more than a little curious about the Soviets' methods, showing openness to Danko's suggestion about how China dealt with its country's drug problem. Danko says they "line up all the drug dealers, all drug addicts, take them to public square and shoot them in back of head." With more than a little rueful lament in his voice, Ridzik says, "It'll never work here. Fuckin' politicians wouldn't go for it." Danko's wry reply: "Shoot them first." His invocation of state-sponsored vigilantism, an act of brutality akin to Stalin's terror, allows Ridzik to at least consider the possibility of escaping from America's democratic norms and indulging in policing fully unmoored from the rule of law and respect for human rights. Ridzik does not cross the line in *Red Heat*, made uncomfortable by Danko's devil-may-care pursuit of Rosta that culminates in a Greyhound bus chase through the streets of Chicago and their "very Russian" showdown in the trainyard. It is Ridzik, for example, who yanks the wheel of the bus to the right, swerving away from the game of chicken Danko is playing with Rosta—he flirts with crossing over, but ultimately steps back. Both Jimmy and Kwon in *Bullet to the Head* engage in similar flirtation, with Bobo turning his sights on the corrupt white-collar criminals of New Orleans, performing a pseudo-law enforcement role, and Kwon, sinking into Jimmy's underworld, play-acting as Mafia enforcer. But, Jimmy and Kwon are more comfortable retreating to the lives they have always known, staying on opposite sides of the law.

The prospect of escape for noir characters is thrilling, but also dangerous. In *Johnny Handsome* and *The Assignment*, two films that rely on the central character's physical transformation through surgery, the idea of detaching from the emotional self through bodily change comes to the forefront. If *Red Heat* and *Bullet to the Head* centralized the relationship of physical borders to ideological ones, then *Johnny Handsome* and *The Assignment* are about the difficulty of separating the inner self from the outer self. Set in New Orleans, *Johnny Handsome* is a dark, unrelenting interrogation of the titular character's ugliness—in its tempting offer of redemption for Johnny (Mickey Rourke) in the arms of accountant Donna (Elizabeth McGovern), however, it is not only Hill's most romantic movie, but also his saddest, aided by a script by Ken Friedman that Hill considers top-notch, based on a novel by John Godley.[18] The disfigured Johnny, an emotionally vulnerable, naïve but supremely clever criminal, participates in a jewel robbery that leaves his mentor dead when some members of the gang double-cross him; in jail, he is given a second chance when the enterprising Dr. Steven Resher (Forest Whitaker) gives him plastic surgery that transforms his face in the hope that new looks will rehabilitate him and help him qualify for special parole. Upon release, Johnny returns to society incognito and looks to get even with the crooks who killed his mentor and left him for dead. Transformative surgery plays a major role in *The Assignment*, as well, as male hitman Frank Kitchen (Michelle Rodriguez) is given gender reassignment surgery without his consent, changing his physical body into a woman's. The culprit is Dr. Rachel Jane (Sigourney Weaver), whose reasons for performing the surgery on Frank are revealed in a series of conversations with a psychiatrist, Dr. Ralph Galen (Tony Shalhoub), conducted while Dr. Jane is incarcerated in a mental hospital.

Hill much preferred to call the film "Tomboy," but it was given the title *The Assignment* by its producers.[19] It generated no small amount of controversy, especially for a film of its size, with a number of LGBTQ organizations attacking it even before it was released as "transphobic."[20] Said Sam Adams, reviewing the film for the BBC,

> The only thing that keeps it from being as damaging as organizations like Glaad feared is that its plot is so fantastic and nonsensical that it never comes anywhere near the real world. It helps that it's so bad almost no one will see it.[21]

For his part, Hill concedes that the film is certainly "lurid" in its subject matter, but he argues that the basic position of the movie is supportive of trans people; fundamentally, he says, the movie ascribes to the notion that "we are who we are inside our head."[22] Whether the film is in fact transphobic is ultimately for trans people to decide, but *The Assignment* is tonally inspired by the short stories of Edgar Allan Poe, who Dr. Jane discusses during her interrogations with Dr. Galen, and is executed in the style of the heavily ironic *Tales From the Crypt*. A far cry from lofty, prestige-driven takes on trans characters, *The Assignment* is a low genre effort that is gleefully unpretentious, featuring plenty of nudity and violence which, to many audiences, and especially those who belong to a group of traditionally marginalized people under threat by dint of their very existence in a society that is often openly hostile to them, seems to trivialize their difficult everyday experiences. And yet, there is another school of thought that suggests that the low film, the genre picture, or the exploitation movie is more suited to explore potentially transgressive territory because they bear no burden of expectation. They are supposed to be tasteless, and in the execution of their tastelessness, unearth some deeper truth. The rape-revenge thriller *I Spit on Your Grave* (1978, Zachi) features an extended sequence in which a woman writer is gang-raped repeatedly, escapes, and then is gang-raped again by the same men when they catch up to her. Taking no vicarious pleasure in her vengeance, critic Roger Ebert called the film "a vile bag of garbage" that is "without a shred of artistic distinction" that apparently inspired men in the audience at the screening he attended to shout their affirmation at the horrifying rape on screen.[23] However, critic Carol Clover offers a defense of the film's adoption of its female protagonist's point of view, suggesting its power at engendering a masochistic identification in its male audience members, who may not otherwise access the feelings of a woman in her position.[24]

Noir too was once considered a low genre, featuring scenes of violence, brutality, and crime that painted American society in a negative light, and only after substantial critical intervention and reevaluation have many noir films come to be seen as among the best made in the Classic Hollywood era. Hill suggests that he considers *The Assignment* his "entry in the *Detour* sweepstakes," referencing Edgar G. Ulmer's micro-budget 1945 thriller that many claim is the pinnacle of film noir, especially for its reliance on the bitterly ironic hand of fate, which dooms its world-weary protagonist, Al Roberts (Tom Neal). Hill looks upon *Detour* with tremendous admiration—it is "one of the very few movies that I actually honestly say to myself, 'I wish I'd made it.'"[25] To him, it is "the noir of noirs," with the "perfection of an existential premise."[26] For him, the films as a whole express through "the visual presentation a perfect synchronization of the idea of being doomed."[27] In both *The Assignment* and *Johnny Handsome*, the transformed protagonists can never go back—Johnny dies, and though Frank survives, he has lost some part of himself which can never be recovered. The cities in which they live— New Orleans and San Francisco—extract a terrible price from each character. Johnny dies, unable to change his nature despite the facial reconstruction that offers him a fresh start, while Frank, having exacted his revenge upon Dr. Jane, is forced to find a way to live a life he did not choose. As in *Detour*, where the road plays a determining role in Roberts' doom, place defines the characters in *Johnny Handsome* and *The Assignment*.

Johnny Handsome moves inexorably towards a conclusion that takes place in a New Orleans cemetery, where the characters meet their fates—Johnny's quest for revenge is, thanks to the trappings of noir, doomed from the start. A brutal confrontation between Johnny and the double-crossers, Rafe (Lance Henriksen) and Sunny (Ellen Barkin), who killed his mentor Mikey (Scott Wilson) and hold Donna hostage, plays out against the above-ground graves and mausoleums that serve as an ever-present reminder of the city's dead. Such settings are common in noir-influenced action movies, blurring the line between past and present. In *Detour*, as in many noir films, this uncertainty is rendered through the use of voice-over narration that produces what Jonathan Auerbach calls "curious shifts in tense, so that we are often uncertain about whether we are listening to present feelings about the present, present (retrospective) feelings about the past, or memories about the past."[28] Two-ness is literal in both *Johnny Handsome* and *The Assignment*: there is the disfigured Johnny Sedley of the film's first act, and his alter ego, the post-operation Johnny Mitchell who attempts to exact his revenge; in the latter film, there is the male Frank who lives blissfully ignorant of his masculinity, and then Frank in-female-body who becomes aware of the performativity of gender in new ways.

New Orleans is central to Johnny's identity. He is introduced in slow motion, walking the wet streets of the city, the shadowy grip of night pierced only by the flicker of neon. Ry Cooder's score, its most prominent feature a wailing blues guitar, lends the film a moody, mournful tone that is intermittently interrupted by chaotic, frenzied action sequences with fast cutting and unconventional framing. Hill's creative experimentation is on full display in *Johnny Handsome*. Wide-angle lenses for extreme close-ups characterize the film's first breathless action sequence, the jewel heist masterminded by Johnny and pulled off by Rafe, Sunny, and Mikey. The ferocity of the close-ups, lent a distorted unease by the use of wide angles, joins with the frenetic cutting to intensify the heist sequence. At one moment, the hapless store manager slams the alarm, drawing the murderous ire of Rafe. In extreme wide-angle close-up that foregrounds the pistol, leaving Rafe's masked face out of focus in the background, makes the violence immediate, achieving a kind of three-dimensional effect; a corresponding shot of the manager screaming in terror, anticipating the bullet, ties the extremity of the gunshot across the edit. As Rafe, Sunny, and Mikey use hammers to smash the jewel cases and grab all they can, the film combines sound and image to create a symphony of shattering glass, harnessing a frenzy of formal techniques to create a chaotic expression of unrestrained violence.

Though not as frequently utilized as San Francisco, Los Angeles, New York, or Chicago, New Orleans has its own noir history. According to Imogen Sara Smith, the New Orleans-set pandemic noir *Panic in the Streets* (1950, Kazan) achieves a sense of setting worthy of its subject matter:

> No city has ever looked less sanitary than this: all sagging tenements, rickety stairs, blind alleys, crumbling houseboats, and cheap restaurants that stonewall health inspectors. The disease is a physical manifestation of the malaise pervading the city, an epidemic of fear, suspicion, lies, petty thievery and casual murder, wife-beating, and everywhere grime, unease, sweat, decay and poverty.[29]

The feelings evoked by *Johnny Handsome* exist in the same tradition—the film is emotionally and physically subterranean, a constant reminder that the whole story seems to take place below sea level. According to Lance Henriksen, one of its stars, the film is "sultry. You can feel it in the hotel, how many times people have had a party."[30] It feels lived in, each scene carrying the history of its characters' sins—Johnny's regrets and quest for revenge, or Rafe's insecurities about his toughness, or Sunny's blazed trail of wreckage.

Johnny Handsome's motif of surgery, which offers the protagonist an opportunity to start a new life by abandoning his criminal past, is a powerful manifestation of a city built in a swamp. The nickname "handsome" is first ironic because it contrasts with Sedley's physical looks; though the surgery gives him a more traditionally appealing face, "handsome" remains ironic because he is unable to renounce his criminal ways and immediately sets about on his quest for revenge against Rafe and Sunny. The parallels drawn between Johnny and New Orleans pose a question central to noir: can a person or a place hide their true nature? According to Eric Lott, "Noir's crossings from light to dark [. . .] throw its protagonists into the predicament of abjection. Noir characters threaten to lose themselves in qualities that formerly marked all the self was not and that unsettle its stable definition."[31] Johnny's new face grants him the freedom to get close to the suspicious Rafe and Sunny, infiltrating their gang with the offer of a new payday. In *The Assignment*, Frank's female body grants him similar license to kill, especially when he embraces the performative nature of his newfound femininity. Though the film was shot in Vancouver, its San Francisco setting associates *The Assignment* with an important noir predecessor, *Dark Passage* (1947), in which Humphrey Bogart plays wrongly convicted wife murderer Vincent Parry, who escapes from prison to clear his name and undergoes plastic surgery to continue his investigation unimpeded. Director Delmer Daves relies on a subjective camera that represents Parry's point of view for much of its first half, which separates Bogart's instantly recognizable voice from the image of his face. *Dark Passage* is keenly aware of its star's face, and Daves uses the techniques of noir—voice-over, heavy shadow—to support its highly unconventional reliance on subjective camerawork.[32] Similar subjective shots throughout *Johnny Handsome* pay tribute to Daves's film. During Johnny's operations, Dr. Resher looks directly into the camera to assure him of the surgery's impending success; by contrast, the cop who arrested Johnny and sets out to prove he is still no good, Lt. Drones (Morgan Freeman), looks directly into the camera upon seeing the post-op Johnny for the first time, stunned if not impressed by his transformation. Resher's direct-to-camera gaze reveals his belief in Johnny's potential to reform, but Drones's accusatory stares pull him in the other direction, down to damnation. Such formal association makes noir less a physical place than a psychological one, achieved through technique.

The Assignment features another reference to *Dark Passage*. After Frank's surgery, he reunites with a nurse, Johnnie (Caitlin Gerard), with whom he had a one-night stand while still physically male. Upon seeing the female Frank for the first time in a diner, Johnnie says, "You had plastic surgery, huh? Just like some gangster guy out of an old movie." The nurse's androgynous name calls attention to the performative nature of gender roles. Just as Johnny Handsome has an opportunity to create a new life for himself with a new face—his choices are his again—Frank's new body allows him to unlock a relationship to outward signifiers of gender that previously eluded him. While Frank continues to hold on to the memory of his male body, he uses black tape to compress his female breasts; in a particularly evocative shot, he stands in front of the bathroom mirror and sees Johnnie stepping out of the shower over his shoulder. Frank silently evaluates Johnnie's nude body not in sexual terms, but in fascination with her physical form, which he now shares. The mirror, of course, is a defining motif in *Dark Passage*, *Johnny Handsome*, and

The Assignment; each film contains a similar sequence, in which the patient wakes up from surgery and, upon removing the bandages, sees his new face for the first time. In *Dark Passage*, the mirror delivers the moment at which Bogart's signature voice and his face finally match; in *Johnny Handsome*, the physical transformation is so dramatic, the revelation brings the sensitive Sedley to tears, which trickle down his reconstructed cheeks; in *The Assignment*, a moment that drew considerable outrage from the film's detractors, Frank lets out a horrified, anguished cry at his gender change.

Judged by this moment alone, *The Assignment* dramatizes Frank's bodily nightmare—the monstrous feminine made literal. However, if the rest of the film is taken into account, it tracks Frank's realization that his body and his mind are separate from one another, and he can decide how best to perform gender through his adoption of its outward signifiers. In a scene with Honest John (Anthony LaPaglia), the crooked mobster who first hired, and then delivered him to Dr. Jane for the operation, Frank ties him to a chair for interrogation. An automatic pistol, a totem of Frank's masculinity as well as his criminality, is ostentatiously shoved into his belt in the space where his penis once was. After getting what he wants, Frank pulls the gun from his belt and shoots John to death, but not before the gangster tips him to nurse Johnnie's involvement in Frank's operation; when he confronts her, she confesses that she supplied drugs to Dr. Jane and then reunited with Frank as a means of surveilling him. Though Frank's anger leads him to put a gun to Johnnie's head, he can't pull the trigger—he spares her, perhaps because, however duplicitous she has been, Johnnie has been supportive and encouraging about Frank's new identity, reminding him that it will afford him a disguise that may protect him from prosecution, as did Johnny Handsome's. Frank's femininity is an asset to his criminal life, but also a liability; just after his surgery, he is attacked by the sleazy desk clerk at his dingy motel, the man clearly intending to rape him, but Frank uses his training as a hitman to fight the man off, beating him with a baseball bat and subsequently using it to smash the motel office in fury. This brief scene dramatizes Frank's newfound awareness that a change in his outward presentation of gender brings with it new dangers. In a study of trans men who live in San Francisco conducted by Miriam J. Abelson, interview subjects "reported that four factors affected their changing sense of safety: the stage of their transition, their location, those with whom they interacted, and their bodies."[33] In these interviews, "several mentioned that they no longer had the same fears from when they lived as women, such as walking alone at night or being raped."[34] Frank's sudden change teaches him a hard lesson about the unequal experiences of men and women. *The Assignment* forces the hyper-masculine Frank to identify with women by making him one biologically, an act of enforced empathy that may extend to some portions of the audience.

Frank uses femininity more overtly late in the film when he infiltrates Dr. Jane's organization, donning a blonde wig, wearing a dress and black underwear that sexualizes his body; he hides a gun in his crotch where it goes undetected by Jane's bodyguards. He also fastens a single bullet to the underside of a high-heeled shoe, which will come in handy during his final confrontation with Dr. Jane, who thinks he is out of bullets after making quick work of her security team, tempting them with the thought of his breasts and vagina. Dr. Jane is in some ways the antithesis of *Johnny Handsome*'s Dr. Resher, who convinces Sedley to participate in the surgery as a means of redeeming himself by appealing to his better angels. In a legal deposition, she also confesses that she wanted to give Frank "a second chance," rhetoric that echoes Dr. Resher's. However, Dr. Jane forcibly subjects Frank to reassignment for two major reasons: the first and most salient is revenge for Frank's contract killing of her brother, but the second, which may sound like a rationalization, is to pursue a research hypothesis. She says, "I wanted to reinforce the theory that if gender is identity, then even the most extreme surgical procedure will fail to alter the essence. And this proved to be true. Frank Kitchen is still very much the man he was, because he believes himself to be the man he was." Dr. Jane already knows what Frank comes to discover—that gender is primarily a matter of performance, which she demonstrates through her close-cropped hair and traditionally masculine clothes. In her deposition, for instance, she is dressed in a black suit, white shirt, and skinny black tie that makes her indistinguishable from the men at the table. The casting of Sigourney Weaver to play Dr. Jane is highly self-conscious of Weaver's screen image; she and Hill began their collaboration in the late 1970s, when Hill's rewrite of the script for *Alien* (1979, Scott) led to the role of Ripley

Figure 8.2 Though *The Assignment* (2016) drew accusations of transphobia, it shows a considerable interest in the idea of gender performativity, as hitman Frank Kitchen (Michelle Rodriguez) dangles his pistol from his belt. *Source: Screenshot captured by author.*

being reconceived as a woman, rather than a man. In Weaver's recollection, Hill fought for her to play the role over studio objections, specifically for the gendered implications a female Ripley would bring to the story. As she tells it, they wanted her because "no one will ever imagine that this girl will be the survivor."[35] Weaver points to the complexity of Ripley's characterization as an indicator of his sophistication as a screenwriter, mostly in his unwillingness to sacrifice depth to appeal to a prevailing trend. She says that Hill's screenplay, written in collaboration with David Giler, really understood "Ripley's voice," which to her means that the part was "not written for a girl." This feature was unlike many scripts she read, which

> would have a strong woman, theoretically, but then they always put in a scene where she cried and gave up for a second because they thought it made the character more sympathetic, and it was very important that women be sympathetic back then. And it is to my lasting gratitude that these guys did not do that with Ripley.[36]

Though more poised and in control than Ripley, who is in constant peril, *The Assignment*'s Dr. Jane is similarly defiant of action's gender norms. First of all, Weaver performs much of the role while wearing a straitjacket, given the narrative circumstances that have her incarcerated in a mental institution and telling the story in flashback to Dr. Galen. She credits her performance in the role to Hill's presence: "I was very glad that he wrote it, and was very glad he was directing it because it was a strange piece."[37] In concert with the gender doubling of both Frank and Johnnie, Dr. Jane's presence complicates the very idea of the femme fatale, an essential component of film noir. *Johnny Handsome* offers a much more traditional, if particularly extreme, version of the character type in Sunny; as played by Barkin, the blonde Sunny is thrilled by violence, a hurricane force of brutality and greed who uses her partner Rafe as a junkyard dog; she is a dangerous threat who, as in most noir films, far outpaces the man with whom she has agreed to conspire. Lance Henriksen thought of Sunny as "the matriarch of a wolf pack" who was in total control of the pair of them.[38] However, she is not granted a privilege that *The Assignment* bestows upon Frank, Johnnie, and Dr. Jane; they tell the story through narration and the intervention of flashback. *The Assignment* is Hill's most non-linear movie—while the story progresses forward to an ironic reveal (Frank has amputated the surgeon's fingers), it is constantly shifting to another time, another place by its narrators. Johnnie's confession about her involvement in Frank's operation is granted a series of supporting images that privilege her point of view momentarily, but most of the film's narration is handled by Frank and Dr. Jane, as they take turns relaying what happened to each of them. As *Dark Passage* consistently disembodies Bogart's voice from his face, the act of storytelling in *The Assignment* underlines the film's interest in the separation of the body from the self, situating it in voice-over. According to Richard De Cordova, "voice-over in film noir works to problematize the body by introducing a variety of disjunctions between the bodily image and the voice."[39]

Though the response to *The Assignment* focused on the film's apparent portrayal of transitioning as a terrible punishment, which it does in the scenes when Frank initially wakes up after surgery, as the film progresses it empathizes with Frank as he learns more about the performativity of gender. His journey to self-acceptance in the wake of surgery comes with an important realization, which he confesses to the camera that records his story in noir-tinged black-and-white. He is glad Johnnie has started over: "I think it was the best thing for her. New city. New place to live. A fresh start. Yeah. I think it worked out for the best." He might well be talking about himself, too. In Johnnie's escape, he sees liberation, which he echoes when he pivots in the final voice-over to his own story, now with a new perspective: "I used to be a guy," he says, but notably does not call himself a woman, an indication that his thought process has moved beyond the conception of binary gender roles. Frank's new fluidity will allow him to experiment with gender as performance as he sees fit. It is an ironically hopeful ending, especially for a noir film, that looks forward to an uncertain future: "change is gonna come," he says. Frank achieves the redemption that eluded Johnny Handsome, whose dying breaths in the New Orleans graveyard are focused on his own looks. Savagely beaten and slashed by a vengeful, punishing Rafe, Johnny lies bleeding, and looks up at Donna: "How do I look? How's my face?" he wants to know. In his final moments, he remains unsure of his moral position. His sense of self is still up for debate, and he goes to his grave without an answer; Frank is more at peace with the inevitability, knowing that the sands of self will continue shifting underneath his feet. In both endings, noir is present.

In his study of several noir films that use images of painting to literalize their themes, author Mark Osteen argues that "all identities are to some degree forged, that human character is too malleable and complex to be framed within a single subject or explained within a single narrative."[40] To Osteen, noir "films indeed suggest that identities are *always* in flux, always a matter of performance."[41] Noir's own identity is "always in flux," as genre, style, mood, or classic noir, neo-noir, or the more contemporary self-referential films that have come in the wake of both. Because noir is so endlessly applicable, it can deliver ideas and themes from another time and another place to a contemporary society. Its themes drive *Red Heat* and *Bullet to the Head*, which foreground partnerships as a means of exploring the limitations of ideologies for protagonists who cross ethical and geographical boundaries. They likewise animate *Johnny Handsome* and *The Assignment*, which use the motif of reconstructive surgery to offer their protagonists a chance to reinvent themselves, detaching from the corporal and unearthing their inner selves. As in most of the noir the results for the characters are mixed. Walter Hill's noir films draw on varying traditions of the form, but, as in his westerns, respect and intensify the themes of earlier works. In his foreword to the book *American Neo-Noir: The Movie Never Ends*, Hill writes of film noir: "When we heard the ominous minor chords of the title music, that told us we were going to watch people fighting for their lives in a story of desperation and anxiety." Though the classic period of noir had ended by the time Hill became a filmmaker, its stories still spoke to him, and he believed that its characters "still had dramatic life even though they may have outlived their time, played out their string."[42] As times moved beyond these noir characters, their fates ironically became even more tragic, trapped as they were forever in lonely places, and getting lonelier all the time.

NOTES

1. Richard T. Jameson, "Son of Noir," in *Film Noir Reader 2*, ed. Alain Silver and James Ursini (Limelight Edition, 1999), 205.

2. Eric Lichtenfeld, *Action Speaks Louder*, 3.

3. This is critic and filmmaker Paul Schrader's timeline, as expressed in his classic essay, "Notes on Film Noir," accessible in *Film Noir Reader*, ed. Alain Silver and James Ursini (Limelight Edition, 1996). One can quibble with the exact years, but it's pretty close.

4. R. Barton Palmer, *Shot on Location: Postwar American Cinema and the Exploration of Real Place* (Rutgers University Press, 2016), 171.

5. Walter Hill, interview with the author, 4 June 2021.

6. Before the actor's numerous plastic surgeries, of course.

7. Imogen Sara Smith, *In Lonely Places: Film Noir Beyond the City* (McFarland, 2011), 19.

8. This seems to be why the two most frequently cited texts on male bodies and the action cinema of the 1980s, Yvonne Tasker's *Spectacular Bodies* and Susan Jeffords' *Hard Bodies*, seem not to know what to do with *Red Heat*. It rates barely a mention in Tasker's book, and is excluded entirely from Jeffords'.

9. Reynolds Humphries, "The Politics of Crime and the Crime of Politics: Postwar Noir, the Liberal Consensus, and the Hollywood Left," in *Film Noir Reader 4*, ed. Alain Silver and James Ursini (Limelight Editions, 2004), 242.

10. Walter Hill, "Last Neotraditionalist Standing," interview by Giulia D'Agnolo Vallan, 54.

11. Raymond Durgnat, "Paint it Black: The Family Tree of Film Noir," in *Film Noir Reader*, ed. Alain Silver and James Ursini, 45.

12. Ibid.

13. Interivew with the author, 12 March 2021.

14. Jeanine Basinger, *Anthony Mann: New and Expanded Edition* (Wesleyan University Press, 2007), 32.

15. Eric Lott, "The Whiteness of Film Noir," *American Literary History* 9, no. 3 (1997), 548.

16. Robert Porfirio, "No Way Out: Existential Motifs in Film Noir," in *Film Noir Reader*, ed. Alain Silver and James Ursini, 85.

17. Smith, 3.

18. Walter Hill, interview with the author, 12 March 2021.

19. Interview with the author, 4 June 2021.

20. Samantha Allen, "Why 'The Assignment' Stinks of Sensationalist Transphobia," The Daily Beast, 25 January 2017, https://www.thedailybeast.com/why-the-assignment-stinks-of-sensationalist-transphobia.

21. Sam Adams, "Is (Re)Assignment 2016's most offensive movie?", BBC, 13 September 2016, https://www.bbc.com/culture/article/20160913-film-review-is-reassignment-2016s-most-offensive-movie.

22. Interview with the author, 5 March 2021.

23. Roger Ebert, "Review of *I Spit on Your Grave*," rogerebert.com, 16 July 1980, https://www.rogerebert.com/reviews/i-spit-on-your-grave-1980.

24. See Chapter 3, Carol Clover, *Men, Women, and Chainsaws*—Updated Edition (Princeton University Press, 2015).

25. Interview with the author, 5 March 2021.

26. Ibid.

27. Ibid.

28. Jonathan Auerbach, *Dark Borders: Film Noir and American Citizenship*, 146.

29. Smith, 29.

30. Interview with the author, 6 February 2021.

31. Lott, 549.

32. A fuller accounting of Daves's formal approach to *Dark Passage* can be found in Matthew Carter and Andrew Patrick Nelson's "Introduction: 'No One Would Know It Was Mine': Delmer Daves, Modest Auteur," in *ReFocus: The Films of Delmer Daves*, ed. Matthew Carter and Andrew Patrick Nelson (Edinburgh University Press, 2016), 35–36.

33. Miriam J. Abelson, "Dangerous Privilege: Trans Men, Masculinities, and Changing Perceptions of Safety," *Sociological Forum* 29, no. 3 (2014), 557.

34. Ibid, 558.

35. Sigourney Weaver, interview with the author, 13 April 2021.

36. Ibid.

37. Ibid.

38. Interview with the author, 6 February 2021.

39. Richard De Cordova, "Genre and Performance: An Overview," in *Film Genre Reader II*, 134.

40. Mark Osteen, "Framed: Forging Identities in Film Noir," *Journal of Film and Video* 62, no. 3 (2010), 17.

41. Ibid, 22.

42. Walter Hill, "Foreword," in *American Neo-Noir: The Movie Never Ends*, Alain Silver and James Ursini (Applause Theatre and Film Books, 2015), 9.

Conclusion
Terminate with Extreme Prejudice

In Sam Peckinpah's *The Getaway* (1972), the film's criminal couple Doc McCoy (Steve McQueen) and his wife Carol (Ali McGraw) sit in half of a junked car after a daring escape from the law that trapped them in a garbage truck and finally dumped them out in a field of smoking trash. In an exchange from Walter Hill's screenplay, but excised from the finished film, McCoy tells Carol that they've got one chance to get out: "We get to Mexico, we can have a life."[1] Across the border, they imagine a life free from the law and their marital problems, where the anonymity can afford them a chance to start over. In Peckinpah's final edit, it seems possible—they pay a cowboy to take them across the line and leave them his truck, and the final shot sends the couple into the proverbial sunset, their newly procured vehicle cresting over the road that disappears on the horizon's edge.

Mexico was a complicated place for Peckinpah who, according to Christopher Sharrett, "depicted Mexico as an idyllic landscape or arid backdrop to test the mettle of alienated men in disfavor in their own land."[2] *The Getaway* is the former, when it held out the realizable promise of a better life; *The Wild Bunch* (1968) is much more the latter, as it becomes a last stand for a group of outlaws whose way of life is dying out. Paul Schrader says that Mexico was

> the ideal place for an old Westerner to go to give his violence meaning. The American frontier has been superseded by the more sophisticated mayhem of the city, but in Mexico there is an ongoing tradition of significant violence. There you can fill a hero's grave, even if it is a shallow one. In Mexico you can extend the external frontier and postpone the conquest of the internal frontier.[3]

Peckinpah's most extreme depiction of the promise and perils of Mexico comes in *Bring Me the Head of Alfredo Garcia* (1974), a deeply confessional and personal film. Piano player Bennie (Warren Oates) is a tortured, anguished, agonized lost soul whose scheme to collect a reward for securing the head of the title character leads him into increasingly fraught circles of hell. To Marhsall Fine, the film is "a poignant if nihilistic tale of a loser trying to salvage a shred of dignity at the end of his life. Its brutal quality has an undertone of sadness and regret."[4] Part of the anguish contained in the film was no doubt a reflection of Peckinpah's personal pain at the increasing difficulty of getting his movies made: "For me," he said in an interview during the production of the film, "Hollywood no longer exists. It's past history. I've decided to stay in Mexico because I believe I can make my pictures with greater freedom."[5] Oates's on-screen presence evokes Peckinpah's own, placing him in opposition to the crooked operators who send him on the errand to collect Garcia's head, stand-ins for an army of producers and executives standing in the way of Peckinpah's art. As seen in *Bring Me the Head of Alfredo Garcia*, Mexico is a place where a man goes to escape his demons, only to have them find him again—taken as a metaphor for Peckinpah's legendary fights with studios and financiers over many of his films, it is a demonic poem about the struggles of a frustrated artist.

To Walter Hill, the Mexico idea is likewise tremendously appealing, but he is well enough aware of its artificiality as a mythic construct: "The idea that if you can just get to Mexico, you can somehow get away from your sins, or your problems, is an old American idea. It's silly in a way, but in another way it's a very deeply held kind of instinct."[6] To an artist, the idea is that a creative paradise exists, somewhere, but is difficult to find. Hill has certainly had his fair share of creative frustrations, especially in the period following the release of *Undisputed* in 2002, which saw a formerly prolific filmmaker (a movie nearly every year in the 1980s, his most fertile period) reduce his output considerably, as well as a step behind the camera in some unfamiliar places. Though seemingly well-suited to his temperament and history with the genre, Hill's direction of the pilot episode of HBO's *Deadwood* (2004–2006) ended in his departure from the project over creative differences with executive producer David Milch. Nevertheless, Hill's personal stamp lingered well into the series' three seasons (and subsequent film conclusion, released in 2019); a number of actors from Hill's stock company appeared in prominent roles. *Deadwood*'s ensemble focus, in which the machinations of the town are more important than any single character, are certainly of a piece with Hill's numerous films about the politics of groups. Despite Hill's disagreements with Milch, his name remains on the credits for the pilot episode, and Hill suggests that his visual template is mostly intact, albeit with some substantial changes to the edit.[7]

Two of Hill's other directorial projects fared less well, both of which were more or less jobs for hire in which he had little personal investment—both ended badly, with Hill removing his name from the cuts of the films. The first and most high profile of these difficult experiences was the science fiction film *Supernova* (2000), credited to the pseudonym Thomas Lee. A science fiction film in the mode of *Alien*, in which an external force threatens the survival of the crew of a space vessel, Hill ran afoul of the studio when he made substantial changes to the script. A disagreement over the use of visual effects led to Hill renouncing the film entirely. The frequent use of canted angles and moving camera exemplifies some of the visual grammar that Hill established with his regular cinematographer Lloyd Ahern, but the final cut of *Supernova* is nearly impossible to follow. Hill's influence remains in a few key ways, including the use of a trope indebted to Howard Hawks and visible in a number of his films; the ship's captain (Robert Forster) is the first to die. Today, Hill dismisses the entirety of *Supernova* as "a lousy episode" that he worried would permanently damage his career.[8]

The other project that Hill stepped away from became a film called *Madso's War* (2011), produced by the Spike TV network, and intended to be another television pilot that became a movie instead.[9] A warmed-over gangster film set in Boston, undoubtedly an attempt to draft off of the success of *The Departed* (2006, Scorsese), *Madso's War* is unfocused and chaotic. The film is credited to the nonexistent Rob Marcus and features messily directed action scenes that are difficult to follow, with cutting far afield from Hill and longtime editor Freeman Davies' usually tight control or finely crafted expressionism. Moments of inspiration in the film are few and far between, with one of its only interesting scenes supplied by Hill regular David Patrick Kelly; the actor's Irish gangster, upon receiving the news of the death of a compatriot, repeatedly and excessively slams a metal folding chair into a chain-link fence. It is a fleeting recall of Kelly's sense of physical environment, a trait Hill encouraged during their making of *The Warriors*.

In the 1980s, Hill's projects were not so few and far between—he made a number of films and experienced his greatest box office successes, cementing a reputation begun in the previous decade as a filmmaker who deserved critical attention. After the offbeat *Brewster's Millions* and *Crossroads* were met with shrugs, he returned to the action genre with *Extreme Prejudice* (1987). Based on a story by John Milius and Fred Rexer, and a screenplay by Harry Kleiner and Deric Washburn, *Extreme Prejudice* stars two of Hill's regulars, Nick Nolte and Powers Boothe as Texas Ranger Jack Benteen and drug kingpin Cash Bailey, respectively. The film's spine is their relationship, which stretches back to childhood, but intervening events have landed them on opposite sides of the law and, crucially, the border between the United States and Mexico. Benteen's stoicism and effectiveness as a law enforcement officer do not prevent him from granting Cash a wide berth—as long as the violence is kept to a minimum, Benteen is loath to pursue Bailey too ardently. The two men end up on a collision course after the nefarious involvement of a group of mercenaries led by Major Paul Hackett (Michael Ironside) brings fresh chaos to Benteen's town; before long, he has no choice but to join forces with the duplicitous Hackett and his gang of ex-military soldiers of fortune, head south to Cash's Mexico-side compound, and settle their differences once and for all.

Throughout this study of Walter Hill's films, I have relied on an observation by Eric Lichtenfeld that action films, which come to fruition in the 1970s in their modern form, are assembled out of a combination of the tropes of westerns and film noir.[10] If Lichtenfeld's thesis is correct, then Hill's action films reveal the degree to which the conventions of westerns and noir are thermostatic, with many of his works cranking up one or the other, according to the demands of the story he is telling in each case. Hill's engagement with the history of both film genres makes his movies exemplars of how the action genre marshals, manipulates, and merges the conventions of westerns and noir. Though a number of Hill's films demonstrate his approach, in *Extreme Prejudice* the western and the noir meet in an action film of that genre's classical period.

Ironically, Hill says of *Extreme Prejudice* that one of its flaws is that "there's too much action in it."[11] He was drawn intensely to the relationship between Benteen and Cash, but his "interest in the soldiers was much more limited," which manifests in the final film; the soldiers are much less compelling than the intense performances given by Nolte and Boothe. The mercenaries led by Hackett supply much of the film's fireworks, especially in the orgiastic violence of its conclusion, when they have their last stand in Cash's compound and are all gunned down by machine gun fire in the tradition of *The Wild Bunch*, a critique that Hill acknowledges has "been said often." But, he insists, the ending does not just evoke Peckinpah's bloodbath, but exists in a larger tradition of westerns that stage their conclusions in Mexico:

> *The Wild Bunch* is the best example of the gunfight of Americanos versus Mexicans in a big plaza while in Mexico, but this is a tradition. If you look at *Vera Cruz* [1954, Aldrich] if you look at *The Magnificent Seven* [1960, Sturges], or all the sequels to *The Magnificent Seven*, they've got the same scene. I was aware that this criticism would be raised. I always said it was just an homage to a tradition.

Hill's interest in his two leads was not shared as enthusiastically by the film's executive producers, who thought the film's emphasis should be on Hackett's mercenaries; the result is a film that runs 104 minutes in its released version, but Hill's preferred course of action was to trim the violence and emphasize Jack and Cash—he was overruled by the producers at Carolco, who followed the reaction of the test audience, which gave high scores to the action sequences, so they stayed in all of their slow-motion, blood-splattered frenzy.[12]

The bloody battle that ends *Extreme Prejudice* intensifies the experience of the films in its tradition through formal excess that almost threatens to parody the apocalyptic gunfight as a convention. The battle is set off by the revelation that Major Hackett is working with Cash as his partner in the drug business, news that completely shatters the already wavering faith in the mission of many of Hackett's men—specifically, his right-hand man, Master Sergeant Larry McRose (Clancy Brown), who has, sometimes with less than full confidence, spent much of the film insisting on the sanctity of the outfit's chain of command. By the time Hackett's greed is revealed in Mexico, McRose has had enough; bullets from his gun, aimed at the fleeing Hackett, ignite a conflagration in the town square that will eventually descend into total chaos. His pursuit of Hackett into the center of the village is deeply personal, fueled by the Major's betrayal of his responsibility to their comrades—the execution that McRose delivers is brutally violent, a shotgun blast to Hackett's chest that sends him flying into a fountain. Its intimacy, fueled by McRose's deep and sudden disillusionment with all he has been fighting for, anticipates the final shootout between the cop Danko and drug dealer Rosta in the following year's *Red Heat*. In both moments, the intensity of emotion cannot be restrained, and can only be given voice through gunfire that purges one man from the other's consciousness. McRose's victory is short-lived, however, as he and the rest of his men are swiftly gunned down in the melee. Their agony as they are perforated recalls the bottleneck shootout of *The Long Riders*, as the fleeing members of the James Gang take hit after hit on their way out of Northfield after the botched bank raid. After the gunfire dies down, there is a close-up of each of the dead mercenaries, paying visual tribute to their newfound equality. In Hackett's shot, his face is covered in blood, water from the fountain trickling onto his head in a final humiliation that turns the physical environment in judgment against such a craven operator. A filmmaker who is constantly attentive to the dynamics of groups offers one of his most dysfunctional in *Extreme Prejudice*. As in *Southern Comfort*, their inability to work together dooms them from the start; lies, secrets, and naked self-interest destroy the mercenaries from within. In this unmoored depiction of a group of ex-military operators who have faked their deaths and live off the grid, Hill invests the outlaw gang trope of westerns like *The Wild Bunch* with an overwhelming cynicism that reflects the outlook of noir. Instead of uniting in their purgative, self-immolating act of violence as Peckinpah's outlaws do, these men turn on one another, their ties severed by their inability to overcome their own selfishness and sacrifice for the group.

Though Hill suggests his dramatic interest in the underdeveloped Hackett and his men was less than robust, his attentiveness to their tragedy, as their commanding officer sacrifices their ideals for a payday, offers a parallel to the relationship between Jack and Cash. *Extreme Prejudice* relies on the conventions of westerns and noir films to explore the two characters as mirror images of one another. In describing their relationship—one a cop, one a criminal—Hill sees yet another tradition of filmmaking, hearkening back to what he recalls as "the oldest Warner Bros. plotline," where "one guy becomes a priest and the other guy becomes a crook."[13] *Angels With Dirty Faces* (1938, Curtiz) places priest Pat O'Brien and gangster James Cagney in just this position. In the Fox noir *Cry of the City* (1948, Siodmak), Victor Mature plays a hard-bitten cop from the neighborhood, who grew up with the gangster Richard Conte, and vows to bring him to justice despite their boyhood friendship. Mature's execution of Conte, a shot fired from the distance that hits the fleeing gangster in the back, brings the officer no honor. He lies wounded on a staircase, haunted by his treachery, which he dares not speak aloud as he slips into the back of a police cruiser—where the perpetrators usually sit—with a young man who admired Conte but has seemingly chosen to go straight. Throughout *Extreme Prejudice*, Jack and Cash are similarly mirrored; in their first on-screen meeting, an arranged conversation in the desert, Jack stands in the dark brown uniform of the Texas Ranger and a white hat, while Cash wears a white suit and hat, the drug kingpin's costume a symbol of purity that not only evokes the color of his product, but offers an ironic comment on the work he does. The two men's demeanors are opposites, as well. Cash is garrulous and easygoing, a mood that masks inner pain that he increasingly loses interest in concealing. Jack is stoic to the point of near silence, his jaw clenched tightly, his lips a humorless horizon. Each man is a performer, and self-consciously aware of the artifice of his image; before stepping out to confront Cash, Jack tells his mentor Hank (Rip Torn) how best to cover him, using something of a winking shorthand: "real western," he says, which Hank, an aging Texas sheriff in the tradition of perennial John Wayne sidekick Walter Brennan, immediately understands.

Two critical scenes of public violence, each one perpetrated by Jack and Cash, further the mirror image. In both scenes, Jack and Cash shoot a man in front of a crowd in a bar, a demonstration of their respective holds on authority. Early in *Extreme Prejudice*, Jack and Hank pay a visit to a saloon during a driving rainstorm. Their police prowler pulls into the saloon lot and they are introduced through rain-streaked glass, their be-hatted profiles visible only in silhouette. It is a quintessential neo-noir shot, designed with the self-consciousness of the history of noir films that have preceded it,[14] given an intensified detail—the driving rain obscures nearly all of their features, letting only their voices serve as an introduction to the characters. They are at the bar to serve notice on T. C. Luke (Kent Lipham), a local drug mule; Jack's entrance into the saloon is real western, rifle stock resting on his hip, its barrel aloft. He passes through a crowd of white and Mexican people alike to find T. C. sitting in the back. When T. C. refuses to go along with Benteen and pulls a pistol from beneath the tabletop, Jack draws from beneath his rain slicker and pumps T. C. full of lead in plain view of the gathered crowd. His repeating rifle, while loaded, has been little more than a prop, an elaborate piece of misdirection that led T. C. to believe he might have a chance against the Ranger—Jack's quick draw makes short work of the suspect. Benteen takes his role as a law enforcement officer very seriously, but came into the saloon expecting to use force, not just prepared for it if necessary. Though the scene is undoubtedly western, it also carries echoes of the relation private detective of noir films have to violence.[15] Jack's killing of T. C. nevertheless has the justification of the law behind it; Cash's similar murder of an underling in the Mexican cantina where he presides over his kingdom does not. After making an uneasy alliance with Hackett's men, Benteen travels to Mexico in an attempt to convince Cash to return to the United States; he is incentivized by Cash's abduction of the woman they both love, Sarita (Maria Conchita Alonso). In Mexico, Cash's white suit shows signs of dirt; he is now unshaven and irascible, his hold on his temper badly slipping away. A break in their barroom conversation leads to Cash noticing the arrival of a courier, Jesus (Larry Duran); Cash calls out to him and stands up to meet him in the middle of the sweltering cantina. Cash stands above Jesus on a set of steps and says, "Well, everything's fine. Just fine, except for one little thing. This'll fix it." He draws his revolver, presses it to Jesus's forehead, and pulls the trigger in one sudden motion, the gunshot silencing the cantina crowd. As Jack demonstrated his authority through violence in the Texas saloon, so does Cash in his Mexican cantina; while Benteen camouflages his use of force in the official procedure of law enforcement, Cash ruthlessly wields his power with the sudden intensity of a despot. Jesus's offense, presiding over an account that came up short, gives Cash the freedom to settle things his way: "This is a damn nice country here. I like it. Man can get away with anything just as long as he keeps payin' his friends."

Both scenes are deeply indebted to the western tradition in their adoption of place (saloons/cantinas) and costuming (the lawman and outlaw), but no more so than in their staging of public violence, which is essential to the genre. In western films, violence is a public act that is undertaken to demonstrate how force can be wielded to express power—Lee Clark Mitchell has shown how men in westerns use violence to establish a sense of self.[16] In *Extreme Prejudice*, these two public acts of violence demonstrate to each man's audience that he is in control, and will use force to maintain a kind of order. Benteen's is marked by procedure, however much of a fig leaf it is for old style vigilante justice, while Cash's is driven by sheer arbitrariness, dealt out unceremoniously to maximize shock. In each case, the act of violence becomes a kind of performance, an extension of an idea that consumes Hill's work, as in the public duels in *Hard Times*, *The Long Riders*, *Streets of Fire*, *Crossroads*, and *Undisputed*.

Public gunfights are essential to the western; they literalize the idea that most often, control over land takes on ideological ramifications. Gunfighters or lawmen protecting a bad town from unsavory elements—as in *Last Man Standing*—use the space of the town itself as their battlefield, making the stakes of the conflict strikingly immediate. Hill's consistent removal of non-combatants from the narrative action in his films turns the public space of westerns into the isolated space of film noir, where violence is almost always conducted in private. Noir characters shamefully hide the evidence of their killings, rather than performing them before an audience; *The Assignment*'s hitman Frank kills and disappears. Hill's combination of western and noir imagery creates a clash between the public performance of violence associated with the former genre and the private murders of the latter. In *Extreme Prejudice*, Jack's private spaces are deeply evocative of noir; a long shot down one of his ranch's hallways at night is streaked with shadow, pocked by squares of bright highlights. He passes down the hallway towards the camera in silhouette, a man returning to a house that feels very little like a home. In a more traditional western sequence, an ambush at a gas station perpetrated by T. C.'s brother Chubb (Mickey Jones), Hank is riddled with bullets while Jack fends off machine gun-wielding attackers. Once the gunfight is over and the dust has settled, Hill and cinematographer Matthew F. Leonetti reference *High Noon*, craning the camera high above the field as the lawman walks alone through the dirt. Zinnemann's shot precedes the gunfight, emphasizing Gary Cooper's isolation in advance of the shootout; when Hill and Lloyd Ahern reprise this shot in *Wild Bill*, it comes in the same dramatic place, in advance of Hickok's battle with the mercenaries who have held him hostage. The delay of the *High Noon* shot until after the catastrophic gun battle at the gas station in *Extreme Prejudice* not only repositions the isolation of the lawman to the point following the violence, rather than anticipating it, but its emphasis on Jack's loneliness carries an undercurrent of noir. According to Paul Arthur, urban space in noir can perform a dual function: "during intensely violent scenes of dramatic action represents an externalization of a character's inner state of mind or whether that look is better understood as a subject's introjection of an overtly menacing, disorienting environment."[17] *Extreme Prejudice* finds another way, as the traditional western shot of a desert landscape and a lone lawman performs a function usually associated with noir. There are no trappings of urbanity, no geometric patterns, no overwhelming shadows, but the isolation of noir, where the heroes and villains alike are destroyed, dominates this image. The lawman is not alone so that he can become the hero we already know he is; in *Extreme Prejudice*, Benteen is alone because he failed to anticipate the ambush, got Hank killed, and had little else to do but shoot whoever remained. He even fails to apprehend or kill Chubb, the architect of the surprise, who escapes in a truck before being killed down the road by Hackett and McRose, who watch the ambush through binoculars and intervene only belatedly and surreptitiously. Benteen is unable to become the western hero in this sequence, and the reprise of the iconic shot from *High Noon* does not empathize with Jack by valorizing his bravery, but laments his loneliness and failure.

Aside from their childhood friendship and their affection for Sarita, Jack and Cash are united by their loneliness. The noir-influenced shot of Jack coming home to his ranch strands him in a lonely place; though Hill says now that he regrets killing Hank midway through the film,[18] the effect is to further isolate Jack, forcing him into a deal with Hackett and the mercenaries. The outward performance of the western hero, however, is irreconcilable with the loneliness of noir, a tension which Jack responds to with characteristic stoicism. Cash, on the other hand, embraces the romanticism of isolation; in his Mexican cantina, surrounded by reveling villagers and his own private army, he is terribly alone in a crowd. Upon Jack's arrival in Cash's kingdom, the drug dealer makes the lawman surrender his weapon, preferring to delay their inevitable showdown in favor of a drink and discussion inside the bar. "This is pretty nice, ain't it?" Cash says. "Two amigos drinking, just like old times." Boothe highlights Cash's vulnerability, simultaneously allowing Jack to see his pain and attempting to conceal it. He wants his friend back, much preferring to ignore their societal roles and retain their personal connection. Throughout their conversation, with Sarita conspicuously seated between them, Cash holds forth much more than Benteen, who remains situated behind Nolte's steely interpretation of the character; in contrast with his combustible Jack Cates in the *48 Hrs.* films, Nolte gives a reserved performance marked by the actor's intentionally flat delivery of his lines. The screenplay is judicious in giving out character backstory, but the little that Benteen supplies culminates in a cryptic revelation: "The only thing that ever scared the hell out of me, Cash, was myself. So I come home and I put the badge on, and things were right. When I got home I looked around for my old friend. And he wasn't there." Jack's brief confession paints an alternative vision of his life, one, perhaps, where he became an outlaw like Cash. It also retroactively shapes the execution of T. C. Luke in the saloon in his first scene, demonstrating his capacity for violence. The badge of a

Texas Ranger has restrained his darker impulses—it hasn't extinguished them completely.

By contrast, Cash makes no apologies for his way of life; he insists to Jack that he "got everything I wanted," but Boothe's delivery is wracked by insecurity; just as his execution of Jesus was a performance, so too is his insistence on his happiness. He also situates his rise to the top of his drug empire in distinctly class-oriented terms: "I'm just a poor boy that rose up! Nobody ever gave me nothin'! Ain't nobody gonna take away what I got!" Cash—here is where the double entendre of his name pays off—is animated by a desire to first acquire, and then preserve, his wealth. Reggie in the *48 Hrs.* films, the firemen Vince and Don in *Trespass*, Brewster in *Brewster's Millions*, the title wheelman in *The Driver*, are all consumed by the security of the money to which they feel entitled, earned through labor, theft, inheritance, or ingenuity. These are the concerns of noir characters, who face similar choices as Cash: How far will they go, how much of themselves will they compromise, to get what they want? In *Extreme Prejudice*, Cash has made these choices repeatedly, compromising himself through serial acts of violence and sadism that have corroded his soul; he is introduced stepping out of a shack south of the border, picking up a scorpion in his bare hand and then crushing it. Jack tells him, "You've gone bad." Though Cash refuses to ascribe moral dimension to his choices, Jack's criticism wounds him deeply because he knows it to be true; while Jack steps away from the table in the aftermath of Cash's execution of Jesus, the drug dealer saves his most personal feelings for Sarita.

Figure C.1 Noir and westerns meet in *Extreme Prejudice* (1987), an action film that pits Marshal Jack Benteen (Nick Nolte) against drug dealer Cash Bailey (Powers Boothe), two childhood friends who find themselves on the opposite sides of the law. *Source: Screenshot captured by author.*

"Yeah, it's true. I go to lunch with the governor of this state. I go to Mexico City for them big charity balls," he tells her. "But I ain't got nobody to talk to, honey. Nobody from home." According to Hill, Cash is "a tough guy, but he's certainly not above self-pity." His willingness to vocalize his despair sets him apart from Benteen, who keeps his pain inside: "He'll say things that Jack would never say."[19]

Cash wants only to forestall the violence between himself and Benteen a little longer: "Just need a little more conversation, Jack. Then you can have your gun back." He knows that surrendering the pistol to Jack will accelerate their inevitable confrontation. When they do step outside into the courtyard, they bring an audience of Cash's soldiers and other townspeople with them, who gather to watch. They are to stand back-to-back and count ten, pacing away from one another in an echo of an old-fashioned duel. In stepping out to face one another, Jack and Cash anticipate the darkness of Jeff Bridges's Anthony Mann-style portrayal of Hickok in *Wild Bill*, whose characters Jim Kitses calls "dark, extreme men trapped in an impossible dilemma, making a neurotic attempt to escape themselves and rise above a past of pain and violence."[20] So too are the men of *Extreme Prejudice*; neither really wants to shoot the other, but they feel compelled to do so by their recognition of themselves in their counterpart. Like the doomed hero of *Johnny Handsome*, Benteen wants to purge himself of the darker impulses lurking within him, and Cash needs to eliminate the conscience that tells him his choices were destructive. Cash imbues the moments before the duel with bitter irony, commenting that "it's a good day for a killing" and promising that they will "blast each other into the land of glory." Jack, as is typical, says nothing. The two men are back to back, and the parodically dramatic music by Jerry Goldsmith kicks in as Cash begins to count and they start to pace away; Sarita interrupts the count and the music drops out, the power of her cries defusing the western climax both narratively and formally. Cash has no patience for it: "If you're gonna cry, it just fucks it all up. Lowers the whole tone!" He knows that there is a dimension of playacting to their staged duel—it is as if the non-diegetic music is playing audibly in the courtyard, investing the moment with the high drama that Cash wants. He desires to make his or Jack's death glorious, so that it might invest the violence with meaning. The further interruption, which comes when McRose turns on the duplicitous Hackett in the hacienda adjacent to the duel, begins the melee and delays the showdown until the film's final moments. The slaughter over, Jack and Cash stand opposite one another, guns at the ready. Cash offers a Hawksian reminder to his opponent: "We gotta do things right, Jack," he says, "Fair is fair." After they make Sarita count to three, Cash fires and Jack puts one in his friend's shoulder, offering him one last chance to call it off. When Cash refuses, Jack fires again, his shots captured in a close-up of his barking pistol.

Cash staggers and then falls in slow motion, the editing emphasizing the moment of pain that precedes death.

In *Extreme Prejudice*, Mexico becomes a proving ground for Jack and Cash, as well as the mercenaries who tear themselves apart over greed and disloyalty—as it was for the cavalrymen in *Geronimo*. Though Jack survives and takes Sarita with him back to the United States, his desire to purge the dark part of himself that Cash represented goes unfulfilled; in exchange for the chance to leave, he bargains with Cash's lieutenant Lupo (Luis Contreras), telling him that now he gets "to wear the white suit." In Jack's mind, there will always be a man south of the border, clad in a white suit—the violent, destructive part of him will never really die. As the chaotic frenzy of violence between the mercenaries and Mexicans recalls a tradition of similar scenes in western films, the showdown between Jack and Cash does as well. In westerns, according to Lee Clark Mitchell, "Violence is the means by which men are encouraged to show their manliness, both as handsome cinematic figures that rivet the viewer's gaze, and as individuals capable of triumphing over adversity as only men are allowed to do."[21] One might say the same thing of most of Hill's films, which consistently put men to the test, asking them to perform in order to demonstrate their worth. They often fail, but sometimes prove that they, as Hawks would say, "are good enough."

Mexico is also the primary setting of the forthcoming *Dead for a Dollar*, Hill's latest project, which is set for release in 2022. It is a western set in 1897 with a propulsive, direct screenplay populated by dialogue written with forthrightness and specificity. As in *The Getaway*, Mexico offers its characters a chance at a better life—their travels south are fueled by the desire to escape, but their arrival in Mexico reveals that there are limits to how far they can run. The story concerns a bounty hunter called Max Borlund (Christoph Waltz), who is hired by a wealthy man to facilitate the return of his wife Rachel (Rachel Brosnahan), who has fled to Mexico with a Black soldier, Elijah Jones, who is also her lover. Joined by another Black cavalryman, Poe, Max travels across the border to bring Rachel back, but runs afoul of an old nemesis, the recently paroled Joe Cribbens (Willem Dafoe), who wants revenge against Max for putting him behind bars. Hill's screenplay evokes not only the kidnapped woman idea of *Streets of Fire*, but also *The Searchers* and especially *The Professionals* (1966, Brooks). Hill is quick to point out that all of these stories have even greater traditional resonances: "it's Helen of Troy, too," he says.[22] Hill's inclusion of Black soldiers adds a racial dimension to this version of the myth, demonstrating a continued interest on his part in the complexities of American history. It also features a public duel that ups the ante on *Bullet to the Head*'s axe fight, as Poe and a villain face off against each other with bullwhips, a scene that a smiling Hill calls "just showing off."[23] The part of Max is specifically tailored to Waltz, taking advantage of the actor's Austrian origins, which invest the bounty hunter with an air of mystery. The screenplay is deliberately opaque about Max's backstory, even obscuring his nationality. While riding south with Poe, the soldier asks him where he comes from: "Well you mind tellin' me—You a Dutchman or a Swede—whatever," he says. Max responds, "No problem. I'm an American."[24]

To Walter Hill, longevity is one of the most important things that a filmmaker can achieve:

> It's the totality of the vision and the uniqueness of the vision, and a body of work, at least to me, is what's the most significant. And making one fabulous movie is not quite what a body of work is.[25]

He has survived in a difficult business long enough to create a sustained collection of films made in six decades, from the streets of San Francisco as the assistant director on *Bullitt* to the deserts of New Mexico for his forthcoming *Dead for a Dollar*. Like any film artist, he has had his share of successes and failures, both artistically and commercially, and dealt with the compromises attendant on mainstream Hollywood filmmaking. His devotion to an older tradition of classical filmmaking certainly did him no favors as the tastes of audiences changed; as mainstream studio productions seemed to be getting bigger, louder, and faster, he seemingly preferred to withdraw further into the past, finding refuge in westerns, an antiquated genre by the standards of most contemporary viewers. Taken together, Hill's films offer a vision of American society shaped by its history as filtered through cinema. Because the medium itself is one of the primary chroniclers of—and distorters of— the history of human endeavors, much of Hill's work is informed by and in conversation with cinematic traditions. Hollywood has, since its very beginning, been a mythmaking machine, and Walter Hill's films interrogate the myths built by cinema; they offer extensions of, correctives to, and new visions of some of the foundational myths of America as expressed by its most influential art form.

NOTES

1. Walter Hill, screenplay for *The Getaway*, dated 23 February 1972.
2. Christopher Sharrett, "Peckinpah the Radical: The Politics of *The Wild Bunch*," in *Sam Peckinpah's The Wild Bunch*, 84.
3. Paul Schrader, "Sam Peckinpah Going to Mexico," in *Doing It Right: The Best Criticism on Sam Peckinpah's* The Wild Bunch, 23.

4. Marshall Fine, *Bloody Sam: The Life and Films of Sam Peckinpah* (Donald I. Fine, Inc., 1991), 274.

5. Peckinpah quoted in Garner Simmons, *Peckinpah: A Portrait in Montage – The Definitive Edition* (First Equuleus Edition, 2019), 255.

6. Walter Hill, interview with the author, 23 April 2021.

7. Ibid.

8. Walter Hill, interview with the author, 7 May 2021.

9. Walter Hill, interview with the author, 4 June 2021.

10. I have quoted from Lichtenfeld a few times, but the relevant passages can be found in Eric Lichtenfeld, *Action Speaks Louder*, 2–3.

11. Interview with the author, 12 March 2021.

12. Ibid.

13. Interview with the author, 12 March 2021.

14. Mark Bould, Kathrina Glitre, and Greg Tuck's handy definition of neo-noir: "made and watched by people familiar with the concept of film noir," in "Parallax Views: An Introduction," in *Neo-Noir*, Wallflower, 2009, 5.

15. John G. Cawelti, "Myths of Violence in American Popular Culture," *Critical Inquiry* 1, no. 3 (1975), 536.

16. Lee Clark Mitchell, "Violence in the Film Western," 178.

17. Paul Arthur, "Murder's Tongue," in *Violence and American Cinema*, 165.

18. Interview with the author, 12 March 2021.

19. Interview with the author, 12 March 2021.

20. Jim Kitses, *Horizons West*, 143.

21. Lee Clark Mitchell, "Violence in the Film Western," 177.

22. Interview with the author, 23 April 2021.

23. Ibid.

24. Walter Hill, screenplay for *Dead for a Dollar*, draft dated 1 May 2021.

25. Interview with the author, 26 January 2021.

Works Cited

Abelson, Miriam J. "Dangerous Privilege: Trans Men, Masculinities, and Changing Perceptions of Safety." *Sociological Forum* 29, no. 3 (2014): 549–570. http://www.jstor.org.cod.idm.oclc.org/stable/43653950.

Adams, Sam. "Is (Re)Assignment 2016's Most Offensive Movie?" *BBC*. September 13, 2016, https://www.bbc.com/culture/article/20160913-film-review-is-reassignment-2016s-most-offensive-movie.

Alexander, Michelle. *The New Jim Crow*. New York: New Press, 2010

Allain, Mathé. "Glamour and Squalor: Louisiana on Film." *Louisiana History: The Journal of the Louisiana Historical Association* 27, no. 3 (1986): 229–237. http://www.jstor.org.cod.idm.oclc.org/stable/4232519.

Allen, Samantha. "Why 'The Assignment' Stinks of Sensationalist Transphobia." *The Daily Beast*. January 25, 2017. https://www.thedailybeast.com/why-the-assignment-stinks-of-sensationalist-transphobia.

"Appendix I: The Hollywood Motion Picture Production Code of 1930." In Thomas Doherty, *Pre-Code Hollywood: Sex, Immorality, and Insurrection in American Cinema 1930-1934*.

Arroyo, Jose. "Introduction." In *Action/Spectacle Cinema*, ed. Jose Arroyo, vii–xiv. London: BFI Publishing, 2000.

Arthur, Paul. "Murder's Tongue." In *Violence and American Cinema*, ed. J. David Slocum, 153–175. New York: Routledge, 2001.

Auerbach, Jonathan. *Dark Borders: Film Noir and American Citizenship*. Durham, NC: Duke University Press, 2011.

Bajgrowicz, Brooke. "The 15 Highest-Grossing '90s Movies of All Time (According To Box Office Mojo)," *Screenrant*, June 5, 2020, https://screenrant.com/grossing-90s-movies-box-office-mojo/.

Basinger, Jeanine. *Anthony Mann: New and Expanded Edition*. Middletown, CT: Wesleyan University Press, 2007.

Baumgartner, Michael. "Underscoring Chased Heroes and Robbing Villains: Music of Immediacy in New Hollywood Action Thrillers of the late 1960s and 1970s." In

Music in Action Film: Sounds Like Action!, ed. James Buhler and Mark Durrand, 99–115. New York: Routledge, 2021.

Bazin, Andre. "How Could You Possibly be a Hitchcocko-Hawksian?" In *Howard Hawks: American Artist*, ed. Jim Hillier and Peter Wollen, 32–34. London: British Film Institute, 1996.

Bean, Jennifer M. "Trauma Thrills: Notes on Early Action Cinema." In *Action and Adventure Cinema*, ed. Yvonne Tasker, 17–30. Malden, MA: Wiley Blackwell, 2015.

Belton, John. "Howard Hawks and Co." In *Focus on Howard Hawks*, ed. Joseph McBride, 94–108. Englewood Cliffs, NJ: Prentice-Hall, 1972.

Bingham, Dennis. *Acting Male: Masculinities in the Films of James Stewart, Jack Nicholson, and Clint Eastwood*. New Brunswick, NJ: Rutgers University Press, 1993.

Biskind, Peter. *Easy Riders, Raging Bulls*. New York: Touchstone Books, 1998.

Bliss, Michael. "Introduction." In *Doing It Right: The Best Criticism on Sam Peckinpah's* The Wild Bunch, ed. Michael Bliss, xv–xxiii. Carbondale, IL: Southern Illinois University Press, 1994.

Bogle, Donald. *Toms, Coons, Mulattoes, Mammies, and Bucks*. 5th Edition. New York: Bloomsbury, 2016.

Borde, Raymond, and Etienne Chaumeton. *A Panorama of American Film Noir 1941-1953*. 1955. Translated by Paul Hammond. San Francisco: City Lights Books, 2002.

Bordwell, David. "Aesthetics in Action: Kungfu, Gunplay, and Cinematic Expressivity." In *At Full Speed: Hong Kong Cinema in A Borderless World*, ed. Esther C.M. Yau, 73–94. Minneapolis: University of Minnesota Press, 2001.

Bordwell, David. "Intensified Continuity Visual Style in Contemporary American Film." *Film Quarterly* 55, no. 3 (2002): 16–28. doi:10.1525/fq.2002.55.3.16.

Bordwell, David, Janet Staiger, and Kristin Thompson. *The Classical Hollywood Cinema*. New York: Columbia University Press, 1985.

Bould, Mark, Kathrina Glitre, and Greg Tuck. "Parallax Views: An Introduction." In *Neo-Noir*, ed. Mark Bould, Kathrina Glitre, and Greg Tuck, 1–10. New York: Wallflower, 2009.

Buhler, James and Mark Durrand. "Preface." In *Music in Action Film: Sounds Like Action!*, ed. James Buhler and Mark Durrand, xiii-xxviii. New York: Routledge, 2021.

Carney, Ray. *American Vision: The Films of Frank Capra*. Hanover, NH: Wesleyan University Press, 1986.

Carroll, Noël. "The Future of Allusion: Hollywood in the Seventies (And Beyond)." *October* 20 (1982): 51–81. doi:10.2307/778606.

Carter, Matthew and Andrew Patrick Nelson. "Introduction: 'No One Would Know It Was Mine': Delmer Daves, Modest Auteur." In *ReFocus: The Films of Delmer Daves*, ed. Matthew Carter and Andrew Patrick Nelson, 1–47. Edinburgh: Edinburgh University Press, 2016.

Casper, Drew. *Hollywood Film 1963-1976*. Malden, MA: Wiley-Blackwell, 2011.

Cawelti, John G. "Myths of Violence in American Popular Culture." *Critical Inquiry* 1, no. 3 (1975): 521–541. http://www.jstor.org.cod.idm.oclc.org/stable/1342829.

Cawelti, John G. *The Six-Gun Mystique Sequel*. Bowling Green, KY: Bowling Green State University Popular Press, 1999.

Clover, Carol. *Men, Women, and Chainsaws* – Updated Edition. Princeton, NJ: Princeton University Press, 2015.

Conrich, Ian and David Woods. "Introduction." In *The Cinema of John Carpenter: The Technique of Terror*, ed. Ian Conrich and David Woods, 1–9. London: Wallflower Press, 2004.

Covey, William. "The Genre Don't Know Where It Came From: African American Neo-Noir Since the 1960s." *Journal of Film and Video* 55, no. 2/3 (2003): 59–72. http://www.jstor.org.cod.idm.oclc.org/stable/20688414.

Cumbow, Robert C. *Order in the Universe: The Films of John Carpenter*, Second Edition. Lanham, MD: Scarecrow Press, 2000.

De Cordova, Richard. "Genre and Performance: An Overview." In *Film Genre Reader II*, ed. Barry Keith Grant, 129–139. Austin: University of Texas Press, 1995.

Desser, "Toward a Structural Analysis of the Postwar Samurai Film," *Quarterly Review of Film Studies* (Winter 1983), 25–41. doi:10.1080/10509208309361143.

Desser, David. "When We See The Ocean, We Figure We're Home: From Ritual to Romance in *The Warriors*." In *City That Never Sleeps*, ed. Murray Pomerance, 123–136. New Brunswick: Rutgers University Press, 2007.

Diawara, Manthia. "Black Spectatorship: Problems of Identification and Resistance." *Screen* 29:4 (1988), 66–79. doi:10.1093/screen/29.4.66.

Dixon, Wheeler Winston. "Re-Visioning the Western: Code, Myth, and Genre in Peckinpah's *The Wild Bunch*." In *Sam Peckinpah's* The Wild Bunch, ed. Stephen Prince, 155–174. New York: Cambridge University Press, 1999.

Doherty, Thomas. *Teenagers and Teenpics: The Juvenilization of American Movies in the 1950s*. Philadelphia: Temple University Press, 2002.

Donalson, Melvin. *Masculinity in the Interracial Buddy Film*. Jefferson, NC: McFarland, 2006.

Durgnat, Raymond. "Paint it Black: The Family Tree of Film Noir." In *Film Noir Reader*, ed. Alain Silver and James Ursini, 37–52. New York: Limelight Edition, 1996.

Dyer, Peter John. "Sling the Lamps Low." In *Focus on Howard Hawks*, ed. Joseph McBride, 78–93. Englewood Cliffs, NJ: Prentice-Hall, 1972.

Dyer, Richard. "Action!" In *Action/Spectacle Cinema*, ed. Jose Arroyo, 17–21. London: BFI Publishing, 2000.

Ebert, Roger. "Review of *I Spit on Your Grave*." rogerebert.com. July 16, 1980. https://www.rogerebert.com/reviews/i-spit-on-your-grave-1980.

Ehrenstein, David, and Bill Reed. *Rock on Film*. New York: Delilah Books, 1982.

Farber, Manny. "Howard Hawks." In *Focus on Howard Hawks*, ed. Joseph McBride, 28–34. Englewood Cliffs, NJ: Prentice-Hall, 1972.

Fine, Marshall. *Bloody Sam: The Life and Films of Sam Peckinpah*. New York: Donald I. Fine, Inc., 1991.

Flanagan, Martin. "Get Ready For Rush Hour: The Chronotope in Action." In *Action and Adventure Cinema*, ed. Yvonne Tasker, 103–118. New York: Routledge, 2004.

Frankel, Glenn. *The Searchers: The Making of an American Legend*. New York: Bloomsbury, 2013.

Friedkin, William. *The Friedkin Connection: A Memoir*. New York: Harper Perennial, 2013.

Galbraith, Jane. "Coincidences Cause Director to Tread Lightly With 'Trespass'." *Los Angeles Times*. December 28, 1992. https://www.latimes.com/archives/la-xpm-1992-12-28-ca-2070-story.html.

Gallagher, Tag. "Shoot-Out at the Genre Corral: Problems in the "Evolution" of the Western." In *Film Genre Reader II*, ed. Barry Keith Grant, 246–260. Austin: University of Texas Press, 1995.

Gilbey, Ryan. *It Don't Worry Me: The Revolutionary American Films of the Seventies*. New York: Faber & Faber, 2003.

Grant, Barry Keith. "Disorder in the Universe: John Carpenter and the Question of Genre." In *The Cinema of John Carpenter: The Technique of Terror*, ed. Ian Conrich and David Woods, 10–20. London: Wallflower Press, 2004.

Grant, Barry Keith. "Introduction: Spokes in the Wheels." In *John Ford's* Stagecoach. ed. Barry Keith Grant, 1–20. New York, Cambridge University Press, 2003.

Gross, Larry. "Big and Loud." In *Action/Spectacle Cinema*, ed. Jose Arroyo, 3–9. London: BFI Publishing, 2000.

Guerrero, Ed. *Framing Blackness: The African American Image in Film*. Philadelphia: Temple University Press, 1993.

Gussow, Adam. "'I Got a Big White Fella From Memphis Made a Deal With Me': Black Men, White Boys, and the Anxieties of Blues Postmodernity in Walter Hill's *Crossroads* (1986)." *Arkansas Review: A Journal of Delta Studies* 46, no. 2 (August 2015): 85–104. http://search.ebscohost.com.cod.idm.oclc.org/login.aspx?direct=true&db=a9h&AN=109051927&site=ehost-live&scope=site.

Hammett, Dashiell. "Nightmare Town." In *Nightmare Town*. 3–41. First Vintage Crime/Black Lizard Edition, 2000.

Hammett, Dashiell. *Red Harvest*. Vintage Crime/Black Lizard Books Edition, 1992.

Hawks, Howard. *Hawks on Hawks*. Ed. Joseph McBride. Lexington: University Press of Kentucky, 2013.

Herman, Jan. *A Talent For Trouble: The Life of Hollywood's Most Acclaimed Director*. New York: Da Capo, 1997.

Higgins, Scott. "Suspenseful Situations: Melodramatic Narrative and the Contemporary Action Film." *Cinema Journal* 47, no. 2 (2008): 74–96.

Hill, Walter. "Edgar Wright and Walter Hill Discuss *The Driver*." Interview by Edgar Wright. *Empire*. March 13, 2017. https://www.empireonline.com/movies/features/edgar-wright-walter-hill-discuss-driver/.

Hill, Walter. "Foreword." In *American Neo-Noir: The Movie Never Ends*, Alain Silver and James Ursini, 9. Milwaukee, WI: Applause Theatre and Film Books, 2015.

Hill, Walter. "Slow Motion: Walter Hill on Sam Peckinpah." On *The Long Riders*. DVD. Kino Lorber, 2017.

Hill, Walter. "Walter Hill on the Anti-Buddy Movie and the Evolution of the Action Film." Interview by Scott Tobias. *The AV Club*. February 1, 2013.

https://film.avclub.com/walter-hill-on-the-anti-buddy-movie-and-the-evolution-o-1798236038.

Hill, Walter. "Walter Hill's Dark Visions." Interview by John Stanley. *SF Gate*. May 27, 2007. https://www.sfgate.com/entertainment/article/Walter-Hill-s-Dark-visions-2558469.php.

Howell, Amanda. *Popular Film Music and Masculinity in Action: A Different Tune*. New York: Routledge, 2015.

Humphries, Reynolds. "The Politics of Crime and the Crime of Politics: Postwar Noir, the Liberal Consensus, and the Hollywood Left." In *Film Noir Reader 4*, ed. Alain Silver and James Ursini, 227–246. New Jersey: Limelight Editions, 2004.

Jacobs, Jason. "Gunfire." In *Action/Spectacle Cinema*, ed. Jose Arroyo, 9–16. London: BFI Publishing, 2000.

Jameson, Richard T. "Son of Noir." In *Film Noir Reader 2*, ed. Alain Silver and James Ursini, 197–206. New York: Limelight Edition, 1999.

Jeffords, Susan. *Hard Bodies: Hollywood Masculinity in the Reagan Era*. New Brunswick, NJ: Rutgers University Press, 1994.

Johnson, Albert. "Moods Indigo: A Long View." *Film Quarterly* 44, no. 2 (1990): 13–27. doi:10.2307/1212655.

Kirshner, Jonathan. *Hollywood's Last Golden Age: Politics, Society, and The Seventies Film in America*. Ithaca, NY: Cornell University Press, 2012.

Kitses, Jim. *Horizons West: Directing The Western from John Ford to Clint Eastwood*, New Edition. London: British Film Institute, 2004.

Langford, Barry. *Film Genre: Hollywood and Beyond*. Edinburgh: Edinburgh University Press, 2005.

Langlois, Henri. "The Modernity of Howard Hawks." In *Focus on Howard Hawks*, ed. Joseph McBride, 65–69. Englewood Cliffs, NJ: Prentice-Hall, 1972.

Lev, Peter. *American Films of the 70s: Conflicting Visions*. Austin, TX: University of Texas Press, 2000.

Lev, Peter. "Movies and the End of an Era." In *American Cinema of the 1970s: Themes and Variations*, ed. Lester D. Friedman, 228–249. New Brunswick: Rutgers University Press, 2007.

Lichtenfeld, Eric. *Action Speaks Louder: Violence, Spectacle, and The American Action Movie*, Revised and Expanded Edition. Middletown, CT: Wesleyan University Press, 2007.

Lott, Eric. "The Whiteness of Film Noir." *American Literary History* 9, no. 3 (1997): 542–566. http://www.jstor.org.cod.idm.oclc.org/stable/490180.

Lott, Tommy L. "A No-Theory Theory of Contemporary Black Cinema." In *Representing Blackness: Issues in Film and Video*, ed. Valerie Smith, 83–96. New Brunswick: Rutgers University Press, 1997.

Maltby, Richard. "A Better Sense of History: John Ford and the Indians." In *The Book of Westerns*, ed. Ian Cameron and Douglas Pye, 34–59. Continuum, 1996.

Mamet, David. *On Directing Film*. Penguin Books, 1991.

McBride, Joseph. *Searching for John Ford*. New York: Faber & Faber, 2003.

McKinney, Devin. "Violence: The Strong and the Weak." In *Screening Violence*, ed. Stephen Prince, 99–109. New Brunswick, NJ: Rutgers University Press, 2000.

Mitchell, Lee Clark. "Violence in the Film Western." In *Violence and American Cinema*, ed. J. David Slocum, 176–191. New York: Routledge, 2001.

Mitchell, Lee Clark. *Westerns: Making the Man in Fiction and Film*. Chicago, IL: University of Chicago Press, 1996.

Mulvey, Laura. "Cinematic Gesture: The Ghost in the Machine." In *Gesture and Film*, ed. Nicholas Chare and Liz Watkins, 9–17. New York: Routledge, 2017.

Murphy, Eddie. "Episode 1207 – Eddie Murphy." *WTF with Marc Maron*. March 8, 2021, http://www.wtfpod.com/podcast/episode-1207-eddie-murphy.

Murphy, Ian. "'Human Frailty Swallowed Whole': On Walter Hill's *Southern Comfort* (1981)." *Bright Lights Film Journal*. October 31, 2012. https://brightlightsfilm.com/human-frailty-swallowed-whole-on-walter-hills-southern-comfort-1981/.

Neale, Steve. "Action-Adventure as Hollywood Genre," *Action and Adventure Cinema*, ed. Yvonne Tasker, 71–83. New York: Routledge, 2004.

Neale, Steve. "Westerns and Gangster Films since the 1970s." In *Genre and Contemporary Hollywood*, ed. Steven Neale, 27–47. London: BFI, 2002.

Nystrom, Derek. *Hard Hats, Rednecks, and Macho Men: Class in 1970s American Cinema*. New York: Oxford University Press, 2009.

Osteen, Mark. "Framed: Forging Identities in Film Noir." *Journal of Film and Video* 62, no. 3 (2010): 17–35. doi:10.5406/jfilmvideo.62.3.0017.

Osteen, Mark. *Nightmare Alley: Film Noir and the American Dream*. Johns Hopkins University Press, 2013.

Palmer, Lorrie. ""Cranked" Masculinity: Hypermediation in Digital Action Cinema." *Cinema Journal* 51, no. 4 (2012): 1–25. http://www.jstor.org.cod.idm.oclc.org/stable/23253574.

Palmer, R. Barton. *Shot on Location: Postwar American Cinema and the Exploration of Real Place*. New Brunswick: Rutgers University Press, 2016.

Patterson, John. "Walter Hill: A Life in the Fast Lane." Interview by John Patterson. *The Guardian*. July 17, 2014. https://www.theguardian.com/film/2014/jul/17/walter-hill-action-movie-interview.

Pinkerton, Nick. "Audio Commentary." On *Ulzana's Raid*. Blu-Ray, Kino Lorber, 2020.

Pippin, Robert B. *Hollywood Westerns and American Myth: The Importance of Howard Hawks and John Ford for Political Philosophy*. New Haven: Yale University Press, 2010.

Pope, Richard. "Doing Justice: A Ritual-Psychoanalytic Approach to Postmodern Melodrama and a Certain Tendency of the Action Film." *Cinema Journal* 51, no. 2 (2012): 113–136. http://www.jstor.org.cod.idm.oclc.org/stable/41341038.

Porfirio, Robert. "No Way Out: Existential Motifs in Film Noir." In *Film Noir Reader*, ed. Alain Silver and James Ursini, 77–94. New York: Limelight Edition, 1996.

Prats, Armando Jose. *Invisible Natives: Myth & Identity in the American Western*. Ithaca, NY: Cornell University Press, 2002.

Prince, Stephen. *Classical Film Violence*. New Brunswick: Rutgers University Press, 2003.

Prince, Stephen. "Genre and Violence in the Work of Kurosawa and Peckinpah." In *Action and Adventure Cinema*, ed. Yvonne Tasker, 331–344. Malden, MA: Wiley Blackwell, 2015.
Prince, Stephen. "Graphic Violence in the Cinema: Origins, Aesthetic Design, and Social Effects." In *Screening Violence*, ed. Stephen Prince, 1–46. New Brunswick, NJ: Rutgers University Press, 2000.
Prince, Stephen. "Introduction: Movies and the 1980s." In *American Cinema of the 1980s: Themes and Variations*, ed. Stephen Prince, 1–21. New Brunswick, NJ: Rutgers University Press, 2007.
Prince, Stephen. "Introduction: Sam Peckinpah, Savage Poet of American Cinema." In *Sam Peckinpah's* The Wild Bunch, ed. Stephen Prince, 1–36. New York: Cambridge University Press, 1999.
Prince, Stephen. *Savage Cinema: Sam Peckinpah and the Rise of Ultraviolent Movies*. Austin, TX: University of Texas Press, 1998.
Prince, Stephen. *The Warrior's Camera: The Cinema of Akira Kurosawa* (Revised and Expanded Edition). Princeton, NJ: Princeton University Press, 1991.
Purse, Lisa. *Contemporary Action Cinema*. Edinburgh: Edinburgh University Press, 2011.
Pye, Douglas, "The Collapse of Fantasy: Masculinity in the Westerns of Anthony Mann." In *The Book of Westerns*, ed. Ian Cameron and Douglas Pye, 167–173. Continuum, 1996.
Pye, Douglas. "Ulzana's Raid." In *The Book of Westerns*, ed. Ian Cameron and Douglas Pye, 262–268. Continuum, 1996.
Rivette, Jacques. "The Genuis of Howard Hawks." In *Howard Hawks: American Artist*, ed. Jim Hillier and Peter Wollen, 26–31. London: British Film Institute, 1996.
Romao, Tico. "Guns and Gas." In *The Hollywood Action and Adventure Film*, ed. Yvonne Tasker, 130–152. Malden, MA: Wiley Blackwell, 2015.
Sarris, Andrew. "Howard Hawks." In *Howard Hawks: American Artist*, ed. Jim Hillier and Peter Wollen, 103–106. London: British Film Institute, 1996.
Sarris, Andrew. "The World of Howard Hawks." In *Focus on Howard Hawks*, ed. Joseph McBride, 35–64. Englewood Cliffs, NJ: Prentice-Hall, 1972.
Saunders, John. *The Western Genre: From Lordsburg to Big Whiskey*. London: Wallflower, 2001.
Schrader, Paul. "Notes on Film Noir." In *Film Noir Reader*, ed. Alain Silver and James Ursini, 53–64. New York: Limelight Edition, 1996.
Schrader, Paul. "Sam Peckinpah Going to Mexico." In *Doing It Right: The Best Criticism on Sam Peckinpah's* The Wild Bunch, ed. Michael Bliss, 17–30. Carbondale, IL: Southern Illinois University Press, 1994.
Schrader, Paul. *Schrader on Schrader & Other Writings: Revised Edition*. Ed. Kevin Jackson. Faber and Faber, 2004.
Seydor, Paul. "Audio Commentary." On *Bring Me the Head of Alfredo Garcia*. Blu-Ray, Kino Lorber, 2021.
Sharrett, Christopher. "Peckinpah the Radical: The Politics of *The Wild Bunch*." In *Sam Peckinpah's The Wild Bunch*, ed. Stephen Prince, 79–104. New York: Cambridge University Press, 1999.

Shotguns and Six-Strings: The Making of a Rock 'N' Roll Fable. On *Streets of Fire.* Blu-Ray, Shout Factory, 2014.

Simmons, Garner. *Peckinpah: A Portrait in Montage* – The Definitive Edition. New York: First Equuleus Edition, 2019.

Sklar, Robert. "Empire to the West: *Red River.*" In *Howard Hawks: American Artist*, ed. Jim Hillier and Peter Wollen, 152–162. London: British Film Institute, 1996.

Slocum, J. David. "Introduction." In *Violence and American Cinema*, ed. J. David Slocum, 1–36. New York: Routledge, 2001.

Smith, Christopher J. "Papa Legba and the Liminal Spaces of the Blues: Roots Music in Deep South Film." In *American Cinema and the Southern Imaginary*, ed. Deborah E. Barker and Kathryn McKee, 317–335. Athens, GA: University of Georgia Press, 2011.

Smith, Imogen Sara. *In Lonely Places: Film Noir Beyond the City.* Jefferson, NC: McFarland, 2011.

Smith, Valerie. "Introduction." In *Representing Blackness: Issues in Film and Video*, ed. Valerie Smith, 1–11. New Brunswick: Rutgers University Press, 1997.

Smukler, Maya Montanez. *Liberating Hollywood: Women Directors & The Feminist Reform of 1970s American Cinema.* New Brunswick, NJ: Rutgers University Press, 2019.

Snead, James. A. "Spectatorship and Capture in King Kong: The Guilty Look." In *Representing Blackness*, ed. Valerie Smith, 25–46. New Brunswick: Rutgers University Press, 1997.

Spoto, Donald. *Stanley Kramer: Filmmaker.* Hollywood: Samuel French, 1978.

Sragow, Michael. "Realized Ambitions." *The Atlantic*. December 1995. https://www.theatlantic.com/magazine/archive/1995/12/realized-ambitions/376504/.

Sragow, Michael. "Sam Peckinpah, 1925–1984." In *Doing It Right: The Best Criticism on Sam Peckinpah's* The Wild Bunch, ed. Michael Bliss, 177–188. Carbondale, IL: Southern Illinois University Press, 1994.

Tasker, Yvonne. "Introduction." In *Action and Adventure Cinema*, ed. Yvonne Tasker, 1–13. Malden, MA: Wiley Blackwell, 2015.

Tasker, Yvonne. *Spectacular Bodies.* New York: Routledge, 1993.

"The Making of *Southern Comfort.*" On *Southern Comfort.* Blu-Ray, Shout Factory, 2014.

"Trailer for *Southern Comfort.*" On *Southern Comfort.* Blu-Ray, Shout Factory, 2014.

Tuska, Jon. *The American West in Film.* Lincoln, NE: University of Nebraska Press, 1988.

Vallan, Giulia D'Agnolo. "Last Neo-Traditionalist Standing." *Film Comment* 49, no. 1 (January 2013): 54–60. http://search.ebscohost.com.cod.idm.oclc.org/login.aspx?direct=true&db=a9h&AN=84855570&site=ehost-live&scope=site.

Walker, Michael. "The Westerns of Delmer Daves." In *The Book of Westerns*, ed. Ian Cameron and Douglas Pye, 123–160. Continuum, 1996.

Wilson, Ron. "The Left-Handed Form of Human Endeavor: Crime Films During the 1990s." In *Film Genre 2000*, ed. Wheeler Winston Dixon, 143–160. Albany, NY: SUNY Press, 2000.

Wollen, Peter. "Introduction." In *Howard Hawks: American Artist*, ed. Jim Hillier and Peter Wollen, 1–11. London: British Film Institute, 1996.
Wood, Robin. *Hollywood from Vietnam to Reagan*. New York: Columbia University Press, 1986.
Wood, Robin. "*Rio Bravo*." In *Howard Hawks: American Artist*, ed. Jim Hillier and Peter Wollen, 87–102. London: BFI, 1996.
Wood, Robin. *Robin Wood on the Horror Film: Collected Essays and Reviews*. Ed. Barry Keith Grant. Detroit, MI: Wayne State University Press, 2018.
Woodman, Brian J. "A Hollywood War of Wills: Cinematic Representation of Vietnamese Super-Soldiers and America's Defeat in the War." *Journal of Film and Video* 55, no. 2/3 (2003): 44–58. http://www.jstor.org.cod.idm.oclc.org/stable/20688413.
Wright, Joshua. "Be Like Mike?: The Black Athlete's Dilemma." *Spectrum: A Journal on Black Men* 4, no. 2 (2016): 1–19. doi:10.2979/spectrum.4.2.01.

INTERVIEWS

Henriksen, Lance. February 6, 2021. Via Zoom.
Hill, Walter. January 26, 2021. Via Zoom.
Hill, Walter. February 5, 2021. Via Zoom.
Hill, Walter. February 26, 2021. Via Zoom.
Hill, Walter. March 5, 2021. Via Zoom.
Hill, Walter. March 12, 2021. Via Zoom.
Hill, Walter. March 26, 2021. Via Zoom.
Hill, Walter. April 9, 2021. Via Zoom.
Hill, Walter. April 23, 2021. Via Zoom.
Hill, Walter. May 7, 2021. Via Zoom.
Hill, Walter. June 4, 2021. Via Zoom.
Kelly, David Patrick. January 25, 2021. Via Zoom.
Remar, James. January 26, 2021. Via Phone.
Sadler, William. February 22, 2021. Via Zoom.
Weaver, Sigourney. April 13, 2021. Via Phone.

Index

20th Century Fox, 79

Abelson, Miriam J., 238
Above the Law (1988, Davis), 46
acrobatics, 22
action-comedies, 25
action films, 5, 8, 9, 18–19, 21–29, 32, 39, 40, 45, 46, 49, 50, 92, 93, 106, 107, 132, 142, 143, 149–51, 155, 171, 214, 215, 235
action genre, 17, 19–21, 23–25, 27–29, 39, 44, 59, 76, 85, 101, 132, 133, 149, 159, 189, 247
action hero, 21–25
action-musical hybrid, 143
action sequences, 22, 23, 29, 69, 102, 142, 143, 247
Adams, Sam, 234
Adjani, Isabelle, 33
adventure films, 17, 43
"aestheticized violence," 6, 7
aesthetics, 4, 26, 27, 86, 88, 144, 150, 216; comic book, 50, 51; rock and roll, 144, 178; visual, 19, 38, 75
African Americans, 108, 111, 168, 182
Ahern, Lloyd, 165, 185, 208, 247, 252
Air Force One (1997, Petersen), 21
Air Force (1943, Hawks), 54–57
Akinnuoye-Agbaje, Adewale, 229

Albert, Eddie, 89
Aldrich, Robert, 89–91, 97
Alexander, Michelle, 170
Alien (1979, Scott), 3, 53–54, 239–40
Alien 3 (1992, Fincher), 54
Aliens (1986, Cameron), 54, 93
Allain, Mathe, 94
allegorical interpretation, 74, 76, 98
Alonso, Maria Conchita, 251
Altman, Robert, 191
amateur video, 186
AMC television network, 27, 189, 207
American Cinema of the 1970s: Themes and Variations (Lev), 3
American Cinema of the 1980s: Themes and Variations (Prince), 3
American culture, 108
American deindustrialization, 183
American Films of the 70s: Conflicting Visions (Lev), 3
Anabasis (Xenophon), 49
Angels With Dirty Faces (1938, Curtiz), 250
Another You (1991, Philips), 172
Apache (1954, Aldrich), 192, 193
Apocalypse Now (1979, Coppola), 93, 96
Aquino, Amy, 166
Aristotelean drama, 163

Arquette, David, 201
Arroyo, Jose, 26
Arthur, Paul, 252
Ashby, Hal, 2
The Asphalt Jungle (1950, Huston), 227
Astaire, Fred, 133, 134, 141, 142, 151
Aster, Ari, 40
Astor, Mary, 225
Atomic Blonde (2017, Leitch), 142
Attack (1956, Aldrich), 89, 91
Auerbach, Jonathan, 235
authenticity, 27, 30, 31, 182, 185, 190
The AV Club, 5

Babe, Thomas, 201
Baby Driver (2017, Wright), 20, 150
Bacall, Lauren, 127
"(The Boys Are) Back in Town" (song), 126, 131
"Bad to the Bone" (song), 149
Baldwin, James, 105, 108
The Band Wagon (1953, Minnelli), 133–34, 141–42, 153
Barkin, Ellen, 205, 235
bar scenes, 121–22, 126
Basinger, Jeanine, 191, 229
Batman Begins (2005, Nolan), 27
Baumgartner, Michael, 150, 151
Bazin, Andre, 4, 69
BBC, 234
Bean, Jennifer M., 142
Beatty, Ned, 94
Beck, Michael, 43, 52, 66
Beery, Noah, Jr., 53
Belafonte, Harry, 107
Belton, John, 55
Belushi, James, 224
Berenger, Tom, 91
Berry, Chuck, 148
A Better Tomorrow (1986, Woo), 22
A Better Tomorrow II (1987, Woo), 22
Beverly Hills Cop (1984, Brest), 108, 131
Beymer, Richard, 152
Bigger Than Life (1956, Ray), 79

Bingham, Dennis, 203
The Birthday Party (1969, Friedkin), 43
Birth of a Nation (1915, Griffith), 106, 122
Biskind, Peter, 2, 3
Black: Americans, 101, 102, 105, 107; bodies, 12, 169, 170; cinema, 111; directors, 111, 181, 182; men, 170, 171, 175, 176, 178, 181; protagonists, 25, 159, 166; representation, 169
Blackboard Jungle (1955, Brooks), 145, 146, 149
Black Gunn (1972, Hartford-Davis), 107
Blackness, 114, 186
Black Panther (2018, Coogler), 111
The Blasters (band), 148, 149
Blaxploitation, 107, 112–14
Blaxploitation films, 106, 181, 182
Blazing Saddles (1974, Brooks), 76
Bliss, Michael, 62, 82
blockbusters, 19, 28, 109
"Blow With Ry" (song), 179
blues music, 171, 176–79
Bogart, Humphrey, 127, 134, 182, 225, 237, 238, 240
Bogdanovich, Peter, 33, 45
Bogle, Donald, 105–9, 113, 114, 116, 118, 126, 127, 172, 173, 176, 181
Bond, Ward, 80, 211
Bonnie and Clyde (1967, Penn), 75, 170
Boorman, John, 35, 94, 95
Boothe, Powers, 25, 91, 98, 247, 248, 253, 254
Borde, Raymond, 137
borderless technique, 22
Bordwell, David, 22, 56, 215
Born to Run (1975, album), 136
Boseman, Chadwick, 111
The Bourne Supremacy (2004, Greengrass), 20
box office, 73, 108, 109, 191
Boyle, Peter, 228
Brackett, Leigh, 44

Brando, Marlon, 93, 145, 146
Brandon, Henry, 198
breakdancing, 142
Brechtian distancing effect, 79
Brennan, Walter, 65, 211, 250
Bridges, Jeff, 10, 27, 201, 255
Bright, Richard, 225
Bringing Up Baby (1937, Hawks), 103
Bring Me the Head of Alfredo Garcia (1974, Peckinpah), 46, 246
British Film Institute, 73
British Invasion bands, 177, 178
Britton, Barbara, 78
Broken Arrow (1950, Daves), 193
Broken Arrow (1995, Woo), 22, 193, 199
Bronson, Charles, 19, 160, 165
Brooks, Richard, 146
Brophy, Kevin, 81
Brosnahan, Rachel, 256
Brown, Clancy, 249
Brown, Jim, 107
Brown, Olivia, 112
Bruckheimer, Jerry, 23
Bruno, Frank, 36
brutality, 18, 45, 90, 133, 138, 192, 230, 233, 234, 240
buddy films, 27, 102, 108–10, 127, 128, 172
Buhler, James, 149
Bullitt (1968, Yates), 1, 19, 30–32, 34, 150, 151, 257
Bunker, Edward, 84
The Bus Boys (band), 126, 131
Busey, Gary, 128
Butch Cassidy and the Sundance Kid (1968, Hill), 102
Butler, Jack, 180
"By Myself" (song), 141
Byrne, Gabriel, 213

Caan, James, 38
Cage, Nicolas, 149
Cagney, James, 250
Cahiers du Cinema, 4, 44

Callie, Dayton, 166
camera movement, 50, 58, 103
Cameron, James, 93, 131
Candy, John, 172, 173
capitalism, 231
Capra, Frank, 45, 102, 119, 174
"Caprice #5" (song), 180
car chases, 19, 20, 29–37
Carey, Harry, 55
Carney, Ray, 174
Carpenter, John, 4, 39
Carradine, David, 80
Carradine, John, 77–79, 81, 98, 199
Carradine, Keith, 90, 204
Carradine, Robert, 85
Carroll, Noel, 36, 50
Carter, T. K., 90
Casper, Drew, 3
cavalry westerns, 192, 196–98
Cawelti, John, 73
cell phone cameras, 186
Chakiris, George, 152
Chan, Caroline, 211
Chandler, Jeff, 193
character(s), 22, 31, 35, 44, 50, 52–57, 106, 163; aesthetic, 75; archetypal, 29; Black, 107, 109–13, 115, 116, 165–66, 186; male, 25, 120, 152; types, 18–20, 74; white male, 108
Charisse, Cyd, 133
Chaumeton, Etienne, 137
Cheng, Olivia, 211
The China Syndrome (1979, Bridges), 164
Chinatown (1974, Polanksi), 223, 232
Church, Thomas Haden, 207
Cimino, Michael, 73, 191
cinematic apparatus, 144
cinematic style, 47, 108, 148, 155
cinematography, 116, 117, 122, 141
civil rights, 102, 105
civil society, 136, 137
Clapton, Eric, 149
Classic Hollywood, 2, 4, 9, 10, 12, 14, 17, 45, 77, 79, 114, 157, 235

272　Index

classical westerns, 75–77, 80, 82, 197, 206
classicism, 45, 48, 75, 76, 208, 213
classic noir, 229, 230, 232, 241
class politics, 169
class structure, 172, 173, 174
Cleopatra (1962, Mankiewicz), 2
Clift, Montgomery, 47, 120
close-ups, 35, 50, 54–57, 63, 83, 84, 93, 103, 142, 143, 147, 157, 200, 209, 236
Clover, Carol, 234
Cobb, Lee J., 135
Coburn, Charles, 65
Coburn, James, 65, 160
Colbert, Claudette, 102
colliding montage, 75
combat films, 17, 19
comedic drama, 174
comic books, 8, 13, 27, 49, 50, 52
comic-book style, 50, 63, 132, 153, 176
Commando (1985, Lester), 9, 21
communism, 231
computer generated imagery (CGI), 23, 26–28, 48
Con Air (1997, West), 149
Conan the Barbarian (1982, Milius), 9
Conan the Destroyer (1984, Fleischer), 9
Conrich, Ian, 4
Conte, Richard, 250
contemporary film, 17, 39, 213
Contreras, Luis, 256
Cooder, Ry, 94, 131, 138, 148, 153, 154, 158, 176, 179, 180, 235
Coogler, Ryan, 111
Cooper, Gary, 135, 174, 206, 252
Cooper, Jackie, 78
Cooper, Scott, 207
Coppola, Francis Ford, 2
Corman, Roger, 67
Costner, Kevin, 194
Covey, William, 183
Cox, Ronny, 94
Coyote, Peter, 54, 90

Craven, Wes, 39
credits sequence, 53, 62, 63
crime thrillers, 10, 18–20, 32, 38
Crisp, Donald, 203
Cronenberg, David, 39
Cronyn, Hume, 173
crossover film, 107
Cry of the City (1948, Siodmak), 250
cultural appropriation, 178
cultural tradition, 176
Cumbow, Robert C., 4
Curtis, Tony, 105
cutting, 31, 34, 57, 103, 122, 152, 153
cynicism, 2, 46, 227

Dafoe, Willem, 135, 147, 256
Damon, Matt, 194
Dances With Wolves (1990, Costner), 194–96, 199
"Danger Zone" (song), 149
Darkness on the Edge of Town (album, 1978), 135
Dark Passage (1947, Daves), 134, 237, 238, 240
Darwell, Jane, 77
Daves, Delmer, 237
Davies, Freeman, 144, 147, 152, 165, 208, 247
Davison, Bruce, 89, 196
Dead for a Dollar (2022, Hill), 256, 257
Deadwood (Dexter), 201
Deadwood (TV series), 189, 246
Death in the Afternoon (Hemingway), 67
Death Wish (1974, Winner), 19, 190
De Cordova, Richard, 241
Deliverance (1972, Boorman), 76, 89, 94–96
Dennehy, Brian, 92
De Palma, Brian, 3, 8
The Departed (2006, Scorsese), 247
Dern, Bruce, 32, 65, 203, 218
DeSouza, Steven E., 126
Desser, David, 48, 49, 74, 132, 213

Detour (1946, Ulmer), 235
De Vorzon, Barry, 63, 160, 165
De Wilde, Brandon, 37
Dexter, Pete, 201
dialectical cinema, 48
Dickey, James, 94
Diddley, Bo, 136, 148
Die Hard (1988, McTiernan), 20–22, 25
digital effects, 7, 28
digital technology, 142
The Dirty Dozen (1967, Aldrich), 107
Dirty Harry (1971, Siegel), 26
disaster movies, 18
Disney, 27
disruptive montage, 63
Dixon, Wheeler Winston, 46
Django Unchained (2013, Tarantino), 122
Doc (1971, Perry), 59
Dog Day Afternoon (1975, Lumet), 161
Doherty, Thomas, 140, 145–47, 146
Donaldson, Roger, 20
Donalson, Melvin, 102, 105, 108, 112
Double Indemnity (1944, Wilder), 134
Downs, Cathy, 193
Drive (2011, Refn), 20
Dru, Joanne, 120
"Dueling Banjos" (song), 94, 95
Duran, Larry, 251
Durgnat, Raymond, 228
Durrand, Mark, 149
Duvall, Robert, 79, 194, 207
Dyer, Peter John, 68
Dyer, Richard, 24

Earp, Wyatt, 206, 218
Eastwood, Clint, 208, 213, 216, 232
Easy Rider (1969, Hopper), 80, 102
Easy Riders, Raging Bulls (Biskind), 2
Ebert, Roger, 234
Eddie and the Cruisers (1983, Davidson), 136
Eddie Murphy: Delirious (1983, Gowers), 126
Edge of the City (1957, Ritt), 106

editing, 46, 152–54, 177; continuity, 56, 58, 143; fragmented, 7; pattern, 31; staccato, 142
Eggers, Robert, 40
Ehrenstein, David, 135, 144, 145
Eisenstein, Sergei, 69
Eisensteinian montage, 61–63, 93
Eisensteinian theory, 93
Elba, Idris, 128
El Dorado (1967, Hawks), 44
emotional effect, 61
The End of History and the Last Man (Fukuyama), 218
epic films, 18
epigraphs, 145, 162
Escape From New York (1981, Carpenter), 75
Evans, Art, 183
experimental approach, 85
experimentation, 141, 142, 157, 161, 171, 186, 236
expressionistic style, 186

Fabray, Nanette, 141
Face/Off (1997, Woo), 22
Falk, Peter, 166
Farber, Manny, 5, 48, 50
Fast and Furious (film series), 101
Fast & Furious Presents: Hobbs and Shaw (2019, Leitch), 101, 128
The Fate of the Furious (2017, Gray), 28
Fathers and Sons (Babe), 201
femininity, 237–39
film: genres, 2, 14, 73, 75, 98, 134, 182, 214, 224; industry, 18, 20, 219; performances, 172; theory, 161
filmmaking, 14, 19, 23, 27, 38, 56–58, 89, 131, 224, 257; classical, 56, 58
Fire, Inc., (band), 144
First Blood (1982, Kotcheff), 9, 92
Fishburne, Laurence, 228
A Fistful of Dollars (1964, Leone), 213, 214, 216
Flanagan, Martin, 20

Fleischer, Richard, 229
Fonda, Henry, 78, 79, 91, 193, 196, 206
Fong, Donald, 211
Ford, Glenn, 146
Ford, John, 1, 2, 4, 6, 9, 10, 17, 18, 33, 45, 46, 50, 68, 77, 78, 91, 132, 135, 138, 141, 190, 192–93, 196–98, 206, 211, 213, 214
Ford, Wallace, 229
Ford, Winston, 154–55
formal expressionism, 171
Forster, Robert, 247
Fort Apache (1948, Ford), 10, 91, 192, 196–98, 201
Foxx, Jamie, 122
framing, 52, 54–58, 152, 168, 236
franchise filmmaking, 27
Frankel, Glenn, 136
"Freedom From Want" (painting, 1943), 214
Freeman, Morgan, 237
The French Connection (1971, Friedkin), 29–30, 34, 44, 123, 151, 161
Friedkin, William, 29, 30, 38, 43, 151
Friedman, Ken, 233
Fruitvale Station (2013, Coogler), 186
Fukuyama, Francis, 218
Fuller, Sam, 78, 79, 87
Full Metal Jacket (1987, Kubrick), 93
Furious 7 (2015, Wan), 28
Fusco, John, 178

Gable, Clark, 102
Gale, Bob, 181
Gallagher, Tag, 77
gangster films, 48, 50, 192, 214, 217, 247
Garfield, John, 55
generic identity, 20
genre(s), 18, 19, 21, 67, 186; conventions, 77, 191, 192; hybridity, 171; musical, 125; revisionism, 13, 92, 208; western, 26, 27, 59, 68, 73, 77, 84, 89. *See also specific entries*
Geoffrion, Alan, 207

Gerard, Caitlin, 237
German Expressionism, 157
Geronimo War, 192–201
Gertz, Jami, 176
gestures, 5, 64, 78, 119, 127
The Getaway (1972, Peckinpah), 1, 3, 6, 8, 19, 20, 45, 60, 63, 161, 166–67, 245, 256
Gibson, Mel, 128
Gilbey, Ryan, 3
Giler, David, 53, 164–67, 189, 240
Gindoff, Bryan, 160
Glover, Danny, 128
Godley, John, 233
Gone in 60 Seconds (1974, Halicki), 20
Gordon, Lawrence, 32
Gosling, Ryan, 38, 39, 149
gothic film, 94
Graf, Allan, 215
Grant, Barry Keith, 4, 9, 77
Grant, Cary, 65, 119
graphic novels, 8
Great Depression, 19, 102, 159, 165, 168, 174, 186
The Great McGinty (1940, Sturges), 104
The Great Northfield Minnesota Raid (1972, Kaufman), 79, 80
The Great Train Robbery (1903, Porter), 61
Grier, Pam, 46
Griffith, D. W., 106, 111–13
Gross, Larry, 26, 126
Guerrero, Ed, 108–10, 117, 124, 169, 172, 176, 180, 182
Guess Who's Coming to Dinner (1967, Kramer), 112
Gussow, Adam, 176, 178, 180

Hackman, Gene, 29, 30, 123, 194
Hadley, Reed, 78
Hammett, Dashiell, 192, 212–14, 217, 223, 225
hard bodies, 20–22, 132
Hard Bodies (Jeffords), 24
Hard Boiled (1992, Woo), 22, 215

Hardcore (1979, Schrader), 135
Hard Hats, Rednecks, and Macho Men (Nystrom), 3
Hard Target (1992, Woo), 22
Harris, David, 56
Harris, Thomas, 38
Harris, Timothy, 173
Hatari! (1962, Hawks), 17, 65
The Hate U Give (2018, Tillman, Jr.), 186
Hathaway, Henry, 190
Hawks, Howard, 2, 4, 5–7, 11, 13, 17, 35–36, 43–58, 60, 63–65, 68, 69, 73–75, 103, 104, 120, 157, 208, 209, 247, 256
HBO, 157, 189, 246
Heaven's Gate (1980, Cimino), 73, 191
Hemingway, Ernest, 2, 67, 68
Henriksen, Lance, 8, 13, 202, 235, 236
Henstell, Bruce, 160
Hepburn, Katharine, 112
Hickey & Boggs (1972, Culp), 3, 8, 161
Higgins, Scott, 22, 24
High Noon (1952, Zinnemann), 206, 252, 253
Hill, Roger, 52
Hill, Walter, 4, 19, 20, 24, 26, 27; *48 Hrs* (1982), 11, 13, 21, 22, 25, 26, 65, 101–28, 131, 133, 143, 147, 152, 159, 172, 176, 177–80, 184, 190, 194, 195, 209, 223, 228, 232, 253, 254; as action director, 17, 19, 28, 39, 40, 50, 186; admiration for Peckinpah, 76; *American Neo-Noir: The Movie Never Ends* (book), 242; *Another 48 Hrs* (1990), 11, 13, 21, 25, 101, 107–28; *The Assignment* (2016), 8, 10, 14, 19, 28, 225, 233–35, 237, 238, 240, 241, 252; as assistant director, 19, 30; awareness of Walsh and Hawks, 44–45, 50, 53, 60; *Brewster's Millions* (1985), 11, 13, 115, 159, 171–77, 180, 184, 247, 254; *Broken Trail* (2006), 13, 27, 189, 191, 207, 209–12; *Bullet to the Head* (2012), 8, 9, 14, 23, 25, 27, 152, 176, 196, 224, 225, 228–33, 241, 256; collaboration with Schwarzenegger and Gross, 21, 26; *Crossroads* (1986), 11, 13, 150, 152, 159, 171, 172, 176–81, 184, 185, 201, 247, 252; *The Driver* (1978), 3, 8, 13, 14, 19, 20, 29, 32–39, 48, 51, 60, 63, 65, 75, 110, 131, 133, 140, 143, 146, 150, 158, 215, 254; employment of Peckinpah-esque techniques, 60, 81, 95, 98, 170, 217; *Extreme Prejudice* (1987), 7, 14, 24–26, 141, 152, 247–56; *Geronimo: An American Legend* (1993), 10, 13, 14, 26, 189, 191, 192, 194, 195, 197, 198, 200, 201, 206, 209, 256; *Hard Times* (1975), 3, 8, 13, 14, 19, 20, 29, 60, 65, 75, 110, 131, 133, 143, 152, 159, 160, 162–72, 176–78, 180, 186, 224, 225, 252; identity as white man, 111; *Johnny Handsome* (1989), 10, 14, 115, 141, 202, 225, 233, 235–41, 255; *Last Man Standing* (1996), 10, 13, 22, 23, 27, 141, 189, 191, 212–19, 224, 252; *The Long Riders* (1980), 3, 7, 8, 10, 11, 13, 21, 23, 26, 48, 49, 54, 65, 73–88, 98, 103, 110, 131, 133, 143, 148, 152, 172, 179, 189, 191, 196, 206, 249, 252; *Madso's War* (2011), 247; "The Man Who Was Death" (TV episode), 157–59; mixed-race partnership in films, 25, 101; *Red Heat* (1998), 9, 14, 21, 23, 26, 27, 141, 176, 196, 224–33, 241, 249; as screenwriter, 160–62, 186; *Southern Comfort* (1981), 3, 7, 8, 11, 13, 14, 21, 23, 24, 26, 48, 49, 54, 74–77, 89–98, 103, 110, 131, 133, 143, 152, 176, 179, 185, 196, 209, 249; *Streets of Fire* (1984), 1, 7–8, 12–14, 115, 125, 132, 133, 135–41, 143–52, 155, 157, 159, 171, 176, 177, 179, 180, 185, 224, 231, 252, 256; *Supernova* (2000),

247; *Trespass* (1992), 8, 12, 13, 24, 25, 115, 159, 181–86, 196, 201, 209, 254; *Undisputed* (2002), 12, 13, 115, 152, 159, 164, 165, 167–71, 175–78, 184, 189, 246, 252; use of white text-on-black screen, 146; and violence, 22–23; *The Warriors* (1979), 3, 7, 8, 10, 13, 14, 21, 24–26, 43, 48–69, 74, 75, 81, 83, 91, 96, 110, 131, 133, 143, 144, 146–48, 153, 185, 196, 247; *Wild Bill* (1995), 8, 10, 12, 13, 26–27, 65, 141, 189, 191, 201–6, 209, 218, 249, 252, 255; working on both westerns and noir, 28–29. *See also individual entries*
hip-hop, 142, 165, 189
His Girl Friday (1940, Hawks), 103, 104, 119
Hitchcock, Alfred, 2
Holden, William, 46, 82
"Holding Out for a Hero" (song), 144
Hollywood, 3, 6, 13, 14, 19, 20, 22, 26–29, 40, 45, 59, 108, 109, 111, 145, 150, 165, 175, 181, 202, 257
Hollywood Motion Picture Production Code, 7, 18, 47, 60, 127, 161, 223
Hollywood's Last Golden Age (Kirshner), 3
Hollywood studio system, 224
Holt, Tim, 183
Homer, 53
Hong Kong, 22, 215
"hood film" cycle, 181, 182, 186
Hopper, Dennis, 2
horror films, 18, 39
Houghton, Katharine, 112
Howell, Amanda, 150
How the West Was Won (1962, Ford, Hathaway and Marshall), 190, 191
Humphries, Reynolds, 227
Hunter, Jeffrey, 79
Hurt, John, 205
Huston, Walter, 183, 184

"I Can Dream About You" (song), 155

Ice Cube, 182, 183
Ice-T, 181, 182, 183
iconography, 29, 74, 76, 90, 92, 93, 125, 132, 133, 141, 155, 192, 214, 219
improvisation, 117
incarceration, 63, 104, 109, 116, 119, 166, 167, 169–71, 223
Indian westerns, 192–96
institutionalization, 170
intensified continuity, 56
interior shots, 31, 32, 34
international art cinema, 2
"In the City" (song), 131
Iovine, Jimmy, 148
Ireland, John, 47, 78
Iron Man (2008, Favreau), 27
Ironside, Michael, 247
I Shot Jesse James (1949, Fuller), 78
I Spit on Your Grave (1978, Zachi), 234
The Italian Connection (1972, Di Leo), 30
Italian Neorealism, 224
It Don't Worry Me: The Revolutionary American Films of the Seventies (Gilbey), 3
It Happened One Night (1934, Capra), 102, 104, 119
I Was a Fugitive From a Chain Gang (1932, LeRoy), 104, 105

Jacobs, Jason, 60
jagged montage, 48
Jagger, Mick, 179
James, Brion, 95, 103
Jameson, Richard T., 223
Jamming With Edward! (album, 1972), 179
Jason, Peter, 122
Jeffords, Susan, 9, 20, 24
Jennings, Brent, 227
Jesse James (1939, King), 75, 77, 78, 85
Jeter, Derek, 167
Jim Crow South, 111
Johnson, Albert, 173

Johnson, Ben, 58, 60, 65, 196
Johnson, Dwayne, 128
Johnson, Robert, 176–78
Johnson County War, 191
Johnston, Shaun, 210
Jones, L. Q., 65
Jones, Mickey, 252
The Jon Spencer Blues Explosion (band), 150
Jordan, Michael, 167
Judd, Robert, 176
Judex (1963, Franju), 49
Jurassic Park (1993, Spielberg), 26

Kamen, Michael, 149
Kang, Sung, 25, 225
The Karate Kid (1984, Avildsen), 179
Kaufman, Philip, 79, 80, 82
Keach, James, 81
Keach, Stacy, 35, 84
Kelly, David Patrick, 7, 13, 52, 65, 67–68, 115, 218, 247
Kelly, Nancy, 77
Kennedy, Arthur, 204
Kennedy-Martin, Troy, 226
Kent, Jennifer, 40
The Killer (1989, Woo), 22, 215
The Killer Elite (1975, Peckinpah), 49
King, Henry, 75, 77, 85
King, Martin Luther, Jr., 105
King, Rodney, 181, 186
Kirshner, Jonathan, 3
Kitses, Jim, 73, 146, 197, 203
Kleiner, Harry, 226, 247
Knott, Robert, 203
Kramer, Stanley, 102, 105–7, 112
Kristofferson, Kris, 65
Kurosawa, Akira, 10, 60, 213, 214

Ladd, Alan, 37, 136
La La Land (2016, Chazelle), 149
Lampley, Jim, 168
Lancaster, Burt, 89, 192
Landham, Sonny, 103
Lane, Diane, 135, 203

Lang, Fritz, 2, 17, 75, 78
Langford, Barry, 22, 28
Langlois, Henri, 52
Lannom, Les, 90
LaPaglia, Anthony, 238
Lawson, Richard, 146
Lee, Robert E., 196
Legend, John, 149
Leitch, David, 142
Leone, Sergio, 191, 213, 216
Leonetti, Matthew F., 252
Le Samourai (1967, Melville), 48
Lethal Weapon (1987, Donner), 128, 149
Lethal Weapon (film series), 101
Let It Bleed (album, 1969), 178
"Letter from Birmingham Jail" (King), 105
Lev, Peter, 3
Levant, Oscar, 141
LGBTQ organizations, 234
liberal consensus, 227
liberal dramas, 107
Liberating Hollywood (Smukler), 2
Lichtenfeld, Eric, 19, 26–28, 50, 51, 190, 224, 248
The Lineup (1958, Siegel), 229, 230
Lipham, Kent, 251
Liston, Sonny, 164–65
Little Big Man (1970, Penn), 59
Locke, Sondra, 210
Loggins, Kenny, 149
long shots, 54, 55, 63, 190, 199, 252
Los Angeles riots (1992), 181
Lott, Eric, 230, 237
Lott, Tommy L., 107–8, 111
"Love in Vain" (song), 178, 179
Lover, Ed, 165
low genres, 4, 39, 234
Lucas, George, 135
Lundgren, Dolph, 227

Macchio, Ralph, 176, 179
MacMurray, Fred, 134
Madigan, Amy, 137

The Magnificent Seven (1960, Sturges), 248
mainstream cinema, 48, 76, 92, 108, 169, 257
Major Dundee (1965, Peckinpah), 6, 46, 49
male bodies, 24, 237
Maltby, Richard, 193
The Maltese Falcon (1941, Huston), 225
The Maltese Falcon (Hammett), 223
Mamet, David, 163
Mandel, Steve, 95
The Man From Laramie (1955, Mann), 203, 204
Manhunter (1986, Mann), 38
Manifest Destiny, 192, 195, 197, 200
Mann, Anthony, 202–3, 229, 255
Man of the West (1958, Mann), 135
The Man Who Shot Liberty Valance (1962, Ford), 33, 201
market capitalism, 169
Marshall, George, 190
martial arts, 18
martial arts film, 50
Martin, Dean, 6, 43
Martin, Strother, 58, 65, 160
Martinez, Joaquin, 89
Marvel Cinematic Universe, 27, 28
Marvin, Lee, 33, 35
masculinist genres, 48, 171
masculinity, 3, 9, 20, 24, 25, 235, 238; Black, 112, 168; white, 124
Mature, Victor, 250
McBride, Joseph, 43, 44, 53
McCabe and Mrs. Miller (1971, Altman), 59, 76
McCallany, Holt, 225
McCrae, Frank, 65
McCrea, Joel, 6, 104
McGovern, Elizabeth, 233
McGraw, Ali, 60, 166, 245
McGraw, Charles, 229
McGuire, Michael, 163
McHattie, Stephen, 199
McKee, Lonette, 174

McKinney, Devin, 23, 216
McKitterick, Tom, 57
McLaglen, Victor, 196
McQueen, Steve, 30, 31, 60, 65, 166, 245
McTiernan, John, 20
Meet John Doe (1941, Capra), 174
melodrama, 22, 79
Mexico, 245–46, 256
MGM Studio, 133
Michos, Terry, 56
Mifune, Toshiro, 213
Milch, David, 246
Milius, John, 7, 131, 135, 247
Miller's Crossing (1990, Coen and Coen), 213
Minnelli, Vincente, 133, 134, 141–42
mise-en-scène, 122, 124, 142, 231
Missing in Action (1984, Zito), 92
Mitchell, Lee Clark, 59, 216, 251, 256
Mitchum, Robert, 134
mixed-race buddy film, 25, 128, 172
modernism, 48, 75, 76, 213
modernity, 46
Momoa, Jason, 225
Monsters and Men (2018, Green), 186
montage, 64, 74, 82, 83, 85, 112, 143, 144, 157; approach, 69; editing, 45, 47, 49, 58–60, 63, 86, 166, 170. *See also specific entries*
Moranis, Rick, 138
Morton, Joe, 177
Moses, Mark, 91
moving camera shots, 31, 213, 247
Mulkey, Chris, 207
Mulvey, Laura, 127
Muni, Paul, 104
Murphy, Eddie, 11, 25, 101, 103, 107–11, 113, 114, 117, 119, 120, 124, 126, 127, 131, 172, 173
Murphy, Ian, 91, 94, 98
musical films, 75, 153
musical genre, 133, 141–55, 157
musical performances, 133, 144, 151, 153

musical sequences, 151, 154
"music of immediacy," 151
My Darling Clementine (1946, Ford), 193, 196, 206, 211, 218

Nakadai, Tatsuya, 216
The Naked City (1948, Dassin), 64
narrative(s), 18, 20, 21, 23–25, 29, 31, 32, 35, 45, 50–52, 57, 58, 68, 80, 91, 96, 132, 151, 155; black, 108; control, 109; doubling, 37; economy, 48; moments, 134; resolution, 80, 96, 97; sequences, 151; structure, 10, 19, 74, 109, 175, 193
The Narrow Margin (1952, Fleischer), 229, 230
Neal, Tom, 235
Neale, Steve, 19, 59, 75, 77, 181
neominstrelsy, 108
neo-noir films, 223, 224, 241
neorealist immediacy, 30
New Hollywood, 1–3, 8–11, 14, 17, 19, 36, 45, 50, 73–77, 89, 93, 96, 101, 102, 149, 161, 190, 191, 223
"The New Jim Crow," 170
New York City, 29, 43, 49–51, 172, 174, 182
Nicholson, Jack, 2, 223
Nicol, Alex, 203
Nightmare Town (Hammett), 212
nihilism, 217
noir conventions, 19, 28, 140, 248
noir films, 1, 9, 17, 28, 75, 132–38, 140, 141, 214, 219, 223–25, 227, 229–32, 234–35, 241, 242, 250, 252
noir style, 141
Nolte, Nick, 11, 22, 25, 101, 109, 110, 120, 127, 172, 247, 248, 253
non-diegetic sound, 147, 151
non-linear approach, 79
non-linear movie, 240
Norden, Phil, 208
Northfield Minnesota Raid sequence, 74, 78–80, 82, 83, 85–88, 148
"Nowhere Fast" (song), 144, 145
nudity, 18, 230, 234

Nystrom, Derek, 3

Oates, Warren, 46, 59, 65, 246
O'Brien, Edmond, 58
O'Brien, Pat, 250
October Revolution (1917), 227
"oddly unclassifiable," 132
Odyssey (Homer), 53
O'Neal, Ryan, 29, 32, 33, 38
"One Bad Stud" (song), 149
Only Angels Have Wings (1939, Hawks), 43, 53
"On the Dark Side" (song), 136
On The Rolling Stones (band), 178
On The Yard (1978, Silver), 65
Open Range (2003, Costner), 207
optimism, 105
Orbach, Jerry, 175
Orlandi, Felice, 65, 88
O'Ross, Ed, 113, 225
Osteen, Mark, 138, 241
O'Toole, Annette, 113
The Outlaw Josey Wales (1976, Eastwood), 208, 210
Out of the Furnace (2013, Cooper), 20

Paganini, Niccolo, 180
Palance, Jack, 89
Palmer, Lorrie, 23
Palmer, R. Barton, 224
Panic in the Streets (1950, Kazan), 236
Paper Moon (1973, Bogdanovich), 33, 75
Pare, Michael, 135, 136
parody, 23, 76, 121, 124
Passenger 57 (1992, Hooks), 20
Pat Garrett and Billy the Kid (1973, Peckinpah), 46
Patric, Jason, 194
Patterson, John, 5, 10
Paxton, Bill, 147, 183
Peckinpah, Sam, 3, 6, 7, 13, 19, 22, 23, 45–49, 58–69, 74, 75, 77, 81–89, 98, 143, 166, 213, 216, 245, 246, 248, 249
Peele, Jordan, 40

Penn, Arthur, 191
Petersen, William, 38
Pickens, Slim, 65
Pierson, Frank, 161
Pinkerton, Nick, 89, 90
Pippin, Robert B., 209
plagiarism, 143
Platoon (1986, Stone), 90, 91
Platt, Louise, 199
Poe, Edgar Allan, 234
Point Blank (1967, Boorman), 35
Poitier, Sidney, 105–8, 112–14, 146
The Police (band), 117
polizieschi, 30
Pope, Richard, 22
Porfirio, Robert, 231
post-war Hollywood films, 78
Powell, William, 172
Power, Tyrone, 77, 79
power dynamics, 48, 109, 127, 171
Predator (1987, McTiernan), 9, 93
Preminger, Otto, 103
Presley, Elvis, 145
Prince, Stephen, 3, 6, 23, 45–48, 68, 81, 86, 213
professionalism, 57, 65, 103, 123
The Professionals (1966, Brooks), 256
Prohibition era, 10, 192, 213, 214
The Prowler (1952, Losey), 227
Pryor, Richard, 101, 107, 171–73
Purse, Lisa, 19, 21, 24
Pursued (1947, Walsh), 134
Pye, Douglas, 89, 97, 203

Quaid, Dennis, 80
Quaid, Randy, 84

Rabin, Trevor, 149
race, 107–28, 170
racial conflict, 102, 126, 127
racial consciousness, 171
racial difference, 11, 25, 102, 120, 128, 179
racial dimension, 102, 124, 171
racial division, 25, 105
racial identity, 123
racial issues, 106
racially motivated crimes, 111
racial tensions, 13, 102, 110, 127, 133, 223
racism, 120, 126, 127, 136
Rafelson, Bob, 2
Rambo: First Blood Part II (1984, Cosmatos), 9, 92
Rambo III (1988, MacDonald), 9
Ramos, Rudy, 35
rap, 165
Ray, Nicholas, 78, 79, 84
Reagan, Ronald, 20
realism, 105, 215
rear screen projection, 30
Rebel Without a Cause (1955, Ray), 79, 153
Red Dawn (1984, Milius), 131
Red Dragon (Harris), 38
Red Harvest (Hammett), 212, 213, 217
Red Line 7000 (1965, Hawks), 53
Red River (1948, Hawks), 4, 44, 47, 120, 207, 209, 210
Reed, Bill, 135, 144, 145
Reevis, Steve, 198
Refn, Nicolas Winding, 20, 38, 39
Remar, James, 7, 13, 22, 25, 53, 65–67, 103
restaging, 37–39, 74, 92, 174
The Return of Frank James (1940, Lang), 75, 78
revisionist approach, 11, 59, 75
revisionist westerns, 77–88, 191, 197
Rexer, Fred, 247
Reynolds, Burt, 94
Rhames, Ving, 25, 165, 189
"Ride of the Valkyries" (song), 96
Ride the High Country (1962, Peckinpah), 6
Ridgely, John, 55
Rio Bravo (1959, Hawks), 6, 35, 43, 63, 181
Rio Bravo, Hatari! (1962, Hawks), 44, 53
Rio Grande (1950, Ford), 10, 192, 197
Rio Lobo (1970, Hawks), 44

Rivette, Jacques, 4, 6, 44, 45
RKO, 104
Robards, Jason, 65
Robertson, Cliff, 79
rock and roll, 7, 131–41, 143–45, 148–50, 152–55, 178
rock and roll films, 135, 144
"Rock Around the Clock" (song), 145, 146, 150
Rockwell, Norman, 214
Rocky IV (1985, Stallone), 227
Rodriguez, Michelle, 28, 233
Rogers, Ginger, 141, 142
Roizman, Owen, 30
Rollins, Rose, 167
Romao, Tico, 29–31
Romero, George A., 39–40
Rossovich, Tim, 84
Rourke, Mickey, 225, 233
Royal Wedding (1951, Donen), 142
"Rumble" (song), 153
Rush Hour (film series), 101
Russell, Rosalind, 103
Russell, T. E., 185
Russo, James, 207
Ryan, Robert, 58, 82, 134

Sadler, William, 7, 13, 25, 157–59, 183, 186
Sallis, James, 38
Sampson, Will, 210
samurai films, 213, 214
Sanchez, Marcelino, 57
Sanderson, William, 218
Sarris, Andrew, 44, 54
Saturday Night Live (TV show), 107
Saunders, John, 61, 79, 81, 87, 90
Scacchi, Greta, 210
Scarecrow (1973, Schatzberg), 102
Schifrin, Lalo, 150, 151
Schrader, Paul, 3, 61, 86, 135, 136, 161, 245
Schwarzenegger, Arnold, 9, 20, 21, 27, 93, 131, 150, 224, 226, 227
Schwimmer, Rusty, 211

science fiction, 18, 93, 247
Scorsese, Martin, 2, 3, 8, 135
Scott, Randolph, 6
Scott, Tony, 23
screen persona, 21, 22, 107, 117, 141, 172
screenwriting, 1, 3, 45, 161, 162
screwball comedies, 33, 75, 102–5, 107, 119, 120, 159, 171, 174, 175, 180
Seagal, Steven, 46
The Searchers (1956, Ford), 21, 80, 132, 135, 136, 138, 141, 198–200, 214, 232, 256
Seda, Jon, 225
See No Evil, Hear No Evil (1989, Hiller), 172
self-censorship, 18
self-conscious approach, 79
self-conscious awareness, 77, 80, 127
Seneca, Joe, 176, 180
The Set-Up (1950, Wise), 134
sexual desire, 112–14
sexuality, 106, 107, 112
sexual themes, 18
Shaft (1971, Parks), 106
Shalhoub, Tony, 233
Shane (1953, Stevens), 37
Sharp, Alan, 89
Sharrett, Christopher, 245
Sheen, Martin, 93
"She's the One" (song), 136
She Wore a Yellow Ribbon (1949, Ford), 10, 192, 196
Shout Factory, 140
Siegel, Don, 229
silent cinema, 29
Silver Streak (1976, Hiller), 101, 172
Simpson, Don, 23
Skerritt, Tom, 54
Sklar, Robert, 207, 209
Slaughter (1972, Starrett), 107
Slaughter's Big Rip-Off (1973, Douglas), 107
slavery, 170, 172
Slocum, J. David, 18

slow-motion, 6, 7, 22, 23, 45–49, 58–62, 74, 75, 81–87, 95, 96, 98, 143, 170, 213, 217
Smith, Christopher J., 179, 180
Smith, Imogen Sara, 226, 232, 236
Smith, J. W., 157
Smith, Lewis, 91
Smith, Valerie, 111, 181, 182
Smukler, Maya Montanez, 2, 3
Snead, James A., 114, 116
Snipes, Wesley, 25, 165, 166
social realism, 49
societal conscience, 49
Soldier Blue (1970, Nelson), 59
Sondheim, Stephen, 67
sonic expressionism, 148
The Sorels (band), 155
sound effects, 147, 154, 155, 162
Southern Gothic, 76
spectacle, 22–24, 26, 27
Spectacular Bodies (Tasker), 24
Speed (1994, De Bont), 20
Spider-Man (2002, Raimi), 27
Spielberg, Steven, 135
Spike TV network, 247
Spiral: From the Book of Saw (2021, Bousman), 186
Spoto, Donald, 105
Spottiswoode, Roger, 126
Springsteen, Bruce, 135, 136, 140
Sragow, Michael, 69
Stagecoach (1939, Ford), 9, 17, 77, 134–35, 192, 193, 198, 199
staging, 30, 46, 48, 57, 58, 104, 122, 202
Stallone, Sylvester, 9, 20, 21, 25, 27, 225, 227
star persona, 20, 134
Star Wars (film series), 145
Statham, Jason, 128
Step Up (2006, Fletcher), 142
stereotypes, 108, 112–14, 168
Stevens, Charles, 193
Stevens, George, 37
Stewart, James, 193, 202, 203

Stir Crazy (1980, Poitier), 101, 172
Stone, Oliver, 90
The Stones (band), 178, 179
storytelling, 17, 22, 44, 48, 80, 240
Straw Dogs (1971, Peckinpah), 86
Street Law (1974, Castellari), 30
Street People (1976, Lucidi), 35
"Streets of Fire" (song), 140
Studi, Wes, 189, 194
studio system, 2, 8, 17, 18, 107, 161
Sturges, Preston, 45, 104
stylistic approaches, 29, 40, 45, 149, 170
stylistic austerity, 32
stylistic conventions, 29
stylistic experimentation, 8, 48, 80
Sudden Death (1995, Hyams), 20–21
Sullivan's Travels (1941, Sturges), 104
Superfly (1972, Parks, Jr.), 106
superhero films, 27
swashbucklers, 17
Sweet Sweetback's Baadasssss Song (1971, Van Peebles), 113
Swenson, Karl, 90
swordplay, 18

T2: Judgment Day (1991, Cameron), 150
Tales From the Crypt (TV series), 157, 234
Tamblyn, Russ, 152
Tannen, Charles, 78
Tarantino, Quentin, 122
Tasker, Yvonne, 18, 19, 24, 39, 181
Taxi Driver (1976, Scorsese), 135, 161
Taylor, Dub, 82
technological developments, 144, 186
teen pics, 145–47
The Terminator (1984, Cameron), 9, 131
Terminator 2: Judgement Day (1991, Cameron), 26
Tessier, Robert, 168
The Texas Chainsaw Massacre (1974, Hooper), 96

The Big Sleep (1946, Hawks), 44, 127
The Defiant Ones (1958, Kramer), 102, 105–8, 111, 120, 126, 128
thematic concerns, 58, 202, 206, 214
Theron, Charlize, 142
Thief (1981, Mann), 38
The Thief Who Came to Dinner (1973, Yorkin), 8
Thieves Like Us (1974, Altman), 75
Thompson, Jim, 1
Thorogood, George, 149
Thunderbolt and Lightfoot (1974, Cimino), 102
"Thunder Road" (song), 140
Tian, Valerie, 212
Tidyman, Ernest, 161
Tierney, Gene, 78
Tighe, Kevin, 113, 195
time-shifting montage, 81
T-Men (1947, Mann), 229, 230
To Have and Have Not (1944, Hawks), 127
To Live and Die in LA (1985, Friedkin), 38
"Tonight Is What It Means to Be Young" (song), 140, 155
Top Gun (1986, Scott), 149
Torn, Rip, 250
"Total Eclipse of the Heart" (song), 144
Touch of Evil (1958, Welles), 103
The Town (2010, Affleck), 20
Tracy, Spencer, 112, 191
"transphobic," 234
Treasure of the Sierra Madre (1948, Huston), 159, 181, 182, 184
The True Story of Jesse James (1957, Ray), 78
Twentieth Century (1934, Hawks), 103
Tyler, Bonnie, 144
Tyler, Brian, 57
Tyson, Mike, 164, 167

Ulmer, Edgar G., 235
Ulzana's Raid (1972, Aldrich), 89–91, 97, 192, 196, 199

Uncommon Valor (1983, Kotcheff), 92
Under Siege (1992, Davis), 20
United Artists, 73
Universal Studios, 143, 181, 224

Vai, Steve, 177
Van Holt, Brian, 230
Van Peebles, Melvin, 113
Van Valkenburgh, Deborah, 143
Vera Cruz (1954, Aldrich), 248
verbal austerity and dexterity, 33
Vidal, Gore, 161
Vietnam War, 13, 47, 74, 76, 86, 88, 89, 92, 96, 191
Ving, Lee, 147
violence, 18, 19, 40, 45, 47, 49, 61, 64, 68, 75, 86, 89, 93–94, 123, 132, 136, 147, 202, 203, 210, 217–18, 234, 251; gun, 22, 23, 37, 103, 202; screen, 6, 18, 19, 23, 45, 47, 48, 60, 74, 85, 86; as social problem, 48
The Violent Professionals (1973, Martino), 30
visual approach, 59, 83, 157
visual design, 144, 165
visual metaphor, 63
visual strategies, 58
visual style, 19, 38, 50, 54, 143, 157, 170
voice-over narration, 133, 157, 194, 195, 197, 232, 235, 237, 241
Voight, Jon, 94

Wagner, Robert, 79
Waites, Thomas G., 53
Walken, Christopher, 216
Walker, Michael, 192
Walker, Will, 35
Wallach, Eli, 229
Walsh, Edward, 65
Walsh, Joe, 131
Walsh, Joseph, 35
Walsh, Raoul, 17, 44–45, 134, 157
Waltz, Christoph, 256
Ward, Fred, 90

war films, 6, 9, 18, 26, 75, 89–98
Warner Brothers, 12
Washburn, Deric, 247
Washington, Kerry, 122
Waters, Muddy, 177
Watts, Charlie, 179
Wayne, John, 6, 33, 43, 44, 46, 47, 65, 80, 120, 134–36, 196, 250
Weathers, Carl, 227
Weaver, Sigourney, 11, 13, 28, 54, 233, 239, 240
Weingrod, Herschel, 173
Weissberg, Eric, 94–95
Welles, Orson, 2
western archetype, 33, 35
western conventions, 26, 27, 98, 124, 140, 248
western films, 1, 18, 133, 135–37, 202, 250, 251
western genres, 189, 191–93, 199, 202, 214, 223
westerns, 6, 9, 17, 28, 29, 33, 37, 46, 59, 60, 73–75, 78, 92, 132, 140, 141, 147, 191, 232, 248
West Side Story (1961, Wise and Robbins), 152, 153
What's Up Doc? (1972, Bogdanovich), 33
Whitaker, Forest, 233
White, De'voreaux, 183
whiteness, 110, 123, 124
white protagonists, 159, 180
white supremacy, 172
wide shots, 30, 34, 37, 56, 57, 122
The Wild Bunch (1969, Peckinpah), 6, 7, 45–49, 58–61, 63, 64, 74, 76, 80–83, 86, 87, 89, 214, 216, 245, 248
Wilder, Gene, 101, 172

The Wild One (1954, Benedek), 145, 146
"Willie Brown Blues" (song), 180
Willis, Bruce, 20–23, 28, 212
Wilson, Ron, 217
Wilson, Scott, 235
Wolf, Howlin', 177
Wollen, Peter, 5, 44
Woo, John, 22, 23, 215, 217
Wood, Lana, 198
Wood, Natalie, 198
Wood, Robin, 35
Woodman, Brian J., 91
Woods, David, 4
Working (Sondheim), 67
World War II, 78, 80, 224, 227
Wray, Link, 153
Wright, Dorsey, 52
Wright, Edgar, 20, 30, 32, 150
Wright, Joshua, 168
Wyler, William, 103
Wyman, Bill, 179

Xenophon, 49–51, 63, 67
X-Men (2000, Singer), 27

Yasker, Yvonne, 149
Yates, Peter, 30, 31, 34
Yeo, Gwendoline, 212
Yes (band), 149
Yojimbo (1961, Kurosawa), 10, 191, 213, 214, 216
youth subcultures, 150
Yurick, Sol, 49, 67

Zemeckis, Robert, 181
Zinnemann, Fred, 252

About the Author

Brian Brems is a professor who teaches film at the College of DuPage. He publishes regularly in academic collections and is coeditor of *Refocus: The Films of Paul Schrader* (University of Edinburgh Press, 2020). In addition, he writes for online film magazines and websites, including Vague Visages.

www.ingramcontent.com/pod-product-compliance
Lightning Source LLC
Chambersburg PA
CBHW021348300426
44114CB00012B/1128